JOURNEY

TO THE

TRUE SELF

Intimate Conversations with Christ Consciousness

LAURA DERR

Seshat Press
211 Pauline Drive #513
York, PA 17402
www.seshatpress.com
Send questions to: support@seshatpress.com

Paperback ISBN: 979-8-9996544-7-2
ebook ISBN: 979-8-9996544-8-9
Library of Congress Control Number: 2026902812

Cover Design and Layout: Ranilo Cabo
Editor and Proofreader: Simon Whaley

Printed in the United States of America

To Cricket, my warrior protector, June 1998–April 20, 2019

Contents

Foreword

by Jon Mundy, PhD

You might be familiar with the story from the Jain tradition about six blind men who each touch different parts of an elephant to try to figure out what the object is. One touches the side and says, "How smooth! Like a wall." The second man touches the trunk and says, "It is round! Like a snake." The third touches the tusk and says, "It is sharp! Like a spear." The fourth touches the leg and says, "How tall! Like a tree." The fifth touches the ear and says, "How wide! Like a big leaf." The sixth man touches the tail and says, "How thin! Like a rope."

The same could be said about our different religions: they have different perspectives, and yet ultimately, they all point to the only truth that can be true: One God, One Love, One Universe, One Mind, which belongs to us all in our Unified state of Being, right here in the Eternal Now.

Laura Derr's new book, *Journey to the True Self: Intimate Conversations with Christ Consciousness*, was composed in conversation with a group of friends, talking to the Christ-Mind as one would speak with any friend.

One person is no more holy than any other, but some individuals have the wonderful experience of waking up and remembering who they are. The rest wander about in dreamlike states, believing their stories, their resumes—daydreams that somehow give them definition.

I was introduced to *A Course in Miracles* in 1975, as *received* by Dr. Helen Schucman. I knew Helen, and I can assure you that, while she was perfectly capable of *hearing* the *Course*, she was not the author of the Course; she was simply the *receiver*. Thirty years later, in 2015, I read *A Course of Love*, scribed by Mari Perron, who, like Helen, describes herself as a *receiver* of *ACOL*, not the author. Now, ten years later, I've been given another book, received from yet another friend, Dr. Laura Derr.

I first met Laura at *A Course in Miracles* retreat in New Hampshire in the spring of 2007. She would later join us as a student at All Faiths Seminary International in New York and graduate as an Interfaith Minister in 2016. During the thirty-five years she has been a psychotherapist, she was also a Buddhist practitioner, and then devoted herself to the path of *ACIM*. Buddhism is similar to our two *Courses* in its assertion that the world is an illusion, and our clinging to a false self, the ego, is also an illusion. Like our modern *Courses*, Buddhism emphasizes transcending the ego's hold on our consciousness.

Laura, like Helen and Mari, is a receiver. The author is Yeshua, or Jesus, or Isa. Regardless of the earthly name, we are talking about "the Christ-Mind" and thus "the Voice for God" speaking to us in the language with which we are most familiar. It is Jesus I knew as a child, and Jesus I choose to understand as an adult. The Christ-Mind, or Buddhahood, or call it what you may, is available to everyone at all times, regardless of their background. Laura is simply someone who, through her practice with Buddhism and *ACIM*, got quiet long enough to allow this eternal Voice to speak to and through her.

The Voice Laura hears reiterates many of the same things found in *ACIM* and *ACOL*, such as the importance of refraining from anger and attack, which creates further separation. The Voice assures Laura that the message it would share is available to everyone at all times. We must, of course, first turn off our personal static machines, our minds, and get quiet long enough to hear clearly.

In Lesson 49 from the *ACIM Workbook*, "God's Voice Speaks to Me All Through the Day," Jesus says, "The part of your mind in which truth abides is in constant communication with God, whether you are aware of it or not. (…) The part that is listening to the Voice for God is calm, always at rest, and wholly certain. It is really the only part there is."

The Voice of Jesus in this book says, "I am One with you who are not yet awake, and I am One with those who are awake. When you are attuned with me, you are attuned with the All in All." He is reminding us that no Soul is not one with the Whole, no matter how separate anyone may see themselves.

The Christ-Mind is everywhere. We are becoming more tolerant of what appears as a paradox: that one mind can be in communication with an infinite number of minds simultaneously without diminishing the awareness of one's personal consciousness. This is not an intellectual concept to be understood; it is a knowing felt in the mind, heart, and body. In fact, Jesus tells us in this book that, "It is through our repeated joinings that knowing of the Truth of Unity becomes ever more visceral."

An expansion of consciousness is occurring all around us, and it's accelerating as modern technology provides us with more opportunities to connect with an increasing number of like-minded individuals. As we become aware of what is not true, what is true comes more into view. Thank God for the gifts that Jesus, through Laura, brings to us. And thank you, Laura, for being willing to listen, hear, and share this joyful news.

Rev. Dr. Jon Mundy
Author of *Living A Course in Miracles*, Publisher of *Miracles Magazine*, Director of *A Course in Miracles* program at All Faiths Seminary International
September 3, 2025

Foreword

by John Krysko, DDiv

This book is more than a testimony of one person's journey into Higher Consciousness through an intimate relationship with the Christ. It is an invitation to the reader to reach deeper, strive higher, and allow their Divine essence to emerge into this world. This spiritual guidebook, by helping us look inward, moves us forward towards distant horizons. As a deeply committed pilgrim on the Higher Way, Laura points to the Way and encourages us to plumb our own depths and soar to the heights that can be achieved.

The story of Laura's expansion into higher awareness provides a frame of reference that says, "You, too, can achieve this Consciousness." It is a glorious and candid mix from an expert diarist. Philosophy blends with experience to provide the reader with a bounteous meal to nourish us as we travel our varied roads.

All those who have had the pleasure of engaging in Divine Dialogues with Laura, as I have over the years, can testify to her honesty, forthrightness, intelligence, and compassion. These *Intimate Conversations* deserve to be re-read, often. Keep this book on your nightstand during trials and tribulations, and reference it in those moments of growth and victory.

By sharing her most personal relationship with Yeshua, Mary Magdalene, and others in that Holy Group, Laura shows us how we, too, can find passage to our own Soul Groups. No one ever journeys alone, so get ready for the next leg of your journey…

Rev. Dr. John Krysko
Founder of Berkshire CenterPoint, Inc., building community through arts, spirituality and healthy lifestyles, Creator of TableRock Sanctuary and Retreat Center for integrative spirituality
May 27, 2025

Author's Note to Reader

This book is an invitation. As you learn about my personal spiritual path, I invite you to reflect on your own unfolding process of awakening. While each of our paths is unique, we all arrive in the same universal Awareness in which the appearance of separate personalities has no meaning.

Through diligent spiritual practice, I have been blessed with receiving and transmitting the teachings in this book. Universal spiritual knowing is the true nature of all of **Creation**, so each one of us is destined to receive and extend it through our own particular gifts. As more of us access this universal consciousness of Love, we create a kaleidoscope of infinite beauty. I hope this story encourages you to continue with your own process of clarifying your inner vision. The rewards appear miraculous at first, but we come to realize that *miraculous* has been Reality all along, always accessible in the intimacy of our own hearts.

The teachings in this book are for the benefit of all who are drawn to them. Some are soothing, and some are quite challenging. You may even find yourself feeling confused as these teachings shake your concepts and assumptions. As you read, please let go of your grip on rational thought and just feel your responses in the heart. These words are absorbed through feeling, not thinking. It is when mind and heart are joined that Wisdom is experienced as the physical sensation of *knowing*. Through this inner joining, and through joining with friends of the Heart, I have trusted the sensation of knowing enough to hear and transmit these words.

These teachings poured through me in the context of joining with a group of friends on the spiritual path, from October 2018 through February 2021, at which time I needed to take a break. Because of the sheer volume of the teachings, they do not all fit in one book. This book concludes in July 2019. Further information about subsequent teachings can be found at www.lauraderr-journeytotrueself.com.

Please note that while the terminology may sound like it comes from the Western Christian tradition, these are just words that focus toward a universal Awareness that is the unified Creation. Every spiritual tradition has done its best to use words to describe this universal totality that exists beyond concepts the thinking mind can grasp, so these teachings are for readers of all faith backgrounds. As the Buddha's raft parable explains, the raft is not the shore. Once you have relinquished your small personal identity and have reached the shore of identification with the totality, the All in All, then there is no more need for the raft of words to carry you. In the meantime, I have included a glossary to help with understanding names and terms that are unfamiliar. When glossary words first appear in the text, they are in **bold**.

In two communication sessions, **Yeshua** shared these messages. "By modeling courage—and you are already modeling courage by being willing to be my Voice—you will be a beacon of Light to other **Souls** who already want to share the Light that they feel so graced to have received.

"You are being called to serve in many places. This is a call that you have responded to, over and over again, in many lifetimes. In this lifetime, you can bring my Love further out into the **world**. Humanity is ready to know that the Truth is **God**'s Love. Your role will be to amplify that confidence in others.

"You are very courageous to be walking in **Christ Consciousness** with the support of your spiritual family, who sees who you are and recognizes the value of what you are offering to the world. You have a choice, always, but it is also ordained. This is the path you chose before you came into this life, knowing this was a time that was a context that would support you.

"There are many Souls here who are hearing my words through you, and many more Souls who will also hear these words. Once you agreed to join me in intimate communication, your Soul agreed those words would be shared broadly. These communications are not personal or private. I began my communications with you by teaching you that you are not special. You have understood well why I told you this in my first communication. If you had thought you were special, we would not be able to work together. My words are not especially for you or your close circle of friends. My words and energies are for whoever is drawn to them."

Dear reader, these words are for you.

Laura Derr

Journey to the True Self

Intimate Conversations with Christ Consciousness

"The name will convey that this is a source of Wisdom that goes directly to the **Source**, which is God, and that it is an interactive Source. My work through my sister is an active communication with any Soul who desires to come and speak with us. The name will convey the endless Source of God's Love, which is always available to answer questions and provide healing—a fountain of Love, Wisdom, healing, care, and blessing. We leave it to Laura to distill that into a title, but that is the energy."

Introduction

Dear friend,

I call you *friend* because I have come to know that anyone who has made a commitment to awakening is truly a friend. If you are holding this book, I trust you are feeling the pull of God, the inner longing we all share to be known, completely known, by our Source. We all long to be known by a human beloved. This longing is the worldly expression of our deepest desire to experience the perfect intimacy of being loved by God, the infinite Beloved. The process of awakening reveals, embraces, and dissolves all obstacles to this pure intimacy. This book is the ongoing expression of my awakening process, a process that can only occur in **Communion** with friends on the Path, and with the All in All.

As the obstacles to knowing Love are dissolved, the Love of God shines through with ever greater clarity and depth. My journey is everyone's journey. The particulars are mine, but it is a universal journey from fear to Love. I share with you here some of those particulars so you can see how it is possible that the Voice of Christ Consciousness can be expressed through the body-heart-mind called Laura. My deepest desire is for you to know that if it is possible for *me* to experience knowing and expressing the Wisdom of God, then it is possible for *you*. We all have our particular gifts, so everyone's expression is different, and everyone's expression is beauty itself. This is the harmony of playing our own part in the infinite pattern of Creation.

How did my journey begin? I came into this life with a deep desire to transmit the healing Love of God. Even though I started kindergarten when I was only four, I was one of the tallest children in the class, and I could also read, count, and behave myself. I don't remember consciously thinking my peers needed help, but I developed a recurring fantasy image of sitting in the center of the school playground, wearing a long, beautiful, pink dress, and welcoming the children to come to me so I could love them, transmit healing energy to them, and bless them.

I grew up in the 1960s and '70s, attending a Protestant church. I remember sitting in the pew with my family, my heart aching, containing my tears, knowing there was more—a deeper Truth, a more profound expression of Love than what was allowed in this intellectual approach to God. These words of Yeshua's always grabbed my heart. "And be sure of this: I am with you always, even to the end of the age" (Matthew 28:20 NLT). What I loved most was singing, where the expression of deep feelings was allowed. As an adolescent, I was passionate about my love for Jesus. I felt the pain of his **death** deeply. *Jesus Christ Superstar* made me weep. My friends thought I was weird. I wondered about myself. Where was this intensity coming from?

I left home and left the church. There did not seem to be a place for my longing there. I found the feminist women's community in Cambridge, Massachusetts, and fell, wide-eyed, into the discovery of our Goddess-centered past. Here was the explanation for the rootlessness I felt in the Western intellectual tradition in which I had been raised: the voice of the **Divine Feminine** was absent, only hints and fragments remained. The women's musical group *Libana* was my home for four years, starting from our first rehearsal in 1979. This family of women working through the process of healing the detritus of misogyny in ourselves opened me up to the healing power of music and community. *Libana* also opened my awareness to the long and ancient history of the Divine Feminine. The reinterpretation of history and culture fostered in the crucible of this group was profound. Now my femaleness could be revived and honored.

In my early twenties, a friend suggested I attend Al-Anon, the program based on the same twelve steps of Alcoholics Anonymous that provides support for those affected by someone else's drinking. I felt instantly at home. Here were people being humble and honest with themselves and each other, and connecting an inner spiritual relationship with their lived emotional experience. Here, I could feel and express my longing for God that I had always had but did not know how to articulate. I loved the program's lack of spiritual dogma, and its encouragement to give up control and develop my sense of trusting spiritual guidance. I began cultivating an inner dialogue with my Higher Power. I also began psychotherapy. I was hooked on the journey of self-awareness. The women's community, music, Al-Anon, and therapy opened up an inner universe I had felt but had had no context to know could really exist.

After completing my Bachelor's in counseling psychology and expressive therapies, and working for three years leading art and music therapy groups in a state psychiatric hospital, I continued my mental health education and earned a doctorate in psychology. I loved the deep dive into the mind through the lens of Western psychology. I was especially fascinated by gaining a deeper understanding of child development, and by the systems theory on which family therapy is based. I benefited from the graduate school's focus on knowing myself first, so I could then best apply the tools learned to helping others.

Immersed in Al-Anon, I wanted more experience with meditation than the program offered, so I found a retreat that fit between my spring and summer semesters. I was enthralled. The philosophy and practice of Buddhism taught by Thich Nhat Hanh meshed beautifully with the Twelve-Step program. The teachings about the lack of a separate self also fit with the systems theory of family therapy that so intrigued me. This Buddhist practice community was my spiritual home for twenty years. I received lay ordination and was given the dharma name of *True Garden of Joy*.

My doctoral dissertation led me, through a detailed look at my subjects' observations of their own minds, to the conclusion that there is no such thing as a separate self. It is a constructed **illusion**. So, I was ready, through my explorations of our Goddess history, Western psychology, systems theory, Buddhism, and the Twelve-Step program, for the next stage of my journey—finding the true **Self**.

I now see how all my life experiences have healed wounds, expanded my awareness, and taught me skills. I am deeply grateful to all my hundreds of psychotherapy patients over the past thirty-five years. They gave me the opportunity to practice articulating the wisdom I was learning from my experience in ways that are useful for others to hear. Even writing thousands of progress notes has helped me bring the human mind-heart-body patterns of confusion and release into clear focus. My patients have also taught me patience.

I can look back at the pattern of my life and see how each experience helped prepare me for the next. Each stage of the journey revealed some new spiritual experience that felt so wonderful I thought I would stay there. But there was always either an inner knowing or an external event that would clarify that I had completed what was necessary for my growth in that chapter, and it was time to move forward. What was to emerge next, when I found a book based on *A Course in Miracles*, was beyond the way of knowing of my rational, psychological mind, but I can see now that it had its roots in my earliest longings.

I invite you on this journey with me. I welcome you into following your own unfolding path as we all travel **Home** to awareness of our Unity with God.

Part 1

The Inner Way

Chapter 1

Inner Knowing is Revealed

When I found the originally published version of *A Course in Miracles* in 2008, the words went like a lightning bolt into my heart. I recognized the vibrational quality of the Voice. It felt extremely familiar. Here was the Jesus (who I call Yeshua, as his name is said in **Aramaic**), for whom I had longed as a child and adolescent, finally speaking the *more-ness* that I had known must be there. Here was my personal teacher, whose presence I felt viscerally, and who was deeply engaged with my learning process, an experience I had never felt in my twenty years of Buddhist practice. I slowly and carefully read through the lengthy *Text*. Though the writing was dense, it all felt familiar and quickly made sense to me. Yeshua's teachings were similar to the Buddhist teachings I knew well—just using language that sounded Christian. I was simply enthralled that the Christianity I had grown up with, which never really made any sense to me, was now being explained with familiar Buddhist concepts. A bridge was being built between my childhood religious training and the spiritual practice community that had sustained me for so many of my adult years.

And then I began practicing the *Course*'s *Workbook* lessons. From this point forward, the reality of my spiritual life gained momentum.

When I was eighteen, I felt a strong conviction that I would be a writer, though it was not clear to me what I would write about. I did some experimenting with words, but it was when I started Al-Anon and therapy in my twenties that I began journaling in earnest. I have spent countless hours over many years writing in my journal, at first to work through my emotional issues, and then to revel simply in the joy of connecting inwardly. I am deeply grateful to my cats, Cricket and Felicity, whose love of staying present with me encouraged me to sit and write for hours—Felicity around my shoulders, Cricket on my outstretched legs, and the journal on my lap.

The *Course*'s emphasis on listening to inner guidance was a natural continuation of the Al-Anon practice of sensing a Higher Power. To cultivate this skill, a *Course* friend encouraged me to write a question and then just write the answer that came to me. This proved easy and startling. My first question, "Why does my cat annoy me sometimes?" (Felicity loved to sit on the *Course* book I was trying to read) elicited a response that was clearly not my habitual way of thinking: "Because you still think there are things that are more important than Love, including reading *A Course in Miracles*."

Halfway through practicing the *Course Workbook*, I felt an intense inner push to write—much stronger than my regular habit of writing. It was uncomfortable, and I avoided it for three days. When my house was totally clean and I finally sat down to write, what poured forth was clearly a Voice that differed considerably from my normal self-observation voice. I did not hear it as an audible voice but as a flow of what I came to call *clear thought*. I just wrote the thoughts as they came to me in a continuous stream, having no idea where they would go. The process of writing brought these thoughts into focus because I had to formulate them into coherent sentences. I was amazed and fascinated by the profound teachings coming into my mind. Here is some of that journal passage.

February 15, 2009

I told Spirit a couple of days ago that I promised to *really* listen now, always really listen. The thought came clearly to get up and write a conversation. I avoided doing so. Yesterday, the same. Today, the same thought. I'm quite aware that **ego** is freaking out, aware that, as I listen to Spirit, its power diminishes. Ego is trying to convince me this is all silliness, not fit for a practical Yankee like myself. But I read today in the *Course* that Yeshua has basically imparted all the ideas I need now, and it's time for me to listen to God because I'm finally aware that I want my will to be in tune with his. Lately, meditation has felt solid and joyous, so I know this is all true. OK Spirit, let's talk.

Finally! You've been resisting me!

Sorry, I know.

I forgive you. Listen, we have work to do. This is important. No more dallying around.

That scares me.

No need for fear. What I mean is, you've always wanted to be a healer, to help people feel happy and blessed—that was your vision of yourself from childhood. You've laid a strong foundation. You've got the external credentials the world requires of you to earn your living at this work. You've always known that words are your gift—you cultivated that gift in your writing group. You wrote an excellent dissertation in which you learned that there is no self as the ego describes a self. You saw that you in the West are connecting with Eastern wisdom in that regard. And now you've found the Course, *teaching you more than Buddhism has taught you, which is that I am here, actively guiding you to experiences that teach you I am real and the world is not. Buddhism laid the foundation for you. You came to trust that there are higher states of awareness, even pure-knowing, aware liberation, but that path is easier in the presence of an* **Enlightened One**, *surrounded by practitioners. You were drawn to that path, but never really wanted to immerse yourself. It took you a while to listen to your experience and learn to let it go. It served you well, but it's no longer yours. But you found Yeshua, whom you have loved for hundreds of years with such a deep longing. This is where you really experience Love. You have total confidence in him.*

I know, I've really missed him. I remember how I longed for him as a teenager, but the church's teachings made no sense to me, and my parents were so unhappy. They were certainly not enacting his teachings about Love and forgiveness. But he was the spiritual Love of my youth.

Yes, and longer ago than that. You had a sense of your connection to **Simon Peter**. *You really understand his devotion and his fear and betrayal out of self-protection. You're feeling that now—that panicky fear people will find out about your Love and devotion, your confidence in Yeshua's enlightened Love, your commitment to his* Course in Miracles. *You fear their derision, that they will laugh at your foolishness, your impracticality. It's OK. I hear you are mad at me for saying all this. I'm just pointing this voice out so you can disagree with it, and stand now with Yeshua. He's so excited to have you back after all your wanderings, looking for him again after you lost him. That was the first grief, where you shut down when Yeshua died, you closed your heart in the grief. Your grief when your friend Pam died opened up this grief and helped you find your path. That is why you found Thich Nhat Hanh two years later—your heart was open, finally, to return to active pursuit of a spiritual path. Are you ready now to fully love Yeshua again?*

Yes, I am.

This direct, internal communication continued the next day.

February 16, 2009

OK, Spirit, I'm listening. In meditation, I can feel you physically, a solid, warm, tingly feeling. I've been thinking about what I wrote yesterday. It seems so outrageous, but when I re-read it just now, it felt true on a feeling level. Emotionally, I totally get that simultaneous feeling of Love and devotion to Yeshua—I can feel it as I write this, there is no way words can express the solidity and expansiveness of this feeling—and the doubt, the attachment to feeling sure about the *truth* of the material world, the feeling that I'm foolish for my devotion. But writing that I also feel your gentle laughter, Spirit, that you know I don't really believe that, that my conviction is now with the Truth of Spirit, the Truth of my being the **Child of God**. I don't get intellectually how this works, but on a feeling level, I know it's true.

Yes, Laura, that's what Yeshua has been working with you on in the Course, *patiently, over and over, telling you the Truth so it can get through your defenses and speak to the part of you that knows this Truth already. He's helping you connect your conscious awareness to your deep knowing—remember he uses the word* **Knowledge** *to mean enlightenment, the state in which all of your awareness is reconnected to everything, including the knowing that there is God and you are God's Child.*

I know your feeling of connection with Peter troubles you. But I know, as you write these words, you are resting in a deeper awareness—that everything is not only connected but is the same, and that all external images are just symbols of your thought. So, Peter is a symbol of your emotional state, which is not ambivalence—your devotion and Love are 100% pure—but is two states simultaneously: your Love and devotion, and your fear that other people will ridicule you. As you make public your Love and devotion, this will attract people. Love and devotion are the true state of people's hearts, and some part of them still knows it and is drawn to it like a magnet.

It's OK that your thought process is slowing down in therapy, and that words don't always come as quickly as they used to. This is evidence of your listening to me better, a skill that is new enough that your brain is a bit slow. It's not quite tuned in to my frequencies. But you can see, writing this, how easy it is for you to tune in when there are no distractions—the words come more quickly than you can possibly write.

OK, we're done for now. I know you think you'll miss me, but I'm with you all day and night—just keep listening. You're doing great. You're in a training period now, tuning up your brain to become a better receiving instrument. I love you.

This process of becoming a better receiving instrument is recorded in hundreds of journal passages over many years. After writing these first two long passages, I continued with the daily practice of asking a question and writing the answer that came to my mind, always surprised that there was another way of knowing that was so easy to hear. The Voice was a clear presence that interacted with me, answered my questions, and provided me with guidance. It was kind, encouraging, and never critical, though it could certainly use humor to show me what needed attention! If I tried to get it to say what I wanted, it simply fell silent.

Thus began ten years of dialogue with the **Holy Spirit**, who helped me process *A Course in Miracles*, then *The Way of Mastery*, and then *A Course of Love* (Diamond Clear Vision 2012, Shanti Christo Foundation 2015, Perron 2014). I am deeply grateful for the human beings who were willing to serve as channels for these gorgeous and profound teachings. With all these texts, I felt a deep intimacy with the Author, a feeling of being known and loved. More and more, there was nothing in my life of greater value than my relationship with this energy of infinite Love and Wisdom.

Chapter 2

Inner Vision Expands

Healing Energy Patterns in the Body

I attended a professional continuing education workshop on body-oriented trauma therapy with the psychologist Peter A. Levine, PhD. He has observed that unresolved traumatic events are continually repeated as subtle motions in the body, and once these motions are amplified, they can be enacted consciously, completed, and released. Learning this technique encouraged me to ask my patients with trauma histories if they would allow me to place my hands on their shoulders to sense this motion. My traditional psychological training prohibited any physical contact, so this was a new lens on my way of understanding how to be helpful to people. It turned out that, not only could I easily sense these subtle motions, but I could also instantly access an enormous reservoir of intuitive information about my patients. In my mind's eye, and sometimes felt in my body, I perceived patterns of physical energy in their bodies, deep psychological patterns in their consciousness, and **past-life** information. In a psychotherapy practice, I could share the first two types of information, but not the latter!

I began sharing this gift with friends and acquaintances, with whom I could be more open with the intuitive energies I was receiving than I could in my psychotherapy practice. Often, while describing what I was seeing and experiencing, the energy patterns would shift, and healings occurred. At times, I felt energy being transmitted through my hands to assist with these healings. Once, while doing a healing session with an older man I did not know, I kept seeing an image that seemed to have nothing to do with what I was sharing with him—a mother holding an infant. At the end, I reported it to him, including that the mother was conveying to the baby that she loved him. He exclaimed, "Oh, that's my mother. She comes through in any reading I have." He explained that, unmarried, she was forced to give him away at birth and always wanted to reassure him that she still loved him. From this, I learned to trust the visual images I was seeing in my mind's eye, not just the bodily energies I was sensing.

On a pilgrimage to Israel and southern France with *The Way of Mastery* community in 2015, most of the group accepted my offer of an intuitive session, giving me lots of practice with trusting what I was being shown. The sessions were strikingly different, which boosted my confidence that I was not just sharing some preconceived idea of *wisdom*, but that the Wisdom was coming from a deep Source. This Source was sharing what would be helpful for each person on their journey. With this confidence that my **small self** had nothing to do with this process, my intuitive abilities blossomed. You will read later on that Yeshua encourages a brother to trust the images that come into his mind as gifts from Spirit. This ocean of intuitive knowing is accessible to us all. It just takes practice trusting what we know.

When the pilgrimage group was in **Mary Magdalene**'s cave in Sainte-Baume in Provence, I had an intense and transformative experience. Inwardly, she and Yeshua made it clear they had a pressing issue to address with me. They needed me to release any feelings of guilt and failure, and to engage with them more fully so I could move on to a higher calling. Inside the cave, I sat over on the right side, down a few steps, where there were some benches in front of her statue. For forty-five minutes, my heart **chakra** burned most uncomfortably. I kept thinking it *must* end, but it never did. During this process, the group was called to gather by a small altar on this lower level. Standing with my fellow travelers, I began convulsing, to the point that someone thought I would fall over, but I knew I needed to stick with it. Suddenly, **Maryam** (Magdalene's Aramaic name) was on my left, and Yeshua was on my right, holding me up. They performed some sort of energetic healing, and I ceased convulsing. I then watched them move among the group, providing whatever healing each person could receive. Then they came back to me, and in my mind's eye, they took me outside the cave to the plaza overlooking the valley. My heart chakra simply exploded. At the end of the group ceremony, I flew down the rocky path, my feet barely touching the ground, never once losing my footing, just high with delight and amazement.

Looking back, I can see that this experience was an energetic shift into being more willing to receive the energies of these Great Beings and to be a more conscious partner with them here on the Earth-plane. For the next two years, whenever the situation called me, I offered healing sessions in partnership with these Beings. This felt so miraculous, I thought I would be content to abide here for the rest of my life.

When Maryam helped me with healings, at first I noticed other Beings with her, but I couldn't see who they were. Then I realized they were other women, simply clothed, who helped her with applying herbs while she chanted. Sometimes I could hear her, a haunting sound that broke up stuck places in people's vibrational fields. The women worked as a group, knowing that joining energies is much more powerful than working alone.

In one healing session, I saw Maryam and her group, as well as other Beings unknown to me, pulling strands of sticky black material from a woman's belly, followed by a careful search for every small black fleck. I realized these were cancer cells. Only after the session was complete did the woman reveal that she had been treated for abdominal cancer. Many years later, she remains cancer-free.

The more I did these sessions, the more the Enlightened Ones appeared in my awareness. A few times, **Mother Mary** helped mothers heal their relationships with their daughters. I could see clearly the small, stone building on a hill outside of Ephesus in Turkey in which she lived and, along with other women, provided healing for all who came to her. I could see her beautiful garden, where she grew many healing herbs, as well as vegetables and flowers, up the hill behind the house and clinic.

Once, in doing a reading for a friend who is a spiritual teacher, I physically felt Yeshua's energy enter my body. I felt my body grow taller, my shoulders broaden, and, most particularly, my hands seemed larger. I felt like holding her hands during the session, a practice I later continued with other people. When he was finished, my hands became feminine again, and I felt his energy leave my body. Her concern was how to help people who are slow to release their obstacles. His response was beautiful. He showed me a parade, with this teacher and others at the head, and a whole stream of people following behind. I remember he said, "Being in the vanguard of the parade, do not forget that there cannot be a vanguard if there is no following parade. For a parade to exist, people have to be at various places all along it. Please remember that the vanguard is connected to the parade, and do not worry that they are following behind." He reassured her that the parade and the head of the parade are one—there is no distinction. It is a continual stream. Her role was to play her part and trust that other people who are drawn to this path are playing theirs. For me, this experience was stunning. It was the first time I felt his presence so palpably.

The clarity of this intuitive knowing felt so miraculous to me that I was sure that offering readings and healings was a sufficient life purpose! But there was more to come. I now know this is the nature of Creation: there is always more. It is a continual process of unfolding into ever greater awareness and ever greater expression of that awareness. You, too, dear reader, are in this process of continual unfolding.

A friend encouraged me to get ordained because it is permitted for ministers to do hands-on healings. Ordination would clarify that I was practicing this intuitive spiritual healing as a minister, not as a psychologist! I dove into the intensive one-year training program of All Faiths Seminary International in New York City, where I received ordination as an interfaith minister in May 2016.

I met my friend John Krysko at the week-long retreat that concludes the program. I later accepted his offer of spiritual guidance sessions and, during joint meditations over a few months in the spring of 2017, we quickly discovered a similar ability to see clearly in the inner planes of awareness. When we first found that we could see and experience our own perspective on the same inner events unfolding, we were rather overwhelmed. This was not an experience we have had with anyone else, but I understand it is a glimpse into what life will be like when we are all able to live in the integration of expanded and mundane levels of awareness. After some initial surprise and adjusting, entering a state of shared awareness became exhilarating!

Our first session revealed my personal spiritual symbol, drawn in the patterns of **sacred geometry** — a bee on a flower. I was unaware of the power of this symbol at that time, but you will see it recur in surprising places throughout this narrative. Many of these joint meditations involved astounding initiations with Maryam, Yeshua, and the **Christ Council** in a cave in the **Himalayas**. Once, I experienced Maryam blowing into my left ear and saying, "**Ethphatha**," the Aramaic word for opening. This has since happened on three different occasions. Many of my encounters with Yeshua were quite tender. His energy is gentler than hers, though I find her directness refreshing and extremely helpful.

Foreshadowing Meditations

One of these meditations with John, in May 2017, was an important step in my process of growing towards joining with Christ Consciousness sufficiently to hear clearly inwardly. In this meditation, it was foretold I would speak in Yeshua's Voice—the Voice of Christ Consciousness.

In our opening conversation, I shared that I had sensed for some time my life's work would change from a full-time clinical psychology practice to interacting with people who are consciously following the spiritual growth path. I could also see that, while I know I have been helpful to many people as a therapist, my personal growth has been about seeing my own constricted beliefs so I could dissolve them, like freeing the toy stuck in the middle of the bar of soap.

One of these constrictions has been an existential despair I've experienced all my life—a belief that suffering is inescapable. Only by absorbing the modern teachings of Yeshua could I connect with the *experience*, not just the *idea*, that the Truth is that we are all Children of God. I had finally learned that all the painful stuff is just a story we're telling ourselves—not that it's not painful, but it is not the Truth. By this time, I could experience the sensation of actually shifting back and forth between those two levels of consciousness more easily than I had in the past, rather than just *remaining* in the pain consciousness while knowing that there's an *idea* of something else.

This still felt quite tender to me. Could I really sustain connecting with the Truth of everyone being a Child of God and all of Creation being the energy of the Source? I could see this is the challenge Yeshua puts before us—to *choose* to be in Christ Consciousness. Knowing this is a collective choice helped to support me in this new tender place of experiencing it.

John then shared that, while I was talking, he experienced an inward communication with Yeshua about the choice to be in Christ Consciousness. Yeshua was showing him the image of a cloth, and the symbolic role cloth played in his life. "When he acknowledged before the high priest Caiaphas that he is the Messiah, the priest tore his robe in two. Later on, when he died on the cross, an earthquake tore the curtain of the temple in two. The tearing of these cloths reflects the basic split that we, as humans, have between our human nature and our Divine nature. Yeshua was saying to me, 'It's your choice. You can experience that split inside of you, or you can join me in having a whole cloth.' **Edgar Cayce** once said that Yeshua's robe was woven by **Martha**, and it wasn't patched together. It was a whole cloth. That's symbolic of Yeshua not having a split between human and Divine. Indicating both of us, he said, 'You could join me in the absolute wholeness of this experience and share it with others and help them find that wholeness, or you could work at patching it up, like a tailor.' I saw him showing me there's a robe for me and a robe for you. 'Do you want that seamless body?'"

Though I answered yes, it was not full-throated. One sticking place was the thought that it felt blasphemous to say I could be part of the same whole cloth as Yeshua. The conditioning to believe he was the *only* Child of God and that I should put myself below him was strong. Yet I had learned enough by then to know this could not be the Truth.

Another sticking place was the shock of realizing my life will look exceedingly different when I live in the whole cloth of the Unity of the human and the Divine. A fear arose of drawing undue attention to myself. I could hear inwardly, "Calm down, slow down. Now is the time to rest in Unity. Now is the time to wear the new cloth, the new sandals, and just rest in this new awareness. The rest will be revealed in time."

With that reassurance, I could declare, "Yes, I'm ready to be part of the whole cloth!" I observed what a big part cloth played in Yeshua's story. He and Mary Magdalene both wore beautiful white Egyptian cotton robes, an image that has persisted through time. At the Crucifixion, his robe was removed, torn, and distributed by the soldiers. **Veronica** wiped his face with a cloth. The burial shroud that was found without the body it had previously wrapped was hugely significant. It is women who weave cloth, so I could see in this symbol the necessity of weaving the Divine Feminine into the whole cloth of Christ Consciousness.

We then entered the space of joint meditation, sharing a complex series of beautiful experiences in the inner planes. We were welcomed into a circle of colorful Beings of Light in the Christ Consciousness in a cave in the Himalayas. The illusion of the dust of time was washed off our feet, and any stain we believed we had in consciousness was washed off our hands, and we were dressed in whole-cloth garments of Light. We were overwhelmed by a feeling of boundless joy.

Yeshua conveyed his gratitude that we were willing to accept Christ Consciousness into our hearts and indicated that he needs people to receive this sharing. Entering this consciousness together is important, just as he said in the Gospel, "For where two or three are gathered together in My name, there am I with them" (Matthew 18:20 NLV). Only through joining can we release attachment to the belief in our smallness. Christ Consciousness is Unity, so when we join in Christ Consciousness, we become aware that we *are* that Unity.

Yeshua conveyed that any idea of stain in consciousness has no reality in this space. He showed John the tremendous suffering and pain in my heart that I had collected and sustained over many lifetimes. I could feel it like a stone in there. It was the belief that I was responsible for alleviating all the suffering I've witnessed over so many lifetimes. I could see I was still enacting this belief in this lifetime by taking on more and more psychotherapy patients. My work had consumed me for years, and now it was time to let this belief go.

Then John made this prediction, which has clearly come true. "Yeshua says he will help you release that pain. You will know when you are releasing it because he, Magdalene, and others, the Christ Consciousness, will speak through you. I have the sense of his hand on your lips. I see that when you are speaking, you should imagine the Christ or Magdalene is there with you and speaking with you, that you are part of that, and to allow yourself to be a spokesperson."

The distinction between the experience of joining with Christ Consciousness versus believing I was responsible for resolving suffering became clear. I could see that practicing accessing this Consciousness by joining with Yeshua and Maryam in my energy field and then just resting there would result in it becoming more natural, and I could do this while living my daily life. Inwardly, I heard clearly, "Yes, this is not a withdrawal resting. It's consciously choosing to just feel that energy and let things unfold without trying to figure anything out." It felt comforting and deeply worthy to be told, for now, to practice just resting in the Unity of Christ Consciousness, and to let things unfold in time.

Yeshua then conveyed that he wants us to put on the seamless clothing of Light, the Christ Consciousness, while being alive in the body now, in our current human lives. It's like putting on a new skin that then allows us to express the New Life. We could feel his tremendous happiness and gratitude that we were allowing this together. It is his deepest desire for all of us to join in this unified Consciousness. It's what he came here to do—to establish the Pathway of Unity.

The meditation concluded with me sensing Maryam putting her hands on my heart and conveying to just rest there, to *feel* the Love of this connection and not feel like I have to *do* anything, to stop my many-lifetimes-old pattern of trying to do as much good as I can.

She told me, "For now, just feel the Love in your heart." It felt such a relief to just hang out with Maryam and rest in the nurturing of the Divine Feminine.

These experiences had profoundly transformative effects on both of us, and we were tremendously energized and encouraged. I share them with you to encourage you, too, to trust your process of unlearning old habits and accepting the Reality of who you truly are—the Child of God.

Living in the Mountaintop Perspective

Two months later, in June 2017, overwhelmed by grief at the passing of a man who had been like a kindly father to me, as he had to multiple children over many years, my heart was wide open, and this vision came to me:

I remembered that, several times in visions, I had been invited to the Christ Council, where there is a seat at the table when I am ready. Each time, I had received the invitation as true, and also as something I did not yet understand. A sense of confusion held me back—my idea that there's some kind of difference or separation between who those Beings are and who I am. On this day, I felt the inward invitation again, but now, no feelings of unworthiness arose, only a bit of confusion that they had not. Wasn't I supposed to believe these separation thoughts? But I no longer did. Instead, I simply felt a sense of growing into this new state of knowing that my true nature, all of our true nature, *is* the Christ, the Child of God, so how could I not be on the Christ Council? I saw that, in Reality, everyone is already there; we are just at differing levels of awareness of this Truth.

With that thought, there was no resistance left, and suddenly I was back in the cave of Christ Consciousness in the Himalayas. There was the round table—open in the middle—with Great Beings seated all around. I was shown to my chair—high back, no arms.

Yeshua was across from me, his Light brilliant. The table dissolved, and we stood before each other in the center. He kissed me and held me with exquisite tenderness. I cried and cried, but softly, with relief at no longer resisting his Love. How can I use words to describe feeling his Love without any resistance? There are no words for the perfection of Divine Love.

My human awareness had a bit of trouble trying to put the next events into a sequence because it all happened simultaneously, but I needed to sequence it to see it, so both the sequence and the simultaneity were concurrent. Words, which are sequential, fail to describe this. I was given my inheritance in the form of many symbols. Maryam came first and put simple sandals on my feet. Then I was given a beautiful light-blue robe, gossamer, made of Light. Then a ring for my wedding ring finger. Then a book of all Knowledge. Finally, a pendant with my symbol—the sacred geometry bee on the sacred geometry rose. I felt like a Divine Being on whom is lavished the most valuable gifts in the **Kingdom**.

Then, I had to come out of this place and go to work. It was so odd living these two experiences at once—the Divine Perfection and the world of (apparent) separation.

At that time, I was in the midst of reading carefully through The Forty Days and Forty Nights section of *A Course of Love* (*ACOL*) and having the repeated experience that what I read each day was a description of what I had just experienced the day before. Without fail, it happened again—what I read the next day, *Day 27*, *The Apprehension of Levels of Experience*, described what I had experienced in that meditation: "You have thus begun to experience on two levels. [...] Now you contain within you the ability to combine both levels of being through the experience of life. [...] You quite literally have a new way of seeing. You might think of this initially as having two perspectives, an internal and an external perspective, a human and a spiritual perspective, a perspective from ground level, and a mountain top perspective. [...] As you continue to practice your apprehension of this situation [...], it will become a trusted ability and, through practice, lose its dualistic-seeming nature and become as intrinsic to who you are as is breathing. In this same way, the dualistic-seeming nature of all of life will be revealed to only seem to be so. [...] What we are speaking of now is being able to experience wholeness *and* the variability of experience that has come through the separated self of form. This is what you are beginning to do through your practice. Your proficiency will change your experience, and your experience will change the world" (Perron, 2014, 607-610).

So, the Divine pattern continued in its exquisite beauty. I had a profound experience, and the Christ Consciousness then described it in the book on the following day, weaving together all levels of experience. I was beyond feeling awe. I just abided in a state of knowing.

Chapter 3

Gathering Speed

By the fall of 2017, I needed to go through a deeper transformation and so backed off from doing healing sessions. During the winter months, I went through what the world would call depression, crying constantly—on waking, all day, and on going to bed—just keeping the lid on when I had to interact with other people. But I knew I was not depressed. This was, rather, a letting go of the thought that there is anything in the world that will bring me lasting satisfaction. Here was the releasing of the stone in my heart Yeshua had said he would help me with, in meditation with John K. back in May. By spring 2018, I began to lighten up and feel Yeshua with me more, supporting me every time I allowed him to. Since then, I have gone through several rounds of these grieving episodes, releasing further layers of belief that the world has to be a certain way for me to feel happy. Seeking first the **Queendom** in my heart seems to have this effect of highlighting what needs to be released! This is the clearing process that allows the establishment of joy. In Book One, Chapter 23 of *A Course of Love*, Yeshua describes this challenging process as the unlearning of old beliefs to make room for the New (Perron 2014).

The Sacred Bee

In July 2018, I felt drawn to do a session with a past-life hypnotherapist I had seen once before. At the session's conclusion, where learnings from previous lives are integrated, the symbol of the sacred bee came up again. I had no conscious awareness of the bee as an expression of the Divine, but after the session, Google quickly led me to the information that the bee was an ancient symbol of the Goddess.

These are my words, in a light trance, from the conclusion of that session:

"I see a bee, and the eye of the bee with its infinite facets, as the representation on **Earth** of God. The bee is in Communion with other bees. They create this beautiful geometry, and they create food from the beauty of the flowers. The bee is the perfection of God, all of it—each facet of its eye, each hair that collects each grain of pollen, the whole hive, their knowledge of the energy patterns that guide them to fly to the flowers—all of it is God. I see the geometric pattern of everything. Everything is in a pattern, and it's all the same, just different manifestations.

"In this life, I'm letting go of the fear that anything can be harmed, including the fear that I have to be alone in order to protect knowledge. I've always had this quality of feeling alone because of holding the secret knowledge, and the fear that I would be harmed if others knew I had the knowledge. That's why I loved being an abbess (late 1400s in Austria) so much, because I was protected there. It was like a beehive. We kept bees. The garden was beautiful, and the meadows with bees and flowers, and the Alps—it was all so beautiful! And my cat!" I laugh. "It was an experience of being able to manifest, in a little spot on the Earth, the beauty in a place of peace. Even though there were experiences also of unhappiness, the beauty was like the honeycomb. It was the latticework that held everything." Then, quietly, I continued. "So I know it's possible.

"I was supported there. Wealthy men supported the church. The women were still respected inside of the church, and the Divine Feminine was respected—but only in that cloistered place, not out in the world. You had to go inside the wall to be respected.

"And now," I said firmly, "being female in the world is especially important. No harm can come to me because now I know *who I am*.

"Now I see the Light is connected to itself. The Source of the Light can't be separated from its emanation. The Knowledge is already there in the heart. There's nothing to figure out. The mind is the servant of the Knowledge in the heart—I understand that now. The mind is the servant of the Knowledge in the heart. I understand, I understand. The Knowledge of Love in my heart is all that's required."

At the end of 2018, after my channeling experiences had been flowing clearly for two months, I reflected on this hypnotherapy session and saw how profoundly transformative it had been. It was liberating to finally understand that the Truth cannot be harmed, and thus I no longer needed to believe that it must be protected. I could follow, through many lifetimes, the thread of belief that I must protect the secret Wisdom from the forces of control—the Wisdom of how to come Home to God. I thought I had failed in this mission. Discovering that Knowledge has always resided, unharmed, in the heart, liberated me to manifest my purpose in this life—to share the Truth that, like **Dorothy's ruby slippers**, we have had the key to the way Home all along, just waiting for us to notice it in our Hearts.

You will see that this theme of needing to protect secret knowledge from persecution comes up frequently among this community of friends. One sister told me in an email that this had been a theme of recurring nightmares earlier in her life. Yeshua will have much to say about the Souls who have been the keepers of secret Wisdom for many lifetimes. Rather than blame the persecutors, he explains that we projected the idea of attack on the Truth to reinforce our own valuing of it. This projection of the need for attack is no longer necessary because we are now finally ready to understand that the Truth resides in the Heart of God, with which we are One. Now that we know the Truth can never be harmed, the time of persecution is finished. It's time to share our Light with the world!

The Hologram of Light

I have met many dear friends through *The Way of Mastery* community. I met John Hempstead, twenty years my senior, in 2014, and he quickly became a close friend. For the past ten years, he has been a collaborator in our individual and joint spiritual growth processes. In early 2018, while sitting alone in meditation, I saw a vivid image unfold on the Irish coast in my mind's eye, which he later confirmed was a past life of his. We had both been planning to attend a *Way of Mastery* retreat in Ireland that fall, so we resolved to find the location I had seen in this vision. With the help of new Irish friends, we did just that. I will share this story in more detail at the end of this chapter.

On the last day of that retreat in Ireland, I had a profound, energetic experience. I confronted an ancient belief that, because life on Earth is filled with suffering, suffering is therefore inescapable. I had not associated Light with life on Earth, which I perceived as dark, cold, and difficult. I then saw that it was the frequencies of fear in humanity that create these experiences, not that this is the nature of Reality, which is actually Light. I could see that it is the healing of our attachment to past traumas that allows the Light to be known here on Earth. Before this revelation, I did not know that I could actually experience the Earth and the body as Light.

With this awareness, that Light can be known in the body, came the physical sensation of falling apart. I immediately knew that what was disintegrating was my limited sense of who I am. My hands were shaking with the sensation of intense power flowing through them. I could feel that the body contains the mapping of the patterns of life and the entire Cosmos. I could feel the Light in me, and I knew it had always been there, just outside of my awareness. Now I *knew*: the body is vibrating at the same frequency as the stars and the planets. I had a feeling of awe, knowing this body contains everything. I have read that physicists understand the Universe is a hologram; therefore, every point contains the entirety. William Blake saw the Universe in a grain of sand. I was now physically experiencing this body as a hologram of the Universe. The *I* who thinks I am a small, egoic, self felt incredibly humbled.

With the disintegration of another constriction of resistance—the belief in my smallness—Yeshua's presence could flow through me with clarity.

Trusting Yeshua

On returning home from Ireland, I joined remotely in meditation with a brother from the retreat, intending to learn to practice sustaining the spiritual expansion I had experienced there. I suddenly found myself climbing onto the stone plaza in front of the cave in the Himalayas, where I had been often with John Krysko. It overlooks a deep valley with snow-covered peaks on the other side. At first, I was aware of my meditation partner's presence behind me and to my left, but I was entirely focused on my own experiences throughout the meditation.

Suddenly, I saw Yeshua standing in front of me—radiant white Light. He embraced me and turned me to look outward over the valley. I felt him surround me, as if his **Light-body** were an outer layer of my body. My heart started buzzing, which at first felt like fear, but the physical experience was so intense it compelled me to stick with it, and I stopped worrying about being afraid. Then my hands started buzzing. Though intense, this was tolerable, and I never felt like I would disintegrate as I had at the retreat. I just sustained feeling these sensations—Yeshua's presence surrounding and filling me, and my heart and hands buzzing—for the rest of the hour. There were moments I drifted in and out of dozing, but every time I returned, the physical sensations were the same. At first, my breathing remained shallow, but towards the end, the breath filled my body, my feet started buzzing, and I became acutely alert. Then I had a feeling of being complete.

Swiftly, Yeshua was in front of me again, and the buzzing subsided. He stepped aside so I could look out over the valley, and he commanded me to fly. I jumped, feeling completely relaxed, like Superman, happily looking at the valley below. I returned. He told me again to fly. We did this three times. Then he kissed me and disappeared. The outside door of my office banged, and I was ready to stand up.

When I emailed a detailed report to this brother, he confirmed he had witnessed what I had described. He observed I had sustained the experience well, with only a few moments of fear (likely when I dozed off a bit). He encouraged me to trust that things would simply unfold naturally. Because I had experienced many joint meditations with John Krysko the previous year, it was no longer startling to me that three apparently separate consciousnesses could be perfectly well aware of each other on the inner planes. I now knew that this is the natural state of the mind.

The Colors of Creation

Shortly after this experience, when a group of friends returned to Magdalene's cave in Sainte-Baume, I joined them in meditation from my home in Boston. After a series of powerful, energetic experiences in Communion with both Yeshua and Maryam in the by-now familiar Himalayan cave, I suddenly had the experience of my consciousness falling rapidly forward and downward. We appeared to fall out of the image of being in the cave and into the star-lit expanse of the Universe. It was as if the density of materiality, even in the inner vision where it is known to be only Light, dropped away to reveal infinity. The breath and bodily energetics continued. It felt to me like the quality of direct experience of the ecstasy of Creation. Eventually, the bodily convulsing in rhythm with the breath quieted, and I felt my energy and breath in quiet Communion with infinity. Words fail.

Then I noticed I was seeing the sky of Earth, filled with the most exquisite colors, like nothing I have ever seen, even in the most beautiful of sunrises and sunsets. The colors were delicious—I felt I could soak myself in them forever. They had an additional quality of vibration, not just what we see with the physical eye.

As I quieted down, still feeling buzzing throughout my body, I noticed that the group of friends was holding hands in the lower open area to the far right of the cave, in front of the small altar there. I joined them inwardly, chanting together in the circle.

My cat, sitting on my lap the whole time, awakened, and it was time to draw this meditation to a close.

The Portal of Gratitude Opens Christ Consciousness

A week later, John Hempstead and I were on a video call, expressing gratitude for the miraculous events that had been unfolding. After speaking for a while, we decided it was time to go into meditation. He asked me to open with a prayer, and by Divine grace, he began recording, which has proved to be a great blessing.

I began by expressing my immense gratitude. Yeshua suddenly appeared in my inner vision, blessing us and transmitting thoughts. I continued describing what I was seeing, speaking his thoughts as I heard them. There was no real distinction between my thoughts and his. This transmission was punctuated by me frequently interjecting things like, "I can feel him saying," or "He's reminding us," or describing my experience. My consciousness was actively engaged with this inner conversation. The full text of this communication is in Chapter 4.

John and I were delighted and amazed. I had known for about a year that I would be channeling Yeshua, but I had no idea about the circumstances, and it surprised me when it happened. John and his wife Marilyn later listened to this recording together. She described my reception as, "a clear glass pipe, clean and crisp—unlike some other channels, who are more like rusty pipes for water." I affirmed I felt clear and clean in the process.

We decided to meet again on November 2 to see if, together, we could attune to Yeshua's vibration and I could hear his messages. Indeed, his Voice flowed through me again. Though that audio recording is lost, I made a brief note that, in a lovely paradox, Yeshua had spoken about there being no loss. Mother Mary had also come through to reassure us that she is taking care of all the scared Souls who are transitioning out of their bodies. Their consistent message was to heal yourselves, be not distracted, hold and transmit the Light. When Yeshua spontaneously answered an unspoken question of mine, I later realized he would be happy to answer other questions.

Word got out to friends, who began joining us online. Even after just a month, I could feel how much more confident I was in my Communion with him, how much more I had allowed his Love into my heart, and how much more I trusted his teaching that **Heaven** and Earth are becoming one state. And I was certain that we each play an important role in expressing that Light.

This small group of friends from three continents slowly grew, at first meeting weekly, then bi-weekly, then monthly. We continued to join for over two and a half years. A pattern emerged in these gatherings of an opening teaching, followed by personal questions and answers, and then a closing teaching. It is these teachings that came through me that fill this volume you are reading. This volume concludes in July 2019. Details of further teachings can be found at lauraderr-journeytotrueself.com.

Growing Into Voicing Christ Consciousness

What was this experience like for me? Learning to hear and express the consciousness of Yeshua was a profound and intense process. I remember sitting in a concert, looking at the sea of people, thinking, *If they knew I was hearing and speaking the words of Yeshua, and transmitting his energies, they would think I was insane.* But the more I engaged with him, the more comfortable I became.

Yeshua's first teaching to me and John Hempstead was about not being special. When he anointed us with an oil made of liquid Light, he was extremely clear that it did not make us special; rather, it was so we could go on and anoint others. The thought of specialness only reinforces the thought of separation, and I could not continue serving as his Voice if I thought that made me special.

For many months, this felt like an unsolvable paradox, but his repeated teachings that we share the same Soul, the same Self, were so helpful to me in learning to allow this transmission to occur, and not make it about my personal self. While seeing and hearing him so clearly may be uncommon (though thankfully becoming less so), the Path of Awakening to Divine Knowing is destined for all of humanity. We are just at different points along the one unified parade. We are all his sheep, the (apparently) lost parts of his Self that he must gather up so we can know that we are all the One, unified, awakened Child of God, and there are no fragments who still believe they have been left behind.

Then there was the energetic experience! For many months during these channeled sessions, it was all I could do to tolerate the intensity of the vibration in which I was immersed. Sometimes I felt Yeshua like a larger, energetic body that formed a layer around me and that also penetrated me completely. In this way, he could transmit information about his own experiences, such as meditating in the desert. Often, I had to sit gripping my knees to keep myself steady, while my speaking voice carried calmly on, revealing no indication of my intense internal experience. Of course knowing what I was experiencing, Yeshua would encourage me to stay with him.

As he was speaking, my own habitual level of consciousness continued on, fully engaged, often making an inner commentary about the words being said—*I have no idea where this is going, how will I know what to say next?* or, *This sentence is so long, I am losing track of where it's going*—but more often about my credibility or worthiness as their speaker. Then, when the session of transmitting the words and energetics was complete, I would simply return to my habitual level of consciousness.

Yeshua has said that what he can teach depends on the level of awareness of the student. He wouldn't use my mind to explain something if I didn't have an inkling of what he was talking about. Often, when I reviewed what he had said, I would think, *That's amazing, I didn't really know that.* And yet, I could grasp it. I believe he wouldn't use my mind to teach something I can't yet imagine. What a great motivator to keep integrating his teachings!

At first, adjusting to his energy was demanding, and I had difficulty reorienting to my daily life. Even as it became easier, it still felt significantly separated from my normal life. Only after transcribing each recording in detail, and then reading the entire text, would I realize the profundity of what was happening. Reviewing the videos and watching this body-mind speaking Yeshua's words made it more real that this was actually happening in my life. I used to believe mystical experiences only happened to other people, and, while I could learn from them, I always kept myself one step removed. Yet here I was watching myself have the experience for which I had been longing for years! My friends on this path have been invaluable in believing in me and supporting me. I am grateful for their presence in my life.

After about a year, my small-mind, inner commentary slowed down and then stopped. One outward sign of my inward adjustment to being more attuned to this high vibration of consciousness is that the words now flow through me with ease, and I feel the intimacy of the conversations in which this Wisdom is engaging. When this channeling process first started, there were long gaps in my speaking as I felt the next download of thought before the words became clear. I would also experience someone else's comment as a disruption to my concentration. Now my experience is of a lively, loving, present exchange between the consciousness expressing in me, and the consciousness expressing in a friend.

Another lesson I had to learn was not to take personal ownership of what Yeshua said through me, but to let each person have their own relationship with him. Even though I could hear and remember his words, they were not coming from my personality. They came from the universal Christ Consciousness and are, by definition, impersonal. Knowing this helps me to have the courage to bring these teachings forward.

At various points, Yeshua clarified that he was only speaking as the "person" of Yeshua because that is what my mind could comprehend, but that "he" was actually a collective consciousness, and he would slowly shift to using collective pronouns. Eventually, my mind could no longer formulate singular pronouns, except to share specific examples, and the consciousness to which I was giving Voice became much larger. Of course, it had always been infinite! So perhaps I should say I could tolerate a larger, more abstract, consciousness.

I quickly understood that this consciousness only manifests as clearly spoken words when I join with a sister or brother. *Where two or three are gathered in my name, there am I with them.* On my own, I feel strong inner promptings and knowings, but the words only come out clearly when I have joined with a friend on the Path. I would like to express my gratitude to John Hempstead, who has been so devoted to his willingness to join with me and welcome Christ Consciousness into our circle of friends. He served the necessary role of emcee, facilitating the flow of our larger group sessions.

We always say a prayer at the start of every teaching session, which aligns our consciousness with Christ Consciousness.

In the Name of the Mother-Father-God,
In the Name of the Daughter-Son-Child of God, the Creation,
In the Name of the Holy Spirit, **Sophia**, **Shem**,
In the Name of Love,
Christ, I am.

Yeshua has encouraged us to know that this prayer is actually the Truth: we *are* the Christ. The true nature of all of Creation is the Christ, the unified awareness that knows it is the All in All. Yeshua has helped me see I am not a small self that serves as a channel for a higher consciousness—that construct just reinforces the idea of separation—but that my true Identity is the universal Christ Consciousness to which I am giving Voice. The phrase I now use to describe this process is *Voicing Christ Consciousness*. I understand this is the Voice of the universal Self that lives in and as all of us. This Self is beyond all thoughts and ideas, but it makes use of them to help us let go of the idea of a separate, small self and come to rest in our true Divine nature.

In early 2021, I needed to take a break from hosting the monthly online gatherings. The demands of my work as a therapist during the pandemic had become so intense that I was exhausted. I had previously stopped taking on new therapy patients and let my work hours slowly diminish, but the pandemic brought back multiple former patients who needed support during this global crisis. When it was finally over, I still was not ready to return to hosting the online gatherings. Throughout the pandemic, my sister and I had been collaborating on the enormous project of meeting the needs of our elderly, disabled mother and her husband, adding an in-law apartment to my sister's house, and moving the elders there. I then worked on selling my house in Boston and moving to the quieter western part of the state. My sister and I continued to devote a huge amount of time and energy to managing our mother's care and resolving her financial complexities until her passage into Spirit in November 2024.

Since taking this break, I have continued to join on and off with John Hempstead for *voicing* sessions, which became personal conversations between us and Christ Consciousness. This intimacy has further helped me let go of the deep, tenacious grip of ego, confronting my belief that I still think I know the conditions required for my happiness. Undoing the ego and listening only to God is a challenging journey!

While I can feel the difference between the true Self and the small self—the former is filled with delight and the latter with concerns for survival—and many small-self concerns have become uninteresting, the belief that I am a separated Being trapped in a body does not let go easily. Yeshua's teaching in *ACOL* (Book One, Chapter 23, paragraph 23) about physical symptoms helps me have patience with them. "[The body] is the composite of your beliefs, the totality. It will continue to hold former beliefs as well as new beliefs until old beliefs are purged. The purging of old beliefs frees space for the new. It allows your form to reflect what and who you are now in terms that coincide with the You who you have always been. There is no quick route to this purging, as it is the most individual of accomplishments. As you learned your beliefs, you must unlearn your beliefs. As you begin the process of unlearning, you may feel tested. You are not being tested, but given opportunities for unlearning. To learn that a previously held belief is no longer valid is the only way to truly purge that belief." (Perron 2014, C:23.23)

The most troubling concern I have been experiencing is tinnitus, a high-pitched, unceasing squeal that started in the fall of 2022, most likely caused by the third Covid vaccine. It helps me to see that this is an opportunity to relinquish an ancient belief, and I have been given insight, but it is a slow process. At least the initial despair and self-pity have subsided. Now I just long for quiet.

I took the vaccine to prevent illness and death, but it has had the effect of weakening my immune system due to a pre-existing, previously undiagnosed auto-immune condition. This humbling experience is pushing me to let the thought of being a victim of the body go. I must confront the foundation of the ego: the belief that the small, separate self is real, is dependent on the body, and is fearful of its death. The noise is pushing me to let go of the in-between state in which, while I do trust God, I still believe that the illusion of the world and its suffering is reality.

In 2023, I was given these words to speak: "Your Creator is giving you this gift to accelerate your process of relinquishing control. Surrender to the sound and it will allow you to return to the Heart of your Beloved, who does not wish you to suffer. When you let go of your grip on control, the beauty of what will flow through you is beyond your current comprehension. We will help you heal. Suffering is not forever."

I understand that this surrender process must be humbling. Were it gratifying, the sticky fingers of ego would grasp onto any progress to feed its pride. Being forced to give up my tenacious grip on being clever and in control, and surrender only to God, is easier said than done; yet knowing that the squeal will slowly subside does help. I continue to affirm, "Thank you that my ears are healed," knowing that all time is now, the separate *I* is nothing, and my true identity is only the Christ Self. This is having some effect. I have moments of knowing that the squeal is not happening to *me*. The bodily experience continues, while my Self-awareness observes. And the squealing has indeed diminished in the right ear.

The teaching Yeshua gave to a sister in the gathering of April 1, 2019, applies to me directly (paraphrased): "You cannot continue to grow *and* stay in your comfort zone. You can interpret uncomfortable physical experiences with fear that there is a problem, or with Love, that the energetics of higher awareness are shaking up a fixed pattern at a level at which you were comfortable. Interpreted through the eyes of Love, the difficulty with the physical ears is to accelerate your process of no longer listening to the narrow idea of being a limited, small self." I do wish the squealing would just go away—but now I know that will happen when I completely let go of thinking that my Being is this body.

Despite these life-in-the-body challenges, I remain committed to what has been given to me to do. What else is more important than sharing the gift I have received? As Simon Peter responded when Yeshua asked his disciples if they, too, would like to leave him: "Lord, to whom would we go? You have the words that give eternal life. We believe, and we know you are the Holy One of God" (John 6:68-69 NLT).

I can see, looking back on all this, that there is a great blessing in not knowing what will come next. Not only would I not understand it, but I would resist it. We need to go through whatever experiences are necessary to allow what is to come to be possible. The impatient part of me has wanted to circumvent the story and just get to the ending. Can't I spare myself and others the suffering, and just get to the lesson? No, we need to go through the emotional turmoil of our stories in order for the pain to be healed and released. And when it is, then the story holds no further interest whatsoever. It's complete.

I am keenly aware that there are multiple players in this story, and that I am only telling my part. We have been told repeatedly that all our parts are important. I am holding up the necessity and beauty of everyone's part, even if I cannot tell everyone's story. I am profoundly grateful for the part everyone plays in the story of our collective awakening. It becomes clear how everyone's experience is intertwined with everyone else's in a vast poetic display of power and grace.

I feel myself resting in a deep sense of trust. And I can see there is more trusting to come. As I have assembled all these writings, I have been astounded by their profound beauty. It has also become clear to me that, just because I can hear the words, it does not mean that I have integrated the teachings. The process of going through these teachings in detail has helped me move forward on my path. I trust that reading them will also be helpful to you.

The willingness to put the idea of a small self aside and inwardly trust the feelings, sensations, insights, and words that arise from loving Wisdom is the power of the Feminine Way, the way of receptivity and openness. The Masculine Way of confident action, the courage to bring this Wisdom out into the world, is also necessary. This experience of inward reception and outward expression highlights that both are necessary and are ultimately the same Unity. Reception without action stagnates. Action without reception is dangerous. There have been many moments in the process of writing this book that I have felt flooded with fear about bringing my story and these teachings out into the world. I have wished I could just forget it all and stagnate. And then I read the news and weep, and I see how much humanity is longing for the bath of Love these words provide.

I also see how desperately the world needs the Feminine Way of receptivity to Wisdom. Action based on valuing the protection of the small self and its tribe has resulted in more suffering than can be comprehended. When the Divine Feminine and **Divine Masculine** Ways are unified, then we are freed to experience the bliss that all great teachers have found to be the true nature of Reality.

I now know the presence of the Source in me as the boundless infinity of my Self, the Self that is the same as all Creation and God. You are holding its expression in your hands as written words. As you read them, may they be as fresh to you as when they were first transmitted. May you also experience the energetics as you are open to receiving them. These teachings are a vital interactive engagement in the present moment, which contains the All in All.

Yeshua said to us, "Whoever believes in me will do the works I have been doing, and they will do even greater things than these, because I am going to the Father. And I will do whatever you ask in my name, so that the Father may be glorified in the Son" (John 14:12-13 NIV). These words are for you, dear friend.

Ireland Story

I conclude Part I with the story about Ireland that I mentioned earlier. I share it in some detail because it illustrates clearly that all consciousness is shared and that all of Creation, including consciousness and what appears to be solid form, is a pattern of Light. This story is also the threshold John Hempstead and I crossed to join in the unified field of universal Awareness.

In July 2018, I was sitting in meditation, practicing knowing that, as a Child of God, I am the creator of all my perceived experience. I welcomed whatever came into the field of my awareness as that which presented itself for healing. I knew by then that, since all minds are joined, it is entirely possible that memories and experiences can arise that are not *mine*, in this life or in any other. All healing is collective.

The following vision unfolded. It had the vibrant quality of a lived memory—I could hear the wind, smell the sea, feel the mist— but I was not any of the characters. Rather, my consciousness was the experience of their connections with each other and with the world. My perspective was the space between the people, the intimate energy of Love. I also knew what they were all experiencing, so my awareness was simultaneously with each of them, their connections, and the earthly context that held them. I had the distinct impression I was in someone else's memory.

The scene is the Irish coast. The image that first comes into focus is incredibly close to the cheek of a small boy, aged three or four, with dark curly hair that is blown in the stiff wind. He can feel the mist on his face as he looks down from a path high above a beach nestled between rocky promontories made of dark rock, almost black. He holds his mother's left hand in his right. He indicates to her that he wants to go down to the beach where the men are getting their fishing gear ready to go out for the day. It is early in the morning.

Mother and son make their way down the rough path. His father sees them coming. He has the same dark curly hair as his son and a close-cropped black beard. He laughs happily in greeting. The boy runs to him, and the father scoops him up, holding him close. He tells the boy he is not yet big enough to come fishing with him. The Love they feel for each other is perfection. The mother follows close behind. She watches her husband and son in quiet delight. The father catches her eye, puts his son down, and draws her to him. The Love between them is dense and joyous, their kiss the perfection of bliss. The boy wants to be included! Laughing, the father picks him up, their faces are all together like a bouquet of flowers. The holy family. The men are ribbing him—time for that later on!

Holding the son, the father turns to look out at the ocean, the rocks, the sky, and the early Sun filtering through the mist. He tells the boy, "This is God. All of it is God, which is but Love." Wordlessly, he conveys that the boy's mission will be to tell the people about the Word of God, which is Love. The Love between the boy and his parents is the foundation for his knowing that what his father says is true.

Then the scene shifts. At first, it seems like the boy is seeing a picture of his future self wearing the long, fitted, black robe of a priest, walking along that same cliff path above the beach. But then the experience is from the adult's perspective, looking down at the beach, remembering that scene and his parents' Love, as he walks to the next village to tell the people that they are loved, that God is Love.

I reached out to John Hempstead to ask if this were a memory of his past life. He hesitated at first, but later wrote to me, "When you first told me about the memory that was not yours of the boy and his father and mother on an Irish beach, I had an unusual feeling. That feeling has continued to grow. I now feel strongly that that life was mine. When I was a young boy, I had dark curly hair. (That, of course, is ancient history.) Your description of this boy sounds similar. This may have been one of my many priest lives."

We had independently decided to attend a *Way of Mastery* retreat in Ireland in September, so we agreed we would try to find this place. At the retreat, John often asked me to tell people the story of this vision. By the third or fourth telling, a local Irish woman thought my description of a beach at the bottom of an extremely steep hill surrounded by rocky promontories sounded like Malin Beg, just beyond the towering Slieve League cliffs, the westernmost point of County Donegal. She showed me pictures on her phone, and it looked right.

John had felt strongly drawn to see the Slieve League (Sliabh Liag in Gaelic) Cliffs, so we had already agreed to travel there after the retreat. We immediately decided to drive on to Malin Beg. When Janet, the retreat organizer, heard of our travel plans, she arranged an expedition to these sites. Janet, John, two other friends, and I piled into her vehicle and set off to find Malin Beg.

After a long drive through upland bogs that are harvested for peat, we arrived at Malin Beg. I was quiet, aware that I was in the presence of mystery. I stepped out of the car and was a bit confused. My vision did not have a parking lot, guardrail, or grass neatly trimmed by sheep, or concrete steps down to the beach. Maybe this wasn't right! I tuned these details out and replaced them with the low bushes and rough path of my vision. I looked at the shape of the land, the beach, and the water. The cliffs on the left were lighter, but I realized that was because in my vision it was early morning, and now it was late afternoon, and the low Sun was shining directly on the cliffs. The ones in shadow on the right looked black, as I had seen them. On both sides, they reach towards each other, creating arms that protect this magical beach. I stood where I first saw the boy and his mother, and, looking down at the beach, I said, "Yes, this is absolutely it." I was amazed that I was standing, a hundred years later, in a vision of a place where I have never been.

I walked down the two hundred steps to the beach. It was broad and could easily accommodate a group of fishing boats. I found a seat at the bottom of the cliffs, leaned back, and breathed. I was in awe, sitting inside of mystery.

On the last day of the retreat, I had experienced the body as Light, a hologram of the patterns of the Universe. I had physically felt that the body vibrates at the same frequency as the stars. I realized that, while I could see patterns of Light in other people's bodies and hearts and past lives, I had not, until that moment, had the *felt knowing* that my body is made of the same patterns of Light. I realized that, for all my lifetimes in the illusion of separation, I have known the miracle of Spirit, and I have even been able to explain how thoughts produce matter, but I have always believed that material reality was somehow different from Spirit—that is, I have been fooled by the illusion. Even Yeshua's demonstration that his body was made of Light was not enough to crack this belief. I thought he was special. I misunderstood.

This next day, sitting at the bottom of the steep hillside at Malin Beg, I saw that the Earth herself is made of Light. There is no way I could have seen John's past life in this place, and still believed that his Soul is made of Spirit, yet this place is, somehow, a solid stage on which the drama of Souls in separation gets enacted. Yes, it is the stage, but it is not solid. I could *feel* that it is made of Light. My awareness, this body, and the cliff were One, just as I had experienced in the original vision. Such *joy!* If I could have, I would have flown back up the stairs. I made it up one hundred steps and had to catch my breath!

On the way to Malin Beg, we had stopped at St. Catherine's Well in Killybegs, where John had fallen while running downhill. This turned out to be a foreshadowing reenactment of his fatal fall in his previous life as the priest. Being on the Donegal coast, memories of that life came back to him strongly. Here is some of what he remembered:

Based on the adult priest's clothing, it had taken place in about 1920. It was a time of poverty and famine in Ireland. He had not been a parish priest but was assigned the duty of ministering to the people far out in the countryside. He visited homes far from churches to perform the sacraments of Mass, marriage, baptism, and funerals. Many of the houses could only be reached by footpath, so he walked everywhere and was welcomed wherever he knocked. He loved the people and loved the land.

He loved walking, and he especially loved to climb the high hills and cliffs. He communed with Nature Spirits and the little people as he walked. But by the 1930s, his superior had had enough of his supporting the people's belief in the **Earth Spirits**. In a confrontation with the parish priest, he was forcefully instructed to give that up. This was not something he could do, since he interacted with these Spirits himself. Distraught, he walked out onto the Slieve League cliffs, a familiar place that cleansed his heart of any troubles. It was a windy day. He lost his footing, caught his toe on his priest's robe, and fell to his death. It was certainly not suicide, but he was finished with what he could do in that life.

As a young child in his current life, John saw and communed with Nature Spirits, though he had cut that sensitivity off, afraid others would perceive him as crazy. He has always loved to walk, run, and climb high places. And he has always had a strong fear, even recoil and terror, at the top of a steep cliff. He could see that these habits, and many others, were carryovers from this previous life. Seeing the personal issues he was struggling with back then helped him to let go of the ways in which those issues had continued into his current life.

After visiting Malin Beg, we drove on to the Slieve League cliffs. Walking along a broad path that led to the top of the cliffs, Janet told us that a smaller path continued on to a high point where the steep cliffs go down to the sea on one side and down to a valley on the other side. John froze and could not go on. To him, this narrow place felt like where the priest had been blown off.

On the way home, Janet stopped at a court cairn, a Neolithic structure in the countryside before the town of Carrick. We arrived with the Sun low in the sky. The layout comprises a courtyard leading to two inner chambers, reached by going under rock doorways. It has side alcoves for chanting or meditating, both inside the courtyard and outside it. The walls of the courtyard are tall and neatly built. I began chanting and heard that it has what is called a *wolf note*, the tone whose vibrational frequency matches the distance between the walls, and so produces sympathetic overtones that amplified the tone I was singing. The sound was startlingly loud and exhilarating. We explored this phenomenon together—great fun!

I suddenly remembered the fall equinox was that night, September 22, and we were there at sunset! We stood at the opening to the court. The setting Sun was exactly in line with this opening and the two inner chambers. I looked behind me and saw a steep hill with a sharp rock at the crest. I was sure that the Sun would rise exactly over that rock in the morning. This must be why the court cairn had been placed there. We all stood in front of the inner chambers for a photo with the Sun setting behind our heads. Magical!

The next morning, John had a powerful experience of releasing fears and being able to allow the Earth **Elementals** back into his awareness, right as the Sun rose and the room filled with Light. And then a rainbow appeared! What a blessing for the closing of this gathering. The timing of everything was perfect—a sequence that allowed this healing to occur just at sunrise on September 23, the morning of the equinox.

John and I shared this miraculous story with everyone who had been at the retreat. Friends who read it were amazed and inspired. John commented, "I still find it totally astounding that you could awaken to vivid memories of a century ago. Of course, the knowledge it is still there in the Light is key to knowing." This whole experience made it clear to me that everything is still in the Light, so there can be no loss. What I found even more astounding is that we are Light-Beings who believe we are trapped in bodies and so go through multiple lifetimes until we realize that it's really true that everything is made of Light and we are Creators!

I felt myself moving to a deeper place of resting in knowing that my life is being perfectly guided to return Home, so I don't need to plan anything. I was also struck by the collaborative nature of the **Atonement**. We are each responsible for our part, and all parts are also in intimate communication with all other parts. Walking the path Home requires this dual awareness of personal responsibility and intimate collaboration.

Returning to Boston from the retreat was emotionally rocky for me, with lots of ups and downs. I felt I didn't want to live in my familiar life, not yet understanding that it is by bringing the awareness of the Light into every experience that I learn to live continually in the awareness of God. This is a slow process that takes lots of practice! Miraculous moments are encouragements to continue on. I also had moments of doubt when I returned to that familiar life, but I kept thinking, how can I possibly have had a vision of Malin Beg and John's life, and have the whole thing confirmed in *reality* if it is not true in Reality?

Writing this story now, I feel awe and gratitude. How can I ever again believe that anything is by chance? How can I ever again believe that our Creator is not aligning all events for our healing, if only we will open our inner eye and heart to see and feel? How can I ever again believe that there exists anything *other* than Light, than

Love? Streams of gratitude to our elder brother Yeshua, who made sure that, as a child, I would remember his words—that he will be with us even unto the end of the age. Thank you to all of my sisters and brothers, named and unnamed in this account, who love and support each other. May we find our Home in the Heart of God.

Now that you know some of how this all came about, the rest of this book contains the teachings, along with the continuation of my spiritual story. Welcome to the Way!

PART 2

The Teachings

Chapter 4

Direct Communications Begin

Clearing Away the Small Self

What I have told you so far about my experiences with the energy of Light and the Enlightened Ones are just the highlights. The more challenging work is being present with my personal psychological issues, feeling all my experiences fully so I can see where I am still holding onto constricting beliefs, and then being willing to let them go. Anyone who is on an emotional growth path is likewise clearing the way for their own direct spiritual experiences. Our true nature is Divine, and this Reality becomes more accessible the more the layers of rigid thinking covering it up are dissolved.

I encourage you to continue with your own clearing process so that we will all come to know that what Yeshua said is true. "Jesus said to them, 'Is it not written in your Law, "I said, you are gods"? The Holy Writings were given to them and God called them gods.'" (John 10:34-35 NLV). The Law Yeshua was referencing here is Psalms 82:6 (NLT). "I say, 'You are gods; you are all children of the Most High.'"

This true nature is there all along, simply covered up by our fearful focus on maintaining a separate self. The image that always comes to mind that helps explain this process is the art project I was taught as a child. Completely cover a piece of shiny cardboard with patterns of brightly colored crayons. Then cover that with black crayon. Then scrape off the black to reveal the hidden beauty underneath. This is like a super-fast time-lapse video of the Child of God being born in beauty, covering up our Self with egoic fear, greed, guilt, etc., and then slowly revealing who we have been all along.

Yeshua explains this another way in Luke 17:20-21 (NIV). "Once, on being asked by the Pharisees when the kingdom of God would come, Jesus [Yeshua] replied, 'The coming of the kingdom of God is not something that can be observed, nor will people say, "Here it is," or "There it is," because the kingdom of God is in your midst.'"

Thomas recorded this incident in Saying 113 in his Gospel. "His disciples said to him, 'When will the kingdom come?' [Yeshua said,] 'It will not come by watching for it. It will not be said, "Look, here it is," or "Look, there it is." Rather, the Father's kingdom is spread out upon the Earth, and people do not see it'" (Meyer 2007).

This scraping away process is simple but not easy, and always requires understanding and acceptance. The foundational acceptance is that covering up our true nature has been necessary to attain awareness of our Self. When we understand this, we can let go of feeling guilty that we have hidden it from our awareness. It was *necessary* to imagine that we created conflict with our Source in order to *know* that we exist, to know ourselves and know God, rather than remain in the primordial One-ness with no *awareness* of our Being. While imagining this separation did create the whole *way of conflict* and all of its eons of suffering, it has also brought us to the point of knowing that, to quote **William Thetford**, "There must be another way." (Foundation for Inner Peace n.d.) This allows us to see the *Way of Harmony* emerging from behind the layers of darkness, and we become motivated to learn what the suffering is teaching us and thus transmute it into Love. Then we see Reality as it is—Love that expresses as an endlessly moving pattern of vibration that includes all aspects of Creation that are simultaneously Self-aware and in communication with All. There is no thought of separation, and there is full awareness of Being, which is the Being of God. This is the **New Creation**.

A car accident in 1988, my second year of graduate school, revealed a deep layer of consciousness that is beyond all thought. This experience has remained a touchstone on my spiritual journey. I was traveling on a four-lane road at the 40 miles-per-hour speed limit. A red light ahead turned green, so I maintained my speed to go through the intersection. However, an elderly woman in a large car, who had been waiting at the light, misjudged my speed and turned in front of me. There was no way I could avoid driving directly into her car. My perception of time slowed way down while I made precise calculations about how hard to step on the brakes and how hard to turn the wheel to diminish the impact while avoiding spinning out or flipping the car over. Once I had that figured out, there was nothing more to think except *I could die*. Then, my thinking mind simply disappeared. I will never have a memory of the impact because the level of consciousness that is perceptual awareness had ceased.

And what was revealed was *bliss*. There is no way I can describe this in words. It was a pure distillation of the most perfect contentment/joy/delight/awe I have ever experienced. There were no flaws, impurities, or variations. It was timeless and utterly peaceful. I only came back to my normal state of awareness because someone was knocking on my window to see if I were okay. I found that I was holding my unharmed head protectively in my hands, and only my right knee hurt where it had hit the ignition keys (remember those?). The calculations had worked well—my car had bounced off of hers at an angle and had landed upright along the side of the road.

Now I knew with a direct personal certainty: beyond the egoic level of consciousness that is focused on survival lies the ceaseless bliss of universal Consciousness. It continues on, never ceasing, outside of our superficial awareness. It was around this same time that I started with Buddhist practice, so when I heard this state of ceaseless bliss described by the Buddha many times during those years, I knew that what he said was true: when I let go of being concerned about my survival, the thinking mind disappears, and the perfection of God is all that remains. Having this state revealed through shock motivated me to continue on the slower and more stable path of releasing stuck places in the mind in order to arrive at establishing the awareness of bliss as the only state.

It is always challenging to let go of the darkness we are scraping off because we made it ourselves! And we are convinced we will die without its protection. It takes some convincing for the small self to let go of its grip on its own creations and notice that the idea of death is nothing, and the vastness of Creation offers far greater rewards. Yeshua opened his first direct communication with us with exactly this instruction. "Look outward—which is looking inward—but look at the vastness of the whole, the completion of everything in its exquisite, ever-unfolding beauty."

I invite you to absorb Part 2 slowly, allowing the energetics of the messages to soften the resistances your small self puts up to the awareness that your Being has been unified with God all along. This Truth is simple, but the softening takes time. I invite you to experience the frequencies of Christ Consciousness directly through the words, and to be aware of your inward experiences through listening, seeing, feeling, and knowing. You might want to speak the meditations out loud or practice them with friends. How you respond to the material is simply your own response, and I invite you to allow it all.

Anointed in the Light

Yeshua's first direct verbal communication through me was on October 27, 2018. Here is what I said, at times hesitant, at times struggling to formulate what I was hearing, but mostly the words flowed as I simply described what I was seeing and hearing. The process was much like all the intuitive sessions I had done with people, just describing my inner experience as it unfolded—only this time, my experience was seeing and feeling and hearing Yeshua!

I begin to speak.

"I feel such gratitude for the grace of being guided to reconnect with Souls with whom I have such a deep and loving relationship. We always support each other in our desire for the awareness of the Truth of Love.

"I see Yeshua, who has now shown up, right in front, brilliant white Light as always, just blessing us. He's got his hands up in blessing. He is bringing his hand forward to touch both of our third eyes, granting us deeper vision, always deeper vision. There is always more to be aware of.

"Now he joins with our energy field and says:"

"Look outward—which is looking inward—but look at the vastness of the whole, the completion of everything in its exquisite, ever-unfolding beauty. And just enjoy it. Just enjoy it. Just enjoy knowing that you are aware of all of this as your Self. And enjoy knowing that you are not alone—you are always in Love. You are in Love with whatever energy you are aware of being close to. And be aware that you are in Love with all energies, whether they are next to you or apparently somewhere farther away. It's such a miraculous unfolding process.

"This is a glimpse of the Queendom. This is a glimpse of where I reside with the other Enlightened Ones. It is so much more than what you think of as Earth. You think of Earth as enormously varied and complex, with so many places, and it's all true. And yet, this is an exponentially different quality of more-ness.

"Just enjoy. Just enjoy being with each other, with me, and the other Great Beings who are so happy to be welcoming you to this state. Our desire is for all of you to become aware that this is your true Home because all of you are the same as all of us. We are not fully content until every last piece of Light that thinks it's separated has traveled its way back up the Ray to the Source. We can't go on into the fullness of Creation if there is any one little piece of Light that seems to think that it is left behind. This is what I meant when I said to you, 'I am the shepherd and I do not forget any of my sheep,' because my sheep are my Self. How can I forget any part of my Self? You have thought that being my sheep meant being something less—just a sheep. That's only a metaphor to show you the depth of my Love, that I forget no one because you are the same as my Self. How can I forget you?

"There is such celebration as more of you become aware that you are the same as me, and you cease putting me on a separate level. That just creates separation in your mind."

I describe what I am seeing inwardly: "He is now putting a kind of anointing oil made of Light on our heads that is coming down over us. This is so we can know we are in the same Christ Light. It is not to make us special, that we are now the *anointed ones*."

Yeshua continues, "All humanity will become anointed in the Light. We are participating in the great anointing of humanity. Everyone is anointed as they are ready to receive the anointment. You will also anoint others. Your power to anoint others is the same as mine. It has nothing to do with being more powerful or special. It's to do with having already received the Light. Light simply shines. The anointing of humanity is the dissolving of the barriers that create the illusion of shadows. Each anointing puts the Soul into Light fully, so it ceases to cast a shadow.

"Thank you for listening. This is exactly the metaphor I wanted you to understand—that the anointing creates a sphere of Light surrounding the Soul, erasing any obstacle that creates a shadow."

"I was feeling, *what a relief to hear this message about not being special!* And he's saying:"

"Yes, I'm glad that you are ready to receive that being anointed into the Light is the fate of all of humanity—to become anointed in Light—so specialness is irrelevant. That's a thought that only exists in the realm of shadow, where some shadows are darker than others.

"Enjoy the feeling of Light throughout the body. It's a physical sensation of ecstasy. Just sustain that physical sensation of ecstasy. Just feel it.

"You are that Light. When you join with your anointed brothers and sisters, your Light becomes brighter. Join with each other as you surround whoever is sent to you with Light."

"Then he reminds me that, when I forget to join with him, I get dragged down by people's darkness. If I could remember to join with my friends of the Heart, that will help me. Walking around in the illusion, I know you are *real*, and sometimes it's easier to picture joining with a friend than with Yeshua, who I know is real, but who I don't see in a body. Connecting with a friend makes the Light of Christ more real because it's expressed in a body I love."

Yeshua continues, "This is why it's so important for the Soul family of **Light-workers**, the Christ-Minded ones, to join with each other, to help us sustain our knowledge that the Light is real and not to be drawn into the darkness.

"I am reminding you of what I have said before, that when the Light of the mind of humanity increases, what you see as the world changes into beauty. Do not be fearful of the pollution and destruction of the Earth. The only thing that will be transmuted is your vision of a damaged world. It is so important to maintain awareness of your connection with your Light-Minded brothers and sisters. It's important to have times to be in Communion.

"I will join you always because I love you, because I *am* you. You and I are the same Child of God. I am so happy that you are understanding this, this morning.

"Go in peace, be with each other. Whenever you think of each other during your day, you are always there with each other, always."

"And with that, he says:"

"**Ameyn**. Be with each other. Ameyn."

I had no idea Yeshua would speak through me in that moment. Nor did I know this communication, which began so spontaneously during that video call with John, would become a process of consistent and direct verbal communications. But once the inner channel was open to receive his words, they flowed through me with incredible clarity and at a pace that was compelling. All I wanted to do was to receive and express his Wisdom.

The gifts of Spirit are, indeed, infinitely greater than the rewards the small self has made!

Shifting the Balance to Light Heals the Dream

I shared this first message with friends from the retreat in Ireland. People were intrigued, and on November 11, 2018, ten of us from different countries gathered on a video call.

After sitting together in silent meditation, I begin to speak.

"Dear friends, may I share my vision?

"At first, I see the Earth being consumed in fire from the inside, and I'm told this is a purifying fire, not a destructive fire, to purify the attachment to the belief in darkness. And then the vision shifts, and there are beautiful waters that pour around the Earth—cool, healing waters of the Mother, a vision of Paradise, waterfalls and animals and birds and plants, all in beauty on the Earth.

"Then Yeshua appears in front of me with his arms outstretched, wearing a large cape. He's welcoming all the scared Souls who are dying—children, adults, animals. He is indicating that there are many Enlightened Ones, and he asks us to join in holding the fear of the ones who are dying and coming into the embrace of the Enlightened Ones. As we hold all the Souls who have died in fear, that allows the Light to play on the Earth and get established strongly.

"Then the fearful Souls are called, a few at a time, to return to the Earth, but the balance has shifted entirely to Light, so that the Light can hold the fearful ones until they are healed. They go through whatever cleansing process they need until their eyes are cleared. I see this image of their eyes being wiped clean, and they can look around and see that they are in Paradise, the state of the Unity of Heaven and Earth. Then they call to the other Souls who are in their families to come and return to the Earth. It isn't the hell that it used to be, that they thought it was. As each Soul comes back, the balance remains in the Light, in this unified state of Heaven and Earth, so each fearful Soul can return and be healed. Yeshua is reminding us that this is what he had said to me before, when he said:"

"You are my sheep because you are part of my Self. I'm showing you this image of my arms as a cape, welcoming all the fearful Souls into my Self to show you that this is true, that all the fearful Souls are my Self. They are not lost. They are not separated. They are just in a state of confusion. And as I hold them in the vastness of my Being, *you* hold them as they return to Earth. In our state of Unity, we heal all the fragmented parts of the One Child of God, which is *who we are*. This is the *process* by which the state of Unity happens on Earth.

"I know you've been confused about how that could happen, since, as a therapist, you know people can be *so* lost in their darkness, very attached. And you know that you've taken lifetimes to work out your own fearfulness. So, I'm showing you, this is how it works. As Souls enter the Light and form the strength of Unity, then the darkness is no longer able to overshadow. It is welcomed into the Light and healed, one piece at a time, as the Light is able to absorb it, and as each fearful Soul is willing to open his or her eyes and look around and realize that they've just been in a dream. Yes, it was a painful dream, but it's passing, and this is how it comes to pass. And you, my sisters and brothers, who know what comes to pass, I am showing you this so that you can know more clearly *how* it comes to pass.

"You are all *so* important. I need all of you. The Ones who are not in bodies, we are *always* working with you to help those of you who are still lost in confusion return to the Light. *Never, ever* think that you are not important. *Never, for one moment*, think that you are not important, even if you think you are only shedding the Light in one little small spot. Remember that every small spot is the same as my Self. Every lost sheep is my Self. Every lost sheep who is returned Home adds to the brilliance of the Unity of Light.

"I love you all *so* much. We all love you *so* much. Can I convey to you our excitement, our gratitude, our party? There is just a celebration that you are hearing my Voice, that you are *feeling* my vibration. More than hearing my Voice, what matters is to *feel* the vibration. Feel it in your *feet*. Feel it within your body, the lower half of your body. That is the energy of the Light returning *into* the Earth. That is how it happens, through your body transmitting Light into the Earth.

"Such joy, we feel such joy! We want you to *feel* the joy so that you don't forget it, and so you don't get pulled off by those distractions that I said will come your way. Just accept them with humor. *Oh, my little distraction, of course, I know who you are! You're the one that I sent to myself to see what I'm committed to. Of course, I'm committed to the Light! I'm not committed to distractions.* That's all they are, even the distractions that look terrible. They're just distractions.

"Feel me in your heart now. I'm sending my presence to you strongly into your hearts. Feel that burning—the desire to create the New, the new expansion of consciousness *into* matter. This is a new experience. You have no idea what's going to happen. Just stay with the experience of *feeling* the Love *in your bodies*. I'm *very* grateful that you have understood about feeling the Light of Love *physically*, and that you're not afraid to experience it. It is *so* important for you to share the glory of Divine energy. It is *so* important to share the Divine creative power because that is the state of ecstatic union. How could union not be ecstatic?

"And with that, my friends, I give you my *blessing*, my *adoration*. I *kneel* before you. You are my beloved sisters and brothers with whom I have been One since before time began. I remind you that you all agreed to work with me before there was such a thing as time, and you have come now to help all of us bring this phase of work to fruition.

"Never for a moment think you are not important. Remember, I have been with you always since before time began, and I am with you always until time ends.

"We send you our joy, our ecstasy, our delight. Such happiness!

"With that, my beloveds, go out into the world, which is in your hearts—there is no separation between what's inside and what's outside. Shed your Light on all who come to you. Everyone is sent to you for a purpose. Just join with each other in your hearts in whatever endeavor you find yourself engaged." Yeshua laughs gently. "Even when you don't hear someone speaking my Voice, you hear my Voice in your heart, *always*. That vibration of Love *never ever* leaves you.

"I *adore* you.

"Ameyn."

I could see that Yeshua's first message was about the unreality of specialness for a reason. Feeling special was an issue I had struggled with for ten years, ever since I first heard the Voice of the Holy Spirit clearly, and I became aware of my profound intuitive and healing gifts. This could all go to a little ego's head! I had known for a while that I would be channeling Yeshua's Voice, but I had required much purification and much humbling. Now that I could hear him clearly, it simply felt normal, natural, effortless—just a flow of loving Wisdom. As I absorbed his repeated message that we all are his sheep, that is, parts of his Self, the thought of specialness steadily dissolved.

I hope you are feeling how important you are as we all participate in our collective awakening. I hope you can feel the difference between the Truth of your importance—you are the Beloved of God—and the unreality of specialness, the ego's attempt to replace Love with its own meaningless value.

Cricket

By mid-November, my beloved twenty-year-old cat Cricket was feeling quite unwell because of his kidney failure, even after having received subcutaneous fluids the previous day. I worked on getting myself ready to let him go. I asked John for astrological guidance on the timing, and I set an appointment with the euthanasia vet. But I felt Cricket hadn't quite told me he was ready, and then he perked up with daily fluids. He seemed happy, just sleeping a lot—he didn't seem to be ready to die. So I canceled the appointment. I took my cue from him—when he let me know he was done with being in his body, then I would help him go.

I suspect he had had a taste of being in the energy field of Yeshua, and he wanted more!

Cricket would ask me to lie with him whenever I could. What an intense experience! In this wide-open-hearted state of preparing for his passing, I would experience Yeshua all through my physical, emotional, and mental being, through the soles of my feet, the palms of my hands, the top of my head, and everything in between. I would take deep, deep breaths, absorbing all of our Love for each other. I heard Yeshua tell me that, when I release my last piece of identity with ego, then I will be with him where he is, reclining only in Love.

The Flow of Light

When I joined again with John Hempstead on December 3, 2018, we were given an experience of consciously working with the feeling of receiving and extending Light. Please practice this along with us.

I share with John that, "I have been resting daily in profound joy. Having had that mystical healing experience with you in Ireland, I no longer have any doubt about the Reality of the inclusiveness of Spirit. *Everything* is included in the Light, everything, even things that look *negative*. Nothing is, in Reality, negative. I've also been keenly aware that all of us are ultimately the same Soul, and anybody with whom I interact is just another aspect of my Self. You, John, are another aspect of my Self. I feel my heart resonating with the profound devotion that we both have to God, to the spiritual path, and to our beloved brother, Yeshua. I know that we have been devoted to the same Pathway since before time began. It's a choice that we all made to bring together our collective Light in order to bring the awareness of Light back into our minds and the minds of all of humanity. It's just a joy.

"I'm seeing what appears to be conflict in the world as a kind of vibration—ripples that are extending out from a point of fear that I don't believe in anymore. I see it with a kind of gentleness, with compassion, not with fear.

"Mother-Father God, this spiritual path is an endless beautiful unfolding. I know there's always more, always more. I'm asking in my heart for Yeshua to come to be with us.

"And now I see him, *brilliant* white, *intensely* white, with his arms outstretched, indicating for us to look upward to the Source of the Light that I can now see—*exceedingly bright*, coming down through our bodies like an endless stream. It's a brilliant white Light. He's indicating that he is the conduit for this Light and that he is grateful that we are also open, that our crown chakras are open, so this Light, like a stream, can flow down through our bodies.

"And then I see it encircling the Earth. It's like a liquid oil of Light that swirls around the Earth. He is the conduit for this Light that comes down into the crown chakras of all the Light-Minded people—and there are many, many of us all around the world. I can see him, with his arms, pulling the Light down from God, through himself, and into us, in an endless stream. And the Earth becomes brighter and brighter. Extraordinarily beautiful.

"I'm feeling his gratitude that we are no longer afraid, because the stain of fear prevents the flow of Light. This *brilliant* Light today is possible because the fear is gone. The fear of death is gone. The fear of judgment is gone. The fear of illness is gone. The fear of loss is gone. The fear of lack, of poverty, is gone. It's all gone.

"Now he is saying:"

"Just sustain being in this brilliant white Light."

"I see our energies as completely expanded. Our bodies are no longer separate bodies. Rather, the energy of this Light is an extension of our body-minds surrounding the Earth and holding it like a net, like a bag of silk—I'm trying to find the right metaphor. He says:"

"Just rest in holding that energy of Light surrounding the Earth. It's more powerful than you know. You have no idea how powerful it is to hold the Earth completely surrounded in Light. There are no gaps in the Light when we join together."

John poses a question. "I have a question about Light. It's been said that each cell has a center point, a prism through which Light is extended and distributed, and that it can extend out in all directions, including holding the world in Light. Do you have any comments on that?"

Through my voice, Yeshua responds. "Each cell is a metaphor for each body, which is a metaphor for each spark of Light. So, each cell extending Light is exactly the same as each body extending Light, which is exactly the same as all of humanity extending Light. This is exactly the same as all of Creation extending Light. The distinction in levels is simply one to help you know that all levels are the same Light. The cells are holograms for your body; your body is a hologram for your Soul; and your Soul is a hologram for our One Soul, which is a hologram for God. So, allow Light to come into every cell of the body, especially places where you feel constriction, and feel it soften those places. Those are just old habits from previous lifetimes when the belief in fear was strong and manifested as knots in the body.

"Today is the day to release all of that as you rest in this endless flow of Light from God, through Yeshua and around the world, which is the same as your bodies. There is no distinction between your body Light and the world Light. Your body contains the same patterning of Light that is in the Universe, that is also in the Earth. It is all oscillating at varying levels of frequency that are in communication endlessly. That is what is meant by the *music of the spheres*. This endless oscillation of Light can be perceived as Light or as Sound. It is exquisitely beautiful. Just rest in it. The closest thing you can perceive on your Earth is the aurora at the poles, the beautiful colors that slowly oscillate."

After a long pause, he resumes:

"The practice is to hold this awareness of the Light of God coming through me, into you, and surrounding the Earth. It comes through me, not because I am higher than you, but because my role is to direct the Atonement. I can see whenever any Soul is ready to receive Light and, immediately, it goes into that person's body-mind. When another Soul is ready to receive the Light, it amplifies *my* awareness of Light, which seems strange to you to hear me say, because certainly I am aware of Light! And yet, when you join with me, it amplifies, because Light is always increasing."

He continues after another long pause.

"Now take that image of the Earth surrounded by its beautiful net of vibrating Light, and imagine that it shrinks small enough that you can bring it into your heart. Hold your knowing that, without fear, you are always holding the Earth *in Light*. Anytime you think of me, I am right there. I am there all the time, but I am reassuring you that you are free of fear, so that when you think of me, it is the Truth that I am there. It is not your idle imagination."

"He is looking us directly in the eye and conveying:"

"I love you *so* much. It is so wonderful to have friends on the Path returning Home.

"I bless you. Go in Peace. I am with you always. Bring the Light of God everywhere you go.

"Thank you, and, Ameyn."

John remarks, "Laura, I'd just like to share with you that, when you were talking about the Light and including the world and all of what you are doing in it, you were just *radiating* Light! It was amazing how the screen changed from a darker screen to a lighter screen, and particularly at some points, the Light just radiated fully from around your face. That was all I could see on the screen—the Light radiating from your face."

All I could respond with was, "Wow!"

In a subsequent email to John, I shared a fear that I was making up the joining we were doing with each other and Yeshua. But right then, I received a call from my friend John Krysko, who had predicted I would serve in this capacity a year and a half ago. He was exuberant after reading Yeshua's first message, and my fear went away. Yeshua told me the previous week that my one remaining fear was of what others would think, so I got to experience it and quickly let it go. Now I could see I am simply sharing the message with all who desire to hear it. I am just being the servant with no personal agenda.

John Hempstead had nothing but affirmation. "I really love the audio and have listened to it twice so far. This is a wonderful joint venture. The role of Bill Thetford (co-scribe of *A Course in Miracles*) suits me fine."

Enjoy the Feast

John and I joined again on December 10, 2018, with our request to communicate with Yeshua.

John starts. "We're on. This is Laura Derr with John Hempstead, and we're waiting for what's next."

I add, "And my cat, Cricket, has joined us because he likes this Communion energy very much!"

I continue. "We were talking just now about the myth of separating from God as a childlike game—we look over our shoulders to see if God is still chasing us, if God still loves us. Even if we're really *bad*, does our Daddy still love and care for us? The answer is, *Yes! It's just a game!* I feel so relieved.

"We also discussed that we each *needed* to run away so we could experience our creative power as our *own* and not as something that is only our Mother-Father God's power. *I* needed to experience it. *I can do this! I am God! I have creative power!* And now God says, *Yes, you have creative power! And I still love you! And you're adorable!*

"Okay, I'm going to take off my glasses. One benefit of being nearsighted, I've understood, is that it enhances my inner sight. It is the strong symbolic message that my inner sight is to be relied on, not my outer perception, which is flawed indeed.

"Mother-Father God, ever-shimmering Light of All, you shine within us when we remember you. Name of names, our small identity unravels in you, and we know that we are you.

"I am asking in my heart for Yeshua to join us. I feel such Love for him. I feel the understanding of his Love for us, that we are all part of his Self, just as we are all part of God.

"Today, I can see him laughing, enjoying that we are understanding the fun of this game of hide and seek, of going in and out of lifetimes, looking for God, seeing if God is still behind our shoulders, and running away again. He is also laughing that we now understand that we have chosen to run away and that it's been a fun adventure. We needed to run into the deepest darkest places of despair to know that, when we come Home, there is no *badness* that has not been experienced, so that there is nothing secret waiting to trip us up and prove that God can't love us. When we've experienced everything *bad*, then we know we are totally lovable, and it has all just been a game.

"He gestures to a table laden with the most amazing food. It looks like food, but it also looks like beautiful Lights. It's in the cave in the Himalayas where I have met with him many times. He indicates it is time for us to take our seats at the table and enjoy the feast of Creation, the endless supply of nurturing and Love and family Communion. There are many other Enlightened Beings. It's a long table, not a round table. Everyone is enjoying feeding each other, laughing and talking with whoever is nearby, and moving around this amazing feast.

"I can see him now, sitting at the end of the table, just radiating *brilliant white Light*. He is indicating to create space because there are more people joining the table. The celebration is ongoing. There's Laura and John, and there are many other people coming up the mountain and into this cave of the beautiful golden Light of the enlightened Christ Consciousness.

"I have a question in my heart for Yeshua: if we spend our time celebrating at this feast, are we not neglecting our sisters and brothers who are struggling in the darkness down below?

"He explains that I have not yet gotten used to being in both states simultaneously. He says that we have had difficulty understanding how he can be in everyone's minds simultaneously *and* be himself *and* be in Communion with all the Enlightened Minds, all simultaneously, because that perspective of the universal **Christ-Mind** is something that we are not yet accustomed to. From the perspective of the ego-mind, the simultaneity of time and space is not understandable.

"He asks us to stay at this feast so that we know where our sustenance comes from. Our true sustenance comes from this feast, and not from potatoes in the Earth. The potatoes in the Earth are necessary within the illusion, but they are illusion. This feast in the beautiful golden glow of the Christ-Mind *is* Reality. When we stay in the delight of the endless supply of the creative power of God, which is our own, then, when we are walking on the Earth, we do not lose awareness of the Source of our creative supply. He says:"

"Yes, you are understanding what I am conveying to you. I know this is challenging for you because of the appearance of separation on the Earth-plane. It is challenging to hold in your mind, always in consciousness, the connection with the nurturing Source of God, while you are walking on the Earth. This is what I am supporting you in practicing now. I have described this before—how to be in the world, but not of the world. You are now at a place in your practice where it is time for you to maintain your awareness of being in the Christ-Mind so you can stay in that awareness while you are in the world.

"Being in the awareness of the Christ-Mind means being in the *joy* of the Christ-Mind. This image of the feast is to help you feel and see and experience the nurturing, the delight, the creativity, the generosity, the satisfaction in sharing and Communion, and never having an end to what is possible. That is the Christ-Mind—the state of mind that you are now practicing staying in as you walk through what appear to be your mundane lives. I am reminding you that your lives are far from mundane. They are in no way ordinary. No one's life is ordinary. You are now understanding what that actually means.

"I am reminding you that I needed to take time away in the wilderness when I walked on the Earth because the pull of the belief in separation is extremely strong indeed. It is important to take time out of time to return to this feast of Communion with Light-Minded Souls. Even I, as a man, had challenges with remaining in Communion with the Christ-Mind with God. This is why it is written that I withdrew often to pray. I was not asking God for anything. I was returning to my awareness of my true Home, which is in the Christ-Mind with God. Only then, when I was fully sure of who I was, could I return to walk among people who were not yet sure about who they are. *I know who you are.* I was an example of a life lived knowing who I am. It is now your time to live your lives *knowing who you are.*

"I am sending you my Love in your hearts for you to feel the burning of the desire that we have for each other. All the separated ones have this desire to be in Communion, to be yourselves *and* be understood, to be known. *I know you. I see who you are. I know you through and through.* Now that you know that there is no stain in your consciousness, anything that you thought was a mistake is not a mistake. It was done on purpose so that you could experience yourselves as completely different from God as you possibly could. In this way, you *know* that you have become yourself, and you know *God loves all of you.* God can love *every single last piece* of everything you think could be wrong with you. And now you can come Home.

"Celebrate all the mistakes! Celebrate that you have gone to the depths of the depths of despair. That has all been necessary so that there is *nothing* left to explore that you think might still pull you away from God. Here is where it is so important to love everyone's *mistakes.* Not everyone has to experience *everything* bad, *all* the despair. We are all aspects of the same Child of God, so all of us, together, have experienced everything there is to experience.

"You can come Home now. Your wanderings are complete. As you come Home to live with me, together in our shared Heart, our magnetic pull becomes stronger and stronger, and we pull in more and more Souls. They tune in to their longing for Love, for God, for understanding, for being known.

"There is such a feast of delight! My message to you today is to enjoy the feast! Walk around knowing that your supply of Love and creative power is endless; there are *no limits* to what you can do. There is nothing anymore to be afraid of.

"I am reminding you of what I told you in our last conversation—to hold the Earth in Light in your hearts. Today, you are experiencing our shared Heart in a more powerful way so that you can understand that, when you hold the Earth in your heart, you are holding it in our shared Heart, the Heart that we share with God. This endless power is what transforms the appearance of a tired Earth into a vibrant Earth. Do not be afraid of the death of the Earth. Your power, as the Children of God, is far too great to allow that to happen.

"Go in peace. Go in joy. Go in great celebration! *Never* forget how much I love you. I am so delighted that you have opened your hearts so that you can *feel* me. I have told you before that, while it is lovely to hear a voice saying my words, it is *far more important* for you to *feel* my vibration of Love in your heart, emanating throughout your body, and down into the Earth, up into the Heavens, around the Earth, and through the hearts of all our sisters and brothers.

"I adore you. I kneel before you. Your power is infinite, and I am filled with gratitude that you are following the Way that I showed you. I am just ahead of you, that's all. I am your brother. I am with you all the way. I told you I would be with you until the end of the age. I have never let go of that promise.

"And with that, go in *great* celebration, bringing the Peace of the Love of God out into the world.

"Ameyn."

John responds. "Ameyn. I will share again, Laura, that the first time you mentioned golden Light, a golden Light flashed on your face, on your throat, and up to the cheeks. Then, when you talked about the feast, it covered your whole face, just a radiant Light. And then it kind of flashed off and on until Yeshua talked about coming Home—then your entire face lit up. When he mentioned the feast again, your face remained just radiant. And now it's back to normal again."

"Wow. Fascinating. I'm sitting in the same spot."

"Yes, exactly."

"For the record, it's not a cloudy day, so the sunlight has been consistent through my window. It's not coming and going behind clouds."

"The other insight was," John continues, "when he talked about the feast, tears came to my eyes, and I realized I'd been told that before, and decided I was unworthy to attend that feast, and that's why I'm back again. That's why I'm so teary, because I know that feast is awaiting me and I just need to accept it."

❧

I shared this message with our group of friends and started receiving encouraging feedback. "Thank you, Laura! I love it all, and I look forward to anything that you will share with us. Blessings and gratitude."

"Thank you, Laura, for a beautiful channeling. I can feel so much Love coming through."

"Thank you for sharing this! So beautiful and inspiring. Bless you. The remembering is getting to be a lived Reality. I feel the gathering momentum in our joining together."

"This is stunningly beautiful. I could feel the feast and the Light and the Love. Thank you for sharing this with us."

He Delights in Answering Our Questions

A week later, on December 17, 2018, John and I joined with two sisters from the retreat in Ireland.

I start this gathering. "I've been thinking about how, in our session last time, I asked Yeshua a question and he answered it. I thought, *Oh, we can bring questions to him*! So, I would like to invite us to bring questions today and be delighted to receive the answers. I wake up in the morning thinking, *Wow, this is fun! This is amazing! In my devotion, I have come to a place where I can hear Yeshua's Voice and I can ask him questions, and anybody can ask him questions! This is amazing!*"

John suggests engaging in a prayer of affirmation of our alignment with God. We decide to recite the prayer three times, through three different voices.

In the Name of the Father, in the Name of the Son, in the Name of the Holy Spirit, Sophia, Shem, in the Name of the Lord, Christ I am.

(The word *Name* is a paltry representation of a much deeper meaning, for which English does not have a word. It conveys *vibrational atmosphere*—a realm made of a pattern of motion/Sound/Light with which we can align.)

I speak first. "The image that came instantly to mind was Yeshua calling us to bring all our heads together in a little huddle, like a little children's game, where you whisper a secret around the circle. He has this playful energy about him. He says:"

"We're all in this together! You're right, this is fun!"

"Then we have our arms around each other, and he indicates for us to let go, step back, and laugh, and the energy explodes outward, like fireworks, like a fountain of Light. He has us do this again— huddle together, heads touching, arms around each other, sharing what we have thought was secret Wisdom. Now that we know it's not, we release our arms, throw back our heads, laugh, sing, and spread the fountains of Light outward into the world! And he says:"

"Once more, everyone huddle, heads together, enjoy knowing that we have known this secret Wisdom for thousands of years, and it's been fun to know this Wisdom! And now it's time—one, two, three!—to let it out into the world! It is no longer a secret. It's not a secret club anymore. No one is special anymore. We have served our function as keepers of the Wisdom, but that has only been because of this erroneous belief that the Wisdom could ever be harmed. How can the Wisdom be harmed? It is directly from the Mind of God. Nothing real can be harmed.

"I told you that at the beginning of *A Course in Miracles*, [p.1] and now you are understanding, on a deep level, that your group of Light-worker Souls has been afraid that the Wisdom you have volunteered to carry, to have entrusted to you, could be harmed. In the world, it did appear that it could be harmed. There were attempts made to destroy libraries, to destroy books, to persecute people who had secret Wisdom—all of these efforts to destroy the Wisdom of the power of knowing that you are all Gods.

"But of course, it was all impossible. Nothing can be destroyed. That's the Truth. The library of Alexandria was burned to the ground. Books were burned in Germany. Witches were hanged. The Cathars were burned. All these were an attempt to destroy humanity's secret knowing in our hearts that we are One with God. Now humanity has let go of that fear, and our longing to be One with God is foremost in our minds and hearts. And you, my dear Light-worker family, are the ones who know what comes to pass when you share the Truth with the world—it is fountains of joy, like the fireworks that just happened when we released our huddle out into the world.

"I hear that you have questions to ask me, and I share with you it is with deep delight that I respond. God does not feel responsible for his/her Creation. Creation is not a burden. Creation is a gift. God delights in responding to his Creation. I, as your brother, delight in responding to you. There is nothing more I want than to share my Wisdom with those of you who have ears to hear."

John steps up. "In George Bernard Shaw's *Saint Joan*, a soldier challenges her and says, 'It's all in your imagination.' She says, 'Of course! That's how God speaks to us!' If you would say more about that, I would appreciate hearing it. Thank you."

"Joan has such courage," Yeshua explains. "She is a **Way-shower**. She knew humanity could only listen through the way of conflict, even though, in her heart, she did not desire conflict. She took great pride in never having killed anyone. She was given a sword and only used it as a beacon to lead the way towards the Light. Joan had the courage to be human and Divine. By that, I mean, she knew her Identity was One with the **Angels**. She had no interest in being praised. She was always in amazement that her people listened to her, especially the battle-hardened generals. She thought, in her heart, that it was hilarious. But she just kept speaking the Truth that she felt burning her heart.

"She could keep her mind clear during her trial because she just spoke from her own experience. She knew she had nothing to defend because she had no agenda. She was devoted to being the servant of God, which she felt in her heart as a burning desire for Unity on the Earth. She came from a long line of lifetimes in which she had to tolerate being amid conflict because that is the way of the ego. Conflict is how the ego believes it exists. And yet, she could bring the Light of the Love of the Divine Mother into humanity."

"What does Joan's message have for us in developing our imagination so that we communicate with God as she did?" John asks.

"She felt her Voices in her heart as a physical burning. It was not her imagination. This is how she knew it was real, because she could *feel* it. Her message to you is to *feel* God's Love in your heart. Feel the Love of Yeshua in your heart, and all the Saints and Angels who have gone before you. When you open your heart, there is nothing more we delight in doing than pouring in Love. We are the connecting link between your hearts and God. You are not quite ready to receive the power of God's Love, so you can feel God's Love through us. I remind you that I said in *A Course in Miracles* the Holy Spirit would not hurl you into Reality (Diamond Clear Vision 2012, 395). You are much closer to experiencing Reality, but for now, just feel our Love for you in your hearts. When you get used to that, then your hearts will expand. *It's delightfully exciting!* Does that help?"

John nods. "Yes, very much, thank you."

The first sister asks, "I experienced today connecting with the Elementals in Ireland. And St. **Brigid**'s Day is coming up on the first of February. My question is, am I right to do something with that?"

Yeshua chuckles. "Of course, my beloved one, you can trust your feelings in your heart, that stirring of pixie dust you feel there. Brigid, with the beautiful braided red hair, is the Queen of the Elementals in Ireland. They love her, and she loves them. She delights in any human Soul opening her heart to honor them. It is your respect for her and for them that brings them such joy! They delight in collaborating with you. Your lack of fear allows them to come forward without fear. They are there all along. They are only seen by people who have no fear. They have been safe all along. They would like you to know they have simply been invisible to those who are identified with fear. You do not need to worry for their safety or their whereabouts. They have been moving about in perfect safety because they are not seen by the eyes of fear. When you see with the eyes of Love, then they show in their playfulness. We Enlightened Ones—though I don't like using that word because humanity has put a sense of kingliness on being enlightened, but for lack of a better word—love the Earth Elementals because of their *playfulness*.

"Now, Mother Earth also loves them. She is in a big transition now. She has not been slumbering, but rather patiently absorbing humanity's fear and negativity. Now she is shaking it off, like a dog that has been asleep and, on waking, shakes itself. This is not to cause harm to humanity but to release the constrictions of fear that have been poured into her body. You have constrictions of fear in your physical body; so, too, she has held constrictions of fear in her body. Because humanity is receiving the Light that is being poured into your crown chakras, through your hearts, down through your bodies, and into the Earth, she is softening, just as you are softening. Her softening of her physical body is a loosening up. This loosening and stretching process can cause some disruptions on the surface, but it allows the Light to penetrate all the way through her mantle, down into her core, and back out again.

"Do not fear the Earth disruptions. I'm reminding you that any bodies that appear to die have eternal Souls. I'm reminding you of what I showed you in our first conversation, where I hold out my arms like a big cape, and feed all the confused Souls into my Heart, which is infinite. I tell you this because the shifts in the Earth energy can appear to be destructive and capricious. It can look as if the Earth were randomly killing people. I am reminding you that this is not the case. Those are Souls who are ready to go. Do not have any worries for them.

"Remember what I have told you about how important you all are. Every one of you is needed to receive and transmit the Light. When I told you, do not distract yourselves, I meant that I, and all of us, are asking you to keep your awareness as open as you can to receiving and transmitting Love Light. This will greatly accelerate the process of the shift out of fear into the awareness of the Truth of God's Love. Is that helpful?"

"Yes," Sister One replies. "Very helpful. Thank you."

The second sister asks, "What about the stuck Souls? Our sister can sense when Souls seem to be stuck or lost, and she plays a role in helping them go to the Light."

"Yes, Souls can get stuck when they refuse to look at the Light," Yeshua replies, "when they are sure that their identity is only on the surface of the Earth. They are attached to needing to be right, to believing that whatever their conflict was is still active, and they still need to win their conflict. You Light-workers know that conflict is not the way. Harmony, beauty, and Love are the way. When you are aware of stuck Souls, all you need to know is that they want to be vindicated in their rightness. The interpretation Love makes of *rightness* is simply being seen and honored for their experience. They just need to know they have learned something from their experience, and being right is not required to learn. Don't argue with them. If you argue, you are simply engaging in the same right and wrong battle, even if you are trying to convince them there is no such thing as being right!" He chuckles. "Just honor that they are stuck in the thought they must prove they were right after all!

"I remind you of how I have instructed you to work with your own stuck places, which is, with humor, to *agree* with your resistance. Of course, you must have this resistance! *This* is what will protect you! That allows you, with humor, to see that it is completely unnecessary. When you agree with these stuck Souls, 'Darling, you needed to hold on to being right and your sense that this would protect you. I will hold you. Yeshua holds you. Your guides hold you. All of those who love you are holding you.' In that way, that Soul can release the need to be right. Is that helpful?"

"Very helpful, thank you."

Yeshua chuckles again. "Thank you, my sister, for that service of helping those Souls that hover around the Earth-plane like a sort of gray mist, looking down, trying to hold on to the past. Your willingness to honor their attachments is what will help them release their attachments and feel the touch that is always on their shoulder to just turn around and look up. If you could remind them to feel the tapping on their shoulder so they can turn, look up, and see the Light-Beings that are ready to welcome them, that would be helpful."

Both sisters exclaim, "Tapping, tapping!"

"They're looking the wrong way," Yeshua explains. "They are looking down on the Earth, imagining that they have to stay to solve the problem there."

"Our friend was helping some Souls in Ireland here," the second sister continues. "There's a constant tapping—that is the way the man described it—on the roof of the building."

"That's just the guides," Yeshua continues. "It's their loved ones saying, 'Sweetheart, look up, look up! Come back to the Light! We will hold you and take care of you until you are more prepared to return to Earth with new Wisdom. You haven't yet learned what you need to learn. You can only learn that when you have come back into the Light and had a chance to rest and reflect.'"

The first sister, who was helping this stuck Soul, becomes tearful hearing these words affirm her experience. "That man was looking down."

Yeshua agrees. "Yes, they're looking down."

She can barely say, "Thank you."

Yeshua continues, addressing the second sister, "Sister! I love you."

"I love *you*," she replies.

Yeshua continues. "I love your steadiness, your devotion to the community, your willingness to always step forward and create the contexts, the environments that hold our sisters and brothers. We are deeply grateful for the work you do in that way. But I'm asking you today to ask a question for your*self*. What is *your* Heart's longing?"

"Right now," says Sister Two, "I would love to know who is the presence that I feel on my right shoulder that I've had for years?"

"The presence on your right shoulder is the **Archangel** Uriel. Your resistance to being open to us and to your friends here with you today is a difficulty for those of you who are humble of heart—to acknowledge your connection with what you call Great Beings. It is difficult, if you are thinking from the ego perspective, to acknowledge that an Archangel is your personal guide. I remind you that Archangels are the personal guides of many Light-worker Souls who have come through *much difficulty* to arrive at this place. There is nothing special about having an Archangel as your guide. All humanity will have Archangels. You are simply several lifetimes ahead of your sisters and brothers, as I am several lifetimes ahead of you. Remember, time *is an illusion*, so there is no value in being ahead or behind.

"I tell you this so you can receive the powerful energetics of the Archangel Uriel. His Light is gold. He shares the Wisdom of **Yahweh.**

He is the Truth-speaker. He carries the Word of God. He is the one who speaks through many of your sisters and brothers, providing you with your direct link to the Father/Mother/Source.

"Do not be afraid of the Wisdom that comes into your mind and heart. It has nothing to do with you deserving it. That concept only exists in the realm of fear, where humans think they have to earn Love. Please let go of the thought of deserving and earning. You have done *many good deeds* to deserve and earn Love! You can now release that belief completely!

"You will become a glowing conduit of the Wisdom of God, the Voice of Archangel Uriel, a beacon of Truth. The staff you hold in your right hand is the staff of Truth. Where it touches the ground, the Truth enters the Earth, and those around you know they are in the presence of the Voice of God. Do not be afraid of this mission. It is not a burden. It is your response. It is the response of your heart to the calling of your sisters and brothers to know the Truth. Everyone wants to know the Truth. 'What is the meaning of life? Why are we here?' You have direct access to that. It is time for you now to speak freely and without hesitation.

"It will help you to practice standing on the Earth, holding a staff in your right hand, and feeling the energy of the Light of God pouring through your crown chakra, down through your feet, through the staff, and into the Earth. Feel Archangel Uriel behind you, touching your right shoulder, transmitting to you the Truth of the Love of God. When you feel strong and tall and stable in your body, you will go forth and speak the Truth without fear. You will have lots of support. Do not be afraid that this is something you must do on your own. You are *never* alone. *None* of you is alone.

"*We delight in joining with you!* I have been telling you for thousands of years that I will never leave you. I will be with you *even unto the end of the age of illusion.* There is *nothing* we would rather do than to *come and be with you! You are part of us.* I have told you before that we cannot go *fully* into the ecstasy of God if there are parts of us that remain lost in the illusion. We cannot tell you strongly enough how *grateful* we are for your willingness to bring the Love of God into yourselves, into the Earth, into your sisters and brothers, into all of humanity.

"Go out into the world—which is going into your own hearts; it is the same—and bring the fire of the Love of God everywhere you go. We are *always* with you. The Source is endless. The joy is endless! You truly have *no idea of the feast that awaits you!* At least I have given you a visual image of it, and a feeling of the *celebration* that happens when you allow yourself to partake. But there is *much more.* I tell you this to encourage you to continue on. We await you when you have released *all* of your fear and just *live* in the delight of the *ecstasy* of Communion with God!

"Ameyn."

As I get these words ready for publication, I notice a few times that Yeshua speaks in the plural, a foreshadowing that he is not a singular *person.* More on that to come.

A week or so later, I hit a snag of doubt and fear, exactly as he told us we all would. Though extremely uncomfortable to be doubting the messages of my beloved teacher through me, I applied his instruction to hold his hand and to remember he is with me always. Thus, a deep fear of being persecuted, though I know I am innocent, was healed.

A brother sent me a sweet message to be gentle with myself in this undertaking and to go at my own pace, reminding me that "God never wants us to move towards him/her faster than our humanness will allow. We hold you in our Love."

Chapter 5

The Circle Grows

The Harmonics of God

We gathered again the next week, which fell on Christmas Eve, 2018. This time, four sisters joined with me and John.

We again recite our prayer of alignment three times.

I share what I am experiencing. "The first experience is of my heart burning, then my right ear, then the right side of my face. I hear the words to Paramahansa Yogananda's song, *I Will Never Forget Thee*. I'm being directed to put my attention upwards and to the right, where there is a celestial choir, what we call Angels, singing harmony that can only be felt in the heart, not heard with the physical ears. It's a song of joy and gratitude that we are attuning to the Angelic realms that surround Earth. My head is slowly turning, experiencing the Angelic vibration of harmony surrounding the Earth. They are emanating *powerful streams of gratitude* to all of us who are attuning to their joy, their harmony, their beauty. The *powerful* streams of joy are aimed, like a laser beam of Light, into the heart. Feel the intensity of the burning flame of the Love of God in your hearts."

(As I re-read this, I remember what Yeshua said about St. Joan feeling the Angelic Voices physically in her heart.)

After describing my experience of alignment with this higher vibration, I can feel Yeshua's words taking form in my mind. He begins speaking.

"Fear not the destruction of the Earth. It is protected by the power of the Love of God, which *you are*. You are an emanation of the Love of God, and there *is* nothing except Love. I am showing you this vision of the Angelic realms surrounding the beloved Mother Earth to remind you of what I've told you before, that you hold the Earth in your hearts. It is the great paradox that it appears things are inside and outside when, in Reality, everything is One. The Angelic realms and the Earth are in your heart, and your heart is protected by the Angelic realms surrounding the Earth. The only reason you think you need protection on the Earth is when you give credence to the belief that there is darkness. Now on the Earth, there is much belief in darkness, so it is not strange that you would feel that belief around you. But I remind you that the Light outshines the darkness. Do not give it any credence, for what you give your attention to increases. Do not give your attention to the darkness. Put all of your attention on the Light in your heart.

"Feel that Light as a golden flame, white and gold, in your hearts. See how it surrounds your body. When you see the Light surrounds your body, then the vibrational level of your body is attuned to the Light of God. There is no darkness possible in the body when you attune it to the vibrational frequencies of the harmony of beauty. It is of utmost importance for you to maintain your consciousness in this state of awareness as much as you can. It feels like magic to the ego, but I'm telling you the Truth that, in this state of vibrational harmony, *everything around you synchronizes with it*. Everything around you is drawn irresistibly into the harmonics of the Divine Angelic choir. This is why the Angels always say, 'Fear not!' When you fear, the vibrational harmonies are disrupted, and a chaotic pattern results. When you do not fear, then you allow yourself to synchronize with the harmonics of beauty.

"In all of you, there is still the temptation to believe in the darkness, to think that what I am telling you is somehow magical. I ask you to tune into your hearts, and not into your thinking. It is in your hearts that you can feel the burning of the Love of God.

"I have told you before that I have been given the role of being in charge of the Atonement. This is why my name is known around the Earth. *Yeshua: God restores the awareness of Love into the mind of humanity.* Any time you say my name, you are attuning yourself to my harmonics, which are attuned to the harmonics of God. This allows you to become more and more finely attuned to the harmonics of God.

"Though time is an illusion, there will come a time when you no longer need me as the intermediary. You can trust me because you know I have lived as a human many times. I have also lived as other life forms, as have you. You can relate to my life experience, and this helps you trust me, whereas God still feels too abstract. I give of myself to you, fully, freely, willingly, joyfully! The more I give, the more I have, the more I am. The more you resonate with the Light, the brighter the Light. There is *no limit to the brightness of the Light of the Love of God.* The human eye thinks this sounds blinding and overwhelming, and to the human eye, it is. This is why we are helping you attune yourselves at exactly the right pace each of you requires so that you are not blinded by God and cast into fear.

"Please trust everything that is given to you in your lives. There are still some experiences that each of you needs to go through to polish the shadows on your flame. Do not resist the polishing. Think of it as my hands caressing you. Know that, as you go through whatever experiences are given for you to facilitate your growth, *I am with you always,* even unto the end of the age of illusion. I am reminding you of this every time you come to me. The more you hear it, the more you will attune to my presence, which is with you always because *I am you.* I cannot *not* be with you. You can only tune out your awareness. But I cannot *not* be with you because I *am* you. I am reminding you of what I told you — that you are my sheep because *you are parts of my Self.* I am reminding you that those of us who are no longer needing to manifest on the Earth-plane remain attuned to you because *you are us.* Only when all the lost sheep have been gathered back into our Heart, can we go in full *ecstasy* into the Heart of God.

"Feel that all the way through your bodies, from the crown to the third eye, to your throat so you can speak and sing the ecstasy of God, to your hearts where you feel nothing but Love, to the solar plexus, where your will is now attuned to the Will of God, to your belly chakra and the root chakra where you *know* that *your Identity in this body is Light and is the creative power of God.* There is nothing else. *The miracle of all our travels is that now we can know this.* We have gone through the depths of the depths of hell, all of us. Now we know that this does not draw our attention anymore. The blessing is that we know that we exist. And now, the glorious moment in the evolution of our minds — *we know that we exist in God.*

"I am asking you to direct your attention to the Pope of the Catholic Church. His little white hat represents the Light of God coming through his crown chakra. He is requesting your support. He is a courageous man who needs to know that the world supports him in speaking the Truth. He has shed all attachment to thinking that the power of the church holds any interest to himself personally. He has been carefully laying the seeds of Light within the church so that he can be heard. He has never been afraid. His carefulness has resulted from his knowledge that too much Light can't be heard. He is asking for your support now as he gets ready to speak more of the Truth. This is the day that he prepares his Christmas message, which is broadcast around the planet. Your support is very helpful to him, to give him the courage that he can be himself without any fear. You have been doing that with each other, telling each other the Truth of who you are. This gives you the power to support him in speaking the Truth of who we all are. That will be his message—that we are all the equal sons and daughters of God, and Yeshua is our brother. These will be his words.

"The fear within the hierarchy of the church is still strong—the fear of the loss of the power of control. The ego still believes that it gains some satisfaction from control. You have all been through that. You know that feeling, so there is no judgment when we hold those in our hearts who are in the process of releasing their belief in the power of control. You all already know that when you release control, not only do you lose nothing, *you gain everything*. Please support the men who are holding the illusion of power in knowing that, as they release power, they gain the Kingdom of God. Each one of you will be given the image of one of these men to be with around the Plaza of St. Peter, to support them in releasing their fear as they hear the good news that Yeshua is our brother.

"This sounds simple to you, but it is profoundly shattering to the power of the church to hear that I am not God. How can I be God? I did not create myself, and that Self is all of us. We did not create our Self. We are an emanation from the Heart of God, and the only proper feeling is gratitude, ecstasy, fun, and excitement!

"Now that we know to no longer fear God, and we know the infinite power of our creative minds, *now* we can *play* in the Kingdom, in the Queendom! You think creating the Earth was amazing—yes, we are amazing! Please stay with the vibration of the Angels, and just know that what comes to pass is more amazing than your human imagination could ever conjure.

"Feel the Light pouring into your crown chakras now. These are the Angels singing to you, filling your mind with the Truth of God's Love. There *is* nothing else. There are no shadows. There are no stains on your consciousness. There is only joy! There is only Love! There is only Peace! There is only harmony! There is only ecstasy! There is only the power of Creation! Now that you *know* this, you can never *not* know this. It has been given to you to know this.

"Speak this Truth in your lives to all whom you encounter. Remember that when you are in the Truth, *other people's vibrations attune to you, you do not need to fear.* The worst that could happen is they won't understand. That's okay. You have shed some droplets of Light into their mind. Do not receive their misunderstanding as any judgment on your knowledge of what is true. The knowledge that you have kept in secret is now out for the world to know.

"I use 'the world' on purpose because the world is the appearance of your thoughts. The world has appeared to be a fearful place, filled with death. When your minds are attuned to the Truth, the world becomes a *sparkling jewel. Rainbows sparkle off of everything!* Everything is seen in its crystalline perfection! *This is the world!* This is the world that the Angelic harmonies are attuning to create. Your attunement contributes to the Creation of *this* world. And then, when the whole world has attuned to the Angelic harmonies, there is no more need for that illusion, because now, the Angelic realms of Heaven and the Earthly realms have become One. There is no more need for them to appear to be separated.

"Oh, my friends, I adore you. Hold my hand. I delight in walking with you everywhere you go. Introduce me to your friends." Yeshua chuckles. "They already know me, but help their eyes to become clear. The animals feel me all the time. The current of Love has been encircling the Earth always. Feel it under your feet, as if it's an electric current, the power of Love in the Earth. Feel it in your crown, the power of Love in the Heavens. Feel it in your heart, as the electricity from the Earth and the electricity from the Heavens joins in your heart and sparkles.

"Go dance, my sparkly friends! Emit your Light! Have fun! Dance like elves, with abandon! And please hold my hand! I love to dance."

Long pause.

"I am just enjoying being with you before we say goodbye. Just feel me with you, however each of you feels me."

Long pause.

"I plant a kiss on each of your cheeks, and each of you kisses everyone's cheeks around in a circle, the circle of Love. And with that kiss of Love, I say farewell.

"I am always in your hearts.

"Ameyn."

⚬❧⚬

I did not grow up in the Catholic Church, so I was quite surprised to find these words forming in my mind, but as I had been coming to trust, the more I just allowed myself to speak, the more freely the words flowed.

John shared later, "Your Light increased again as the channeling progressed."

Supporting the Pope

Since Yeshua had specifically asked us to support the Pope during his Christmas message, we all watched him speak. As he had predicted, the Pope had indeed emphasized Yeshua's message, "that we are all the equal sons and daughters of God." That had, in fact, been his entire message! And though he had said, "The face of God has been revealed in a human face," he fell short of stating clearly that Yeshua is our brother. The night before the broadcast message, I had the intuition that he had felt the need to tone it down. John also observed how careful the Pope was in presenting the humanity of Yeshua.

Here are some passages from the Pope's message: "What is the universal message of Christmas? It is that God is a *good Father* and we are all *brothers and sisters*. This truth is the basis of the Christian vision of humanity. [...] By his incarnation, the Son of God tells us that salvation comes through love, acceptance, and respect for this poor humanity of ours, which we all share in a great variety of races, languages, and cultures. Yet all of us are *brothers and sisters in humanity!*" He then described many places in the world that are in distress, and his wish that those places could experience their brotherhood and sisterhood (Vatican.va 2018).

Yeshua had told us we each would be given one man in the church hierarchy to support. Twelve of us gathered again on New Year's Eve, 2018, and shared our varying yet similar experiences supporting the men in the Pope's orbit. We all reported similar images of darker figures to whom we had sent Light. I had felt drawn to a man who I sensed enjoyed being shrewd with power and control, in this and in many other lifetimes. Knowing that a softer touch draws people in, he had advised the Pope to use this as a tool to maintain control. Yet for a moment during the Pope's message, he had felt the warmth in the heart that comes from feeling part of the mosaic of humanity. Rather than being controlled, Francis was softening him.

One sister observed, "This Pope is there to create as much change [within the church hierarchy] as he can. Holding him in the Light consciously will help him. This will also help shift the anger we have been holding here in Ireland towards the church. As we move into forgiveness and hold that anger in the Light, we will help the greater consciousness."

I had spoken earlier about my doubts and insecurities about the accuracy of my inner listening. Was I really hearing Yeshua or just my own fantasy? I so appreciated John's question about St. Joan. How did she know to trust her visions? It was by how they *felt*. I could confirm that the feeling of delivering the messages was *electrifying*.

Another sister had some reassuring words. "I feel really grateful that you're naming your vulnerability and fears around channeling. For me, that makes you real and human." She shared about the importance of just relaxing into what I was hearing so I would not try to control it. "Yeshua says that each of us can hear him if we prepare the place in our heart and our mind. For me, it's inspiring and encouraging that you have the courage to listen and to share that with friends. Wouldn't it be lovely to take the specialness out of hearing Yeshua and acknowledge that we all can hear him, too, if we have that desire and allowance and surrender enough? You have my full and total support. I came into this feeling that I'm going to bring, at the same time, 100% belief that this is really Yeshua, but also discernment, because I know it's easy when someone is channeling to give up one's power and hand it over to the channeler. 'Oh, you tell me what to do.' That can be scary for the channel. 'My God, these people might hear my answers and go off and change their lives, and what if I wasn't clear at that moment!' I remember a friend who channels saying, 'There's always going to be some rust in the pipes when you start channeling, and you're clearing out the rust. If anybody receives a piece of rust in the channeling, then that's exactly what they needed to receive for them to practice their own discernment.'"

This reminds me of what the Buddha said in the *Kālāma Sutta*. He advises his listeners not to go by what other people have said or by intellectual thought in discerning the veracity of his teachings. Instead, "When you know for yourselves that, 'These qualities are skillful; these qualities are blameless; these qualities are praised by the observant; these qualities, when adopted and carried out, lead to welfare and to happiness' — then you should enter and remain in them." Ultimately, the means of discernment is the effect of practicing the teachings on your life (Dhammatalks.org n.d.).

Before we began, I had one more thing to share, echoing this sister's words. "This is what I heard in my mind this morning. 'Laura, *you* are *doing* nothing. Just relax, and just listen. That's it.'"

As you absorb these teachings, please trust your own discernment, which is a felt knowing in the heart.

The Consuming Campfire of God's Love

We recite our opening prayer, and I begin by sharing my inner experience.

"Yeshua is asking us to draw our attention to the flame of Light that lives on our crown, which is a visual representation of the Sun. He draws my attention to the Sun, as the source of our life on the Earth, and as a symbol of the Source of the flame of Light in our hearts. He reminds us that the appearance of things being external or internal is how the projection of the illusion of this Universe works, so that the Sun, which appears to be many miles away, actually lives in our hearts. It is not a dangerous fire that will consume. It is a loving fire that will transmute every shred of attachment to fear that we still believe in. He says:"

"You can picture feeding your fears into this fire in your heart, exactly as if you were standing around a campfire with your friends, singing songs, and throwing things you want to burn into the fire, and watching the beauty of the transformation that happens in the fire."

Long pause.

"This is Laura speaking. I'm resisting telling you that he is showing me roasting marshmallows because I have a judgment about marshmallows. He's saying:"

"I'm showing you marshmallows to remove your judgment about anything in Creation. Whether it be the plastics that people are cleaning up, or the sugar that you put into your body, if everything is taken care of in Love, there is no harm that can come from anything, so enjoy your marshmallows."

"He is also drawing my attention to the camaraderie around this fire. It's in the circle of friends that the joy comes in the transformation."

"This is not a singular process of burning our fears in the fire," Yeshua continues. "Every time someone throws something into the fire to be transformed, everyone sings and dances. The bigger the fire gets, the better, so it can burn bigger fears. Anything can be burned in this fire of the Sun, which is God's Love—nothing is bigger than the Love of God. This is why the Sun is such a good symbol for you, because, obviously, there is nothing that could withstand being burned up in the fire of your Sun.

"It's time to tell your stories so that each place in the story where there is something that is unhealed can come forward. This is not to be attached to your stories, but it is in telling the story that the attachments become clear."

"Yeshua is asking this circle of friends who have gathered around the transmuting fire of God's Love if there's anyone who would like to come forward and throw one of your fears outward into the fire. He says:"

"Please, friends, have the courage to bring forward a fear and name it. I am here with you in this circle and can help you transmute whatever the fear is that you remain attached to in this moment. I feel someone who has an elvish energy itching to dance forward."

⌇⌇

Sister Three speaks up. "I don't know if that's me, but I would like to throw into the fire the fear of being completely vulnerable and exposed, including to the Love of God. It's a fear of being abandoned or betrayed. If I didn't hold something back, I could be completely lost."

"That is a familiar one, my sister," Yeshua acknowledges. "I think all humanity shares the fear that if we completely trust God, what might he do to us? And so, we hold one piece back, just in case! Just in case God's Will for us is not perfect happiness. Just in case he has some destruction in store, we hold on to a little piece of cleverness.

"Here is the Truth. God imposes nothing. God simply awaits your acceptance, your arrival at the gate to Heaven. Beyond that gate lies the fire of the Love of God. But before that gate is the thought that you must protect yourself because you might be injured. This is the ego's belief that, if it does not protect itself, it will be destroyed. This is the final letting go because the ego is correct. When it ceases protecting itself, it is, let's use a softer word, transformed. Because the ego is the power of the Child of God to use our creativity to create whatever we would like, humanity has lots of pride in what the ego has created. 'Look! A whole Universe!' How could the ego not have pride in that? And so the ego, masquerading as humility, says, 'Oh, I'll just still hold on in case you need me.'

"This is a challenging stage in letting go because it looks to the ego as if you are saying, 'Everything that the ego made is worthless.' The *fear* has no value, but the power of Creation *is* value. It is *All*. You have simply distorted your power to create what we call ego, which is the appearance of separated bodies—planetary bodies, star bodies, earth bodies, and human bodies. There is creative power behind manifesting all of that! Do not be afraid that, in letting go of the ego, you lose your creative power. This is what the ego is afraid of—that its hard work will not be appreciated.

"We can all say to ego, 'We *do* appreciate your capacity to show us we exist!' By creating a sense of a separated self, we can *know* that we are the Child of God. If we did not have that sense of a separated self, we would never *know* we are the Child of God. We can appreciate all the hard work the ego has done for more time than we can understand to create the awareness of being a self.

"My sister, this feeling of vulnerability is your deep awareness that, in letting go of defending yourself, you become aware of your Unity with God, and the ego is afraid that this means returning to that primordial place where you lose awareness. Yet this is not so. All the hard work of the ego is now paying off, so to speak, because you retain your awareness of yourself when you return to your awareness of God. Do you understand?"

"Yes."

At this point in the session, visible in the video recording, an orb appears, covering my left eye and ear, and then expands to rest over my left shoulder, still covering my left eye and ear.

Yeshua continues, "You are courageous in putting forth this deep vulnerability of letting the ego relax and be appreciated for its efforts in creating your awareness of your individuated self. Please appreciate its efforts and reassure it that your awareness of who you are not only does not disappear but amplifies to a level of magnificence that you cannot possibly imagine at this point. I reassure you that this is the Truth. Please enjoy the ride!"

"Thank you," says Sister Three.

"Ameyn."

The orb is now quite distinct and has a flickering quality.

John then addresses his fear. "The one with elvish energy is going to get in. Through the first eight years of my life, I played with elves. After I turned nine, I shut it off and triple locked it, because I was afraid I was going crazy. The fear I'm going to cast in the fire is that I won't be able to unlock and listen again." He becomes tearful.

The orb is now unmistakable and brilliant! There is a distinct, bright white, inner shape like a head, surrounded by a lighter circle.

Yeshua responds. "Your fear is that your ability to tune into the little people has been destroyed. Nothing is destroyed, my brother. Even your physicists know that. Everything just changes form. Your tears show you that you have not lost your ability to attune to the most subtle vibrations of Love. You have an exquisite affection for the beauty of the vulnerability, of the innocence, of all forms of life. You even appreciate the delicacy of little moths. You have an ability to attune to subtle vibrations that you feel in your heart, which in this life, comes out as tears. You think the tears are that you have lost something, but they are not. They are a sign of your sensitivity. You have an exquisite sensitivity. This is why people come to you for guidance."

A lighter orb now appears over my right shoulder.

"Because you care so deeply for each one of their journeys, you can see the pattern of their Soul's journey—where they have come from, where they are headed, what guidance they need—because of your sensitivity.

"You fear you have lost your attunement to the Earth Spirits. You know perfectly well where that comes from in this life. So, the healing for that will happen when you sit in the woods in the very places where, as a child, you felt that attunement and you again *feel* the energies of the Earth Spirits come to you. Just the way people come to you, my brother, so the Earth Spirits come to you. They recognize a peacefulness in you, a gentleness, a welcome, a delight in their Light. They know you mean no harm, that you have no interest in causing harm. You have let go of any wish to control.

"Your gentleness is like water. It flows outward from you, like an ever-expanding pool, welcoming all it touches in its caress, creating a sense of calm in those who come to you who are touched by your peaceful Light. Your Light is a light-blue color, quite gentle. When you sit in the woods, just rest in your gentleness. You can start by remembering all the people who have come to you for guidance and how helpful you have been. In that state of knowing your helpfulness, you can become aware that the Earth Spirits are also drawn into your gentleness. They will come to you. You are like your story of Snow White, who sits in the woods and the animals come to her. This is your energy, only there is no evil queen in your future, fear not.

"I feel your Love as such a devoted gentleness, my brother. I am so grateful for your compassion for all with whom you come in contact. I am sending you my compassion. Please release your fear that you have locked away your attunement. You have not done so. Your attunement is keen. Please release that last shred of fear into our communal fire. It will be easily transformed. You have no need for it anymore. Is this helpful?"

"Very much, thank you. I think I'll be casting it several times before it's gone."

"My brother, you only need to cast it in as many times as you still believe that it's true," Yeshua clarifies. "Your attunement and sensitivity are finely developed. This fear that you have lost it is much smaller than you have given credence to. It only feels big because you latched onto it when you were a small child. Bring that small child self of yours to you for healing. He is the one who needs to be healed. The fear is tiny. He just needs reassurance that, not only is there nothing wrong with him, but his attunement is a beautiful gift from the Father. Bring into your heart now that little boy who needed reassurance. We can all hold him in a big circle of Love.

"I am sharing with you that my energy is expanding into a sphere of Light holding all of you and this little boy who needs to be reassured that he is God's Child. Bring him to sit by the campfire and give him a marshmallow. He'll be fine." He chuckles. "Is there anything more you would like to share, my brother?"

"Thank you. That's perfect. Thank you so much."

"Enjoy your marshmallow. Ameyn."

"I feel the same way as Laura does about marshmallows," John comments, "but I'll enjoy some."

Yeshua laughs. "It's for the little boy. No worries, he'll enjoy it."

Sister Four shares her fear. "I've recently felt a connection with the Soul of Joseph and with Archangel Uriel. My fear is that I don't know what to do with the feelings of not being good enough. Also, how can I live with the bodily tiredness I experience? I'm open to whatever I'm being asked to do."

"I'm glad that you are asking this question. I have the deepest gratitude to the Soul of Joseph. The tiredness needs healing from the lifetime of Joseph, where he labored in the shadows. He was a wise Soul, quite elevated in wisdom, with a high degree of humility, and did not expect others to pay attention to him. And yet there is a sadness about the Soul of Joseph, not because he was not in the limelight, but because his care and protectiveness could not prevent what appeared to be a series of tragedies, culminating in the dispersal of his community that he had worked so hard to protect. At the end of his life, he couldn't express his feelings of grief because there was no one left who understood them. So he only did what he knew, which was to help the community where he remained.

"The protectiveness of Joseph is what needs transformation. This burden of feeling responsible for protecting everyone is weighing you down. Humanity's energy has changed, and the energy of protectiveness is no longer required for those who work with the Light. The Light has increased in the hearts and minds of humanity sufficiently that you no longer need to protect those who work with the Light. They have enough awareness of the Light within that they do not need you to protect them from the darkness.

"Can you feel the lightening in your Soul as you release the energy of protectiveness? It's like a heavy cloak you have been carrying on your shoulders that you can shake off and let fall to the ground. You can trust those around you in this circle to follow their own Light, which is everyone's Light. Everyone has their own particular threads, ropes, knots, and entanglements of fear that need transforming, but that is now their responsibility and not yours.

"I want you to know that the community that you worked so hard to protect, that ended up being dispersed all across the Earth, is aware of its gratitude towards you. There is no Soul that does not appreciate what you did to create protection and safety. This has allowed all the other Souls to go off in their own direction. It is time now for you to release that function completely. It is no longer needed. Dropping that heavy burden of feeling responsible to protect your brothers and sisters is what will release the heaviness that you now feel in this life of feeling tired.

"Notice in your mind anytime you think you are responsible for creating an environment that someone needs so that they can grow properly, because this is your habit. Notice that thought, and then simply think, *I trust their own Light*, and let go of your habit of creating an environment of protection. Their Light is strong enough that they can go out into the world now, on their own.

"I would like to share that there is a strong feeling of pressure in the third eye and the crown. This is to convey to you that, when you let go of this heaviness, you will see *clearly*, and you will receive the Light *clearly*. Do you feel complete?"

"Yes, thank you," Sister Four confirms.

Before another fear is shared, Yeshua speaks. "I want to amplify the message of Love, that the power of Love is never failing, that humanity, as a collective, has become aware that the power of Love is greater than the power of fear. In this community, that balance is *far* shifted towards acknowledging the power of Love, so in this community, when you join together, you really can trust each other's Light. I told Laura and John at the start, simply to be together. Think of each other during your daily lives. You know you exist in bodies, and you know you are devoted to the Light, so all you have to do is bring any one of you into your mind, and you have re-created this circle of Love, surrounding the power of the flame of God in the center in your Hearts. It is an extremely strong power. There is nothing equal to it.

"As you practice connecting with each other, you will be amazed at the transformations that will happen now in all of your lives. It is really quite exciting for all of you in bodies, and for all of us not in bodies, because we are with you always. It is such a delight that you can feel our presence anytime you think of us. Anytime you think of each other, you can feel it in your heart immediately. Please notice any little twinge in your body. The body is an energy field, so if any little physical experience draws your attention, focus on that and simply ask, what is it telling you? That is the energy of Love bringing your attention to something that either needs care, is a message, or is a power that you can tune into. Your power is infinite, I remind you. Do not be afraid of it."

Sister Five seeks help with her fear. "I would like to know how I can let go of my feelings of mistrust. I have difficulty to trust. I fear I don't trust enough."

"That depends," Yeshua begins, "on what you have placed your trust in. Not trusting can be wise. Use your discernment to look at what you are placing your trust in. If you feel a sense of caution, this is to be honored. Do not generalize that to thinking you must stay in your fearful corner and trust no one and nothing. Honor that as your keen awareness of the energies that are trustworthy and the energies that are not trustworthy.

"Where you get drawn off course is when you find an energy that is not trustworthy and you put too much value in it, you give it too much power. I have told you before, do not give your attention to the darkness. When something comes into your path that is not trustworthy, think of it as a messenger that says, 'This is not the way.' That is all. It does not mean that there is *no* way, it just means trusting that energy—for example, trusting the belief that you need other people to approve of you—is not the way. Just bless it for showing you to head towards Love. Love is always the way.

"Notice where you feel at ease. Even if you are not at first feeling Love, there is a sense of ease that happens when you head towards an energy you can trust. Sometimes the form will be surprising. Do not put any value in the form, just notice the feeling of ease in your heart, and become accustomed to that feeling. That is the feeling you can trust—the feeling of ease in your heart. That is the Holy Spirit showing you that *this* is the path for you to take. It does not mean there won't be rocks on the path, but there will be a feeling of ease because those are the particular rocks that you need to turn over. Is that helpful?"

"Yes, thank you."

Sister Six joins in. "I have a fear of being genuine. I get so confused, and I forget everything. Then I feel I just don't know what to believe and what to do, and I get so confused." She begins to cry.

"Let the tears come," Yeshua encourages.

Sister Six composes herself. "I feel I'm not genuine, and I'm not good enough. I believe for a while, and then I don't know what to believe, and I just swing all over the place."

"The answer lies right within your own question. You said you fear to be genuine. That's because you long to be that genuine energy you think you don't have. I'm reminding you that you cannot long for something you do not already know exists. Your longing for genuineness is because you know you have that energy in your heart.

"There is a long history in this Soul of persecution for knowing the Truth, so that kernel of what is genuine is as if it were a magnet that repels things instead of attracts them, which creates this feeling of bouncing around everywhere. The history of persecution for knowing the Truth is familiar to this group of Souls. They can continue to help you with releasing this ancient knot. The knot is in your mind; it is not in your heart. When you were speaking, the skull was highly energized, as if the thoughts were being scrambled.

"The reason that persecution occurred was because the ego still believed in the need to defend itself, even when it had a hold of the Truth. There is a deep confusion between holding the Truth and believing it needs to be defended. This is a paradox that this group of Souls knows well. It is difficult to let go, at this time, of the belief in the need to defend the Truth because it is something that you have reinforced over so many thousands of years. The Child of God is a collective mind. As a collective, it created this drama of knowing the Truth and attacking the Truth, in order to defend the Truth, to know the Truth, and to be sure about the Truth. All parts of the drama have been necessary for the mind of the Child of God to feel confident in the Truth. When you have defended something with your life many times, it becomes precious. The time is ripe now to let go of the belief in the need to defend this precious jewel. You know the Truth well enough now that you no longer need to project the drama of attack and defense.

"My sister, you have gone to a deep and important place for all of this group of Souls to hear that the Truth no longer needs to be defended. In the past, you have kept yourself away from society with small groups who knew the Truth, maintaining it in the Earth so it would not be lost. There is a great fear in you now, as the Truth comes up to the surface of the Earth and into the minds of humanity, that it is vulnerable and can be attacked again. It will help you to spend time with your sisters and brothers who work with the Light to show you that the Light is safe on the surface of the Earth with your sisters and brothers. As you let go of your thought that the Truth has to be defended, so you will cease drawing to you any events that look like an attack. This is why I am telling you to spend time with your sisters and brothers, because releasing this fear on your own is too great. The belief that you have to defend the Truth is so strong that if you tried to let it go on your own, you could not do so.

"Turn and face into the center of this circle of Love, where the Light of God shines so brightly. Now, all of you, cast into the fire your fear of persecution, your belief in persecution, and your thought that the Truth can be harmed. *How can the Truth be harmed? It resides in the Mind of God. Nothing can harm the Truth.* Here you still all are, able to know the Truth. It has not been harmed all these years. This is of great significance. It represents no longer manifesting on the Earth-plane the experience of being attacked and persecuted. It does not mean that individual Souls will not still need to heal some fears from past traumas. It does mean that, as a collective, you now know the Truth can never be harmed, and you do not need to invest energy in protecting it. Your roles now are to share the Truth, freely, without fear, all of you.

"The fear of the darkness has been in your own minds. You have projected it outward as entities and energies that can attack you, but now it is time for you to know the whole drama has been going on inside of your minds.

"I am drawing your attention again to the Angelic realms that surround the Earth, singing the most exquisite harmonies. These vibrations of Love break up the denser vibrations of fear. And because on the Earth you are now able to tolerate, as a group, the vibrations of Love, the Angelic realms, and your Love vibrations amplify exponentially each other's power that shatters the vibrations of darkness. They simply dissolve. And the layer of Light around the Earth becomes deeper and stronger.

"It is with immense gratitude that those of us in the not-embodied realm receive your willingness to know that the Truth is the Truth, and it is safe not only in your Hearts, but out in the world. I am reminding you that the world is a projection of your belief about it, so when you believe the world is an out-picturing of the beauty of the Love of God, that is what you will see and experience. That is what I mean by bringing Heaven to Earth.

"It is with great gratitude that I say thank you for bringing that fear forward. Is that helpful to you, my sister?"

"Yes, yes, thank you."

❧

"Yeshua," a brother begins, "I would like to know how I can step forward and start teaching. I am feeling drawn to teach, but I do not know how to teach or what to teach."

Yeshua chuckles. "Of course you know how to teach and what to teach, my brother. You are my friend. You know my teachings intimately. That's not your fear. The fear you have is in believing in your ability to be a teacher. I am asking you to articulate that fear. What is the block that keeps you from believing that you can teach?"

"My fear is standing in my truth."

"And what will happen if you do?"

"It's the risk of rejection."

Yeshua agrees. "Yes, my brother. This is the same fear your sister just brought forward. The fear of rejection in this life is a lower amplitude vibration of the fear of being killed that you all share. You have all experienced that in some form—people turning against you. In your case, because your promises of the Love of God did not magically manifest and fix everything, people turned against you in their misunderstanding that the Love of God is something to cultivate in their own hearts, and that this is what transforms their lives. They thought you were preaching about how the Love of God would transform things without their having to do any of their own healing work, and so they turned on you. This is your fear of rejection.

"For you personally, it is important to teach inner awareness. This is the Way, but it also corrects the misunderstanding that happened for you in the past when people did not understand inner awareness, and they thought God's Love would magically transform their outward experiences. When you teach the Way as an inner awareness of inner fears, an inner transformation, *that* will remove your fear that other people think you are promising them a million dollars, or a million pounds, or whatever you call those silly things. If you approach your teaching in a more psychological way, this will be understandable to people. The world understands psychological healing, so you will not experience any resistance by approaching your spiritual teaching from that vantage point. All you need to do is add in the deeper Truth that, as the psychological obstacles are healed, the Holy Spirit reveals herself as the healing agent.

"I love you very much, my brother. I am with you always. I have told you this before. Is that helpful?"

"Yes, my brother, thank you."

Yeshua continues, "Thank you so much for your devotion. Remember that the proper devotion is to the Love of God in your own heart. Remember that I am simply your brother."

"Thank you, Yeshua. Ameyn."

"Ameyn."

~ⓔ~

Yeshua offers some final thoughts. "I'm happy and grateful for everything all of you do to help all our brothers and sisters drop their fears and shine more brightly. I remind you of what I've said before, that as you shine more brightly, so does my Light, because there is no limit to the Light of the Love of God. Every time each one of you shines more brightly, I shine more brightly, and my gratitude for you increases. Never for one moment think your Light is insignificant. I repeat. Never for one moment think your Light is insignificant.

"I love you all so much! My Heart is burning in Love for you.

"Brothers and sisters, please join your hands around this beautiful campfire. Join with the Elementals, and the children, and the marshmallow sticks, and the fear of persecution that is now consumed in the flames. Look around the circle. Feel our gratitude for each other, my gratitude for you, your gratitude for me, your gratitude for each other, your devotion to the Way. It is in these gatherings that the healings occur.

"I feel such Love in my Heart for all of you. I feel I could speak with you forever, and I'm telling you the Truth—I do speak with you forever. Remember to notice the sensations in your body. That is the most direct means of communication that we have with you. Sometimes there are words in the mind, but more often there are sensations in the body.

"Now come in closer and remember that the fire is a transforming fire. It can't burn you. Put your arms around each other and put your heads together. We're going to do the same ritual I had you do a couple of weeks ago, where all the Wisdom, Knowledge, experience, and Love that you share is now connected in a circle, your heads touching. Then throw back your heads, release your arms, and release the Truth of the Love of God into the world. Then return to our huddle. In the center of the circle, feel your Love of the burning

Love of God in your hearts, your heads touching, the Wisdom shared. Then open out your arms, lift your heads, and let the sparks of Light fly up into the atmosphere of the Earth. And once more, for the third time—feel the power of our connection, and then the joy in releasing it out into the world.

"I adore you, my sisters and brothers. I am with you always.

"Ameyn. Ameyn. Ameyn."

The next day, I joined a New Year's Day promenade in the Blue Hills, a huge public nature reserve south of Boston, where I have spent many hours hiking during my years living in the city. This communal event was filled with happy people celebrating the start of a new year as we followed the circuit around Ponkapoag Pond in glorious, sunny weather. I remember the scene vividly, feeling such awe and gratitude and amazement that I would not have found the words to speak to anyone. I just conveyed my deepest Love and appreciation to the Earth, to my enlightened brother, my friends, and God. My habitual small mind was thoroughly shaken.

After this transmission, one sister wrote to thank me for acknowledging, allowing, and embracing my doubts and fears, and still making the choice for the Voice of Love, not the voice of fear. While she imagined I must be experiencing some disorientation, she encouraged me to be gentle with myself. She saw I was doing amazingly well with the whole process, and that my allowing this opening would make it easier for other people to let go of fears and hear Yeshua in their hearts. She observed that, under the fears, I knew at a deep level that I had come into this life to do this. I responded that I could take this risk because I was feeling loved and supported by my spiritual family in this miraculous experience.

Four days after her email, Yeshua confirmed her observations. "More of you are listening, which makes it possible for even more people to listen. There are other people even now who are listening to me. You are all spreading the Light, which grows stronger every moment." In this same conversation, he said about me, "She is one of a group called the Messenger Souls who bring the Word of God to humanity, [...] a role she has played many times in the past."

Another sister wrote me a similar message. "Your demonstration of sharing your Communion with Yeshua is a reminder for us all of our own ability to hear Christ-Mind directly as we open and listen without fear. Thank you for being a Way-shower as we collectively stop hiding our Light under the infamous bushel basket!"

Her message relieved me of any concern that others would see me as special. I don't feel special. I feel quite ordinary—the same kind of human as every other human being. I am just playing my part in the collective process of humanity coming to abide in Christ Consciousness. How wonderful I imagine that will be! In a unified field of awareness, all would be transparent—no hidden agendas, no controlling. Everyone would be encouraged to express their own flavor of creativity, and no one would need to win or be right!

Yeshua is *so* consistent with his messages that awareness of his presence is for all of us. Awareness that we are the One Child of God is for all of us. Awakening is for all of us. In his name/vibrational atmosphere, I encourage you to keep listening and expressing your true Self.

Chapter 6

A New Year Opens with Intimate Communications

Releasing Unworthiness

I told another friend on the spiritual path about the events unfolding with me, and he asked if he could engage in a conversation with Yeshua. I do not include here the parts of the message that are personal to him, but I have included the parts that are universal. Yeshua makes this universality clear when he says to this brother, "This is not an unusual problem. Do not believe that you are alone with this. The belief in unworthiness is common in humanity—that we must do something to make up for our *guilt*, for something *bad* that we have done, in order to earn back God's Love." This brother's journey is everyone's journey.

Yeshua's opening message to me clarifies that, just as he is helping me, so does he also help all of us with whatever it is we currently need, whenever we are willing to ask. "Ask and it will be given to you; seek and you will find; knock and the door will be opened to you" (Matthew 7:7 NIV).

Our conversation takes place on January 6, 2019. I begin to describe my experience. "The first image is of Yeshua looking me in the eye, smoothing down my hair, kissing my forehead, and sending me reassuring energy—the energy of, 'It's all okay. It's going to be okay.' Then he gives me a walking staff, turns to stand next to me, and shows me a landscape. It looks sort of like Israel. He indicates that I should walk out into the landscape, but I resist him. He comes to sit next to me and says, 'It's going to be okay.' Then he puts his energy around me and says to me:"

"We're walking together. You are not alone. I have told you so many times that you are never alone. I told you before you came to Earth that I would be with you *always*. You heard that as a child. You know I am with you *always*. That means in every moment. There is not a moment that I am not with you. You cannot be alone. It is not possible for you to be alone. Feel my Love for you in your heart, which is burning. I feel such tenderness towards you, such gentleness, such gratitude for your beauty and devotion. Truly, all is well, all is well, all is well.

"Now we can turn towards your friend and ask him to ask his questions."

The brother presents his situation.

"Wisdom is in the feeling in your heart," Yeshua explains. "This is something you know in your mind, but you have difficulty relaxing your heart enough to feel it. When you let your energy relax back down into your body and your heart, that is when you can feel the impossibility of ever being alone. It is true, with a small *t*, that on the Earth-plane it appears that you are a separated body.

"You are using the tool of the intellect to convince the ego to let go of itself. All of my teachings have been to calm the ego, to cajole it into letting go of itself. This is not easy. It is like convincing a child to give me his lollipop. It doesn't work to tell the child that, 'The sugar is bad for your teeth.' The child doesn't care. The child is going to get a new set of teeth anyway, so why does it matter? The lollipop you are holding onto is your image of yourself as effective and competent in the world. This gives you great satisfaction that you can accomplish things. There is nothing wrong with accomplishing things. I am simply pointing out to you that you have *identified* with accomplishing things. You believe this is who you are. If you are not accomplishing things, then you feel lost. You say, 'I don't know who I am.' It is in those vulnerable moments that you sink down into your heart and feel the loneliness.

"Here is something I have told you before. You can't long for something that you don't already know exists. In the loneliness, you are longing for connection. How can you long for connection if you don't know there is the experience of connecting? When you stop your busy doing-ness and rest in the loneliness in your heart, that is the portal to feeling connection, to honoring your longing for connection with me and with God.

"The loneliness is scary for you. The child part of you believes that it's true you're alone and no one can ever understand you, that all the big people are too busy being lost to see you. And so you project that thought onto me as if I were one of those lost big people in your life. I am not lost. I have found my Self, and in finding my Self, I offer my Self completely to you because we are the same Self. By giving my Self to you, I lose nothing. I gain more Light because when I give you my Light, your Light shines more brightly, which amplifies mine.

"I have been teaching this because people have been thinking that I am a static entity, and I am not. I am an extension of the endlessly creative power of God—how could I be static? When your Light amplifies, so does mine, because there is no limit to the Light of God. When you relax and feel your heart, you can, as they say in California, go with the flow. It is fun. It is easy.

"In your identification with being a doer, you forget one of my teachings has always been that you need do nothing. When you relax and you feel the power of my Love for you, you receive the power of the Love of God, and there is nothing more energizing. How could there be anything else than the Love of God?

"The fear of failure places your worth in the minds of other people. Your worth resides in the Mind of God. There is no question about your worth. There is nothing you need to do to prove your worth. It is only because of your fear of your unworthiness that you give the power of granting your worth to other people's minds. Then you are afraid because their egos do not have the power to grant the worth that comes from the Mind of God. You know that you have put yourself in an extremely fragile position—one ego seeking to be told it is worthy by the egos of other people. At any moment, the whole delicate balancing act could fall into the abyss.

"My brother, picture that abyss as the burning fire of the Love of God, not as hell. When you let go of believing that other people's egos have the power to grant you worth, and drop the whole balancing act into the fire of the Love of God, *you* still exist. You are watching that whole delicate structure fall away into the fire and disappear. You are still here listening to me. You are inherently worthy. It is not possible that you are not worthy. If one shred of the Kingdom of God were unworthy, then the whole Creation would be unworthy. This is not possible. It is, in fact, vanity to believe that you have the power to be unworthy and drag down the whole Creation. That is the ego saying, 'Look at me, I am as powerful as God! I can destroy God's Creation with the belief in unworthiness!'

"Throw that into the fire. It is an acutely painful toy that you have been playing with. It has been burning your hands. The ego does not know that there is anything else, so it thinks it has to continue to suffer burnt hands in order to experience the power of being able to be as creative as God. I tell you the Truth: you are as creative as God, but you cannot destroy God. You can enjoy your creative power without fear that you can destroy God. The Truth cannot be harmed, my brother. The Truth is that God's Love is everything.

There is nothing else. Your thought of unworthiness is a passing fancy that you have turned into a monster that you imagine could eat up the entire Creation. It is a trifle. It is a feather in the wind, a piece of paper, instantly consumed by the Love of God.

"Reach out and hold my hands, with your sister, in a circle around the fire of God's Love in the center, which also resides in your heart. Feel that feeling, the inevitable Truth that you cannot escape the power of God's Love because I am holding your hand tightly, and your sister is holding your hand tightly. You can pretend to run away if you would like. We will be here waiting for you whenever you return.

"Everything I have been saying is around the challenge of changing the deeply held thought that other people's egos hold value. You are identified with the belief that you are unworthy and must accomplish *anything* to make up for it. This is not an unusual problem. Do not believe you are alone with this. The belief in unworthiness is common in humanity—that we must do something to make up for our *guilt*, for something *bad* that we have done, in order to earn back God's Love. This is why I taught the parable of the prodigal son so many years ago, because it is the Truth of the journey of the Son of God. He identifies with his *ability to leave* and create whatever experiences he wishes to create until he realizes there is nothing in the external world that brings the satisfaction of being at Home with the Father. And the Father awaits you patiently, knowing you are off on your adventure, because the Father has given you the creative power to do whatever you choose. The Father admires your ability to create whatever you want to create.

"Listen! The ego is afraid that you hate it, so it is putting up a fight. If you can, let the ego know you *appreciate* its enormous gift, which is the ability to know that you are a Self. That is the gift of ego—Self-awareness. Where the ego is confused is that it has taken one step too far into believing that *Self-awareness* means *separated self-awareness.* And yet, we have all needed to experience feeling separated in order to truly know that we exist. But in this lifetime, you are desiring to come Home because you have suffered enough. You know you exist. Your suffering has taught you that. You can tell your ego, 'Thank you so much for showing me I exist. Now I'm ready to come Home.'

"Indeed, all Wisdom resides in your heart. The intellect is merely a tool used to express that Wisdom. Wisdom knows itself and doesn't require the intellect in order to exist. Wisdom is just existing. The intellect is like a mouthpiece that taps into Wisdom, and Wisdom pours forth through the intellect, but the intellect is not creating the Wisdom. The intellect allows Wisdom to express itself in forms. Wisdom itself is primordial; it has no form. The intellect is the funnel through which the Wisdom pours, creating forms. And I don't mean physical forms, I mean thought forms, emotional forms, and anything that is apparently a smaller piece of the whole.

"The key to transitioning to being in your heart is your identification with your mind. The heart is always going; your heartbeat continues; the Love of God continues. There is nothing you need to *do* to be in your heart. You cannot exist if you are not already in the Heart of God. This struggle to be in the heart just continues your identification with 'one who does.' The key is to notice every time the thought comes into your mind of, 'I must *do* something,' and to be aware that, underneath that thought is, 'I am not worthy.' And ask yourself, 'Is it truly possible that I, a Child of God, could be unworthy?' And see what happens when you ask yourself that question. When you have let go of all the arguments of why you are unworthy, then you will simply know that you are resting in your heart.

"I remind you that I am always holding your hand. I know your worth because you are me. There is no question of worthiness in my mind.

"I would like to share that there is strong pressure in the third eye, which is to indicate to you the hope that, when you do this practice, you will see clearly.

"Ameyn."

The Courage of a Lion

Whenever I completed a transcription and read it through, I was in awe of the clarity of the words and the teachings of Love they were conveying. It was overwhelming for me, and the chattering in my mind, doubting myself as I went, was making it difficult for me to concentrate. I also felt overwhelmed by the responsibility of bringing Yeshua's teachings out into the world. So, in advance, I sent John several questions to ask for me during our next joining to help me maintain my concentration during channeling. John also asked some questions of his own. Our conversation takes place on January 7, 2019.

I begin after we recite our opening prayer.

"The first thing I see, instantly, is Yeshua lifting my chin and making a little cross on my third eye, which now feels strong pressure. He holds his face *extremely* close to mine and maintains eye contact with me."

Pause.

"The message he is conveying is to not move away."

There is a longer pause.

"My heart is burning, and there is a golden Light all around, like a fire."

Another pause.

"Yes, *stay with me* in this fire," Yeshua begins. "This is God's Love. There is nothing to be afraid of. This fire does not consume you. This fire is a blessing."

There follows another long pause.

"And then his face suddenly transformed into the face of a lion! Wow! That was dramatic!"

After a further long pause, he says, "That is to convey the power of God's Love, which you all have. It's the same power that resides in the Child of God. I am showing you this to make it clear that you are as powerful as I am. The only difference is that I have remembered who I am, and you still waver. You still have a doubt that you could have the same powers I showed as a man. But I am telling you that you *are* that power. That is who you *are*.

"I see you fear that if you demonstrate that power, you will be crucified and reviled as I was. It took me many years and many lifetimes to have the courage of a lion, to come forward into the world with my knowledge of the Truth of who I am. I will not push you. You will grow into your own knowledge of who you are at your own pace. I am here to help you transform each fear as it arises. I hear your question—do I do this for everyone? And the answer is—yes, I do this for everyone who is listening, for those who have ears to hear. No—I hear your question—I do not get discouraged, because more of you are listening, which makes it possible for even more people to listen. There are other people even now who are listening to me. You are all spreading the Light, which grows stronger every moment."

I again pause and then continue in my own voice. "I am reassured by his words that I will not be pushed, that there are other people listening, not just me, and those of us who are listening are helping to spread the Light in our own way. I'm ready to hear my questions."

John begins. "All right, the first question has to do with Israel. Laura is considering going again this year. Also, can she be open to going in 2020 with the Laura Tour?"

"My brother, I hear in your voice how much you love this sister."

"Yes! Fiercely," John replies.

Yeshua chuckles. "Yes."

"And her face just lit up!" declares John.

"Your Love shines in the resonance of your voice. This question has to do with what is Laura's role in the Atonement. When she went to Israel before, it was to help her increase her confidence, not only in who she has been, but who she is now—a teacher of the Word of God. She has learned that she is one of a group called the Messenger Souls who bring the Word of God to humanity. She needed to go to Israel to confirm for herself that this is indeed her role, a role she has played many times in the past.

"There is a part of her that has wanted to be more humble and in the shadows in this life. She declined some opportunities to be more prominent in her profession. Her inclination has been to serve as the healer of people's minds, so she is now quite skilled in that function. It is this finely attuned skill that she now brings to the next level of working *with me* to help heal people's minds. This is a powerful role. She commands respect because of her profession. She is respectful of other people. She does not get lost in people's problems, so when I work with her, there is no risk that she will take on feeling responsible for other people's journeys. Her profession has taught her well to let other people have their journeys, including her own friends and family. Those are the hardest lessons.

"When she asks if I request her presence in Israel, what she is asking is, 'How can I best work with you to help heal people's minds?' And I say to you, you could be helpful on that trip, but there would be an energy of distraction. It is not the kind of deep healing journey you are most skilled at doing. There would not be a problem for you to go on that trip, but you would have a sense of frustration that your gift would not be used as well as it could be. That is sufficient."

Pause.

John breaks the silence. "No comments on the Laura Tour?"

There's a longer pause.

Yeshua answers, "You could well be prepared for that, but there are experiences that are required first, so one step at a time. You are growing into this role of being my helper in healing people's minds. As you become more accustomed to doing this work together with me, then it will become clear if a tour to Israel to facilitate healing will be the next step. I am telling it to you this way because Laura has a fear of moving too fast. I have told her I am with her every step of the way, and I will never push.

"But to you, my brother, you see her strength and beauty and have almost more confidence in her than she does. You see that this is easy, that she could do this easily, and there are many people who would be happy to do a healing tour of Israel with her because of her gentleness and her focus on healing people's minds. She has quite a single-minded focus on that. She has no need to be famous or important. Her wish from a small child has always been to draw people to her so they could be healed. So keep encouraging her to have confidence in this growing process she is going through with me. Does that answer your question, my brother?"

"Yes," John agrees, "and with pleasure. I will be *happy* to do that. I enjoy encouraging my beloved sister and seeing her face glow with your presence. I'm going to ask her next questions together. Who am I to you in this relationship? Why have you chosen me? What do you want me to do with this gift of being able to hold your energy and hear your words? I can picture myself traveling to meet groups of friends to do healing workshops. Is this my path?"

Yeshua chuckles. "I just answered those questions. Yes, this is your path.

"Who are you to me? My beloved friend.

"We have woven in and out of each other's lives over many thousands of years, you always wanting to be where I am, but holding yourself back through your own feeling of unworthiness. I am *so* grateful that, in this life, you have devoted yourself to healing that feeling of unworthiness. You still have a way to go because you still perceive me as more worthy than you. At least you have given the power to decide your worth into the Heart of someone who truly knows your worth."

Pause.

"I am returning to your heart the knowledge of your worth. I will guide you in how to use our partnership for your role in the Atonement, which is to help heal people's minds. You were right when you realized as a child that you did not want to become a medical doctor and heal people's bodies. You sensed that was not the way."

There is a long pause.

"I have been with you since you were born, guiding you on this path of becoming a skilled healer of people's minds. Stay with me. There is much to unfold. That is sufficient."

"All right," John continues. "I will ask two more of her questions together again, as they seem to be related. What do I need to heal so I can hear your Voice throughout my day, not just in sessions with friends? And, I have a fear of judgment for coming forward as a mouthpiece in service to God. How do I heal my fear of judgment?"

"My sister," Yeshua begins, "as you stay in presence with me, your fear of judgment will fall away. As you practice feeling me in your heart *always*, you will be certain there is *nothing* else that matters. You will see other people's doubts with kindliness. *You* have had doubts, so you have no judgment about other people's doubts. If they sound like they are judging you, it is simply from their own doubt that it could be possible that I could be *so* present in your life or in *their* life.

"There is a belief in the modern, practical, scientific mind that mystical experiences happened in the past, that humanity has grown past that stage of childlike wonder. In a way, this gives you protection because people do not give the same power to mystics they did in the past, so there is less fear that is projected onto people with mystical knowledge. Because of the predominance of the scientific way of thought, people have a craving for mystical knowledge. This is a different energy than in the past, when mystical knowledge was seen to be powerful and, therefore, threatening to those with social power and control. Now, those with power and control do not feel threatened by mysticism.

"You will certainly receive the projections of people's doubt that might come across harshly. All you need to do is remember that, in their hearts, everyone longs to return to God. As you become accustomed to being in my energy, there will be no resonance in *you* of judgment to receive other people's judgment. In my energy, there is no judgment. I give myself fully to you because you are my Self. I do not judge my Self, nor do I judge you. We are One. As you rest in feeling this sense of *loving with abandon*, you will simply notice people's judgment as if it were a statement from a child who simply does not know how things really are. You do not judge a child for not having adult wisdom, so you will not judge people who do not yet have mystical Wisdom. That is sufficient."

"Laura and I have talked about doing a Magdalene tour this year." John states, "I would welcome any comments on this."

Yeshua chuckles. "You two will have much fun frolicking around the countryside. The purpose of this tour is simply to have a feeling of joy and delight. I hear your question. 'Will I be delivering messages through her?' Yes, the answer is yes. You will go to certain power spots, and I will give her messages. These are simply to encourage your brothers and sisters to know that the Truth of God lies in everyone's heart and is easily accessible. There's nothing magical about it. If the Truth can come through your joining, the Truth can come through anyone's joining. Yes, go, have fun! And I will meet you in Scotland."

"Any comments about Laura's face glowing? It is just radiant!"

"How can Laura's face *not* be glowing when she rests in *trusting* that I, who know who I am, and am awake, am residing in her, around her, through her, above, below, to the left, to the right, ahead, and behind? I am the All in All. When all of you have let go of any feeling of specialness and separation, you, too, will know that you are the All in All. That is what is meant when I say I am the Alpha and the Omega. So, too, are you the Alpha and Omega. You are the beginning and the end. In the beginning is God, and God extends herself so she can have a traveling companion. There is no end, there is only the end of illusion. There is only the end of the traveling companion believing that he was separated. That is what I mean when I say I am the Alpha and the Omega. I simply know this. You, too, will come to know this. I am not the only one who is the Alpha and the Omega. The Child of God is one collective consciousness, and all parts that seem to be separated will come to know that they are the Alpha and the Omega.

"This takes some getting used to while being in a body, the understanding that your mind is connected to mine, and my mind has no limitations because I am aware I have no limitations. Your mind still believes in limitation, so the adjustment process that you have been going through is an expansion, where the limitations that you have set are cracking so that your Light can *burst forth* through the cracks. There is an adjusting process as the shell cracks off. It can be tiring, but do not worry. You will have vastly more energy. It has taken a lot of energy to hold the shell in place.

"We will go at your own pace. I am with you every step of the way to help you understand what is happening."

John asks some questions of his own. "First, regarding your recommendation that I take little Johnny outdoors—I have been enjoying our trips to the marsh. It has been wonderfully healing. Also, when Laura ends her session, are there any interactions I can offer that could help her come back into daily life more smoothly? Thank you."

"That is such a beautiful question! Your tenderness towards her is so clear. You can help her with *your own faith*. Your process of learning to trust your intuitive knowing, your confidence in the Earth Spirits, is the same as her coming to trust her confidence in knowing my energy. These are both growing edges for you where you have had doubt. You don't have doubt about her, and she has no doubt about you. Just receive each other's confidence.

"Regarding going into nature with your little boy, you know perfectly well that you are having a wonderful time. I am reassuring you that every human Soul who connects with the Earth Elementals and the Mother is helping revitalize the Earth. The Earth, I have told you before, has absorbed lots of darkness, lots of fear, from the human mind, so every time a Soul goes out into nature and sends the Mother Love, *appreciation*, and *awe*, this helps her balance these energies. Be aware, as you sit with your little boy, throw rocks into the stream, collect leaves, and do whatever you are enjoying, that you also hold the awareness that you are giving Love and appreciation to the Mother. In this way, you are helping to heal the entire planet. She sends her gratitude to you for your blessings. That is sufficient."

"Thank you, Yeshua, for your Love. And I thank you that I can return your Love."

Yeshua laughs. "It is a miracle! It is a miracle! I enjoy participating in the awakening of your minds. What a joy."

John addresses his next question. "If you have any comments about my life as the Irish priest, I would love to hear them."

"He chose to be in Ireland, *not* so he could be part of the Catholic Church," Yeshua explains, "but because there was still a belief in the little people there. The Catholic Church was simply a vehicle through which he could maintain his cover, so to speak. By carrying the garb of a priest, he could travel safely, in Love and protection. The people knew he saw the little people and the Spirits, and they loved him for that because he was not conveying to them the message of the Catholic Church that those energies should be shunned. This is why he chose to be *so far out*, away from the center of any church power, where the knowledge of the little people was strong. Please appreciate that he made this choice to support the knowledge that people carry in their hearts their Love for the Earth Elementals and the Mother.

"He allowed and encouraged people's practices that included honoring the cycles of nature, the springs of water, and the little Beings. He was part of all of that, and the people loved him for that. This is why he struggled with the Catholic Church, because he knew they did not support what he was doing, and he tried to keep it under cover. But when he heard the church being harsh towards the Mother of Nature and the little people, it hurt his heart. This is partly why he was ready to go. He felt he had done what he could. Is that helpful?"

"Yes. Was it Slieve League where he fell?"

"A great wind lifted his Soul up," Yeshua declares. "It was a great whirlwind that caught him and pulled him upwards. The body fell, but the Soul came upwards. It will help you, my friend, in that moment of memory, to focus on your knowledge that the Soul goes Home and does not die with the body, so that you can let that body go, as a leaf in the wind.

"Focus your attention on the knowledge that the Soul was greeted joyfully, was held, caught, and lifted up, in safety.

"He left at the right time so he did not have to carry the message of the Catholic Church to abandon the old ways. Is that helpful?"

"Oh, very much so. It explains so much in my early life, and in the healing now. Thank you."

"Thank you for your devotion, my brother, your sensitivity, and your care for all Beings."

John becomes tearful. "Thank you for your relationship and support."

"I am with you always."

"I love you, Yeshua."

"I give you my blessings. I hold you both in tenderness."

Pause.

"There is always a little resistance when a gathering comes to a close. We will meet again. Ameyn. Ameyn. Ameyn."

"Ameyn," John replies.

✺

John later remarked about this session that, "Yeshua is so gentle and complete when coming through you because you are so open to receive him. Thank you so much for the opportunity to join with him through you."

We both noticed that, although John had read my questions in a different order from what I had prepared for him, Yeshua answered them in my original order. John started with his own agenda about wanting to know about travel to Israel, but by the time he got to the questions about what I should do with this gift, Yeshua had already answered in his response to the question about Israel.

A Magdalene Tour

In late December, John had sent me this email. "A wild idea came to mind. Both of us have read the book *Anna, The Voice of the Magdalenes* (Heartsong 2010). How would you feel about taking a *Magdalene* tour of Britain? Anna identified several sites where the Magdalenes lived: Glastonbury, Devon, Cornwall, and sites in Wales and Scotland. It would be an adventure! We could visit all the sites we might be called to. Ponder this and let me know if that is a possibility."

This fit my desires perfectly. "When I read those books," I responded, "I started making a list of all the locations because I wanted to visit them! I absolutely love this idea."

Through the next months, it emerged that the idea of going to Scotland had come independently to many minds in our extended circle of friends, and we arranged a gathering there, with little need for coordination.

Chapter 7

The Infusion of the Energy of Love Increases

Being the Christ in the Body

After this last session, John and I continued meeting with Yeshua weekly, when possible, and formally invited friends to join us every other week. Our next larger online gathering of friends took place on January 21, 2019.

After we recite our opening prayer, I begin the communication.

"Yeshua is drawing my attention to my body. I have a strong feeling of pressure everywhere—pressure on my crown, in my eyes, my heart, and all the way through my body, down to my feet. My hands are tingling. My feet are tingling. He is conveying to me his pleasure that I have been practicing the awareness that he is with me *always*, in every circumstance. Through this physical experience, he is showing me he is actually in my felt experience of this body. My muscles are twitching."

"Stay calm," he says.

"He is asking us to tune in physically, exactly as John instructed before our opening prayer, and feel his presence in our bodies. Because the mind and the body are Light, and he is identified with the Light, he asks us to take a minute and feel our physical experience of the power of Light."

Pause.

"He tells me he is pleased I have been practicing what he told me and John, that I shared with you last time, which is that *we are* the power of God. *We are* the power that he demonstrated as a man. He is pleased I have been repeating in my mind *I am that power*. He is helping me, and all of us, to dissolve any thought of specialness, because I cannot say, 'I am that power,' if I think I am special.

"This is a challenging process for the ego to notice that the mind-body is becoming more aware of its true Christ nature. The ego still has an attraction to trying to *use* Christ nature, which is impossible. He is showing me an image of a scale. The balance is shifting, one little piece of awareness at a time, from identification with ego that thinks it can use spiritual power, to identification with Christ, where there is no thought of using anything because Christ is already everything, so the thought of use is meaningless."

Pause.

"He is conveying that these gatherings are extremely important to help us all shift this balance from identification with ego to identification with Christ because, when we walk around in the world on our own, it's so easy to slip back into egoic habit. These gatherings create an energy Communion where we feed and energize each other, along with him. Please, feel your bodies right now. He is transmitting a strong power into all our physical awareness."

Pause.

"He is communicating to me that I have a habit of being an intellect, and he is giving me and us this experience of physical sensation today to demonstrate that full awakening means being fully the Christ in the body, not being fully the Christ in the intellect. The body is an emanation of Light, just as the intellect is an emanation of Light, so awakening requires the awakening of every cell of the body, as well as the awareness of the thoughts.”

“Awakening is a process because it is about increasing the vibrational level of the body, and it induces fear if there is a desire to go faster than the body and mind are ready for. He asks us to be patient with ourselves as he works with us to increase our vibrational levels.”

Pause.

“In the silence, he is conveying:”

“Stay with me. Feel the intense vibration in your heart, the crown of your head, the soles of your feet, and the palms of your hands. Notice the power in your root chakra, in your belly chakra, in your solar plexus, in your heart, and in your throat. Feel the pressure in your third eye, and the power of the Holy Spirit that rests on the crown of your head. Invite the Holy Spirit to settle down like a mist, slowly seeping into every cell as it descends through your bodies. Enjoy this healing vibration of Shem. When you feel the power of the Shem in your body as you walk in the world, no harm can come to you.

“I remind you that you do not judge a child for not having adult wisdom, and so you will not judge adults for not having mystical Wisdom. It is simply a level of awareness that people are growing into. There is no need to judge others if they, in their doubt, convey judgment toward you. When you feel the power of the Shem in your body, there is no judgment in you, and no place for the judgment of others to resonate. This is why you can walk in the world fearlessly. When there is no fear or doubt or judgment in you, you do not resonate with those energies that are projected towards you, and you can see them fall away, like little rubber darts from a child’s toy.

“I want you to feel this power today to give you the courage to continue in all the teaching and healing work that you are all doing, each in your own way. This is an energy transmission today to raise your vibrational level as high as you can tolerate. As each of you raises your vibrational level, it raises everyone and allows people whom you do not know to begin to trust their inner knowing. They may not use my name, because people use different names for Christ around the world. But as you receive this power without fear, it allows other people around the world to receive the same power without fear. It is simply called by different names.

"I remind you that you are all extraordinarily important. Never doubt that. Please repeat this phrase: *Never doubt for a moment how important you are—to me, to all the* **Awakened Ones**, *to all of your brothers and sisters.* Remember the effect that I had on the world when I appeared as one man. You, too, can have the same power and effect on the world. Each one of you is extraordinarily important.

"I do not mean to sound so terribly serious. I am speaking to you firmly because I know that each of you has doubted you are important. A human being looks so small, especially when you look out at the Heavens. But you *are* the Heavens. You cannot be small except if you think you are, and only then do you appear to be small, but it is passing."

Pause.

"Please join me in this image of your beautiful Earth, with all the people whose minds are awakening, holding hands around the Earth in a network. Each place a human Soul receives the Light, that Light immediately connects with another Light, and it creates a pattern of Light connecting around the Earth. Please see this in your mind's eye. There are even people on boats in the ocean whose minds are awakening, so there are connecting links everywhere.

"Please remember what I have told you many times, that every time you know who you are, and you send gratitude to the Earth, this helps her. She, too, is waking up from a deep slumber of receiving the darkness. She, too, is shedding the darkness. I gave you an image last time of your minds having a shell on the outside, created by your thought of limitation. As you are willing to increase your vibrational level, that shell cracks, and the Light bursts forth, like a fountain. I have been showing Laura an image of a fountain of Light throughout our talk. The Earth, too, is cracking her shell of darkness, and energy is pouring forth. This sometimes can look like destruction, but I remind you that everything is in Divine order. Please remember that when bodies die, their Souls do not die. Do not worry that if the Earth, in her process of awakening, appears to kill bodies—do not worry for their Souls.

"I have told you before that your role in the Atonement as a family is to maintain the Light so strongly that, when the fearful Souls are reincarnated, they are held in your Light. Their fear can no longer overtake the Light. It is a cleansing process that humanity is going through at this time. This is why you are *so* important. Everyone who can hold the Light is called upon to do so now. You think there is much darkness on the Earth because of environmental degradation and political unrest. But I am telling you, please do *not* get stuck in those fears."

There is a long pause.

"I pause because each of you is being conveyed messages from your own Enlightened Ones who work with you. They are not necessarily all the same Beings, though we are all One. We have different vibrational qualities, and each of you has Enlightened Ones who work with you, too. Please, each of you, listen within for the messages that you are being given. You each have your own role in the Atonement. Please do not be jealous of anyone else's role. Everyone has their gifts. All parts are necessary.

"I am pleased that all of you are *so* willing to drop your fears and take on the courage of the lion. It takes courage to go out into the world and teach and heal. Because I showed that courage, that portal has been opened, and it is easier for each one of you to walk through the portal of the courage of the lion.

"I am ready to hear if there are any questions from any of you, my beloved sisters and brothers. I am *so* pleased you have gathered. I am *so* pleased to be with you."

Sister One begins. "I have a strong feeling in my heart of great pressure. Is this a healing taking place or just a resistance? Also, I feel I am blocking hearing what needs to be heard. If you could, please help me, as you are doing already." She cries. "I know you are constantly with me. Thank you."

Yeshua replies, "My sweet sister, your devotion is so pure. The pressure in your heart is something all of you are experiencing. I have been working with Laura to help her understand it is not fear. The human heart can feel fear, and so confuses my presence with fear. It is *not* fear. My presence is powerful. I have no limitations on my mind. Nor do you. You only think you do. Because I have no limitations, my power is infinite, so when you feel me in your heart, it is *intense*. It is a *strong* pressure. It can feel like shaking. It can feel like tears. Allow all of those feelings to come! What you are doing is shaking off the layers of fear that you have encrusted around your mind."

"Thank you," this sister responds, through her tears.

"My sister," Yeshua continues, "you struggle with the thought that you are unworthy. This is a common thought. I remind you of something that I have said before, which is you believe the thought that you have more power than God. God creates nothing that is unworthy. God simply extends herself, because God is in Communion with her companion. If the companion believes she is unworthy, that is an arrogant thought that she can have more power than God and create something that God cannot create. God cannot create unworthiness. Nor can you, my sister. It is only a passing thought that I urge you to throw into the fire you feel burning in your heart. It is an impossibility that you could ever be unworthy.

"I have shared with you before that the reason the ego has gone through the depths of the depths of despair, is so that when you return Home, there is no place left you might go to that God might still yet find unacceptable. You have all gone through hell. This is so you are *sure* that when you come Home, God has forgiven everything. And I assure you, *every hellacious thought and action* has been already forgiven because, in the Mind of God, these things cannot exist. So there is nothing to forgive, my sister."

"Thank you," she says. "You have me laughing. Thank you."

"Never forget that I adore you. Do you feel complete?"

"Yes, I do, and I am grateful for your presence, patience, and Love, and all the other Beings who accompany you. Thank you."

Yeshua encourages another question. "Please, my friends, I am giving you the courage of the lion to speak."

A brother speaks. "Good to feel you in my heart. There's been a lot of struggling going on ever since I posted the website. Do you have any pointers for me?"

"My dearest brother," Yeshua begins, "your desire to transmit the Word to the world has not gone unnoticed. I need people like you to spread my teachings as far as possible. Please be aware that I have the deepest of gratitude for everything that you do to convey my Word.

"I am specifically grateful to you for conveying the sound of my Word, because the Shem is a vibration, and you have the gift of tuning into the sound of the Shem. When you sing for people, it elevates their vibration in ways that they may not understand. This is your gift, to elevate people's vibration through the sound of the Shem, which softens their minds so that then they can hear my teaching.

"Your struggles are simply a little patch of doubt. Who are you to be conveying Yeshua's words? You are my beloved brother. You are the Child of God. This is who you are. In your heart, you know this, and this is why you have stepped forward to share my teachings, because you know who you are, and your deepest desire is that all whom you come in contact with will also remember who they are.

"All of you in this family have had persecution in the past, so all of you, when you struggle with doubt, some connection to the fear that you will again encounter persecution has emerged. This is why I told you at the beginning of our meeting today that those arrows of persecution that will be shot towards you are like children's darts with a rubber tip that will simply fall away.

"Your only healing, my brother, is to let go of the doubt about whether you are anointed. You *are* anointed. You have my blessing to go forth in the world and share the vibration of the Shem and teach people my words. I am *so* grateful for all of your efforts in this.

"The website is merely a link for you to communicate with people. Your great power is the power of sound. I remind you that all the mystical civilizations on the Earth were aware of the power of sound. I am sure you are all aware of the Vedantas, the Egyptian mysteries, and of the Mayan use of sound. There are also places in Polynesia that you are not aware of, and the Mongols. Many people have known about the power of sound. Remember that the Earth is a vibrational frequency of Light. When you tune into the sound vibration around you and in the Earth and emanating from God, you are in the flow of the most powerful energy there is, which is the Love of God. It is like a magnetic pull that is *irresistible*.

"And you, my brother, have succumbed in the most *beautiful* way to the ecstasy of this magnetic pull of the power of the vibration of Sound, Light, and Love. Let that power pull you; take it where you are pulled to go. *Always*, I am with you.

"One thing that is important in your work is to gather with Souls who are willing to feel the vibration of my Love in their hearts and are willing to let go of their constrictions. You are going to sing to soften people's minds so that then they are more willing to let go of their fears. Make sure you are invited into a circle of Souls who wish to let go of their fears."

"Is it so that after they can hear the words better, it sinks in better?" the brother inquires.

"Exactly, my brother. You have understood exactly."

"Thank you very much."

～☯～

Sister Two asks which healing method is more helpful—an energy method focusing on feeling positive, or a spiritual method teaching about feeling the fear and going through it, leading to freedom on the other side. "How do I go forward in the way that I feel authentic? I want people to get to know their own Truth. You also mentioned sound, and I would love to hear you talk more about that. I have discovered the Solfeggio [tones used in Gregorian chants that are believed to have transformative effects on the body-mind], and the 528 Hertz, and I find that fascinating. Thank you."

"My sister, you are asking an important question: how important are techniques? The answer is—only as they are useful. It is such a beautiful thing that humanity is willing to listen and come up with different ways of loosening the constrictions of fear. There are different ways that work for different people. The mistake people make is they then become attached to the method. This is a common story that you are aware of over many centuries. The energy healing method is a beautiful little tool to break up energy blocks in the body-mind, but it is simply a tool. Remember, the strongest power is the only power, which is the fire of the Love of God. There is nothing greater than the fire of the Love of God.

"You, as a Soul, have been involved with many techniques related to elevating consciousness, including sound as a healing tool. Of course it attracts you in this life because it has a familiar resonance for you as a Soul.

"Your question answers itself when you ask, 'How can you be genuine? How can you be authentic?' You can only desire to be genuine and authentic because you already know that being genuine and authentic exists! The answer is simple. You know when you are genuine and authentic when you feel that way. If you feel you are trying to be clever and force the use of a particular technique, even if it is useful for someone else, if it doesn't resonate for you, then it doesn't resonate for you. There is no judgment whatsoever about the technique.

"There are different Soul families. There are different Soul groups. There are different vibrational levels. There are different levels of awareness. This is why there are so many different techniques. They are all useful for the people for whom they are useful. All you need to do, my sister, is listen to that feeling in your heart for what has resonance for you.

"It is entirely possible that something has been useful, and then it is no longer needed. Remember, I am helping you increase your vibrational level, so if a technique that you needed to increase freedom in the past is no longer necessary, let it go. There's no judgment about the technique. It's simply no longer necessary. You do not need to read a children's storybook in order to practice your English—it's that simple. Nor do you judge the children's storybook as something that was ineffective because now you don't need it anymore. You needed it when you needed to learn to read. Now you know how to read, you don't need to practice reading your children's books. When you are learning a foreign language, it is highly recommended that you read children's books because the language is pitched—and I use that word advisedly—at the correct vibrational level so you can receive the meaning. When you're new to a language, you have to start at a simple vibrational level. When you understand how to read French children's books, you no longer need to read French children's books; you can move on to Baudelaire.

"So you, my sister, are in the process of increasing your vibrational level and learning that some tools that have been helpful for you are no longer needed. However, you can still keep them as useful for certain people, even if they are not primarily what you always use. What you will use is your knowledge that you are God's Child, and the fire of God's Love lives in your heart. When you emanate the fire of the Love of God, *it does not matter what technique you use!*

"There are stories in your Gospels of people saying their children would be healed if I said the word. I did not use any special technique. All I did was attune to their faith. It was *their faith* that did the healing, *not me*. When someone touched my robe, it was *their faith* that caused the healing, *not me!* I could not impose my will. Only those people whose minds were *open* to receive the energy of God's Love could be healed.

"Techniques are merely tools used to help people because it is something that their mind can hold on to and make sense of. Eventually, my sister, you will not need any tools. You will simply be a beacon of Light. For this, I send to you my deepest gratitude.

"Have you understood?"

"Yes, I have. Yes, thank you. I completely resonate with everything you said. I have a question still. Do people need to go through the purification of their minds, or is it possible to just choose to be in a chosen energy and create from that?"

"Yes, and yes. It is possible to simply wake up and say, 'I know who I am. I am the Child of God. I have the powers that Yeshua demonstrated on Earth. I can go forth and tell people they are the Child of God. I can be a beacon of Light and spread Love everywhere I go!' However, most Souls need a purification process. If you suddenly became fully aware of your true Identity, it would be overwhelming for you at this moment. Purification has a satisfaction to it, my sister, because there is always a feeling of resonance when you figure something out and it starts making sense. 'Oh, that's why I have always believed this', or 'That's why I have always felt that', or 'That's why I have always had this physical problem', or 'That's why I have been drawn to this teaching, or to that place on the planet.' There is such a beautiful feeling of the pieces falling into place. Please enjoy your purification process. It is quite delicious! And by the way, speaking of delicious, I enjoy your cooking! It always smells good.

"Do you feel complete?"

"Yes, although I would like you to expand sometime on sound and the different frequencies. Thank you."

"My message for you is that because you have been involved with sound to create matter and to heal matter, I encourage you to rest in your own heart and let images from your past come into your mind and into your body. I ask you to trust your own awareness of the patterns of sound vibration. I also encourage you to do chanting. This is something you have done in previous lifetimes. Just play with sound and notice where you feel each sound in your body until you are accustomed to those sensations. This is something you will be able to share with others—that certain sound vibrations will loosen up certain blocked places in the body. This is also what I was telling my brother before you, that the sound vibration is something you can enjoy. Please practice it on your own. I will be with you. Enjoy!"

"Thank you," says Sister Two. "Thank you. That's incredibly helpful."

⌘

"I have a follow-up question about the heart," says John. "I've had atrial fibrillation for some years, and my cardiologist says I can drop dead at any moment. He wants me to take medications, but I'm not going to do that. I've decided to just let my heart be, so I've fired him. Any comments on freeing up the heart would be welcome. Thank you."

"So you have fired your medical doctor because he wants you to take medication that you don't want to take?" Yeshua chuckles. "You have always been an independent thinker, always outside of the control centers of power.

"Freeing up the heart! My brother, you are having such a good time freeing up your heart! Now that you have released so many fears—the fear of death, the fear of judgment for knowing about all the spiritual Beings who live in the Earth and on the surface of the Earth with whom you have been having such a good time dancing in your little fairy circles in the woods—you are already freeing up your heart!

"Of course, the only constriction there, for anyone, is fear. You have been letting go of some ancient fears. To let go of the fear of death, my brother, is a *profound awakening*! You are *free*! If you do not fear death, then there is nothing else you can be afraid of. It matters not if other people know you enjoy dancing in the woods. If you are not afraid of death, let them think what they think. The more you dance in the woods, the lighter your heart becomes, until eventually, such a time comes when your Soul dances off with the Spirits. It will be that simple for you because you have no fear. Do not worry about your heart. Just keep feeling me in your heart. Because you have had a medical concern, there is always the possibility that you could feel me in your heart and be afraid that this is a medical problem. I'm telling you what I have been telling Laura. The sensations in the heart are *my Love*. They are not fear. Do you understand?"

"Yes, thank you. That answers my question about the night I woke up every hour with something going on in the heart that was unusual. I believe I know now."

"You are much fun to play with, my brother. You are Light-hearted, so your heart is becoming en-Lightened!" Yeshua laughs. "Puns intended."

"Thank you. Thank you for the information on the Irish priest. That helped free up that fear of death."

"It is such a joy to participate in your awakening. Truly, letting go of the fear of death, my brother, is a profound release. I am welcoming you Home."

⮾

"Yeshua," asks Sister Three, "is there any advice you can give me to help me remember the Truth of who I am?"

"That is a profound question. How to remember the Truth of who you are? One way to understand my purpose in manifesting as a man on the Earth was to be an example of someone who remembered the Truth of who he is. I walked on the Earth to show you what it looks like, and what it *feels* like, when a human being *knows* that he is the Child of God. Now people misinterpreted that to think that I was the *only* Child of God, but you are *all*, as you know, the Child of God.

"So, my sister, one way that will help you remember the Truth of who you are is to remember that I knew the Truth of who I was as I walked on the Earth. Now there are other human Souls who have manifested on the Earth who also remembered the Truth of who they are. What holds you back is a common belief that those Souls are somehow better, more important, or of a different caliber, quality, or category of Souls that have the capacity to remember who they are. There is no such thing as a different caliber or quality of Souls. All Souls are emanations from the Love of the Light of God. What will help you remember your Truth, my sister, is to understand that you are the same power as I am. Just rest in that. Repeat that awareness. Let yourself become accustomed to understanding that you are the same as I am. Do you understand? Do you feel complete?"

"Yes, I understand. Thank you very much, yes."

"I am with you always."

⌇⌇

"I am now conveying to Laura's mind the image of a magic carpet in the beautiful, starry sky. You are all on this carpet together, going for a wonderful ride. It is the ride of your lives. It is truly happening. Your minds truly have the capacity to awaken. It is not magic. It is not something that happens only to other people. It is not something that only happened in the past. It is actually happening *now*, and you are participating because of your willingness. I am giving you *courage* to know that this is true, that your minds *truly* can awaken. It happens in community like this, where you share your energy, and your Light, Love, and belief in each other, and your encouragement of each other, and your encouragement to let go of your doubts.

How is it possible that one sister or one brother could hear my Voice or could hear my song and that not be possible for all of you? It is possible for all of you. You can all hear my Voice. You can all hear me in your hearts. *Truly*, I say to you, I am with you *always*. All you need to do is feel my Love and let it dissolve your fears.

"I am so glad that Laura has been trusting her heart to take the time that she needs to attune to my vibration. Taking a week to just connect with me and John is helpful for her in this process, as I guide her through the elevation of her mind and body.

"All of you have your own gifts, each one of you. I am reminding you again, please do not be jealous of each other's gifts. It would be too much if you each had every single gift, and the pattern would not come together in such beauty. You are like a mosaic, each piece fitting together, creating the most exquisite harmony of Light and Sound and Love.

"And with those words, I anoint you with my Love on the top of each of your heads, as the drop of fire that is the Holy Spirit. Again, feel it going down through your bodies. Feel that power through every cell, vibrating in the palms of your hands and the soles of your feet. Sense the Unity of Love in each of your bodies and minds, and collectively, as a spiritual family, the body of Christ.

"I *adore* you, my sisters and brothers. I have *such* gratitude for your devotion and your commitment to continuing on this path, on the Way of Awareness.

"With those words, I say to you, we will meet again.

"Go in Peace. Go in great joy. Go in power, the power of the lion.

"Ameyn. Ameyn. Ameyn."

Three sisters sent me loving emails after this gathering.

"It was such beautiful energy today, such a blessing. I felt I allowed myself to drink it in deeply! Thank you, my sister. It came to me that it was because we had all opened the space together that we were able to receive, more than ever before, the Love of God pouring through Yeshua."

Another sister wrote, "This was a rich channeling for me. I had had two conversations the previous day, and Yeshua went straight to clarifying my questions in his opening teaching. I hope the integration is getting easier for you. I felt like I had a caffeine rush for quite a while afterwards!"

The third sister shared a vision that was helping her move past a stuck place she had asked about in the New Year's Eve session. "In his response to my question, Yeshua had referred to the gate before Heaven, where I was still holding a piece of me back. Last week, I had the image of me and another person opening the floodgates, with Yeshua looking on. An initial little fear came that, if this is water pouring through, will it drown people in the way? Then I laughed as I recognized it was Love pouring through, and it will give all the more power to those who are in its way! In the last few weeks, I am sensing my *God-essence*, my *Christ-ness*, as something that I already have, and that I had only put blinkers on my awareness. Holding back doesn't seem to make sense at all now. Thank you for what you are allowing through. It is priceless."

"Thank you so much for this news!" I responded. "The living waters of Love flooding out of Heaven—I love it! How wonderful that it no longer makes sense to hold back."

For me, Yeshua's repeated message to have the courage of a lion was helping me push through my tendency to withdraw, to go back to some *normal* state before I could hold him and hear him. I was slowly becoming more comfortable living inside the miracle of knowing that he lives in my heart and loves me passionately. I could feel his gratitude for my willingness to be his Voice.

A brother agreed. "It is indeed a miracle of epic proportions which I am looking forward to witnessing unfold."

The Purpose of Memory Is to Heal, Not Grasp

As Yeshua mentioned above, John and I had planned to meet the following week. A brother who had been in the group session asked to join us to explore the intriguing phenomenon of both of us being aware of emotional memories of Simon Peter. He and I had had what we agreed was a fascinating and weird conversation, in which we shared memories that had come to each of us independently. I wrote to him, "It helps me be less attached to a personal identity and more identified with who I know I truly am, the Child of God with no personal identity."

One of the fascinating challenges of this channeling process is that my consciousness stays perfectly alert while I hear Yeshua's thoughts in my mind, much in the way **Helen Schucman** described receiving *A Course in Miracles*. In the early weeks and months, any time the information was about me, a vigorous commentary of my own unspoken thoughts about what Yeshua was saying went on in the background, while I was calmly speaking his words. When I did not have an opinion about what he was saying, the words simply floated out of my mouth. (With five years of practice now, the voicing process flows simply, even when I have been in great personal distress.) Since I had no way to understand this shared memory phenomenon, I was concerned that the commentary of my consciousness would interfere with my ability to hear Yeshua's thoughts, so I wanted John to be present, along with this brother, to help ground me, to amplify Yeshua's energy amongst us, and thus keep me steady and hearing clearly.

In Communion with these two brothers, Yeshua joined our conversation on January 28, 2019.

I begin to speak after our opening prayer. "Yeshua says:"

"Be aware of the body."

"There is a strong buzzing in my heart that's been going on since we started to speak, a sort of buzzing pressure on the top of my head, and a strong buzzing on the back side of the heart chakra, and also in the lower two chakras. He continues:"

"It is not a coincidence that two of my brothers have joined with a sister. It takes a lot of courage for men to relinquish their ego enough to join with me on this Pathway. This is why there tend to be more women, because they're inclined to be less rigidly attached to an idea of a separate self. Thank you to you two, my brothers, who are willing to relinquish your idea of separation. You cannot be aware that you are a creator if you are not open to receiving the power of God and allowing that power to extend through you. It is both a receiving and an extending process. Males have had great difficulty with the receiving aspect of the process of Creation. So, my brothers, it is with gratitude that I express to you my *joy* that you are willing to be receivers of the creative power of God."

Long pause.

"I am pausing to allow Laura to experience that energy of receiving and extending the creative power of God. I am showing her the image of a high-voltage electrical wire that has to be held by a tower that is prepared to receive the electrical wire, or else it would melt. So it is with receiving the intense electrical charge of the creative power of God—you must be prepared to receive it. I am showing her the specific image of a clamp that holds the wire. This is your mind. It is like a channel into which the wire is laid, and the electrical power flows through the wire. It is not static. Your mind allows the receiving and passing through of this creative power.

"There is much fear associated with this creative power because, just like a high-voltage electrical wire, the fear is it could kill you if you touched it. There is some truth in that. If the body is not prepared to receive the power of God, it would be jolted and unable to sustain it. This is something I have shared with you before in *A Course in Miracles*. I am telling you again so that you will not have any shame that you cannot sustain the power of God on a regular basis. It is quite an attunement process.

"I am still holding the image in Laura's mind of this tower that holds up an electrical wire to convey the steadiness of the tower. It does not move. It is strong and stable. In our regular Communions, I am helping you establish your stability so that you can be better prepared to withstand the power of God without being tipped over."

Pause.

"I am now showing Laura a broader vision. The electrical wires are carried over long distances, tower to tower. This is a metaphor for the transmission of the power of God from one stable mind to another. It is this network of stable minds I am now working with humanity to create, so more and more of the power of God can be withstood and transmitted. I remind you how incredibly important each one of you is. Each one of you is necessary to be a stable transmitter of God's Love, to receive and transmit, receive and transmit, and receive and transmit. The more of you who can do this, the stronger the network, and the higher the vibration level.

"The image of the electrical towers that stand on the Earth also represents your ability to transmit the power of God's Love down into the Earth. As the Earth receives God's Love through you, then she can transmit the creative power of God's Love through her own creativity.

"There is a strong temptation to be pulled into despair because of the current state of the world. In fact, humanity's ability to receive Love is at a much higher level now than ever before. The disturbances on the Earth are partly in reaction to that, and partly a catalyst to help humanity become committed to giving and receiving Love. Things that appear to be distractions serve the purpose of reinforcing your commitment to being the receiver and transmitter of Love."

Pause.

"I am pausing again so Laura can feel the intensity of the fire in her heart. Every time she receives my presence, she can withstand more of the power of Love."

Long pause.

Yeshua chuckles. "I am laughing because Laura's cat is highly energized by my presence and is jumping up and down on the bed. Laura wants to convey that the feeling of the fire of Love in the heart is almost uncomfortable, and I am asking her to just stay with it. Your presence, my brothers, is extremely beneficial to help ground and sustain this energy. Do you have any questions?"

John starts off. "The insulator on the wire that prevents the electrical energy from burning up the tower—do we need to develop that insulator in some way? I suspect you're helping us do that."

"Yes, that is correct. The image in Laura's mind of the holder that holds the wire does have insulation on it so the electricity does not melt the tower. What I am doing is helping you create that feeling of stability so that you don't resist the power flowing through you. If you resisted it, then the power would get stuck, and it would melt you, just the way the power line tower would melt if it said, 'No, I don't want to transmit electricity. It has to stay here!' Then it would just be destroyed. The power of God's Love is not for you individually. It flows through you endlessly. Where the metaphor of the insulator is not quite correct is that there is no wall between you and God's Love. It's more like an insulator that is being slowly adjusted to allow into your body-mind the amount of Love power that you can tolerate. The place to start is to understand that the power of Love is flowing through you constantly. Is that helpful?"

"Yes, thank you. Is it time to go to our question about Peter?"

"Yes."

Our brother asks, "We would be curious about the explanation as to why Laura and I have become aware of similar understandings and feelings about the life of Peter."

"I have known the Soul of Peter for many thousands of years," says Yeshua. "We did not meet in Palestine. The Soul of Peter has been plagued by the thought of unworthiness, mixed with a deep devotion to God and to saving humanity from its belief in hell and sin. The Soul of Peter has been conflicted by these competing purposes—to be a messenger of God's Love, while simultaneously believing that he is unworthy of the task. This conflict has often manifested in a feeling of despair. 'How could it ever be possible to save humanity?' The unworthiness belief has kept Peter at a distance from me, thinking that he is less worthy than I am."

Pause.

"The Soul of Peter is determined. This Soul has made a determination to release the belief in unworthiness, to release the belief in guilt, and to understand that all Souls are responsible for their own choices. I am reminding Peter that even I could not heal people if they did not agree to be healed. This is a great leap for the Soul of Peter—who has believed that maintaining the thought of unworthiness was somehow respectful, that it would have looked like a usurpation of power to say that he is equal to me—that Peter has made a determination to stop holding himself back in this life.

"I am showing Laura the image of a prism that receives light and then splits it off into many different aspects. This splitting-off appearance happens when Souls are determined to make progress and will take on lots of experience to move through obstacles quickly. It is entirely possible that one Soul can manifest in multiple bodies. I have told you before that you are all my Self, that we are all the same Soul. It's just a matter of levels of perception. There is nothing strange at all to say that one Soul manifests in multiple bodies. Currently, the Child of God is manifesting in billions of bodies. This is as miraculous as to say one Soul is manifesting in several bodies.

"The Soul is much larger than a body. The Soul can never be disconnected from God. I have shown Laura this image before, that on the *back* of the Soul it is at One with God, and on the *front*, it looks as if it's a separate entity. On the back, there's no barrier. The Light of God shines through it as if it were a costume. The front side looks like it's animated as a separate awareness, but the back side is completely open to the Light and the Love and the fire of God. All Souls are connected to the same Source. This idea that the Soul is a rigid entity is false. There are simply differing awarenesses of how much connection there is.

"Sometimes two people will be aware their minds are connected, and they can easily share thoughts and information and feelings. Lots of people have this experience. This is nothing strange. Sometimes these two Souls have been together many times. Sometimes they are aspects of the same Soul. This does not matter. What matters is that each Soul is taking responsibility for his or her own growth. That you and Laura share the same memories simply means that you are looking backward through the same prism and seeing the same original Light. Ultimately, all of humanity will know you share everyone's memories. Again, this is nothing strange.

"The ego grabs onto the awareness of memories to say, 'Proof of my separation!' What I am showing you is that awareness of memories is the opposite. It is proof of your unification. The more you release the idea of specialness and separation, the more you can easily travel in and out of other people's experiences as you are aware, as I am, that they are simply aspects of your Self. The idea that the Soul is a separate entity with one thread of memories going backward in time that is impermeable to other Souls is false. All Souls interweave with each other. Each Soul has a collection of memories that it uses to reinforce its self-awareness, but it turns the idea of a story into the idea of a rigid entity. This is false."

Pause.

"I am showing Laura images of many different people coming in and out of her mind to illustrate what I am saying—that it is easy to go in and out of the experiences of every individual in humanity. You could spend your life going in and out of the experiences of billions of people, so this is not a good use of your time, even though it is possible. The best use of your time is to heal whatever constrictions you are aware of in your own mind, and also, in meditation, to hold and bless any constrictions that you have become aware of in the minds of others. As these constrictions are released, more and more people will become aware that they share memories simply because they will know they are the same Self.

"It is tempting to grab onto a memory and say, 'This is me!' That is not the purpose of being shown memory. The purpose of being shown memory is to hold the feelings associated with those memories and to hold in Love whatever emotions are causing difficulty, *not* to hold on to the idea of a separate personality. This is difficult for the ego-mind to understand. Ego still wants there to be strict boxes that each little *I* is put into, and never shall there be feeling-Communion between the boxes. This is false.

"I only speak to you as a first-person individual because that is an artifact of your minds that helps you to understand what I am saying. When you are ready, I will convey to you, as a group-mind of the Souls who are awake, thoughts and ideas, feelings, and impressions that will come to you as your own experience. It will not be your own *individual* experience. Is this helpful?"

"Yes. Thank you."

Yeshua continues. "I am showing Laura the image of a branching tree. Remember that time is a fiction. If you go back to the beginning of time, the Child of God was One but split into thousands of pieces. Yet all the pieces go back to the same root. Each little twig appears to be separated, but each awareness can follow its history back on the twig, the small branch, the larger branch, the upper trunk, the lower trunk, and all the way down to one unified root. Many people can end up following back the thread of their own experience and uncovering that they have the same memories, as their Souls have split off at various points in the history of time. I caution you again that all time is simultaneous. I am just explaining it this way to help your minds understand this concept of the appearance of separated Souls which are not, in Reality, separated. Is this helpful?"

"That it is. Is there time for further questions?"

"Yes!"

"Is there a specific way I could introduce myself as a teacher of your teachings?"

"You are asking, what is the particular symbol that would engage people's attention for them to want to hear what you have to say?"

"Yes."

"The best symbol is your own personal experience," explains Yeshua. "It's the transformations that you have experienced by devoting yourself to this Pathway: to be humble and feminine in your presentation; to be honest about where you have been, what you have gone through, and where you are now; to share from your own lived experience the process of letting go of egoic attachments and embracing pain. This is *extremely* powerful coming from a male body-mind. Women are much more willing to acknowledge pain, to be humble about mistakes, and to be open to their own emotions. For a man to model this kind of humility, of learning from his emotions and his mistakes, is what will draw people to you, because you will not be presenting yourself as someone who is already all together, but someone who has let go of enough fear that the Light can shine through.

"Joining with other men to help heal men will be an immensely powerful role for you. Not that women are not welcome, but modeling for men your ability to be humble and tolerate your emotions, to be what is called weak but is actually a strength—this modeling is what the male energy desperately needs in the world. This is where you can most be helpful in the Atonement."

"Thank you."

"There is much healing for men to do because they have been trained to have the upper hand and to abuse power, so there is *much shame* in playing that role. It is difficult for men to feel their own hearts because of the shame. We who are here not in bodies are grateful for your commitment to help heal the shame that men carry in their hearts. Is that helpful?"

"Yes, thank you."

"I feel there is another question. The energy has not quite come to a close." Yeshua says to John, "I know you have brought forward the question about traveling with Laura, and your question of whether I would transmit messages, and the answer to both was yes. I remind you I said I would meet you in Scotland. There will be a large portal opened there for you. Perhaps other Beings will be called to join."

Pause.

"I am showing Laura the image of a funnel of brilliant white light aiming down into northern Scotland. The reason it is northern Scotland is that the interference energy is minimal there. The atmosphere is less dense, including the Earth's atmosphere, the atmosphere of thought, and the atmosphere of all the radio and microwaves you humans have put into the Earth's atmosphere. It is much clearer farther north. I am showing her the image of a vortex of white Light aiming down into a valley in northern Scotland. I will meet you there."

Pause.

"I am showing her the image of also many animals, large and small, coming to join, being drawn to the Light of the Love of God. It is the restoration of the awareness of Love in the minds of every living Being, human and animal."

"Just knowing that you helped us accomplish the impossible of finding Malin Beg in Ireland," says John, "I know we're going to find that valley, and I'm so grateful for all of this. Thank you."

"Nothing is impossible for those who love God. You have heard that before, my brother." (cf. Luke 1:37, Romans 8:28.) Yeshua chuckles. "It is with great joy that those of us who are not in bodies provide you with guidance. There is nothing more that we want than for your minds to know the Truth of the Love of God, and we will help you in whatever way you are open to receiving our help."

Pause.

"It is time now for me to ask the three of you, please, when we are complete here, to go for a walk out on Mother Earth, not on the pavement, but on the Earth, and transmit to her this electrical power of the creative energy of God. Transmit that to her with my blessing, with all our blessings, and encourage her to express her own creativity with your gratitude. She is excited to be given permission for this new phase of her creative expression. Everything is new. This new awareness of consciousness that humanity is developing—of being aware of yourself as an individual, and aware of your Self, with a capital S, as the unified Christ-Mind, simultaneously—this is a new experience in the development of consciousness. So, too, the Earth is having a new experience of being aware of herself in her own creative power. Go out into the world, plant your creative energy down into the Earth, and express it through your eyes as an electrical spark into the Light that you can see in everyone, even if it is dim. Every transmission of the electrical spark amplifies whatever is there in each Being."

Pause.

"Before we close, I ask you to rest in your hearts. Feel the intense vibration of God's Love. It is in your heart where the joining of the fire of Spirit and the Earth of Mother comes together. Feel it not only in the front but also in the back. This power of the joining of Spirit and matter permeates your being, front and back. Also, feel it in your hands and feet.

"Go now and bless yourselves, and bless all of those whom you encounter. It is with *deep* gratitude for your willingness to join me on this rather amazing journey that I say to you, I *love* you. I *adore* you. We will meet again. We will meet again, in this form, and when it is accomplished that Heaven and Earth are one unified state.

"Ameyn. Ameyn. Ameyn."

I followed his instruction and walked to the nature center that is a mile from my house in Boston. I felt I could walk forever on its trails through wetlands and farmlands. I could feel the deliciousness of the flow of life from the Earth to the Sun and back again, from the Father and the Mother into my heart and out again. My entire body-mind felt highly energized!

This brother and I later got to spend several days together during our spontaneous pilgrimage to Scotland in June. The journey through this world is certainly fascinating! Though our outward expressions could hardly be more different, we both felt comfortable around each other. When talking about Peter, we had the same emotional resonances, a feeling of how obvious it was that we understood what we were talking about, including many moments when it felt like our minds were joined as one. Such a joy to feel understood at such a deep level! He remarked how "graceful and easy, direct and simple, it felt to connect. It feels good to know what we are both doing, individually and collectively, for the full restoration of the shared Soul of the Christ-Child we are. Know I am here with and for you all ways." While outwardly each of our journeys is healing differing aspects of our Souls, inwardly, we are healing the One Soul of all of humanity.

I later became aware that the manifestation of the Soul of Laura during the time of Yeshua was as a woman in the Essene community. Older than Yeshua, she was in the role of teaching herbalism and meditation practices, including singing and circle dancing, as well as supporting those playing more visible roles. She later escaped with many other Essenes to southern France. She was in intimate Communion with the Soul of Peter, joining him on the inner planes to support him in his extremely challenging outward mission. It is from these experiences that the vivid memories of the life of Peter emerge. I could relate so much to Peter's feeling of unworthiness and of having failed. He felt guilt at having abandoned his family and being unable to save Paul, and he felt abandoned himself, dying alone in a foreign country. I was also aware of his jealousy of Maryam's closeness with Yeshua, and his fear that, if she took the lead after his Resurrection, the movement would not be respected. This ability to join with the awareness of other Souls has happened multiple times in my current lifetime. That I have developed this ability in previous lives explains why it is so effortless in this one.

Being aware of Peter has reinforced for me what Yeshua is teaching. What matters is healing the emotional/belief issues involved from an earlier life, not becoming attached to an identity. The journey Home is about releasing all attachment to the idea of a separate self, after all!

Going through all these teachings and experiences for this book, I see how firmly entrenched is our belief in our small identity, so much so that even evidence of our universal Identity as the One Child of God is misinterpreted as evidence of how special our small identity is. Letting go of being concerned about a small identity definitely takes getting used to, and the process of dis-identification takes a long time, but it also brings us to freedom.

Chapter 8

The Unity of Being with Creation

You Are the All in All. What Is There to Lose or Gain?

John and I joined again the following week, February 4, 2019. I was beginning to feel that this Communion with Yeshua was so compelling that there was little else I wanted to do.

After our prayer of alignment, I quickly begin to speak and describe my experience as I go.

"The distinctly clear image is of Yeshua sitting on a rocky promontory in the desert—the rocky desert of Palestine, not a sandy desert. I am surrounded by his energy, experiencing my body as he was experiencing his body when he was going through his purification experience for forty days and nights there. Our energy fields have merged. It feels as if we have aligned our body energy fields so that I am experiencing physically what I experience mentally when I channel—being at One with his consciousness, while simultaneously being aware of my own. He is directing me to notice the experience of the groundedness of the energy in the legs sitting on the rocks, and being attuned with the rocks. He says:"

"This was the stage of the progression of awareness in the desert when I had released the thought of separation, and I *knew* that my body was the same as the rocks."

"I can feel that the legs are the same as the rocks in the desert."

He continues. "This was only possible when I had released my fear of death, that the body might die; and I had released my fear of God, that God would harm me; or my anger at God, that I had to be put through this challenge in the desert. I had released all of that, and I knew it was a falsehood, and I was resting in the Communion of God's Love. I suddenly looked at my legs, and I could see they were the same as the rock on which I was sitting. I could look down into this crevasse—I was sitting high on the edge of the crevasse—and I could see that it was the same as my own body, as if my body were lying in the crevasse, and the crevasse was my Self, as a container for God's Love. The calling birds flying around were also extensions of God's Love. I could feel the experience of my body being completely in union with what appeared to be outside of me. I *knew* there was nothing outside of me. I was experiencing the Unity of my physical body with the Earth's physical body and all the living Beings on the Earth, or above the Earth, and in the Earth.

"And there was a complete Peace. The sound of the wind in the desert brought this enormous Peace because the thought of harm had evaporated. How could harm come to me when I knew I was at One with the rocks of the Earth? There was no separation between my Self and the Earth.

"That Peace of knowing that the Mother and I are One is something I could then bring forward when I went back into the world—and I use that word advisedly—the world that humanity projects.

"And Maryam [of Magdala] also knew this experience of Oneness with the Earth. We knew that we both knew it, and so, just catching each other's eye, we could immediately go back to the physical sensation of knowing that our Beings were in Unity with the Mother.

It was such a delight! I longed in my heart for everyone to know the joy of this Unity. Someday, I said, I will stick around, and humanity will know what she and I knew."

Pause.

"I am just resting in the beauty of that Communion. I want to share with you that it's this beauty of the Communion of knowing Unity with the Earth and the Father that makes the idea of jealousy an impossibility because jealousy is a word that implies rules, boundaries, limits, ownership, use, and need. When we are in Communion with each other and the Earth, the Mother and the Father, we are the All in All. There is no need. There is nothing that needs to be owned. I am sharing with you that this is the ecstatic state in which we abide—the knowing of Unity—because we know that there is nothing else except Unity. It's not a practice. There is nothing to *practice* because there *is* nothing *else*.

"Now I have shared with you this feeling-Communion of the knowing of the legs being the same as the rocks on which they are sitting, this is an image and a sensation to which you can return at any time. This will ground you in your Communion with the Mother, and open your mind to receiving the Light of the Father, and the knowledge that nothing can harm. I am reminding you that no one needs to be crucified. There will be no danger that is anything like that challenge. There will be challenges, but when you return to this awareness of the Unity with the Mother and the openness to the Father, all is well.

"Now I would like to say something about the little girl because I hear Laura's question about her." (I had become aware of the death of a small child.)

"Laura is experiencing right now the *pain* in the second chakra that the mother of this child is experiencing, this *intense grief*, that the fruit of her womb, which she bore for nine months, and this little being that she took care of, is no longer in her body. She feels this intense loss and futility that all of her care and devotion is apparently evaporating. I ask you and John to please hold this mother in the circle of your Love so that her grief does not poison her.

"In this way, she can allow the grief to run through her body. This is a great opening of her heart that she agreed to allow herself to go through. The grief of the loss of a child is such a heart-opening experience. Her asking for support shows she knows she is ready to allow the grief. Letting go of this feeling of futility will allow the grief to open her heart."

Pause.

"Yes, you are giving her the willingness to believe there is still a blessing in living. The little one is someone in this woman's Soul family who agreed to play this role of opening her heart. The mother now understands this little one has given her this enormous opportunity—she is feeling it as a responsibility, but let's help her see it as an opportunity—to express her open-heartedness in the world in a way that would never have been possible before. With your support, she will let this grief open her heart and expand her consciousness in a way that would have taken many lifetimes." He chuckles. "She sees her little one as an angel. She is showing you the image that she sees of this little cherub with wings."

Long pause.

"All will be well. The mother is able to look upwards now and release the little one, and in her looking upwards, she can receive God's Love.

"For you and John, please receive God's Love through the crown. Feel it burning in your hearts, and hold this woman in the center of your circle of Love.

"All will be well."

"Yeshua," says John, "I was feeling out of sorts and chastising myself for still feeling these negative feelings I have felt all my lifetime, and your Voice came through. 'You're feeling it because you still want to.' And I had to laugh at myself because I am sure it's true. I welcome anything else you have to say."

"The ego uses emotion for its own nefarious goals. It is a currency it uses, a bargaining chip with the Soul, so it thinks it has some leverage. 'If I make you suffer, then I will get some gain.' It is quite funny, my brother, because you do not need this any longer. You still think there is some merit in suffering, that it will get some recognition, or some advancement, or some admiration. You think the suffering is a sign of your courage, devotion, and commitment. But that is only from a place of the ego thinking that other egos can give it something it is lacking. Because it lacks its own courage, admiration, and commitment, it thinks it needs that from other people.

"If you would, go back to the image that I just shared of your body being One with the Earth. There is *no* separation. None. When you can feel this—the earthiness of your body, the lightness of the Earth, the fluidity of your body, the motion of the Earth; all of it is One—then the thought that there is some gain in suffering is meaningless. When you are the All in All, what is there to gain?

"Remember, my brother, I am not a unique… person. I am trying to find a word that works in the human mind. I know I am One with all of humanity, so when you are attuned with me, you are attuned with the All in All, not just with me. Thinking of me as your elder brother is helpful, but that is not only what I am. Look at the images in your mind and see how much is there, how much you *do* know that you are at One with so many Beings.

"Do you see, my brother, that you *do* know of your Unity with all there is?"

Long pause.

"I am sharing with you that you are suffused in a brilliant red color, which is the color of the root, that you are bringing your knowledge of your Oneness down to the root, which is *all* the way down into the body, to the deepest thought that the body *must* be separated. You are bringing your awareness of your Oneness *deeply* within the body, hence this red color that is now suffusing your field.

"Once you allow that awareness, then the power of God can come through your crown and throughout your body. Feel the intensity of the power of God's Love, right now. Don't resist.

"My brother, you serve an important function in the Atonement because of your deep attunement to the Mother of Nature. Your ability to bring the power of God's Love into nature is more of a blessing than you have any idea. Your channel of willingness to bring Love into the Earth is *extremely* important. I express to you my deep gratitude.

"Maryam is here, wanting to say to you, since she has *such* a Love for the Earth, 'Thank you so much, my brother, for your devotion to the Earth herself, to all the little Beings on the Earth, the microscopic Beings, the dance that they all play together, the patterns of Light that show up as leaves and insects and little animals. Thank you *so* much for your devotion. I am *always* with you because of your sweet sensitivity to the Earth. Your gentle, feminine energy is so attractive. This is why I am drawn to being with you.'"

I speak in my voice: "I can see Yeshua and Maryam as these two orbs of Light that are overlapping and surrounding you. They have slightly different vibrational qualities. Yeshua's is a little cooler, and Maryam's is a little warmer. But it is as if you are their child and they are just loving you, together, in their Unity, and your willingness to be at One with them and the Earth, and to be open to God. There is *nothing* more beautiful!" I chuckle. "They want you to know that anytime you go out to play, be aware that they are holding your hands, and they are running and skipping along with you, just enjoying the Earth."

"Is that helpful?" Yeshua asks.

"No wonder I have so much fun in the marsh!" John laughs. "No wonder it is such a privilege to go out and send Love, send sparks of Light, to the Earth!"

"The Earth is receiving your Love. It is a dynamic communication."

I continue: "Yeshua is conveying the same image to my mind as to yours, which is the image of you being in the desert at Qumran and your Love for the delicacy of that environment that looks barren, but you have such an ability to see the life that is bubbling in the desert. There is a clarity that the desert offers. It is as if you are, yourself, an Earth Spirit, and you can attune to the energies of different environments around the Earth. Where you are now is like water Spirit energy, and the desert at Qumran is like fire Spirit energy. I am also being told you have Wind Spirit energy. I can see this wind blowing across the desert.

"Yeshua confirms that, yes, those are all the four elements—your ability to connect with the Earth, the water Spirit energy where you are now, the fire energy in the desert, and the Wind energy in the desert. He says:"

"You are close to letting go of the thought of separation in your ability to know that you contain all the elements of the Universe. What need is there to hold on to an idea of separation? That's what those little wisps of suffering are doing—ego's last stand! The ego is saying, 'Oh no, I'm disappearing!' And you can say, 'And now I have everything!' Is that helpful?"

John laughs. "Oh, very much so. Thank you so much. During each of our sessions together, I feel a release, and this is wonderful."

"I feel your release. It's wonderful for me also. There will still be little bits of fear, my brother, as you dissolve your identity into the Light. There is still a bit of fear that this means that *you* disappear. Just keep holding my hand and holding Maryam's hand because you know that *we* have not disappeared."

"Yeshua, I am an Enneagram fear-type," explains John, "and this makes it difficult to let go of fear. Any tips you have would be welcome."

"This is why I began with the image of my awareness of my body's complete Unity with the Earth, and I told you that this was only possible after I had released the fear of death, the fear of God, and the anger at God. You do not have to go through the desert. If you can trust me, that I have gone before you and experienced my complete Unity with the Earth, let yourself know that I have done it for you. I have released the fear of death." Yeshua chuckles. "This is one thing Christianity *almost* got right. I did not die *for* you, but I *did* release the fear of death. So, if you join with me, you can walk through that portal that I opened. You do *have* to face your fear of death. When you join with me, who has demonstrated the transcendence of death, then you can let your fear go. Is that helpful?"

"Yes, thank you. The idea of the portal and you letting go of the fear of death for me is helpful. It's a pathway to follow."

"You have understood perfectly." Yeshua pauses, then continues. "Laura and I are enjoying being in the same body." He chuckles. "Laura is noticing her body feels much larger and more masculine, and my body feels smaller and more feminine, and we're just sort of enjoying being here together, playing in the energy field, which is Creation. I am showing you that this is Creation, this playfulness of enjoying Communion and expressing anything that we wish to express. There's no fear because nothing can cause harm, so we can express anything—flowers, light, birds, delicious food—all of this stuff we can project and create, knowing that it's not *out there* projection, it's within the Unity. You are experiencing what it means to play in the sandbox of Creation.

"My heart is *burning* with the desire for all of humanity to know this experience. I am asking you, my brother and my sister, to go forth in the world and share this delicious Communion, the burning Love of God that *is* our Unity.

"I ask you to hold in your hearts the fearful leaders of the world, the ones who think they have to defend themselves and defend their countries, their acquired power. They are afraid of death. They are simply the ego dynamics writ large. I am asking you to hold them in this *enormously powerful* field of unified Creation in which we are resting at the moment. Bring in *all* the world leaders who are in turmoil, and there are *many*, I assure you, who are in turmoil. We have the power to hold them.

"And then let them go!

"Now, my sweet brother and sister, I want to be *totally* clear that the Communion we are experiencing *never ends*. It does not end when we cease speaking. This power, this complete unification of *all* the elements of Creation, *never ends*.

"In the world, there are clocks, and day and night, apparently, and this communication in this form must end, but the experience of Unification *cannot* end. We love you *so much*, with such a gentle, sweet, powerful Love. There is no need to say goodbye since we are with you *always*. Until we meet again. Ameyn."

"Ameyn," says John.

"Ameyn."

The Source of Action Is in the Heart

I was feeling slightly more comfortable with the experience of channeling, though I was still apprehensive about putting myself in such a position of total trust and vulnerability. Here were all these friends joining together, and little old me just trusting I could hear the inner Wisdom I was given to share, having zero clue beforehand of what would be said!

On February 18, 2019, ten friends and I joined together and invited Yeshua to join us.

After our prayer, I begin.

"Yeshua asks us to pay close attention to our bodies today. He is transmitting the energy of the awareness of Creation, from the soles of our feet to the palms of our hands, all the way through the root chakra, the first chakra, the second chakra, the third, the heart, the throat, the third eye, and the crown of the head. He says:"

"I am starting with your attention on your feet to help you attune to the Mother. The Mother has been neglected in spiritual communities. There is an idea that Spirit is somehow transcendent and is not a part of nature. The Truth is that Spirit manifests through what appears to be the material world. Your bodies are the expression of Spirit in the material world. Your bodies and the Earth are made of Light; they only appear to be solid. In the knowing that everything is Light, you can experience the Oneness of everything—Light has no boundaries, Light inter-penetrates everything. I have shared with you before that Souls also have no boundaries; Souls interpenetrate one another.

"The healing journey involves releasing painful feelings from past memories. These memories can be from this lifetime or from many other lifetimes. When you are gifted with memory, the purpose is to feel the emotions from that memory so you can release them into the loving embrace of the Holy Spirit. The purpose of recovering memory is not to identify with it and make your identity something fixed. Your true Identity is the same as mine—the Child of God. You have heard this before. I am asking you today to feel it in your bodies, particularly in your feet and your hands, and in the preciousness of the breath. You have heard me share about the preciousness of the breath so many times, but it's so easy to forget that the breath *is* the Holy Spirit. It *is* what enlivens you. Just take a moment to feel the deliciousness of the breath moving through your body in whatever currents are yours. Everyone's body-mind has a different pattern of energy, so you will experience the current of breath in your own unique way."

Long pause.

"I have so much to tell you, but the most important thing is that there's nothing to *do*. I am resting in silence with you so that you will notice the Communion of all of your Souls, and I am expressing to you my deep gratitude that you are continuing to join together. I taught you before that when two or more are gathered, I am present. When all of you are gathered, it reinforces your Light and allows me to communicate clearly with you, my sisters and brothers, whom I *adore* deeply. You are a part of my Self.

"There is much to do in the outer world, so it appears. But when you take time to rest in your Communion with God, the knowing what to do comes easily. There is no planning. This is strange to the ego that needs to plan. But when your mind is attuned to God, every step is laid out in front of you, and the *feeling* that arises is ecstasy!"

Pause.

"Laura wants to share that as soon as the prayer closed, she was feeling ecstasy, this vibrational energy of the Light in the body. The crown of the head, the third eye, and the voice are all *highly* energized, the heart is expanded, the will is attuned with God, the Identity is the Child of God, and the root is the creative power of God. All of this is *awake*!

"When you are likewise awake, everything will flow smoothly. That doesn't mean there will not be challenges, but when you know you are in the current of the Love of God, the challenges are surrounded by God's Love, and they simply dissolve. There is nothing to do except to love whatever arises as perfection. This is difficult for the ego to understand — that *all* is perfection. Every difficulty that arises is *for you* in particular, to heal exactly what your Soul requires for healing. Healing is merely the release of attachment to identifying with the suffering. The ego has lots of pride in its suffering — its proof of everything that it has gone through. It is like a little child who shows you the scars on her knees to say, 'Look how many times I've climbed up the tree and fallen and skinned my knees! I'm so brave!' And the ego *is* brave. That initial impulse of Creation, to *jump* into the abyss and say, 'Let me try it myself! Let me see what it's like to be my own creator!' takes *enormous* courage. And now, humanity is ready to know that *always* there has been a cord connecting the Soul back to God, even as it appears to free-fall into the darkness of space."

"I am showing Laura's mind the image of parachute jumpers who have the courage to *jump*, and then hold their hands in a ring, and float gently to Earth. This is what you are doing now. You have had the courage to jump out of the Mind of God into space, not knowing what would happen, yet in your hearts, knowing you have the parachute of God's Love, always. Now you are *aware* that the parachute of God's Love has been holding you up forever. When you join hands, then the landing on the Earth is soft and beautiful. Where your feet touch, grasses spring up, water flows, butterflies flitter around—it's Paradise. When you land in a community of Love, your feet spread Love into the Earth. I have shared with you before the importance of walking on the Earth and transmitting to her *your Love*—the Love of God through you and into the Earth—telling her she is loved and encouraging her creativity. Humanity has been sending Earth fear, and is afraid she is dying. Please do not give her this message. Please give her your Love and empower her with your belief in her creativity. She is also a Soul with creative powers, just like yourselves.

"I draw your attention again to the Angelic realms surrounding the Earth. The Angelic realms are patterns of Light, and they focus the Love of God into places on the Earth that require support. When you receive the Love of God and of the Angels, you are assisting with this project of focusing Love into the Earth. Every time we meet, I tell you that you are important; never for a moment forget your importance. Each one of you is a receiver and a transmitter of God's Love. I shared before the understanding that you are like a tower that holds up the electric lines of God's Love. Every time we meet, you are softening your resistance, so you can receive God's Love without melting down, and transmit God's Love, both to each other and down into the Earth."

Pause.

"I pause for a moment so you can experience the ecstasy of the power of this Love that comes through the crown of your head, down through your body, and through the soles of your feet, down into the Earth. Be aware of every point of power in your body and its electric aliveness."

Long pause.

"The last time I met with Laura and John, I shared my experience in the desert, when I had released all fear, all anger, and I knew, physically, emotionally, and mentally, that my body was the same as the Earth. In that moment, I knew no harm could ever come to me because I was not separate from anything. Knowing I am the All in All, there is no *thing* outside of me that could cause me harm. My beloved Maryam also knew this, and I have shared before that all it took was making eye contact, and we would know, physically, that we were One with the great All in All. My deepest desire is that all of humanity will come to know this experience of the ecstatic awareness of Unity with God and the Earth and each other."

Long pause.

"I repeat myself only because the ego is subtle. The intellect understands concepts, but the ego still needs softening. So I repeat myself like a song repeats the chorus. And every time it comes around, it feels more familiar and even more beautiful. The heart sings along and says, 'Oh, yes, I know that song, I have sung it before—the ecstatic awareness that I am One with the All!' Just like a familiar song brings joy to sing in the community, it brings me joy to sing this song to you of the transmission of God's Love. Sing this song to yourselves every time you remember God is but Love, and so am I.

"Only Love heals. Anything you do when it is motivated by Love is healing. This is why it is so important to attune to each other and to God before you take any action. Then you will know what to do, and it will flow easily."

Pause.

"I am delighted to help each one of you in any way that you need. If anyone has a question, I am happy to help."

❧

John starts off. "At nineteen, I decided to leave the Christian church. When I asked myself, 'What do I do now?' this booming Voice came from the area of my heart and said, 'Seek the Truth.' That sounded good! A few months later, I met my future wife. She asked me, 'What are you going to do with your life?' And I said, 'Seek the Truth.' I thought she'd think that was pretty freaky and be out of there in a minute. Instead, she said, 'Me too.' Well, that was the start of something, and we have been doing it for fifty-eight years. But we also push each other's buttons regularly. I guess the question is, how can we work together, rather than at cross purposes sometimes?"

"The way through any conflict is to understand that the irritation comes from within your own mind," Yeshua clarifies. "Your brother or your sister is not the cause. Your brother or your sister is like the irritant in the oyster that creates the pearl. When you understand your irritation is yours and yours alone, then you can withdraw the energy of blame. Blame is a universal habit of the ego. When you withdraw the energy of blame and you understand that your irritation is *yours* to be held in Love, then you are free to let the other one go on their own path.

"The ego has rather fixed ideas about how other people are supposed to behave. Sometimes other people are inspired to behave in ways that seem quite illogical and even zany to the ego. When you trust that each person's Soul has their own path and follows their own Light, then there is great liberation. What is liberated is the ability to truly connect. There is the connection of the ego, which is a negotiation, compromise, contract, agreement, and expectation. The connection of Spirit has no constrictions whatsoever. When you allow each other to be yourselves, suddenly you are aware that your

Lights are always in communication. You can even be helpful to each other in shedding Light on the source of your own irritation. That can only work when each one of you does not blame the other for being the source of your irritation. Is that helpful?"

"Yes, very helpful, thank you. And I'd just like to say that I enjoyed the halo around Laura when you were doing the introduction."

Yeshua chuckles. "Laura, through her work with me, is improving her attunement to my energies, so her physical sensation is of a high vibratory quality when she allows me into her energetic space. If you could see her aura, it would be brilliant white at the moment because she and I have made an agreement to be in communication with each other."

Sister One asks, "Three times recently, I have heard you asking for healing of leaders, in another group, through another channel, and through the channeling with Laura. Could you tell me more about how best I can bring forgiveness to them?"

"First," Yeshua begins, "remember that every Soul is an aspect of the One Child of God. If one Soul has taken action based in fear, it does not differ from any action based in fear that any Soul has taken. Remember, the One Child of God has a deep desire to know herself in all aspects, in every possible way of manifesting Creation. This has taken some dark turns, as the One Child of God explores all the different ways of being a creator.

"Start by knowing that any Soul taking action that appears to be hurtful is a part of your Self. Once you know they are a part of your Self, then you surround them with the Love you know you have in your heart. In a gathering such as this, I have asked several times that you bring in leaders, such as the Pope of the Catholic Church, who is even now working to heal the problem of sexual trauma. He and I have a close relationship, I assure you. I asked you to bring in the leaders of the political world, many of whom are caught in fear.

By bringing them into this circle of Love, you help them catch even momentary glimpses of the Truth, which is that they are One with all of humanity.

"The leaders of the Inquisition had a confusion about power, which the ego has always had. The ego perceives power as the ability to make things happen on the Earth, to be the puppet master who moves materials and other human beings around. The leaders of the Inquisition confused this power with spiritual power, at first thinking they were helping people find the way Home to God. Please remember that this was the original source of their actions, trying to find a pure pathway Home to God. It was just confused with the attraction of the power to move people in their own way. Those Souls are longing for forgiveness because they are a part of you. If you hold them as separated—those people who did bad things—you keep yourself separated at the same time.

"I have shared before that when Souls manifest in male bodies, they are given power to enact control, and there is much shame connected with this egoic empowerment. If you hold those Souls in resentment, you entrap yourselves as well as them. All Souls have been male and female, so maintaining anger towards Souls who have manifested in a male body and fallen prey to the attraction of worldly power only keeps you entrapped.

"It is when you see Souls who have caused harm as *separate* that you can be afraid of them or angry at them. When you understand, as I did in the desert, that I am One with everything—every Soul, every molecule, every beam of Light—then there is no harm. So welcome every Soul who appears to have caused harm into this brilliant circle of white Light that is the Love of God. Is that helpful?"

"Yes, very helpful. Thank you."

∾҈∾

Sister Two presents her inquiry. "I have recently come to see that I have created experiences most of my life that justify hiding and being small. Could you speak to how I might work with this?"

"My sister, Laura wishes to express her gratitude to you that you are here in this circle, because she, too, has struggled with that problem. She appreciates your support in the courage it takes for her to welcome my energies and speak through her. She is modeling for you what you can also do.

"You have an energy of ecstatic joy, my sister. There is a belief in spiritual families that there is some value in holding oneself back, that it is somehow respectful of great teachers to stay behind them and let them shine. This is not respectful. Great teachers want you to know you are the same. You are the same Light. Your Source is the same God. There is no difference. When you know that your Source and my Source are the same, then you know there is no value in holding yourself back.

"Humility is a useful word because it means letting go of ego. It does *not* mean keeping yourself small. I modeled humility every time I said, 'Without my Father, I am nothing.' I modeled what the ego thought was the ultimate pride when I said, 'My Father and I are One.' I want you to understand that those are the same statement. They are both humility. I am One with my Father because I do not pretend that I am separated. 'Without my Father, I am nothing,' does not mean I am unworthy. It means I can have no life without being enlivened by my Father. My sister, ponder those teachings in your heart, and you will achieve a great liberation. Is that helpful?"

"Yes, thank you."

Sister Three asks, "How can I best help my son?"

Yeshua chuckles. "By modeling yourself on the Father-Mother God. The Source of all Light helps all of us by letting us have free will to be our own creators, while *never* letting go, because letting go is impossible. So it is between any parent and child. The connectivity of Love can never be let go. And yet, the great paradox is that children are their own Souls who have sovereignty before you agreed to allow them to come through you.

"My mother had great difficulty with this lesson, as you can imagine. She had an enormous challenge letting me go. She is an Enlightened One, so her presence never felt to me like a constraint, but she was always present. I knew she was working out her own challenge about mothering, which is to love and be present, and to let the child go on his own path. You can imagine that she wanted to counsel me not to go on the path I was choosing. And yet she knew that, had she done so, she would have interfered with the course of the evolution of humanity.

"Likewise, my sister, please trust your son's judgment. Model yourself on my mother, who saw me walking to my certain death and did not interfere. She can be a great blessing to you if you attune to her in this profound lesson about mothering. Mothering is the deepest of services. You know from your own life what a great devotion it is to commit yourself to raising up small humans into grown ones who can then go on their own path. It is a challenge for every parent to let go when the child walks across the threshold for the last time. And even when they come back, they don't come back in the same way. They come back as themselves.

"Your role is to honor his process of becoming himself, and never for one moment let your Love waver. Your Love is like the Love of God, which never wavers, but also never controls or directs. God does not interfere because God has free Will, and we are the Child of God with the same free Will. It would violate the Laws of Creation to impose God's Will in a controlling way. God's Will is only Love, and God extends that Will endlessly. There is no limit on the Source of Love. Likewise, my sister, there is no limit on your Love for your son. Just be in Love, and not in worry. Then you will know what to do. That is sufficient."

"Thank you very much. That was extremely helpful."

Sister Four asks, "How do I love myself more?"

"My sister, how wonderful to hear from you! How do you love yourself more? There is the ego version of *more* and there is God's version of *more*. God's version of *more* is endless. There is always more. There is always more Creation, more extension, more ecstasy, more possibilities, all ceaselessly unfolding. The ego's version of *more* is a grasping, holding on, collecting, piling up, accumulation—a building up of a treasure house that is then protected like a dragon protects its hoard. Those are your two options of the *more-ness*.

"When you seek more self-love from the point of view of ego, it looks like a beautiful jeweled bag into which you keep placing more jewels. The ego imagines these jewels can then be shared, but only for its own recognition. I say to you, my sister, cast those jewels to the wind. They are like drops of dew.

"The *more-ness* that you seek is the infinite Love of God. The energy that you seek is the awareness that it flows *through* you. It is not an accumulation. It is like an electric current that is ever-flowing. You receive and extend the Love of God, and as you do that, your body becomes progressively better attuned to the energy of Love. But there is no need to hoard it or accumulate it because there is the knowing that there is always more. If you hoard and accumulate the thoughts, 'I am loved, I am special,' you will run into difficulties. When energy is dammed up, it can cause various difficulties. It can cause stagnation in the form of illness, or an explosion. My sister, just experience the flow of the Love of God *through* you. The more you extend Love to others, the more you will experience yourself as loved, as the Lover, and the Beloved. It is such a beautiful question because all the Children of God are the Lover of God and the Beloved of God. You are all God's Beloved. Is that helpful?"

"Yes, thank you."

"My sister, you have so much Love to give. Just keep giving your Love, and you will receive more. That is how it works. Don't have any fear that, if you are giving Love away, you are somehow losing Love for yourself. Just remember the distinction I have made for you between the egoic holding onto jewels, and God's Love, which is ever-flowing. That is sufficient."

Long pause.

"The energy has not quite come to a close. I feel there is a further desire to speak."

*　❧　*

Sister Five seeks help. "All my life I've struggled with the message, 'You can't do that.' I've listened to it, and I'd like to let it go."

"That is the same question your sister asked about keeping herself small, is it not?" Yeshua suggests. "There is no benefit in keeping yourself small. That message is given from a place of loving protection, but it comes from the place of egoic control, of one ego thinking it knows better than another about what is best. When you are a child, you absorb these messages because you want to please the people on whom you are dependent. But I have given this message before here today—there is no respect inherent in keeping yourself back. It does not help great teachers that you hide your Light. It does not help your parents that you keep yourself back. It does not help your community to hold yourself back. That you are asking this question is a beautiful sign, my sister. You no longer feel comfortable holding yourself back. Your desire to expand your wings and fly is a true one. It comes from the heart. It is the most respectful thing that you can do for yourself and for all of those around you. All of those around you have nothing but desire that you fill out your wings and fly!

"I can feel your joy in listening to these words. This is the permission that your heart is longing for but has always contained within itself—to fly! Follow your own desire, my sister. It is completely worthy of your trust. Is that helpful?"

"Yes, thank you."

*　❧　*

Yeshua concludes. "Please notice your bodies. Please notice the vibration in the palms of your hands, your legs, and your feet. Please notice the pressure on the top of your heads, the crown that is open to the Holy Spirit. Please notice the pressure in the third eye, which allows you to see truly. Please notice the expansion in your throat that allows you to speak Truth. Please notice the vibration in your heart, where Father and Mother join—the fire of Spirit and the Earth of Mother join in the heart and express outward as Love. Notice the energy in your solar plexus, the desire to enact the Will of the Truth, which is God's Love. Notice the fire in your belly, the joy to be embodied, to be here on the Earth, and to experience ecstasy. Notice the fire in the root, the liveliness of Creation. And particularly notice your hands. My message to you here today has been about action, and the hands are the expression of action. But the source of action is the heart. Notice that the energy comes from the heart and travels down the arms into the hands. Again, notice the currents of Love that move through your own body in your own particular way.

"I wish you could see yourselves as I see you. You are like shimmering jewels, always moving, always in communication, always in an exquisite pattern of Light and colors that are not seen with the human eye. My longing is for you to know the ecstatic joy of being fully aware of your Communion with each other, and with God and the Angels. I draw your attention again to the Angelic realms, who are always singing around the Earth. Again, receive their pure vibration of Love and Wisdom, and extend that Love and Wisdom down into the Earth."

Pause.

"Go forth and act in the world! Now is the time to bring the message and energy of Love out into the world. But make haste slowly. Always take the time to sit in Communion with me, with the Enlightened Ones, with the Angels, and with God, so that you always know you are in that place of Creation, in the awareness that you are an extension of God's Love. Then you will know what action to take as you go forth into the world.

"And never forget—I tell you this every time—I am with you *always*. Every time you remember I am with you, it brings me joy. It is like having your lover reach out her hand to say, 'I know you're there.' How wonderful it feels to be acknowledged. It is in the touch that the joy is experienced. Feel my touch in your heart and throughout your bodies. Allow yourselves to be with me, as I am with you. Please receive my loving embrace. I adore you, each one of you, and all the sisters and brothers who are important to you in your lives—I extend my Love through you to them as well. It is an endless outpouring of a fountain of Love and Light from our Source, Mother-Father God, ever-shimmering Light of All.

"And with those words, I say to you, we will meet again, in this form, and when Heaven and Earth manifest as One unified state.

"Ameyn. Ameyn. Ameyn."

Later that day, John wrote about this gathering. "How amazing that your connection with Yeshua becomes ever deeper with each session. Today, you joined and came through even more strongly."

For me, the more I engaged with this process, the more the physicality of Yeshua's teaching struck me. This was not all an intellectual exercise. It was an attunement of the entire body-mind field, which he makes clear, is a unified field with all that is.

When I shared the transcript of this gathering with the group and expressed my gratitude to them for supporting me in growing into my life's mission, I received lots of gratitude in return.

"We are so fortunate to be the beneficiaries of your life's mission. I am deeply grateful to be included in this process. May Yeshua's Wisdom be a gift to ever more of his beloved ones."

"Love and blessings and deep gratitude for this work you are doing."

"What a powerhouse of a channeling. It is amping up, sister! Hallelujah!"

Giving and receiving are, indeed, one. There was nothing more rewarding in my life than offering this channeling service, and participating was certainly a blessing for all involved.

Chapter 9

Sympathetic Vibration Between Souls

Changes Are Necessary for the New to Be Born

One week later, on February 25, 2019, John and I joined together again to invite further conversation with Yeshua.

As in every previous session, John starts with guidance to focus on the breath. Learning to soften the body and relax the grip of ego helps to allow in Christ Consciousness. After we say our prayer of alignment three times, the internet freezes. When we are live again, I continue.

"I suspect the freezing has to do with what Yeshua was just saying, which is to notice the strong wind that's going on outside of my house. He said I could see it in fear as destructive, or through the eyes of the Holy Spirit as transformational. This is symbolic of the current state of humanity and the Earth. We could either see it with fear—all the political leaning towards control that's going on, and the fear of environmental degradation and collapse—or we could see it as a moment of sweeping out of the old and what does not work, so that the New can be born. He reminds us again:"

"Please, do not send fear to the Earth."

"He has said this before, from the beginning of his work with us: there will be Earth changes, and we are not to be afraid of them. They are necessary for this transformation that is going on. He continues:"

"It is tempting to go back into fear, to look at environmental problems, and people dying, and think that this is somehow bad. Please do not give in to that temptation to see the world through the eyes of fear. Instead—"

I interrupt. "I am resisting letting go of seeing the world through the eyes of fear, and so I was asking, what's the alternative? His answer is:"

"*Joy!* See the world through the eyes of joy, through the heart of joy. Be excited that the old is being swept away to clear space for the New. You can see this in the political atmosphere in this country, where the old is desperately clinging on, but there's a huge, powerful energy of newness coming in to sweep it away. Of course, there is resistance in that process, but it is inevitable—humanity is open *so much* to the power of Love that the power of control does not look as attractive as it used to. We are coming to the end of the age of the power of control.

"I am reminding you again of the importance of staying in communication with your friends of the Heart. We are in communication with them at all times, but the body-mind derives benefit from being in tangible communication.

"That's the message for today: to be in joy and not in fear."

My cat is highly energized and bouncing all around! I address John. "Yeshua wants to know if he can provide you support today."

John replies, "Yeshua, I'd like to ask about what I call the out-of-bounds personality. From an astrological point of view, out-of-bounds is a planet that appears to be beyond the Sun's orbit. Both Laura and I have planets in this type of placement. Almost everyone who listens to you, not just recognizes your presence, but listens to you, has this out-of-bounds consciousness. We can feel pretty freaky at times. Do you have any words for us? Thank you."

Yeshua laughs! "The image in Laura's mind as you are speaking is of a lion cub. It has the qualities of playfulness and lack of self-consciousness. It has confidence from being cared for by the parents and from being born into a confident family. It has the lack of need to follow the rules because the family of lions follows their own rules and does not take directives from anyone else. This is the symbolic energy of being a spiritual leader—to be playful and to know that you are out of range of anyone's ability to harm you. Being within bounds is simply not at all interesting. There's no benefit to staying at a lower vibrational level, following the rules, and then finishing your life without having moved the developmental needle very far forward. There's just no attraction to that.

"It can seem freaky, to use your word, if there is a perceived value in fitting into social rules. But those of you who are not interested in following the social rules can see there is the vastness of infinity that becomes available, so why would social rules have any attraction compared to the vastness of infinity? It is a comparison that has no meaning. There is nothing to even say about that comparison.

"The benefit of being older is that it doesn't matter so much what other people think. You've earned your living, you've followed the rules, and now you are completely free to do as you choose. People will be drawn to you, no fear about that. Maybe the people who like rules won't be drawn to you, but that's OK. You don't need everybody in the world to be drawn to you. Is that helpful?"

"Yes, thank you." John then explains about a recent trip in which a rental car agent lied to him. "I have had a little trouble letting go of having been overcharged. I'd be happy to hear anything you have to say."

"It is whatever emotion that has been stirred up that requires care. If you were to fix the overcharge in the external world, you would miss the opportunity to heal the feeling of being deprived, of not having enough. This is your opportunity to know in your heart that the Source of everything is God. You have heard me say before, 'Render unto Caesar what belongs to Caesar.' Having money is only what appears to be necessary to get by in the world. When you are in tune with God, all of your needs are met. This is *very* difficult for the ego to believe. When I taught about this, about the lilies and the sparrows, I was conveying through parable that, when you are truly in tune with the Will of God, there is no worry about material need.

"Contemplate that fear of not having enough, so you can *know* that you can let that one go. You are in the flow of God, so there is always enough.

"This is a deep paradox that is so difficult to live inside of when you are in a body because the body has demonstrable needs for clothing, food, and shelter. And yet I say to you, your Soul has need for *none* of those things. When you can live in total trust in God while here on the Earth-plane, the physical needs become less and are met with ease. This is so difficult for the ego to understand because it seems to strike at the base of survival.

"But look at my life. I did not grow my own food. I traveled over thousands of miles. I was fed. I was clothed. I was given shelter. When I arrived at my destinations, I was fed and welcomed. When I came back to Palestine, I was fed and welcomed. Never once did I earn my living. You might say, 'Well, somebody had to grow the food.' And I say to you, truly, when all of humanity is in line with the Will of God, the food will just manifest without toil. Then the need for separate bodies that need food will disappear, and all will be seen as it is, which is Light. Is that helpful?"

"Very much so," says John. "You have supported my decision to just let this issue go. Also, I understand that true responsibility is to listen totally to the Mind of God."

"*Oh yes!* I have been giving this message repeatedly, that the most important thing is to be in tune with God. Then everything just flows naturally."

Pause.

"I hear Laura has a question: 'Should we plan our trip to England and Wales and Scotland, or does that just flow naturally?' The answer is that you do need to show up and get yourselves there, but then events will unfold in a miraculous way. It will be fun!"

Long pause.

"I encourage you to continue to move forward with your training with each other in preparation for our journey together. I so enjoy working with Laura and with you, helping you dissolve your mental obstacles and attune yourselves to my energies. It brings me great joy. Please continue on your path of mutual training.

"We await you in Heaven. We await you on the other side of the belief in separation. When you get there, you will see how easy it is. You will be astounded that you held onto separation for so long.

"So, with those words, I will say farewell. Until we meet again. I love you both.

"Ameyn."

John replies, "I love you, Yeshua. Thank you."

The Vesicle of Holiness and Safety

The following week, March 2, 2019, I met with a sister in Ireland to communicate with Yeshua.

We recite the *In the Name* prayer three times, and then I begin.

"He is showing me the image of a boat and asking me to notice the sympathetic vibration between your Soul and mine. The resonance between us amplifies our own growth and confidence in knowing that the prayer we just said is the Truth—that we *are* the Christ. He is showing me the boat on which Maryam came to France. I ask why. He says:"

"I want you to go there. You had a question about whether it was too much to go to southern France and the British Isles. But I want you to go there.

"The image of the boat is a symbol of the vesicle that holds the holiness of the Child of God. It is a magical vesicle because it can carry any number of Souls. As each Soul comes into this boat that carries all Souls safely to Heaven, each Soul becomes aware that he or she belongs to this family, which grows larger all the time. It started out as a small family that I guided across the Mediterranean to safe harbor. Do not think that it is an exclusive family. All Souls will someday be held by this same vesicle of holiness, and there will be nothing outside of the holiness—no thought of anything that is impure or unacceptable.

"This image of the vesicle is carried through the history of Christianity in the form of the Grail. It is the same symbol as the boat. They both hold the sweetness of God's Love. When Souls know they are in this vesicle, they know they are perfectly safe, just like the Holy Family was perfectly safe crossing the Mediterranean with no mast, sails, or oars. It seemed impossible that they should survive, but when Souls are in tune with God, then no harm comes.

"I am also sharing this to help the Soul of Joseph rest. In that time, it could not have been known whether the family had arrived safely. There were rumors, but I am addressing the Soul of Joseph so that he can rest, assured that the role of protection and safety was carried forward, even though he was no longer required to serve in that role."

Long pause.

"The intense devotion of the Soul of Joseph is what I am showing to the mind of Laura in that silence, trying to convey the tenderness of Love and care, of holding the family in the sweetest of embraces. It is like a Light in a dark place that creates a perfect sphere all around the Source of the Light, a warm glow that protects all who are in its realm. That warm glow of Love and protection is eternal and cannot be harmed by the illusion of time. I am telling you this so you can let go of any past worries and feel free to move forward with lightness in your step, and the feeling of springtime and grace.

"Sister, you have a question about moving forward as a teacher of this Pathway. Knowing that the protective embrace of God's Love has never for one possible instant ever diminished, despite the appearances of things, you can move forward with a sense of calm and confidence, from a place of *deep* knowing that the loving protection you cultivated with such diligence is with you. It is an energy that you put outward, and it draws people into its circle, like that Light in the darkness, creating a sense of safety and comfort. You can have confidence in this. It is deeply about *feeling*."

Long pause.

"I paused for a long time so Laura could experience the exquisite, tender beauty of this feeling of loving protection. When you stay in that tender place, then all decisions are simple. Any decisions that support the extension of this tender, loving protection are the correct decisions. You can have complete confidence that this feeling never goes away. And like the boat, the more people you include in the circle of this tender, loving confidence, the stronger the force field of this Love vibration becomes. You will know that it is not only *you* who is the originator of this energy. You will know the Source is God. The more Souls who fall within the sphere of this glowing Love, the stronger it becomes.

"Is this helpful to you?"

"Yes, it is," replies the sister. "Very helpful, thank you."

"Is there anything more that you would request as you go forward on your path to being a teacher of God?"

"What would help me most is, how can I know and practice that what I am hearing coming through me is your guidance on what wants to be shared?"

"That is a beautiful question about practice. Focus on your heart and bring into your mind the image of the warm glow of an oil lamp in a dark room. The emotion that this image evokes is the emotion to practice. The Light itself creates a feeling of protection and invitation. Stay in that warm Light in your heart. When you have that feeling, it is a delicious feeling. It is a feeling of complete calm and confidence, relaxation, warmth, and care. How could it be but from me and from the Father? There is no other Source.

"The key for you is to rest and not put effort into this practice, but to rest in that warm glow of loving protection. Is that clear?"

"Yes, thank you."

Yeshua continues, "Put attention on your third eye at the moment and notice that you have the power of insight. You ask, how do you know it is from me? You will know because you can feel the energy in your third eye. When your third eye is awake, you know that what you are experiencing is a gift from Spirit. Right now, notice that feeling in the third eye. It is a feeling of pressure, as if someone were pushing their finger on your forehead. When you have that feeling, you are receiving the energy of the Holy Spirit. Can you feel that?"

"No, I can feel a tingling on my back, but I can't feel the pressure on my third eye," she responds.

"Put your finger there and press so that you have that sensation of pressure. Then, take your finger away and notice the residual feeling. Practice as you breathe. When you breathe out, let the breath come up the channels in the center of the body and pool in the head so you can feel the Light behind the third eye and in the center of the brain where the pineal gland is. Consciously practice filling your pelvis, the root chakra, with your breath, the Breath of God, and, when you breathe out, see it pool and fill your head, activating your third eye and your pineal gland."

"I can feel it now. While I was practicing breathing earlier today, I felt a little flutter, as if it were right in the center of my head. It was the first time I ever felt that."

"Yes, that is the Light of God awakening the pineal gland, which is the organ in the brain that receives the transmission of Light. You are awakening your Light-receiver.

"Please remember you are surrounded by guides and Angels. When you practice this, bring into your conscious awareness that you are *not* alone, that you have a circle of friends who are sustaining the energy of Love and Light so you can amplify it in your physical body. I am going to say what I always say to you—I am with you *always*. When you practice this, visualize my energy surrounding yours, and we can become one vibrational field. This will help to amplify the awareness of Wisdom in your mind; the Light of God, the feeling of loving tenderness, in your heart; and the power of Creation in the root. It's all One.

"I love you with such sweet tenderness, my beloved."

"When Laura and I started talking," the sister continues, "I felt this really intense heat that fully enveloped me, which is not something I ever experience. And then Laura took her jacket off because she became hot as well. I am curious what that was. Were we somehow connected?"

"Yes, that was not a coincidence that you both felt heat at the same time. Laura has often shared that taking on my energies is on the verge of uncomfortable. The intensity of my vibration is not the level at which she operates day to day, but she is willing to receive this vibrational level, even if it feels just past the edge of what is comfortable. So when the two of you—and remember, I shared at the beginning that your Souls have a strong sympathetic vibration— when you align your energies, it amplifies your own vibration. This is experienced in the body as heat. It can be quite uncomfortable, but as I have said to Laura many times, stay with me. Each time you experience this increased vibrational level, your body adjusts, and it becomes easier. Is that helpful?"

"Yes, thank you."

After a long pause, Yeshua says, "I am just enjoying being here together with you, and so is Laura's cat, who has joined us. He says, 'I don't want to miss the party. I might be old, but I can feel a good time when I feel one!'"

Pause.

"Laura is asking, would you share her question?"

"What is my role?" asks the sister. "What is helpful for me to do or not do?"

"By modeling courage—and you are already modeling courage by being willing to be my Voice—you will be a beacon of Light to other Souls who already want to share the Light that they feel so graced to have received. So continue to step forward and play a leadership role in helping to provide loving support for all those who feel the call to be teachers of God. I am with you always.

"Many riches await you, my Beloved. You are being called to serve in many places. This is a call that you have responded to, over and over again, in many lifetimes. In this lifetime, you can bring my Love further out into the world. Humanity is ready to know that the Truth is God's Love. Your role will be to amplify that confidence in others.

"I am with you always, guiding your every step. You do not have to figure anything out. I am enjoying working with you. I request only that you play a little bit more! I have enjoyed the walks in the woods.

"That is enough for now. There are many, many things that I could tell you. One step at a time, my Beloved. You have an energy of impatience, of always wanting more. Just rest in the delight of my Love for you. You are my Beloved, and I am yours. There is nothing more that you need to know. When you are the Beloved of one who knows that he is the Child of God, then the vastness of infinity is open to you.

"I say to both of you, my beloved sisters, that I hold you in the warm circle of my loving embrace. Such tenderness I feel for you. It becomes easier to say goodbye since I know you now understand I am with you always.

"Until we meet again. Ameyn. Ameyn. Ameyn."

When John read the transcript of this channeling, he could feel its power. "I looked up the word *vesicle*. It is a biological term that describes how material is transported within cells from one place or state to another. This speaks loudly of the work you and Yeshua are doing with the rest of us: transporting us from one stage of consciousness to another—from world consciousness to the heavenly feast shown to you and promised to all of us."

In my wildest dreams, I had seen myself channeling Yeshua. I was amazed the dream had manifested. What I had not imagined was that his presence would manifest in Communion with friends on the spiritual path, but I now understood this to be a teaching in itself—the nature of Christ Consciousness is Unity, so it manifests when friends join in the intention to awaken. What miraculous joy! I felt blessed beyond measure. I had glimpsed this miracle would come, but once it arrived, it surpassed any idea I ever had of it.

I wanted to spend every waking minute channeling our beloved brother, but I knew I needed to integrate his teachings and energies into my everyday life. He was right about my energy of impatience!

Chapter 10

The Intimacy of Christ is Everywhere

The Holy Family Ripens: Becoming Aware We Are All the Christ

On March 4th, 2019, fourteen friends gathered online to converse with Yeshua.

After lots of happy conversation to be in such a large gathering of friends, John brings us into focus. "We started out just the way Yeshua likes us to—in joy, enjoying each other's presence. Let's start with feeling-Communion. Take a deep breath in, then let it out, let go, and relax. Fill that space with gratitude. I feel gratitude that all of us are together. Feel the breath on the inside of the body. Feel the radiant joy of Yeshua's presence, the intimacy of the presence of God, through Yeshua, in the body, the presence of Love. The presence of Love radiates out to each one of us here."

We recite our opening prayer three times, and I begin.

"Yeshua wants to share his utter delight at John's opening meditation because it allowed us to all experience the Truth that the Christ-Mind, which he represents, is everywhere. We are becoming better able to tolerate what appears to be a paradox to the ego, which is that one mind can be in communication with an infinite number of minds simultaneously. This does not diminish the awareness of one personality's consciousness. Both the awareness of the personality and the awareness of all minds can be simultaneous. Yeshua has shared with us before that this is difficult to understand, and he is delighted we are understanding this at an experiential level. It is not an intellectual concept that can be understood. It is a knowing that can be felt in the mind, heart, and body. He says:"

"It is through our repeated joinings that the knowing of the Truth of Unity becomes ever more visceral."

I continue. "He paused to encourage us to experience this awareness that we all are attuned to him simultaneously. It may be that one person is speaking his Voice, but we are all experiencing his presence. This is what he has meant when he has said the purpose of his teachings is to allow the expression of a multitude of Christs. We are well on our way to becoming aware Christs. The ego thinks that is the most grandiose thing that could be conceived. It takes a while to soften the ego so this teaching can be absorbed as the Truth—that who we all are is the Christ. He is asking us:"

"Tune in to your heart chakra, and just notice whatever sensation you are experiencing in your heart. Remember, the chakras are on the front and the back of the body, so you might also experience sensations on the back side of the heart chakra. It is in the heart that the energies of the Mother and the energies of the Father join. The heart is like a loudspeaker that broadcasts the vibrational frequency of Love in all directions. It sends out a message, and it is received by any willing heart who picks up the message and conveys it again, like the child's game of telephone.

"Please notice your heart, because any little quiver of sensation you feel means you are receiving a Love message. You may never know who sent it to you, but as the power of Love amplifies, you will receive many more Love messages. Please notice them, because it is the power of your awareness that amplifies the consciousness of Love.

"Please bring into the center of this circle again, the leaders of the world. I have asked you this in the past. They continue to need your support. Each one of you will receive fleeting images of faces and places around this beautiful Earth that need your particular support. Put those leaders in the center of this circle and surround them with the pure vibration of Love. In the vibration of Love, there are no flaws, nothing is impure or outside—everything is included in the vibration of Love. Remember that a leader always has the thought of protection—hopefully of their country, sometimes of a smaller segment of their country—but they bring a quality of protection to their role. I am asking you to infuse that quality of protection with the energy of Love so that it is a loving protection, rather than a fearful protection.

"I recently shared with Laura and a sister the image of the boat on which the Holy Family traveled in safety from Egypt to France, even though it had no mast, sails, or oars. It was carried on the wind of God's Breath, following the Light. So even in what appears to be dire circumstances that would surely lead to bodily death, when you are in tune with the vibration of Love, then protection flows naturally. This sounds like magic to the ego, and from the ego's perspective, it is magic. However, from the perspective of Love, everything is possible, and everything arises in the mind.

"All time is simultaneous. One of my purposes in bringing to your mind this image of the boat of the Holy Family is to help those Souls see into the future in which you appear to reside, so they can see that their spiritual practice, their community creation, their loving protection of one another, bears fruit. Your appearance in the future helps them gain the courage to continue on in what appears to be the past. But there is a permeability of time. What you are doing now encourages them. Because of their great Wisdom, they can see into the future, which is now. This is not so strange when you understand that what *they* do also encourages you. You look to your spiritual leaders of the past for inspiration and guidance, but I am sharing with you that they also look to you in the future for inspiration and guidance.

"This is a time when Souls who have been supporting each other in the quest for Truth are ripening. When fear is shed, the glowing nugget at the center of the fruit is revealed. It is sweet beyond any sweetness. Now is the time of the ripening of the Holy Family, which has expanded exponentially. I had shared before with Laura and our sister that the boat is not just a physical boat, but it is a symbol of the loving protection of God that holds all Souls on their journeys towards safety, towards Home. The boat is infinite and can hold all Souls; there is always room for whoever is ready to come on board. I am reminding Laura of the image I shared with her at the beginning of our work together—of the heavenly feast, the table that has room always for more Souls. Whoever is arriving is welcome.

"These visual metaphors are simply to help you transition from the limited perspective of the illusion of a material world into the expanded perspective of Christ Consciousness that has no limitation and is filled with joy! I wish I could convey to you the sweetness that is beyond any sweetness you have ever tasted, the tenderness that is beyond any tenderness you have ever felt."

Long pause.

"I am conveying to you a felt image of the glowing quality of your Souls—they are always shimmering. When they join together, this exquisite pattern of color, design, movement, and dance happens. See if you can see it out of the corner of your eye, in the center of your mind, in your heart, this ever-shimmering pattern of Light that is always in communication with itself. When you can see this pattern, you will know that you are all of it. It is not that you have one spot in the pattern, but that you are simultaneously in one spot *and* all of it. You are all the All in All.

"Now picture this ever-shimmering pattern of Light, Sound, music, sweetness, and tenderness. Picture it holding the Earth, this ever-shimmering beauty and harmony. Hold the Earth in the tenderness of your Love for her. Practice seeing all of her wounds being healed, all of her injuries being knit back together, all the toxins being transmuted into Love, all spots on the Earth in communication with all other spots on the Earth, under the sea, and in the atmosphere—all One, all in motion, a never-ceasing celebration of the power of God. It is helpful that your physical bodies are in different places on the Earth. This helps anchor the awareness of this beauty into the Earth. It is my deepest wish that all of humanity will know the ecstasy of the awareness of union with God. And I will never leave you until no sheep have been left behind.

"Now is the time for me to offer guidance to whichever one of you would like to step forward with a request."

Brother One begins. "I have a question Laura asked me to ask for her. 'Is it time for me to be more public with your teachings through me?'"

"My beloved sister, this gathering today is also more public," Yeshua clarifies. "There are many Souls here who are hearing my words through you, and many more Souls who will also hear these words. Once you agreed to join with me in intimate communication, your Soul agreed those words would be shared broadly. It is clear these communications are not personal or private. I began my communications with you by teaching you that you are not special. You have understood well why I told you this in my first communication. If you had thought you were special, we would not be able to work together. My words are not especially for you or your close circle of friends. My words and energies are for whoever is drawn to them.

"Your feeling that it is time to share my teachings more broadly is to be trusted. You would not have that feeling if you did not have that feeling! I have told you before that I will go slowly with you because it will take time to adjust to your new role. When the time is ripe to make my teachings more easily accessible, the assistance will manifest to help you do that. It will become a larger task than what you are capable of on your own, so when the time is ripe, I will send you the support. That is sufficient."

Brother Two asks, "What is the best way for me to cultivate my inner eye or ear so I can experience a more direct connection with you?"

"This is a beautiful question. You are all experiencing that somewhat here today. The power of the group helps amplify the inner awareness of each Soul. I have been showing you the importance of feeling the energies in your body. Right now, just notice any spot where there is buzzing, tingling, heat, a fluttering feeling, or anything like that. The more you notice it, the stronger it gets. Do you see?

"The other thing that is important is to trust every image that comes into your mind. This is why Laura is able to work with me, because she has learned over the years—before she trusted herself enough to hear my Voice—to trust the images that come into her mind. Likewise, my brother, you are adept at seeing images, but you have discounted them as if they were just mind-wanderings. They are not mind-wanderings; they are gifts being given to you. When you see an image, explore it, amplify it, bring curiosity and Love to it, and simply report what you are seeing, and you will be astounded at the doors that are opened.

"It is a process of amplification. It is not that, suddenly, the Heavens open and you see the Truth and you hear the Angels. It is a slow attunement process. You have been receiving many signals and have not noticed that they have been sent to you. Take time to practice trusting whatever comes into your mind. Often, you will be sent a signal that seems meaningless. Later in the day, you will remember you saw that signal in your mind, and here it is. This is to reinforce for you that you can trust what it is you are seeing in your inner vision.

"Continue to practice trusting all sensations, feelings, and images that come to you. These come first. Words come much later. The words are harder to trust because one's own thinking can get mixed up in the thoughts being transmitted from the Christ-Mind. Images have a purer quality. Is that helpful?"

"That it is," says Brother Two. "Thank you."

Sister One inquires, "How can I best make the most of my trip to Spain in a couple of days' time?"

"Ah! The Souls who live in the North have ever been drawn to the South to receive the warm expansiveness of the Sun. This is not just for creature comfort, but to enable the feeling of relaxation and allow in the Light of God. I have shared recently the teaching that the pineal gland, which is in the center of the brain, is the organ designed to receive Light. In animals, this gland tells them how to adjust their behavior according to the season. In humans, it also serves this function, but it has a higher vibrational-level function as well, which is to receive the Light of God.

"When you are in the South, practice placing your awareness on the top of your head. I have shared through many of my channels that this is where the Holy Spirit resides at first. When you soften the crown and let the Holy Spirit's energy sink through your body, as if your body were a sponge and its cells were soaking in this beautiful liquid Light, pay particular attention to noticing the Light in the center of your brain. I am sharing this practice of bringing awareness of the Light into your mind, so you can know that the Light simply shines away the darkness.

"Also, my sister, when you can feel the Light in your mind, allow it to soak into your throat, your heart, deeper down into your body, down to the root chakra, and into your feet. Continue to practice this absorption of the Light of God's Love into your mind, into your knowing, your speaking, your heart, your intentions, your identity, and your creative powers. As you practice this, your sense of being lighter will increase. This is the Path of Enlightenment. Is this helpful?"

"Very, thank you."

"It is beautiful to see your Light increasing, my sister, very beautiful. There is a lovely rose color about you now. I am sending you the loving quality of rose. Please enjoy."

John makes a request. "To build on what you just shared with our sister about the pineal gland—are there other organs that Light should be shined upon?"

"My brother, the pineal gland is simply the gateway. Light should be shined on all organs. The body is made of Light. That ever-shimmering Light I have spoken of so many times is a hologram. In your body, every atom, every molecule, every structure within the cell, each cell, each collection of cells that forms each organ, and each organ communicating with each other organ—all of these are made of Light. This is the Truth. You can believe otherwise. You can believe the body is solid and made of something called *matter* that is somehow separate from Spirit. But this is only your thought about it. It is not the Truth. The Truth is that your body is an ever-shimmering pattern of Light, and the only practice I encourage you to do is to be aware that this is the Truth. If you catch yourself thinking that some structure or other in your body is a solid thing, just hold that thought with gentle humor, then replace it with this image of the ever-shimmering Light of God that is simply manifesting in the particular appearance of John. Is that helpful?"

"Yes. There are those who connect the glands to different chakras. For example, the thyroid to the throat chakra, the thymus to the heart chakra, and so on. Do you have any more to say about that?"

"I do, my brother, which is that ego is always tempted to get clever! There is certainly truth in each gland having a corollary with each chakra, depending on where it is in the physical body, but I tell you, when you bring the awareness of Light throughout your body, it matters not if you know which gland is associated with which chakra.

"I am reminding you that this manifestation of the body has an ancient history and, because all time is simultaneous, you can bring into this body some fairly rigid patterns from previous bodily experiences. I have shared with Laura not to judge these patterns. If there is a particular place in the body that has formed such a habit of how it holds itself, for example, if a bone is in a certain place, angle, or is misshapen, this is *possible* to be healed, since the body of Light is perfect, but it is not *necessary*. I have shared with Laura not to worry about the patterns in her shoulder and in her knee because they will not cause her any harm in this life, and they do not restrict her growth.

"Truly I say to you, when you are attuned to the Love of God, then there are no physical problems, even if it appears that way to an outside observer. The lived experience is that there are no problems. Even if a person is in a wheelchair, they will know they have no problems when they are attuned to God's Love. Is that helpful?"

"Wonderfully helpful, thank you."

Sister Two asks, "In my next vocation, I want to help people remember who they are. I recently had an image of using my gift of photography and sound healing to make portraits of people by first breathing and doing vocal toning with them, and sounding crystal bowls, and then taking their portrait. I want them to see the radiance that they are. I wonder if you could speak about that."

Yeshua laughs. "My sister, you do not need any encouragement from these words. You already know how gorgeous and beautiful this vision is. When you attune people's bodily experience with sound vibration, their auras become stronger, and you will be amazed that, when you take pictures, you will see qualities of their aura around them. I am so delighted you are joining your Love of photography with your Love of sound. Please experiment with different photographic equipment that has different light sensitivities, so you can practice capturing people's auras. This is affirming for people to see that they extend past the outside limits of what appears to be the body. That alone is encouraging. You are going to have so much fun. I will enjoy participating with you. When you tone your beautiful crystal bowls, I know you will call on me, but please call on me, because I would like to participate. I am with you, my sister, in your joyous exploration of this creative path. How wonderful!"

"Thank you so much."

"I am also sharing with you that it is important to bring flowers into your photographic work. Flowers have different vibrational qualities, so when you attune people with sound, it will be helpful for them to choose flowers they resonate with, so your portraits include them holding a flower with which they share the same vibrational frequency. Many people throughout the history of humanity have had the capacity to feel the vibrational qualities in flowers and plants, so I encourage you to develop that awareness, my sister. You might go to a place where there are lots of different plants, like a greenhouse or a flower market, and with your inner eye, sense the vibrational energy of each plant that you come in communication with. They will become brighter because they know you are in communication with them. You are going to have so much fun with this, my sister."

"That is so helpful, thank you."

"My blessings."

Sister Three describes a conflict in a spiritual group in which the perception of attacking arose. She wonders if she had not seen someone's upset as a call for Love and remembered to be forgiving. "Could you address that for me? Thank you."

"This is an important question because the ego, as it is softening, is also reacting and defends its last gasp. It is not at all uncommon in spiritual families for there to be conflicts that emerge. This is an important question for everyone to understand how to soften your way through the conflicts.

"I have shared many times that everything is Love. There is nothing except God, and God is Love. The Child of God decided to see what it would be like to be separated from God. You are now realizing that you have always been held by God, even though you had your eyes closed to that Reality. There is a long history of fearfulness in each Soul because the feeling of being separated from God is the most terrible feeling there is. The feeling of being alone is so frightening that the ego will defend itself if it feels at all impinged upon because it is afraid of death. In its delusion, it thinks it is separated from the Source of life and that it can actually die. This is impossible. Any time there is the experience of being attacked or defending oneself, it comes from the fear that the ego will die because it has done a terrible thing of separating itself from its Father. Be aware that when the energies of attack and defense come up, there is tremendous pressure behind them, an intensity that can feel overwhelming. But when you know it comes from this fundamental fear that the ego is lost, can never be found, and must survive on its own in the wilderness, then you can understand why there is so much intensity around feeling attacked and needing to defend oneself.

"When you hold this in Love when it arises in a fellow traveler, you will help that person feel they are not actually alone, and nothing needs to be defended. Each Soul longs to know that it is not alone, so this Soul does not differ from any other in its apparent need to defend itself. That need to defend itself is simply the wish to be alive. When you convey, silently in your mind and heart, that you know this Soul never died and can never die, then you do not need to engage with the fearfulness that it might die, because you can simply hold it in tenderness and know this thought is false. It has no merit. If a Soul comes to you and says, 'You are attacking me,' your response is only to convey Love because you can see that all the Soul desires is to know that it is alive.

"I am also reminding you, my sister, of something that I said in *A Course in Miracles*, which is, never correct a brother (Diamond Clear Vision 2012, 205). Each Soul has to do its own healing of its own misperceptions. This particular Soul is on its own healing journey, and if you feel called to point out that there is a hole in their pathway, that is only what you are called to point out. You are not called to help that Soul avoid the hole or get out of it unless that Soul asks you for help. Certainly, do not engage in any attacking or defending. This is not helpful for anyone involved. Just hold the Soul in Love and know that she is on her own healing journey to let go of her fearfulness that she might be killed. Is that helpful?"

"Yes, it is, thank you."

～◎～

"Are there any other questions?" Yeshua asks.

Silence.

"My Beloveds," he continues. "You are all so precious. Each one of you is a unique jewel, like your own star in the beautiful Heavens. All of you are also the same. All of you are my Self. Where I am is a vibrational level that includes all vibrational levels. You are beginning to know that this is also your birthright, as an extension of the Child of God. The Child of God is like unto God in every way save that it did not create itself. That is each one of you. You are all Gods. You all have the same infinite creative power of God, the same infinite Wisdom, the same purity, beauty, and harmony, the same lack of flaws, the same delight and joy, and the same infinite creative potential.

"The belief in separation that created the feeling of fear also created the manifest world that is multifarious and miraculous.

Now, begin to imagine the Creation without fear—the multifarious, miraculous quality of Earth expands into infinity. So much awaits you! And remember, you have never died. So, have no fear about whatever comes around the next corner in your lives. Look at the miracles that are unfolding now. There will be many more for all of you. You are all the Child of God. You are all worthy of receiving and extending miracles. None of you is any different from any other of you in your worthiness and ability to receive and extend the creative power of God's Love. You will all just do it in your own beautiful way. Just like there are so many different flowers—they are all beautiful, they are all an expression of the creative power of God, and they are all different. Each one of you is like a flower. I enjoy your being able to receive how valuable you are, how beautiful you are, how cherished you are, and how important each one of you is.

"And Laura's cat, who had left us until now, is sitting here, purring loudly and saying, 'Yes, I, too, am cherished and valuable and beautiful!'

"When I have said to you, go forth into the world and extend the Love of God, sometimes you are not sure how to do that. Today, it is becoming clearer that the way each one of you does that is perfection, by following whatever is most fascinating to each one of you. Whatever draws your attention is the form through which you will express God's Love.

"Remember, I am speaking to you always. The more you gather and hear my words, the more you can hear my thoughts, feelings, and sensations in your own bodies, and the less dependent you are on hearing someone else say my words. We do not have to say goodbye, because now you know I am in the same Light with you always. This is why I started our gathering today as I did, so you could feel your growing awareness of my presence throughout your own body-mind. This never goes away. It is only your awareness that flickers. Keep your awareness of my presence as steady as you can, and you will be amazed at the miracles that flow forth into your lives.

"I send you my blessing. I send you the blessing of the Father and of the Mother. I send my blessings through you to all with whom you come in contact so that each one of you is a glowing ember of God's Love that is forever extending Love. Whenever you hold one another in your mind, you amplify your awareness that each one of you is the Child of God. If one of you crosses into your mind, stop a moment and just say to that sister or brother, 'I adore you. I adore you just the way Yeshua adores you. He has said so many times how much he adores us, so I am saying to you, my sister or my brother, that I also adore you.'

"There is so much more I could say! I will end as I always do. Please go out into nature, and send my Love into the Mother, and into the animals, the birds, the furry ones, and the insects, so that all Beings can partake of the chalice of God's Love. We are One. There is no separation.

"Ameyn. Ameyn. Ameyn."

Experiencing the Body as Light Is Experienced as Death to the Ego

John and I met the following week, March 11, 2019.

After John shares an opening meditation and we recite our prayer, I begin.

"The first thing that comes to me immediately is the knowing that I have the awareness of many of my own lifetimes, of other people's current and past lifetimes, and of accessing the messages and energies of Ascended Masters. It was as if all of that was conveyed to me in an instant download. The message is, 'I *am* all of that. I can know all of that because it resonates with the Truth of who I am.' And then the analytical mind steps in and says, 'Well, how can I have an identity and be also all of that?' Yeshua's response is instant:"

"All that downloaded instantly to bypass the analytical mind so you would know from your own experience the Truth that you are the Christ, the Child of God, so *who you are* contains all of those experiences. This includes experiences you think you can identify as your *current* life, but also includes the inner knowing of the experiences of what appear to be other lifetimes of your *own* Soul, and experiences of *other* Souls in other bodies and their past lifetimes. The Truth is, you are all of that and more.

"This is what I meant by, 'Love your neighbor as yourself,' because your neighbor *is* your *Self*. Who you *are* is all Beings—and that includes everything that appears to be projected in solid form— because all Beings are Light.

"'Love your neighbor as yourself,' was something people heard as a proscriptive ethical command. 'Imagine that your neighbor is somebody similar to you, and then treat them the way you would want to be treated.' This is a beneficial first step, but it is not the inner meaning. The inner meaning is that all of your neighbors *are* your *Self*. People practice with the insight that there is the Light of God in everyone, and again, this is a beneficial step, but it is not the Truth. The Truth is, everyone *is* the same Light.

"The attempt to keep things separated is strong. The habit of trying to cover up the Truth of the Oneness of everything with the thought of separation is extremely strong.

"I would like you to rest in that flash of knowing that everything you have seen, inwardly and outwardly, is the same. It is your Self. It is the extension out of the Mind of God into Creation. And there is only One Creation that is extended from the Mind of God, and you *are* all of that."

I jump in to say, "It's *quite* uncomfortable. I have the sensation of my mind being blown up to create room for this sensation."

John makes an observation. "And I would like to add that you look more serious today than I have seen you before."

Yeshua continues. "You are playing on the edge of the ego's grip. It has softened but not dissolved, because there is still an idea of separation. This download of knowing you *are* all the experiences of what appear to be yourself and other people's selves *is* challenging.

"I have been conveying that I speak to you as if I were an individuated personality, but the Truth is far vaster than that. I am One with you who are not yet fully awake, and I am One with those who are fully awake. We appear to be a collection of awakened minds, but we also appear to be one personality. This is difficult for you to understand, but if you can just stay with the sensation of—"

Yeshua's words become unintelligible in some background noise. There follows another long pause. I resume. "Suddenly, an image flashed into my mind of a deer's face lying in the snow, clearly dead. Why am I seeing the face of a dead deer up close?"

"This is a symbol on many levels," Yeshua explains, "and one of them is that it represents your fear of death and your sadness that innocent creatures should die. On a deeper level, it is a symbol of transformation. What appears to be the creature part of you is dying, and what emerges from that is the greater awareness of the Truth."

"As I am speaking these words, my body is becoming increasingly heated and *extremely* uncomfortable, as if I were in a blast furnace."

"Stay with me," Yeshua urges. "Every time you join with me is an opportunity for you to tune your energies physically to a higher vibration level. This is a profound teaching of letting go of the creature part of you, the animal part of you, the body part you are attached to as a separate *thing*. Please notice that your awareness has not gone away as you experience the image of the death of the animal part of you. Also, notice that your consciousness does not go away as you receive mine. I would like you to feel in your body, both of you, the knowing that you *are*, not just in communication with, but that you *are One* with all Lights.

"Even though you both understand these words, this is difficult to stay with as an experience energetically. There is the feeling of wanting to get out of it—to escape, to distract. I ask you to stay with this energetic experience of knowing that the body itself is One with all Light, and that includes all awareness of every other apparently separated mind. I have shared before that you could spend your life going through the awarenesses of every single individuated Child of God, but this is not a good use of your time, though it is possible. What I am sharing with you now is more effective—the experience of the Oneness of your mind with all of what appears to be separated minds. Once you can include all of that in your awareness, then you do not need to explore the thought processes of everyone else's minds."

Long pause.

"I am showing you the intimate Communion I have with the Soul you know as Mary Magdalene. When we were on the Earth, we knew that our energetic fields were the same *and* that we had our own individuated awarenesses, though it was not possible for either of us to have a thought that the other one was not aware of. It is a paradox that the individuated self can tell the difference between its thoughts and the thoughts of another individuated self, and experience them both simultaneously.

"The reason I am sharing about the death of the body with you today is so that you can fully experience the totally intimate Communion of the Child of God with its Self. If there is any attachment to the idea of being a separated body, this interferes with that total Communion.

"Even though Maryam knew perfectly what I am describing to you, she also had human feelings of loss and struggle. All human feelings *must* be fully experienced and *fully* understood as One with all Lights. This can be a challenging process, but I remind you that I am with you always, even when you are experiencing what appears to be a loss. Never forget, your ability to be aware of my presence by its very *knowing* means that there is no loss.

"Please continue to be aware of each other's presences, even when you are not in direct communication, because there will be what appear to be losses ahead. As I have shared with you before, everything that is birthed in time must end in time. It is necessary to experience these losses so you can know there is no loss. Do not resist them. I am holding up Maryam as your example of this because there were many times when she experienced what appeared to be my loss acutely, and many times she was fully aware I was with her with no separation.

"Tune back into your bodies and notice the physical sensation of being in Communion with Light. Notice that every cell of your body is Light. This is experienced as death to the ego, which thinks of the body as a material thing. You might even visualize layers shedding off of your true nature, which is a Being of Light.

"Can you feel that?"

Pause.

"When you feel complete, resting in that sensation of knowing the feeling of being Light, then I am happy to answer your questions."

John shares an observation. "Yeshua, I feel that experience powerfully, and I'm continuing to experience it. The exercise you gave us on January 28 of feeling the Holy Spirit's flame on our crown chakra, and then feeling Light going down through the other chakras, has helped immensely to awaken a feeling of Light going through the energetic pathways in the body."

"Beautiful. Excellent, my brother. You have definitely understood. Very good."

John continues, "Laura and I talked about inviting others to join us in our Magdalene tour. Do you have any observations about that? Also, do you have any observations about the timing of this tour? Laura felt being in Scotland at the summer solstice would be good."

"As you spoke, I was sharing a bright color of yellow with Laura's mind. Yellow is associated with the Sun and with the will. Aligning your tour with the summer solstice is aligning your energetics with the Sun, which represents, on Earth, God. Aligning your tour with the summer solstice also represents aligning yourselves with the

Will of God. You are both aware that there is no higher calling than to align yourselves with the Will of God. I am glad this feels more *normal* to you. It is this feeling of aligning yourself with God being *normal* that allows continued progress.

"It is much like in child development. When a new skill becomes visible, the child wants it, feels frustrated when they can't get there, practices, practices, practices until they arrive, and then it feels normal. Then they have fun at that level until they realize there is something more. The fact that you two sense that attuning with God feels normal is an excellent sign that you have integrated much of the teachings and energetics that I have been transmitting to you.

"It is also a sign that you are ready for the next level. This tour will push you strongly through several next levels because you will be at sites of power on the Earth that amplify your own physical experience of the Truth of the Lightness of Creation. But you will also transmit power *into* the Earth and help to move the evolution of the Earth forward. By connecting with other Souls, you will create even stronger vortices of energy at each of the places you visit. Please do not take all of this seriously. Just know that when you join with your brothers and sisters, and with me, Maryam, the Angels and Archangels, the Elementals, and all the Beings who adore you, you can't help but create a vortex of Love where you are.

"I remind you, it is difficult for the ego not to plan. All you need to do is communicate with your brothers and sisters, and the planning will happen by itself. I have told you this before, and you haven't quite believed me." Yeshua laughs.

"Is there anything else?"

John says, "I feel so rich today, having experienced the energetic pathways of Light in the body, and experiencing our bodies as One in Christ."

"It takes continuous practice, my brother, to *know* in the body and mind the *actual sensation* of being in Oneness with everything. It is such a temptation to think of it as an idea, but it cannot rest only at the level of an idea. That is a helpful first step. Please keep practicing the energetics I shared with you today of *knowing* that every experience you have had that includes other Souls *is in* your own body-mind. *That is where you hold that knowing,* and therefore that *must mean* all their body-minds are One with yours. How could you know those experiences otherwise?

"Remember, I am with you always. And remember, I am not a separated *I*. I only speak to you as if I were an individuated person because this is a tool your body-mind can use. But please remember that I speak for, and *am*, the entire Christ Council. I also remind you that both of you have been invited to join the Christ Council. We see you with us, sometimes more strongly, sometimes a little faded, but you are materializing, so to speak, in the Light energy of the Christ Council. Do not doubt your experiences. This energetic practice is *real*. Please feel these energies in your body. Please feel your *knowing* that you are One with the trees, and you are One with the Earth and all Beings. This is not fantasy. This is not imagination. When I say that you two have been invited to the Christ Council, I mean that specifically. Others are also invited to the Christ Council—this does not make you special. I simply observe the Truth that, in your practice, you are close enough to your awareness that you are the Christ to be invited into the Christ Council. I put it to you as an invitation, so you know there are Beings who exist already at the level of full awareness of Christ to *help* you remember that this is also *who you are*. It is not because they are higher Beings who are special and have issued an invitation. It is the energy of welcome—that is why I use the word *invitation*. It is inviting. It feels *delicious*, like a beautiful waterfall that you cannot help but slip under. That is the energy of being invited to the Christ Council. Is that helpful?"

"Yes. I have one other question today," says John. "Occasionally, when I get emotional, I shut down. I would be grateful for any comments. Thank you."

"Notice the feeling of a line at the top of your head coming down your face. It's a place where you constrict, where you withdraw and recoil, a sort of fear of being hit. In my practice with you today of *feeling* the body as Light, *know* you can *receive all* emotions because they cannot hurt you. You have a thought that intense emotions are too much for you to bear, and so you fold in on yourself as if you were an accordion or a book that closes shut. Because you are Light, you can open and receive all emotions without harm. My brother, look at yourself. You are alive. You are aware of other lifetimes that you have been in a body, and aware that your experience of being a Being of Light continues without the body. So you truly *know* that you do not need to be afraid. Welcome any emotion as something that simply needs to be picked up and held. It *cannot* harm you. Is that helpful?"

"Very much so, thank you."

"I am conveying to you both," continues Yeshua, "the colors of lavender, light blue, and green. Lavender is the energetic color of the Spirit, light blue is Wisdom, and green is the Heart. I am conveying to you that you are surrounded by the Love of the Holy Spirit, the Wisdom of Sophia, and in your heart, the Christ Council and I reside. We reside in each other's hearts. All your brothers and sisters reside in your hearts because they are your Self. Feel the physical sensation of those words. *All your brothers and sisters reside in your heart because they are your Self.*

"Notice in your mind's eye *all* the colors of the spectrum because your body is made of Light, which is all colors—those you know, and those you don't yet know. All the Beings who appear as your separated brothers and sisters have their own energetic patterns of Light. They all fit together in the most beautiful dance. You, my brother and sister, are aware you *hold* the dance because you *are* the dance. And I am dancing with you. We are all dancing with you. There is such joy in the joining of the dance! One never grows tired of this dance.

"Go into the world today with great celebration and dance on the Earth. In your northern parts, the Earth is getting ready to wake up. I have been sharing with you all winter that it is important for you to bring the energy of Love down through the crown of your heads, through all of your chakras, and down through your feet into the Earth. Now that the vernal equinox is approaching, *please* send the energy of the Love of the Christ Council, the Love of God, into the Earth, so that she, too, can wake up, and her energetic patterns can come to a higher vibrational energy. Just know that what I am saying is true. Don't question how it works. When you know you are One with everything, you do not have a small function. When you are bringing your awareness that you are *The* Christ Council, and you bring that awareness through your feet into the Earth, please believe me that this is an *extremely* powerful action. You are not a small human body. Never for one minute think you are a small human body.

"We do not have to say goodbye because today, when you go out into the world, *you* will carry with you the awareness that I am with you, Maryam is with you, and *all* the Enlightened Ones are with you, because now you *know* in your bodies that *they are you, we are you,* and your brothers and sisters *are you.*

"And with that, and with *great* celebration, we convey to you our *endless streams of Love,* and we say, Ameyn. Ameyn. Ameyn."

"Ameyn. Ameyn. Ameyn," John repeats. "Thank you. Thank you. Thank you."

"I want to go out and dance in the Arboretum!" I exclaim.

"Good idea!" agrees John. "I would just like to say that you are *glowing!* In all other channeling sessions, you have been unserious and glowing during most of it. During this one, you were darker and serious until we came to this last part. Then you started to glow, and you continue to glow."

I respond, "I *felt* serious because he was walking me through this fear I have about death. When that dead deer's face appeared, it shocked me. I wanted to resist it. I wanted to say, 'I just made that up.' But it presented itself *really* close! I *do* have the feeling that it is tragic animals die—they are so innocent! I have always felt that way, ever since I was a kid. So it did feel serious that he was showing me I have this attachment to being afraid of death. That's a deep one. I am going to stop thinking about it, and I am going to go out for a walk."

As a therapist, I know well that emotions are the energetic reactions to thoughts that are then carried into every cell, and that what causes suffering is our *identification* with our thoughts and those emotional reactions. I was now beginning to understand that simply the assumption that I am walking around in an *external* world, which I believe is filled with dangers and threats to survival, maintains the belief in the appearance of being a separated self. But the more time I spent with Yeshua in the deep Heart that we share with God, the less interesting the external world became. That could sound like depression, but it is actually just a gear shift to focus inward where true vision lies. I have subsequently gone through a few episodes of progressively letting go of placing any value in the external world. The result is having a stronger feeling of identification with the Self I truly am, the One Self that is the Child of God.

Chapter 11

Living Inside the Circle of Christ Consciousness

The Way of Harmony Resides in the Heart

My growth process was being pushed forward with great vigor by all the spiritual experiences happening in my life. Attuning my body-mind-heart to Christed energies was certainly having a powerful effect on me, especially making visible my deeply held stuck beliefs. But it didn't automatically transform them. Some active willingness was required on my part. Yeshua has shared that not all the healings he facilitated in his life as a man stuck. People needed to do their own inner transformational work for the healing to last. Likewise, his presence in me could only heal me if I actively engaged in transforming my beliefs, so John's offer of a guided healing conversation was most welcome.

This transformational conversation took place on March 16, 2019. By following Yeshua's repeated guidance to allow whatever I am experiencing and stay with it, an inner process unfolds, with John offering helpful questions and guidance along the way.

I start by sharing, "During my morning walk, my heart was beating strangely. I could interpret this with fear and think something is wrong, or I could interpret it through *feeling* and know my heart is waking up. The feeling-knowing is that Yeshua is working directly with my heart. This discomfort in my heart is a beneficial stretching, just as the on-the-edge-of-uncomfortable experience of channeling him is beneficial.

"Certainly, I cannot stay in what feels familiar and comfortable if I truly desire to know that I am the Christ. Just like physical birth, being birthed into Christedness has to entail discomfort. But the discomfort bears fruit. The perceived benefit of what is familiar inside my little egoic box is nothing compared to the revelation of the infinity of the Queendom!"

Suddenly, I start coughing. "What arises is the physical sensation of holding in my voice, and the emotion of restraining myself because of the fear that, if I speak the Truth, I will draw a counter-reaction and create conflict. I feel strongly that this is not the outcome I want."

Intense energy then arises, and my heart begins to flutter and burn. "I can see directly into the foundational belief of the egoic thought-system that *requires* conflict. 'I exist as my separated self *because* I am in conflict with another.' I feel strongly that I can no longer agree with the belief that speaking up about my existence *must* elicit pushback from somebody else."

Next to arise are images of a fundamental bodily fear of not having the resources to survive. "I fully embrace that I hold the belief in an external world, which inevitably produces the belief that it is possible I could be harmed, and so I must protect myself. I realize this belief is the foundation of ego. 'I have to defend myself in order to exist.'

"The contrast between this belief and all my recent experiences of *joining* with *other* consciousnesses is palpable. This joining terrifies the ego. 'What are you doing? You are going to die!'

"My response is, 'Yes, that's right. *You* are going to die. This *is* about the death of the ego!'

"The ego is not happy. I can feel, intensely, how nasty it is, how it is always willing to get into a fight."

This ego dynamic had arisen just the day before during a psychotherapy session. A patient was repeatedly saying false things about what I was doing, projecting her anger at her mother onto me. For a second, I felt a familiar angry need to defend myself, but I instantly realized I did not need to convince her that what she was saying was not true. I could then see the ego in her was trying to get me to enact attacking her to justify her anger, and, at that moment, I could step out of the game.

"You're doing a great job telling me everything I'm doing is wrong," I said. "You're doing a great job defending yourself!" I was quite lighthearted about it, and she stopped attacking me.

I continue reporting my inner process. "It suddenly becomes clear that if I don't need to defend myself in order to exist, then the opposite is true. I exist because of my *connection* with other Beings—with life itself. You might think this would feel good, but my breath shortens and discomfort arises. Knowing *my* heart is, in Reality, a shared Heart, is uncomfortable! If the Heart is shared, then I have to trust whoever is in there with me! But the fearful ego will never trust the other Beings in this shared Heart. 'What are they going to do? Are they going to manipulate my heart? Are they going to take over? Are they going to have their own nefarious agenda?'"

I have learned, when feeling stuck, to ask the Holy Spirit for help. "Holy Spirit, please help!" I cry.

Who shows up? My cat!

"My heart remains agitated, uncomfortable, burning. Then a vivid image appears of me throwing large chunks of a wooden wall into a fire, which clearly represents my desire no longer to defend myself. I know I can allow this because I have asked the Holy Spirit for help, and I do actually trust the Holy Spirit to whom I do not attribute any egoic plotting.

"Suddenly, the feeling of shame comes up, along with the image of Great Beings sitting around the fire. It is now daylight, which makes me realize that everything that has gone before has been in the dark, or a dim light at best. I experience myself as off to the side, and I can see the Great Beings waiting for me in their circle. My heart is *so uncomfortable. So uncomfortable!* The cause of the shame is clear. I just burned my walls in the fire of God's Love, and now you can see every mistake I have made! You can see all the battles I have been in, all the mean words I have said, all the judgment, selfishness, fear, keeping myself small, thinking I'm better—all that ego drama. I did not know I held so much shame. It's not a feeling I tend to experience."

John reminds me of *Workbook* Lesson 153 in *A Course in Miracles*, "In my defenselessness, my safety lies" (Diamond Clear Vision 2012, 281). He asks if I will talk to them.

"These are Beings who have been incarnate, so I know they have all been through the same profound shame about doing mean, self-protective, selfish things, but I am still keeping myself off to the side.

"I see they are wearing a range of clothing styles from different cultures and eras. The one who is drawing my attention is an older man in Chinese clothing—silk brocade with a pillbox hat. This is not a Being I have ever seen before. He is designated to welcome me into the circle when I am ready.

"Why him?" I ask.

"'Because as an incarnated human, he did many bad things,' I hear, which I neither want nor need to know. He has turned towards me and lets me absorb that he, too, has burned through shame. He shows me that, if he wants, he can access his memories of having done bad things, but where he is, he knows they are a dream. That is the *key!* He can look back and not feel shame because he knows with complete certainty they are dreams that did not happen in Reality.

"As I allow the discomfort of feeling shame, my heart becomes calmer and beats more evenly, though it still trembles a bit. Then I hear Yeshua's Voice."

"The purpose of this experience is for you to know that *you* are a Great Being, and what you are projecting into what appears to be the world is a dream. You have heard this idea before. It is a belief that makes sense to you, but this experience is happening because you have asked to physically experience it."

"I can see that, to be fully in my true Identity, I cannot believe in separation. Reality and the world cannot be true simultaneously. Yeshua says many times in *A Course in Miracles*, 'You can have Reality or you can have the illusion, but you cannot have both.' I can see the illusion is held in place by shame, and I have a much deeper appreciation for how hard it is to release this feeling. I can hold on to the shame about all the bad things I have done and reinforce my thought that they have actually happened. Or I can receive the thought-transference from this Chinese man and know it has all been a dream.

"I understand the psychotherapy session yesterday was also important because I could see clearly that my patient was experiencing a dream. She was sitting on my couch, perfectly safe, writhing in agony. Now I am being reminded about our Malin Beg experience—that was only possible by knowing that the whole thing is a dream.

"My awareness is back with the Chinese man who asks, 'Are you ready to let go of the cause of your suffering—holding onto your beliefs that you are separated and bad, and you cause trouble to other people? Are you ready to let that go? Are you ready to step into the Kingdom?'

"As I shift my attention towards the circle of Beings around the fire, I hear singing, and I suddenly understand—here is the *Way of Harmony* where everything is in harmony instead of conflict! I feel a wave of sadness and relief. This is what I have wanted ever since I first came to Earth. I came to find the Way of Harmony! Ever since

I came into this Universe, I have been feeling done with the way of conflict, yet coming into the Earth-plane, that was still the only way I knew. Now I am *definitely done* with the way of conflict. Back then, it was a *desire* for the Way of Harmony. Now I have *stepped into it.*

"I go towards the fire and commune with the Chinese man and the other Beings. I can identify Mary Magdalene, Mother Mary, and Germaine. They are all seated while I remain standing."

John asks an excellent question. "As you go into the circle, can you, within this Way of Harmony, totally embrace the way of conflict and say, 'Thank you, I learned a good lesson from you?'"

"All the conflict—which I now deeply *feel* as a projected dream, rather than just an *idea* of a dream—can be brought into this embrace. The projections have become light and shadow images that can be played with, like patterns in the campfire's smoke. They are not dangerous. As I see that I can play with them, have adventures, and do what I want without fear, they become much more beautiful—endlessly flowing, shifting patterns in which anything can materialize or dematerialize.

"In the way of conflict, I thought that, in order to be alive as myself, I had to defend myself. Now I have let go of placing value in conflict, I know I am simply always alive, and that can never change. I can continue exploring what it's like to be a living Being, but without fear. With nothing to fear, I can become my Self even more. The awareness of my Being remains, but I am also aware of all the other Beings, simultaneously. This is just like when I channel. I have my awareness and Yeshua's awareness at the same time, and it's not a contradiction.

"Love can allow all things because Love knows that all the conflict is but a dream from which Souls are learning. Love can embrace all things because Love knows these things are not dangerous. It's what Yeshua learned in the desert when he knew his actual physical body was the same as the Earth. There was nothing outside of him, and therefore, no harm could come to him. Now I understand how Love allows and embraces all things because there is nothing outside. All the dramas coming and going in the campfire's smoke can look like a battle, but it's just smoke that is being held by the circle of Love, by the circle of Beings who adore and respect each other. Now I understand.

"I have been mesmerized by the images in the smoke, but I am now ready to take my place. I simply sit down in this circle of Beings who know at all times that they are the One Child of God, and they never have a thought of doubt. I see several Native Americans and people from all around the world—every costume of clothing that humanity has ever worn is in this circle.

"I become aware that all these Beings are projected images of consciousness. They are presenting themselves as they appeared in the lifetime where they awoke in order to help me, but they can also choose *not* to project the appearance of a body. That there is nothing fixed about this image of the Beings around the campfire is really quite striking. This feels perfectly safe. The ego-mind would have thought, 'They are shape-shifting, so they could be anything, and it could be a trick!' But I am no longer afraid.

"Once I settle in, I again notice the constant murmuring of music flowing ceaselessly. I am the focus of their attention, and their attention is everywhere, simultaneously. I am told that they are with me always, supporting me in helping others attain this awareness, so this circle can expand. Suddenly, my understanding of *how* it is that they are with me shifts. It's not that they are *with* me in the dream; it's that *I* am with *them* in Christ Consciousness. We are always together in Christ Consciousness. Everything else is illusory images projected into smoke.

"I become acutely aware of the whole heart area, and I know with certainty that this is where Christ Consciousness resides. It is in the heart, not in the brain. The physical experience of this knowing that I am in Christ Consciousness with them *resides in the heart*—this is not a metaphor.

"The heart area is burning, and I see it as a brilliant Light composed of many colors. I feel the heart filled with multiple, apparently different, Beings, and I experience a sensation of endless bubbling as I confirm that all possibilities reside in the heart. I realize that all possibilities anywhere in the Universe are the Christ, whether or not they are aware of it yet. The Beings in the circle are simply fully aware of who they are.

"The burning sensation is now expansive, like a balloon that lifts me up. I feel I could sit here for hours; I am so completely comfortable. I am aware of the life in my heart, and that it has never *not* been there. I had only lost awareness of this feeling-knowing.

"I am also aware of my feet tingling—the same burning sensation in my heart is also in my feet. I then become aware of this sensation on the top of my head as well. My cat says, 'I want more of that too, that feels good!' as he jumps around on the bed."

John speaks for both of us. "Wow. That was beautiful. That was a wonderful thing."

"I feel like I was just born. This feels like a birth day! (The sixtieth anniversary of my birth date was just one week prior.) This is my birth into knowing that I am living in the Christ, and everything is included in the center. All the projected thoughts that produce the three-dimensional Universe are held in the center of the circle of the Christ-Mind. I remember Yeshua uses the image of the circle of Light that includes everything in *A Course in Miracles* (Diamond Clear Vision 2012, 501). I feel fresh and new, like a little baby."

"Wonderful, beautiful," says John. "That was quite a journey."

⌘

I went out for a long walk in the Arboretum, often in tears. What I have been longing for ever since I came to Earth all those eons ago is all inside of my heart! I felt like Dorothy, who had just discovered her ruby slippers. I scrambled over some steep rocks, a mini cliff I had never gone down directly before. At one point, my foot slipped (barely, I'm part mountain goat), and I saw the temptation to believe that the world *out there* can bring danger. So I just reminded myself, like Yeshua in the wilderness, there is nothing outside me, so there is no other *thing* that can bring me harm. I could see right away how true it is that vigilance is required to remember at all times that perfect vulnerability results from perfect trust in God, which is far better placed than trust in ego.

Chapter 12

Trust and Rest in God, the Creation Is Safe

The Power of God's Love Flows Endlessly Through the Body Into Creation

Two days after that transformational journey into my true Identity with John's support, the larger circle of friends joined online again on March 18, 2019.

John starts the session. "We know that we all need to prepare ourselves to open to receive Yeshua. Let's all take a deep breath, and in your mind say, 'I choose to let go,' and just let go of all the concerns of the day. Do that twice more at your own pace. As you enter into the breathing, pay attention to the feeling of the breath inside the body. Now allow yourself to open and receive Love from the Father, through Yeshua, into your heart. Allow whatever comes up and just recognize it. Within your mind, say, 'I open and receive the Love of God for myself now,' and just rest there. Then, the first person to speak the prayer will break the silence."

Our prayer is recited three times.

I begin. "Continuing on from John's opening meditation, please, everyone, pay *close* attention to your physical experience. Notice the energy on the crown, which is where the Holy Spirit enters. Notice the pressure in the third eye, which is where deep Wisdom is known. Notice the opening in the throat, which allows for the expression of Truth. Notice the fire in the solar plexus, which is the motivation to be attuned to God's Will. Notice the expansion in the belly, the willingness to be fully identified as the Christ *in* the body. Feel the power in the highly energized root chakra, which, in complete communication with all the chakras, allows for the expression of God's Will in Creation. The chakras all work in concert. None is more important than the other. All are necessary. Yeshua has been teaching us, over and over, of the importance of softening the crown to receive the Holy Spirit and bringing that energy into the lower three chakras, which have been neglected. It is when the power of God's Love flows *all* the way through the body and out through the creative outlet of the root chakra that we can manifest the Truth of who we are, here in the body. The dream can only be transcended *in* the dream where we *think* we are. Just take a moment to *really feel* all the energetic qualities throughout the body.

"I can see Yeshua clearly today, a brilliant white. I can see his face extremely clearly. He is standing above us, and he wants to be clear that this doesn't mean he is more important, but energetically, he is above us. His white Light energy is also coursing down through each of our bodies. He is conveying that this visual image and visceral sensation are to make clear what he means when he says he is in charge of the Atonement. He is the conduit through which the Light of Shem comes into the body. Pay attention to the heart, which gets highly energized when his presence shows up.

"He is again conveying gratitude that we continue to meet. It is through the joining of our minds that he can extend his power and Love to other minds. He says, 'Do not be afraid. This power I am transmitting today is of a higher vibrational quality. It is a strong white Light. The heart chakra is extremely energized. It is uncomfortable. Do not be afraid.'"

Pause.

"He is showing me that, when there is no fear, the mind can travel freely to any place on Earth—in the past, in the future, anywhere in the Universe—because there is no fear of being lost. He is giving me a taste of the perfectly unfettered travel that is possible when there is no fear. The feet are highly energized with this image, which is symbolic of travel.

"The image remains of Yeshua, brilliant white Light above us, and the white Light is pouring down. It is a constant flow."

Long pause.

"He reminds me of his teaching about the power of God's Love being like high-voltage electricity that can induce fear because it is so strong. Again he says, 'Do not be afraid.' This whole process of working with us is to attune our energies higher and higher so that we can transmit God's Love into Creation more powerfully.

"He asks us again to please bring the leaders of the world into the center of our circle. He shows me the image of the Pope again, who is beset by fear—not his own, but fear surrounds him. Please transmit loving support to the Pope. He asks me to bring in other world leaders and reminds me they form a sort of community. They are their own circle because they have all stepped forward to be the focus of the political power of their own countries. Some are far more evolved and are also the focus of spiritual power. If we can, bring in all the world leaders and notice who among them are drawn to the Light. Send them Love and Light to help them transmit Love and Light to the other world leaders who share their circle of political power. This is to help them receive the loving will of the people, and not receive the fearful will of those with financial power. Our support is helping them soften their hearts and receive the will of the young people. There is such a passion in the young people to love the Earth and to believe they will be heard. There is enough of a perception of crisis that even the rigid leaders are, in fact, listening."

Yeshua speaks. "I have shared with you before that when you transmit the Love of God into the Earth, the Earth actually heals. Please again, visualize the Earth, who is her own Being, in the center of this circle of Love, and transmit to her your complete confidence that she, like all of you, can transform her woundedness. When she knows that we all believe in her capacity for healing, that awakens her self-confidence, and she becomes able to use her creative powers to heal whatever needs to be healed. Again, I say to you, send her your Love and not your fear.

"I am showing to Laura's mind the image that I am with you in this circle, and that we are all joining hands and dancing in a circle on the Earth with great joy and lightheartedness. Where our feet step, flowers spring up. This is a vision of Creation without fear. See if you can hold that in your minds—the vision of Creation without fear.

"I encouraged you the last time we met to pay attention to the visions that come to your minds. These are gifts from the Spirit. When I tell you to imagine Creation without fear, please look at the visions that come into your mind. The inner eye sees with purity.

"You are probably noticing pressure in your third eye as we speak of this. Now imagine that all of you share a vision of Creation without fear and that you focus your loving attention on creating that vision. Imagine the power that becomes possible because other people are drawn into that vision. There is nothing so attractive as Creation without fear. Again, notice your hearts as I speak about people being drawn into the power of Love. Feel it in your hearts.

"Those of us who reside in the dimension in which we know all dimensions are included participate in your dimension with the greatest of curiosity. We join with you in whatever way you allow. We see that you allow us to join with you more and more. It is with great curiosity that we observe the sleeping Child of God awakening on the Earth-plane. When creative and awake minds are in communication with each other, anything becomes possible.

"I am sending to each of you the image of traveling to different places with joy in your steps, a kind of lightheartedness, an eagerness to go out into the world and bring this visceral experience of God's Love into the body. I remind you of what I have said many times — when you think of each other, send each other Love and gratitude because your presence in each other's lives is helpful in encouraging each of you to become fully aware that you are, each, the Christ.

"In the eyes of the world, saying that you are becoming the Christ sounds outrageous and radical. In the eyes of the Christ, it is also radical, but not outrageous. It is so important to have a community in which all Souls know that their deepest desire is to manifest Christ Consciousness. Then, when fearfulness is encountered, there is no need to defend the Truth. Having a circle of Souls who are aware of the Truth helps each Soul as you navigate your way in the world.

"I am conveying to Laura's mind the image of other Enlightened Ones. I have mentioned that they are also with me, and we communicate as one Mind. I convey this today to encourage you. It is not just Yeshua who attained Christ Consciousness. There are many Beings who have attained full awareness of their true Identity. It is not something mysterious and far off. It is something that is truly possible, even for those who believe they have become lost in fear, shame, and guilt.

"I am open now to receive your questions, with the guiding thought that I would like to help you remove whatever obstacles are in your minds that keep you yet from knowing fully your true Identity as the Christ. There is *nothing* more we desire than to welcome you into our circle."

⚬

John asks for further guidance. "In the last few days, Laura made a big step in her process of entering the circle of Enlightened Ones when she faced a deep fear. You have given us practices to help us remove the fear, guilt, and shame of the past that we have carried with us for lifetimes. I would love to hear more. Thank you."

"I gave the most important key to Laura's mind a few days ago, which is to feel fully, in the body, that anything you believe you have done wrong is simply an image projected onto the field of Creation through the lens of fear. That understanding—that no harm has happened—*is the way* to release shame and guilt. When you understand what I have explained during previous gatherings—that you are all the All in All, and therefore no one part can be separated from another and cause harm to another—when you truly know this, then shame and guilt are released because you understand that, in Reality, you have caused no harm. You also understand that those Souls towards whom you think you have done harm are actually part of the same Soul, that is, all the Souls, the Child of God, then you realize it has been a mutual decision to enact this drama. No part could be played without the willing cooperation of other parts. When you see that all of this drama is within the circle of the Christ-Mind, and it is simply a shifting pattern of ideas and images, then you know there can be no concept of sin. Nothing has been done that cannot be undone because nothing has actually been done.

"How do you get to that understanding? I have given you many, many tools. The most important is never to run away from your experience. Whatever you run away from will come back again and find you—not because it is trying to harm you, but because your Soul requires this experience in order to let go of a deeply held belief in the mind. When it is understood that any emotional problem results from a belief, and those beliefs can be changed, then embracing emotional problems becomes much easier to do.

"For example, if you believe that you have harmed someone in a previous lifetime, then there are feelings that flow from that—shame, guilt, fear, remorse, maybe a sense of power, gratification—all sorts of feelings can flow from the belief that you have harmed someone.

Those feelings, when they are held in the circle of loving friends, reveal themselves to be the result of the fundamental mistaken belief that you can harm someone permanently. When you understand that all parts are playing this drama together, and all aspects of the Child of God remain in communication with all other aspects, then you can let go of the thought, 'I have harmed someone.' Is that helpful?"

"Thank you. I feel that is useful. Thank you."

"Pay attention to your hearts at the moment," Yeshua advises. "This question of how to heal guilt and fear stirs up lots of feelings. Put those feelings into the center of this circle. Look around. Hold hands and see that you have never died. All is well."

Brother One inquires, "I have a group of men coming to do some healing work amongst one another, healing the betrayals of one another, and all that is present with men. Do you have some tips or specific practices that we could do? I have some practices already prepared, but your input would be welcome. Thank you."

"First, I want to express my deep gratitude to you, my brother, for taking me up on my encouragement to focus on your healing work with men. The previous question about healing shame is also pertinent to healing the misuse of the masculine. When Souls manifest as males in the current era, they are welcomed into a world that tells them they have the right to control. The ego thinks this is something wonderful. The Soul recoils. There is always a conflict within those who have been taught that control is a benefit because the deep Heart is perfectly aware that those who are being controlled, including the Earth, are simply a part of the Self. In your work with men, there needs to be permission to acknowledge the temptation to be attracted to the power of control, and there needs to be permission to allow the shame that is underneath that.

"Then there needs to be permission to feel the deeper level of longing in the heart for connection. The heart longs for connection, and when the only tool given to men is control, they try to form connections through control, which, as every one of you is perfectly well aware, never works. And so men have felt confused that the tool of control handed to them doesn't work in the way the packaging instructions indicate it will.

"Men have also been told that if they *drop* trying to control and allow themselves to feel vulnerable, then they will be injured. Here is where your own personal experience will be so beneficial for you to share. It is through vulnerability that genuine connection becomes possible. In this circle of men, it is important that there is a vow made that no shaming or attempt to cause harm will be engaged in because men need to practice being open and receptive, or they will never experience loving connections with other Souls, with themselves, or with God.

"The techniques I have been sharing in this circle to become aware of the body will be helpful. Men have been taught not to be aware of emotions, yet to value the body, so bodily awareness is a path that still remains open to men. They will need support in amplifying their awareness of whatever physical sensations they are experiencing, and support in noticing the emotional quality that is associated with that—but that will be a most beneficial practice. And of course, the breath. The practice of noticing a physical sensation and then directing the energy of the breath to that location will bring emotional release. Is that helpful?"

"Yes, thank you."

"My brother, not all the men will be comfortable with breathing and singing, but since you are, I have shared with you before that when you begin a gathering with your voice, it helps to soften the resistance in the listeners. So use your voice, even if the other men are cautious about joining you. They are welcome to join, but just listening to your voice will be of great benefit."

"Most of the men who are coming are men on the Path of Awakening, but I will definitely sing. Thank you very much."

"And I will be singing with you."

"As I know," says Brother One. "Thank you."

⌇⌇⌇

"I feel as if I have a blockage somewhere," explains Brother Two, "and I'm wondering what is the best way of getting through the blockage to connect better?"

"My brother, the place to start is to notice where you feel that blockage in the body. Does it feel like a block in your head, eyes, jaw, throat, neck, shoulders, and so on? Go down through the body and identify the actual place where you feel this block. When you identify that place, since you are here in this circle, you can visualize offering that constriction into the center of this circle, where Love can be directed to soften it. Any block comes from the thought, 'I must defend myself.' Bringing the block into the center of the circle is already a statement that you are willing to let go of self-defense and trust the loving intention of your friends on the path. Just that experience of offering the block to the Love of your friends will help to soften the belief that you need to defend yourself.

"What will then emerge are memories of times when the block was reinforced because of experiences where you felt the need to defend yourself. It will be helpful to share some of these memories or write them down. Hold them in the context of Love—and by that I mean, understand that you chose these experiences as a Soul to reinforce some deeply held beliefs about needing to defend yourself, in *order* to transmute those beliefs. Asking how to let them go shows you are ready to do this transmutation work.

"The place to start is to honor the belief that you needed to defend yourself. Then honor that, from a more expanded perspective where everything is One, there is nothing to defend yourself against. The visual image is of holding the need to defend yourself in the center of the circle of Love. When you can lift your eyes up from the self-defended vantage point and see around you the circle of Love—of friends on the Path and Enlightened Ones who are already sure of their Identity as the Christ—then you can see how tiny the thought, 'I need to defend myself,' is.

"Just enjoy that practice, my brother, with any block that arises. It will require some support because undoing blocks always releases emotions that the blocks have held back. But do not be afraid of this process. Welcome it as the release that you have been seeking. Is that helpful?"

"Yes, thank you."

"Thank you for asking. I am grateful for your willingness.

"Are there any other questions?"

Silence. Yeshua continues. "I am showing to Laura's mind the image of a wolf's face. This wolf is paying close attention to what is happening here. It is aware of its interconnectedness to the other wolves in its tribe, but also to all the other animals and plants in its environment, and to the thoughts of the people. The wolf listens intently because it knows its intuitive awareness of the connectedness of everything is something people have forgotten and require. The wolf listens with a hopefulness that this will be regained and a willingness to offer this deep knowing of the interconnectedness of everything. It is aware of this because, for its survival, the whole ecosystem has to be functioning properly, and so it is conveying to the human minds that the same is true for humans. But for humans to survive, the whole ecosystem of the Earth has to be functioning properly. Fundamentally, this is a spiritual message. This is not an ethical imperative to take care of the Earth. This is a spiritual Truth that, because everything is One, any obstacles to the knowledge of Oneness will cause the energy of Love to become blocked and diverted.

"Please tune in again to your bodies. Notice anywhere where there is tension, a holding, a resistance, and remind yourself that you do not need to defend yourself against anything. Truly, when you let go of any resistance, that is when you *know* you are the All in All. And then there is a big celebration, and the dancing circle becomes wilder and wilder, and is a great feast of joy!

"My brothers and sisters, as always, when you go out into the world, go with joyfulness and light steps, with eagerness to share the Divine joy that lives in your hearts. I am bringing you back to the image that I shared with Laura's mind at the beginning—my energy as a brilliant white Light above all of your heads, a conduit for the endless power of God's Love. This power is pouring through your bodies now. Please feel it on the inside of your bodies. Then look around and notice that I have joined you, as have all of my beloved friends who are no longer in bodies, who communicate to you as one Mind, because we are *all* one Mind and we are all dancing together in this circle of joy.

"And with those words, I no longer need to say goodbye, because now I know you know that we are always dancing with you. Until we meet again in this form, but in between times, I am going to enjoy the dance!

"Ameyn. Ameyn. Ameyn."

∽⊚∾

I received an email from a sister right after this gathering. "Thank you, Beloved, for a beautiful joining today. I'm really feeling the energy still!"

I agreed with her about the energy, which had been extremely intense for me physically. This was her response to my comment that this was all such an amazing, unfolding miracle.

"Wow, yes! As Yeshua says, 'When minds are joined in Love, nothing shall be impossible.'"

The Safety of the New Creation

John and I continued our weekly online joining on March 23, 2019.

We recite our opening prayer three times, and I begin.

"Sitting here, holding my cat, the image that instantly comes to mind is Yeshua holding small children and the *beautiful* tenderness he had towards them. I can just feel this sensual warmth and why the children were naturally drawn to him."

"It's that easy," he says. "It's that quality of innocence children have that is your true nature. They are drawn to Love with no self-consciousness. It's what I was saying to you before about the attractiveness of Creation without fear. Souls are simply drawn into that because it's warm, delicious, and safe. The Creation is safe. The Creation is a safe, nurturing, and encouraging Universe. You are entering this new phase of *knowing* who you are *and* being able to explore every possibility so that you can continue from where you started all those eons ago—wanting to explore every possibility on your own while not feeling controlled by your Father. But now you know you can explore every possibility on your own, *and* your Father won't try to control you, so you don't have to separate yourself in order to explore. You can explore *and* be connected. This is the new awareness that is developing in the Child of God. It's a new and delicate feeling for you—to imagine Creation without fear, harm, or danger; to imagine exploring anything that intrigues you and seems possible, and have no danger associated with it.

"I am showing an image strongly to Laura's mind."

"As an aside," I say, "my first assumption is still that I'm making up what I see, but when it persists, I'm aware it's persisting."

Yeshua continues, "It's an image of the Himalayan Mountains from a vantage point above the mountains on a *brilliant* sunny day, with the wind blowing the snow up in wisps. The energy there is extremely clear. There is little interference from the energy of fear because human thoughts don't tend to project themselves up to that height. Instead, they tend to be at a lower level of consciousness, on more survival and greed issues. When you bring your consciousness up to the level of the mountains, it is much more expansive, lighter, clearer, and freer. This is why great sages go to meditate in the mountains, because they can rest in Christ Consciousness without interference. My great challenge as an awakened Soul was to leave those mountains behind, knowing that I was coming down into the denser layers of human consciousness, and that I would need lots of help to maintain that higher level of consciousness."

Pause.

"I am showing you that I never doubted I could do that, and I had complete trust that the Holy Spirit would send to me all the Souls necessary to help me maintain my high level of awareness. But I had a quality of not knowing what would happen and just going in trust because I knew I was the Child of God and God is but Love, so there was nothing to fear."

Pause.

"I am conveying to you the excitement of that quality of not knowing what's going to happen, while completely trusting everything that's going to happen because you know everything is in line with God's Will, which is perfect happiness for all of us.

"When you glimpse that state of not knowing what's coming next, it's difficult to stay in the Christ Consciousness of excitement because the ego steps in and says, 'It's possible something fearful could happen next, so let me try to control and plan.' One layer you are currently being pushed through in preparing for this trip is precisely that quality of letting go of the fearful thought that you must plan. Practice trusting me when I have said all the pieces will fall into place. Keep communicating with your sisters and brothers. Even this preparation process is an initiation for you into trusting the Christ-Mind.

"I have mentioned before that there will be losses ahead because everything birthed in time ends in time. Don't recoil from those losses because going through the feelings will help you release the belief in loss that creates the feelings. For example, Laura did well looking at a news item about the suicide of a young lady in Florida. She knew that Soul is not dead, but it was influenced by fear. That's not the Truth of the Soul, who will have further opportunities to release her fear, just like all aspects of the Child of God will have opportunities to release their fear. I remind you of something I said towards the beginning of our work together. Do not be upset about the many Souls who pass on because I am welcoming them into my Heart. Remember, this is part of the grand plan that fearful Souls should leave the Earth-plane, so the more trusting Souls have a chance to create a more enlightened society, which can then welcome back the fearful Souls so they can heal. Do not think of it as a tragedy if a fearful Soul leaves the Earth-plane. They will be well taken care of.

"Laura was just asking, 'Would it be helpful for her to know anything about when her cat is going to pass on?' The answer is no. There is no information to be shared about that. He is a teacher to you, showing you the evolution of your beliefs, and therefore your feelings, about death. You will know when it's time for him to pass on.

"Is there anything that you, John, would like to address?"

"I have a question about my disrupted sleep patterns," says John. "I tend to sleep three or four hours and then wake up for a while. I listen to recordings of you through Laura, and then maybe go back to sleep briefly. I guess it's fear that creates these sleep patterns. I've thought maybe I should take sleep aids occasionally. I'd be happy to hear any comment about that."

"My brother, it is not fear. It is a natural consequence of the aging of the body that sleep becomes less deep and more interrupted. This is your opportunity to notice your belief that you have fear about physical manifestations. It is not unhealthy to sleep in shorter segments as you get older. In fact, most bodies sleep in shorter segments more often as they age. Don't be afraid that this is a problem. It's simply part of the softening of attachment to an image of what the mind-body should look like as you age. If you can experience aging as a softening process, that will help you prepare for when your Soul completely lets go. It's much easier to let go when the perception of the body is soft, instead of some idealized, perfect thing that the Soul thinks it's attached to. Does that make sense?"

"Yes. What about sleeping aids, then?" John inquires.

"Chemicals interfere with sleep patterns, and I am speaking to Laura as well, who has taken Benadryl for the last two nights to clear up her sinus congestion. She is perfectly right to say that while in a body, there are certain biochemical patterns that manifest, and using chemicals to help interact with those biochemical processes is part of the material plane. There is no judgment about that. But it is not helpful to use a chemical regularly because the message to your mind-body is that you believe it is not functioning well enough, and it needs to be pushed around in some way. Ultimately, that's a message to yourself that you believe you are falling short or inadequate. If you would like to use some sleep aids, I encourage you to use herbal or non-drug sleep aids. You can consult with Laura about this later. The key here, my brother, is for you to be gentle with accepting the changes in your mind-body as you approach the last chapters of your physical appearance in this body. Is that helpful?"

"Yes. I feel like I am accepting the last chapters gracefully, but maybe not. My toes tend to tingle, the big toes. I have been massaging them, and that seems to help, but it is a strange feeling."

"Remember that in my energetic transmissions to you, I have given you experiences of receiving Light through the crown and then all the way through the body and out through the feet. Therefore, just as with the experiences of your heart, you *could* interpret the tingling in your toes with fear as evidence of a problem. However, I encourage you to interpret this as evidence of energy moving in your body-mind. Remember, I have said that the Light-body is perfect, so do not put a lot of effort into making the physical body perfect. The physical body is a projection of ego, and it's only the ego that thinks its physical manifestation has to be perfect. I have said that your creations await you, including the body. What the body awaits is your loving acceptance of however it manifests, without trying to impose an idea that it is imperfect and needs to become perfect. Is that helpful?"

"Yes. I'd like to hear more about the perfect Light-body. You have taught that the connection of Christ-Mind to ego/body/physicality is evolving and, at some point, the Soul, the mind as the Christ-Mind, and the body will be One. It sounds to me like it's the Light-body that becomes One with the Christ-Mind and the Soul. I'd love to hear about that."

"Yes. You have understood that I manifested this by showing that my body was Light in what was called the Resurrection. I demonstrated that it is the Light-body that is One with the Soul. The physical body was transmuted into the Light-body because the physical body has no separate existence. It is not a separate thing which the Soul inhabits. It is actually a projection of the Soul, and the Soul's only material to work with, so to speak, is Light. So ultimately, yes, all bodies will become perfected as Light. They will not become perfected as physical bodies.

"Great healers are aware of the perfection of the Light-body. They attune themselves to that level of perfection in the person with whom they're working in order to attract the lower vibrational level of the mind-body to synchronize with the perfected Light-body. In this way, true spiritual healers can perform what look like miracles because they have been able to make the perfection of the Light-body accessible to the person who requires healing. A great healer knows that they themselves are Light, so they can synchronize their consciousness with the Light-body consciousness of the person who has requested healing. The person's mind-body thus has a vibrational model with which they can bring their own resonance into synchronicity. This amplifies the strength of the person's own Light-body, so the lower level of the mind-body can trust that there is an aspect of *themselves* they can rely on to be the source of healing. Does that make sense?"

"Yes."

"In Scotland, your awareness will be closer to an experience of yourselves as light-bodies. I have been helping you experience the energies of Christ Consciousness, of the Light of God, physically, so that your bodies become increasingly accustomed to that higher level of vibration. Thus, when you are in Scotland, you will withstand a much higher level of vibration than you have experienced heretofore.

"Thank you for your diligence and interest. I have said many times that the greatest desire of those of us on the Christ Council is for all Souls to know they are also the Christ and are in ecstatic union with God. This is why we are happy to respond to any request for guidance.

"I hear Laura has a question about her mother: 'How best to be in relationship with her in this chapter of her life?' Laura is already perfectly well aware of the answer, which is to see her as the same Child of God that everyone is and to see her struggles with deeply held beliefs that do not serve her with compassion. Everything I have taught in *A Course in Miracles* applies, including, never correct a brother, each Soul has its own path, and anything that does not appear to be Love is a cry for Love. Just remember, I am with you, and you can ask me for help at every turn. That is sufficient.

"You had a question, my brother."

John talks about what he calls *collapsing* when sad. Yeshua clarifies this is simply feeling sad, which he expresses more easily with his wife. Then John asks, "I am wondering why it happens with her and not other people."

"It is a great blessing that you are aware of your feelings with her, that you feel safe to be so vulnerable with her, and that it is an energetic field in which she is comfortable maneuvering. The question is not, why does it happen with her, but why do you think that level of vulnerability should be avoided in other circumstances? Do you have any insight about that?"

John recounts when he burst into tears when given the gift of the personal rosary of an elderly nun who had just passed. "I guess you're saying it's not a problem."

"All feelings are useful information about an underlying belief. There is a quality of relief when you allow the tears that are triggered by, for example, this gift of the rosary. There is a belief that's deeply held in your mind about the power of the rosary. When one is given to you under special circumstances, that belief is triggered, and you experience a flood of feelings of relief, humility, and gratitude, and you question whether you are worthy to receive this gift.

"Please practice with this feeling just as I have taught you with other feelings, which is to pick it up, hold it with loving curiosity, and ask, 'What does it need? What's underneath? How can you help?' There are definitely past lifetimes in monastic service, so receiving something symbolic of that triggers a kind of longing for those lifetimes because they did resonate with your Soul. The orderliness, peacefulness, and spiritual devotion were quite to your liking. The tears have something to do with a longing for that structured container in which you can express your spiritual devotion.

"In this lifetime, you have had a less-structured container, which is important so that you can follow your own inner promptings and not be told which way to express your spiritual awareness. The rosary simply opens a portal in your heart that has always been there—a longing for God, and remembering that this has been a Truth of your Soul for many, many lifetimes.

"The tears also arise from knowing that you are closer to awareness of God in this lifetime than you have ever experienced. Of course, there have always been moments, or flashes of awareness, of that connection. So embrace this experience, just like any other experience.

"Your last question to me, my brother, was, 'How do you heal shame and guilt?' One thing I said to you was, do not recoil from any experience. If you do, it will simply present itself again, because your Soul requires it for healing. Embrace the sadness that arises when there are symbols or reminders of your past yearning for God. Is that helpful?"

"Very much, thank you. That's perfect. I feel you have given me the tools to explore much of the past and release it."

"Yes, you have the tools. Just feel me with you and trust your own Wisdom. Remember what I taught in *A Course in Miracles*. The Holy Spirit is in your own mind. It's not external. It's always there, always ready to help whenever you ask."

"Yes," says John. "Recently, from the *Workbook*, I put together, 'God is in everything I see because God is in my mind,' with, 'My meaningless thoughts are showing me a meaningless world' (Diamond Clear Vision 2012, 47, 18). There are two sides; one is the Spirit side, and the other is the ego side."

"Of course, the ego manifests still. Embrace every manifestation of ego with joy and gratitude. Here is another piece of ego that needs care and transmutation. Be excited that it's being offered to you for healing. The more you heal and let go, the closer you are to God. It might help you, my brother, to just open the lessons of *A Course in Miracles* because there are some simple, direct mantras in there that are touchstones to keep you grounded in the Truth of who you are.

"The energy feels complete here. There's a sort of gentleness today. I'm conveying to you the quality of just being able to rest in the Love of God and cease striving. One *Workbook* lesson in *A Course in Miracles* is, 'I rest in God' (Diamond Clear Vision 2012, 193). So I remind you today, both of you, just rest in God.

"I am with you always. We will meet again in this form, but in between times, just keep inviting me into your experience, because I enjoy participating in your process of awakening.

"And with that, I say, Ameyn. Ameyn. Ameyn."

"Ameyn. Ameyn. Ameyn," repeats John. "Thank you. Thank you. Thank you."

I went out to the Arboretum, where I often walked. Being with Yeshua was helping me feel energetically the union of all the elements—earth, air, fire, water. I could feel the forest and the whole Earth as a unified Being that is waking up.

Chapter 13

Joy Increases Around the Earth

God Herself Exults That Her Children Are Coming Home

By this point, we had established a pattern of holding a larger gathering every other week, which we called *Mondays with Yeshua*. It had been a most amazing and miraculous winter for me as I opened to hearing his thoughts and sharing his words while in Communion with friends. The teachings and energetics were simply extraordinary. He was clearly paying attention to all of us and was aware of what was going on in each of our lives and in our community. Through this intimate communication, we knew he was truly our spiritual brother. I finally felt what he repeats, over and over, sinking in. "I am with you always."

On April 1st, 2019, a larger group of about fifteen friends gathered online.

Since there are several new friends present, I explain that John will start with a guided meditation. I encourage people to come forward with questions because the collective consciousness of the

Christ Council, speaking as Yeshua in a form we can apprehend, has as their deepest desire for all of us to awaken. They are thus happy to provide guidance to help each of us in our growth process. The responses are always amazing, and they feel simultaneously personal and universal. I share that I'm humbled to be in this role and that this whole process is a miracle.

John guides us through a beautiful meditation practice that helps us feel our union, as physical sensations in the body, with the Awakened Ones who reside in Christ Consciousness. We visualize the glowing Light of Spirit, like the golden flame of an oil lamp, gently soaking from the crown chakra down through to the root chakra, and out through the hands and feet. John places special emphasis on joining the will in the solar plexus with Love in the heart, so the will is an expression of Love. "The heart is the place where the Father and Mother join, where we join with the Christ Consciousness in God. It's the place where we all join in Love. Allow this Light to glow through the entire body as we listen to the recitation of the *In the Name* prayer."

We recite the prayer three times, and I begin.

"The feeling today is of ecstatic joy," Yeshua observes. "There is such celebration in the Christ Council that so many of you are willing to drop the belief that you are but a small self. There is such celebration that you have been listening to the teaching that you are not just a small human body and that this is not your true Identity. There is such joy that you are not just understanding the *ideas*, but *feeling* the *knowing* throughout your body of who you truly are. It is not a small thing to be the Child of God. It is ecstatic beyond anything the world can comprehend. Such joy awaits you!

"You have been told so many times that joy awaits you. It is always present. It just waits on your awareness of it. It is a continuous stream, ever-flowing through your consciousness, just waiting for you to clear away the debris, part the veil, and step into the flowing waters of ecstatic union with God. The words ecstasy, joy, celebration, and union are strong words to the human mind. But these are just a shadow of ideas about the genuine experience of *knowing*. I use words because that is what can be understood at the present moment, but you are all doing well *feeling* the words as the vibration of Truth throughout your body.

"This New Consciousness of retaining your own awareness while experiencing Christ Consciousness does take getting used to. The old consciousness believed that this Christ Consciousness was reserved for the few Exalted Ones, so it takes some adjusting to understand you are all exalted. The ego has the image of *exaltation* being something akin to being on a pedestal, but this is not what *exaltation* means. It also means exultation, celebration, and union among equals. We are grateful you are adjusting your self-perception from the small mind that thinks it is either worthless or more special than others, into the new awareness that you are all equally exalted as the Beloved of God.

"Just feel those words—*you are the Beloved of God*. Any egoic thought of a beloved is simply the idea of grasping to fill the fear of separation. Being the Beloved of God has no grasping. It is a complete letting go into Trust, into knowing that the Father's Will for you is perfect happiness. Why would you ever hold anything back? It is a state of being wide open—you can imagine the body with legs and arms open to receive the energy of the Beloved. Just receive the power of God's Love throughout your bodies. Notice that it is not a static energy, but a flow continually coursing through your bodies. There is no need to hold on to this experience because there is always more from the Source. This is why there are images like the living waters, or the Sun—images that the human mind can understand as ever-flowing, never-ceasing.

"Though it may sound strange to hear this, God herself is exulting that her Children are coming Home. Please know that you are desired by God. Your presence in her awareness is everything she desires. If you can imagine, from a human perspective, the joy you feel when you think you have found your beloved—that is a tiny shadow of the experience of God finding her Beloved, which is *you*, and you not resisting that *she* is *your* Beloved. *Everything* is possible in this ecstatic union. The Earth herself will be transmuted.

"I have told you many times, pay no attention to fearful thoughts about the Earth, or about the leaders on the Earth. You have all been children. All you have to do is remember that feeling of your parents being worried about you to know it is not an energy you wish to receive. No child wished to receive their parents' worry. This is a constricting energy that conveys doubt and a lack of confidence. Likewise, the Earth does not wish to receive your worry about her. Just like a human child, she wishes to receive your confidence in her creative powers, in her ability to trust the Holy Spirit, in her ability to receive God's Love, and in that union between the Mother Earth and the Father Spirit, produce the ecstatic Creation of the New Consciousness. This is why I have told you repeatedly to go out onto the Earth and transmit to her your Love.

"This is an important time in your Northern Hemisphere because the spring equinox has just passed, and now everything is bursting forth into life. When you transmit to the Earth your confidence in her ability to continue to grow and evolve her awareness, much becomes possible. You will be amazed at the transformations that will occur, toxins that will be neutralized and prevented from entering the atmosphere of the Earth, environments that will be healed and rejuvenated, animals that will take on new abilities, and people who are inspired to create environments that heal the Earth. It is a powerful time.

"The same is true for your families. There is rejuvenation happening in each one of your small families. This spiritual family has much rejuvenation occurring, but I am referring to your biological family. Because of your presence in each of your families, please be aware that all of those to whom you are connected are feeling a strange—to them anyway—stirring in their hearts, a new energy, a new hopefulness. This is because you are receiving and transmitting God's Love. I remind you of the image I shared of God's Love being like a high-voltage electric wire whose function it is to receive and transmit, never to hold, the Love of God. Those around you are receiving the Love of God through you because you have become more stable and can tolerate a higher voltage of God's loving power.

"We wish to express to you our extraordinary gratitude for your devotion to increasing your stability so you can receive these higher and higher levels of the power of God's Love. I shared with you before that we are working with many people to create a network of stable minds to allow for the increased transmission of the power of Love around the Earth. You are all playing an important function in that transmission. We wish again to express our deepest gratitude for your willingness to play your part.

"Please, in your minds' eyes, picture the Earth and all the stable minds around it. The Christ Council works through many religious traditions. This spiritual family has a strong connection with Yeshua and his devoted Maryam and his mother Mary. The Christ Council also works through other Enlightened Ones who have cultural connections in other places around the Earth. We share this with you so you do not feel burdened by taking on the thought that you are more responsible. There are many people whose minds are open to receive the Light. The more Light they receive, the more they are encouraged because the better the ecstasy of God's Love feels to them.

"You can picture people in China, Korea, Japan, the Pacific islands, the far northwest of the North American continent, all the way through that continent, the Central Americas, and into the South American continent. There are many old Souls in these two hemispheres who have been carrying the Love of God and the Wisdom of the Truth for many centuries. Never fear that it has been lost. Picture in your mind's eye the African continent with its ancient roots to the beginning stirrings of human consciousness and its deep devotion to the Earth. Send particular Love to this continent, and hold your gratitude for the origin of your ability to wake up, which lies in Africa.

"Hold the Middle East in your Love also, because there is the flowering of so many religions in Mesopotamia, Israel, Egypt, Iran, and Iraq. Then turn to Nepal and the Himalayas. This has been the hotbed of awareness awakening, and therefore, it also stirs up much fear in the ego, so in this area of the world there seems to be intense contradiction. Please hold this area in your Love. Your consciousness has elevated sufficiently that, by all of you holding this area in Love, you can influence a decrease in tensions in that part of the world. Please believe that what I'm telling you is true. Do not let your fear of the conflict overwhelm you.

"Bring your awareness to the continent of Europe, where many minds are waking, who are connecting back to their Earth-origin roots and the devotion of the old people to the Mother. Hold the Asian continent, an area of the world where so much Wisdom has been transmitted to so many minds. Please hold these minds in gratitude for their willingness to receive Love. Then bring your minds down to the Asian subcontinent, where there have been millennia of Wisdom received and transmitted. Please hold in gratitude all the Souls who have been willing to be devoted to the Path of Awakening. Then bring your minds down to the islands that make up such a beautiful part of the world, Southeast Asia, and then to the Australian continent with the beautiful people who know there is no distinction between the outer and the inner, who travel easily between the worlds.

"Imagine this beautiful Earth spinning in your hearts. See all of her colors as sparks of Light that dance and shimmer.

"Because you are all the All in All, you can hold the Earth in each of your hearts, and you can hold the Earth collectively in the

Heart that we all share with God. Be aware there are Beings you would call extraterrestrial Beings who are also holding the Earth in Love and protection, and watching with great compassion as the Child of God wakes up. Please send your gratitude to these Beings who are in different dimensions and holding the Earth in the Light of Love. Now turn your attention again to the Angelic realms, who are always singing, because Creation is a vibration that appears as Light and Sound. Feel the sound of the Angels singing in your hearts.

"Again, we extend to you our gratitude that you are willing to come with us on this amazing journey today of visualizing the Earth and all of her peoples, animals, plants, waterfalls, insects, rocks, oceans, and the creatures in the ocean, on the ground, and in the air. It can all be held in Love. Please remember that, even though it looks like a vast array of diversity, it is all One. It is not possible that any part could be separated from any other part." He chuckles. "This includes each one of you, my Beloveds.

"We are grateful that when we say we know you intimately, this feels delicious to you and not threatening. We are aware of each of your intimate thoughts, and we hold them in compassion. Since we have all been human and have transcended shame and guilt, when we encounter such a thought in you, we simply hold it in compassion. There is no judgment. We have all experienced these feelings ourselves. The only difference between us and you is that we know that anything that appears to be negative is simply a projection on a screen created by constrictions in the mind that produce shadows. That is all.

"Hold in your hearts anything you think you should be ashamed of or feel guilty about, even the most fundamental guilt of having rejected the Father. These are simply constrictions of thought that produce a shadow. Hold those thoughts of guilt and shame in your hearts, and feel our Love surrounding and dissolving them. They are merely shadows. They have no power. Release yourselves from any belief you have in guilt or shame. Allow yourselves to express your creativity freely, in whatever form comes to you, just as the Earth is freely expressing her creativity. Do not hold yourselves back. This question has arisen in this group. 'Is there a benefit in holding myself back?' And always we say to you, no. There is no benefit in holding yourself back.

"It is with great joy we ask you to please ask us for guidance. What is it in your hearts today that we can help you with so you can let it go?"

◦◦◦

John inquires, "You have said that, in a sense, *A Course in Miracles* is incomplete because Helen edited out all of her personal interactions with you. Is there any way we can increase awareness of your interaction with us and with others, including those in *A Course in Miracles*?"

"That is an important question, my brother, because what happens when my words are put into books is they become static, just like the Bible has become static. In fact, as you are all experiencing, my presence is anything but static! As I have been working with you over these months, the energies have shifted and grown as you have shifted and grown. The most important thing to share with students of any of my words is that it is for them to *feel* in their hearts the softening effect the words are having on them, to know that my teachings are always to open the heart. *A Course in Miracles* had to start with the intellect because the world is so identified with the intellect. This identification makes it prone to elicit intellectual arguments, even though I cautioned against that from the start. But that is fine, because the intellect has to work its way through until people realize there is no satisfaction there. There is no judgment about that.

"Truly, the most important teaching is that this is a lived, felt, experience in the body. Whatever you are *feeling* is the most important thing to pay attention to because your *life* is your teacher. My words simply point the way for you to honor your own inner teacher. If you would like to help others who are also students of mine, just share your *own* experience of how my teaching has transformed your life. Is that helpful to you, my brother?"

"Very much so. Thank you."

"It is important not to pass judgment on people who are at differing levels of awareness in their working with my teachings. I have provided several teachings so that people who are at differing levels of awareness have a point of entry. Many of you have experienced going through different levels with my teachings, and I know you do not pass judgment on your earlier self when you first found my teaching. Likewise, do not pass judgment on any of your sisters or brothers wherever they are on their Path of Awakening. That is sufficient."

Sister One asks, "One night I woke up and heard, 'I encourage you to follow the mustard seed instead of the Father.' Is there anything you can tell me about that?"

"The Father is an abstraction to the human mind," Yeshua reveals. "The Father is the All in All of the All in All and can barely be grasped with words. The mustard seed is easily understood because it can be held and be seen. It can be apprehended. The image of the mustard seed is so helpful because it is tiny and it grows into quite a large bush. If you would like to choose a different seed that is appropriate for wherever you live on the Earth, please do so. All you have to do is think of a tiny seed. For example, a birch seed is tiny, yet it grows into an enormous tree. When I say to you, focus on the mustard seed, all I am saying to you, my sister, is to start with what you can understand. Do not overwhelm yourself with something that makes little sense to you. The idea of the Father cannot be understood with the intellect. We began our teaching today by guiding you closer to the physical, known experience of the ecstatic union with the

Father-Mother God. The idea of the Father is not a place to start. Is this helpful?"

"Yes, thank you very much."

❧

Brother One shares about his recent retreat. "I would like to thank you for your guidance on the men's retreat. Your presence and everything that happened there was super amazing—a miraculous flow. It was out of this world! Thank you. It was beautiful. We're going to have more of them!"

Yeshua laughs. "It *was* out of this world, my brother. That is the correct turn of phrase! The world—I am sure you have noticed that I distinguish between the *world* and the *Earth*—is the collective consciousness that is constricted. Therefore, yes, your gathering was outside of the constriction of social consciousness. In fact, your intention was to soften and burst through those constrictions, especially in the male consciousness. We extend to you our deepest gratitude that you are following the path of helping men soften their constrictions so they can be part of the Earth and not just contained in the narrowness of the world."

"Thank you."

"Much joy awaits you, my brother, as you continue on this path of stretching the constrictions in the masculine heart. Please continue. There will be many rewards for you on this path. We are always with you. Just feel our gratitude for your courage. We extend to you our blessing."

❧

Sister Two shares about two different psychological healing methods she is learning. "One posits that focusing on the positive heals without having to address past underlying beliefs. The other teaches that going into old beliefs is necessary. I'm just confused. Could you throw some Light on that, please?"

"That is an excellent question, my sister. The first course you reference is onto something important, which is that pain has a habit of drawing the attention of the mind. There is a purpose for that. It is not to wallow in it and feel attacked by it, or feel self-pity because of it. It is so that you can notice what the problem is and take care of it. If you do not have pain when you break your leg, you will not know that you need to get help to heal your leg. The first course understands there is a strong habit of becoming overwhelmed by pain and thinking it is truer than joy, when the opposite is the case. We shared at the beginning that the ecstatic joy of the union with God flows ever-onward through your consciousness, waiting for your awareness. It is the Truth that joy is the Truth. Not only is it more powerful than pain, but it is simply the Truth.

"However, the temptation in that first course would be to deny the power of the constrictive force of fearful beliefs. Fearful beliefs can operate at a deep level of the mind and create quite strong constrictions. For example, a fundamental constriction is the fear of death, which you all must face before you can awaken to the full awareness of Christ Consciousness. Just saying, 'Joy flows on forever as a stream in my mind,' does not heal the fear of death. It must actually be *experienced* and *held* in the flow of joy that flows on forever in your mind. When the two are *brought together*, then the Light simply shines the darkness away. The temptation in that first course is to deny that the constriction of fear *does* exert power on the mind. This is why I have been teaching you that you *have* to discover, look upon, and feel *fully* all the fearful constrictions that you have in your mind. I taught two thousand years ago in the second Beatitude, 'Blessed are those who fully feel their deep, inner emotional turmoil.' [cf. Matthew 5:4.] It cannot be healed unless you feel it fully. This does not mean wallowing in it in self-pity or identifying with it. But it cannot be denied. Is this helpful?"

"Yes, it is helpful. Thank you."

☙

Sister Three seeks guidance. "I want to practice being fully present, experiencing the eternal, and all that you've been teaching us, but I am feeling overwhelmed by the sense of too many things to do and not enough time."

"My sister, we wish to convey to you the tenderness we feel for you and your consistent devotion to the Way. You might translate your feeling of overwhelm into a feeling of excitement that there is *so* much to be done, because it is so *amazing* that you can be helpful to so many people, and they are waking up! Rather than feeling overwhelmed by it all, please notice the excitement lying at the heart of that feeling of overwhelm. You are feeling it even now as you hear these words. It's as if there is a jewel in there you forgot to notice. It is beyond the human egoic experience to comprehend the vastness of Creation. As you get in touch with that, the ego aspect of your mind experiences it as overwhelm. Be grateful that you are not experiencing it as death, illness, or any number of other more intense constrictions. The ego has softened enough that it only experiences this infinity of Creation as *overwhelm*.

"You might also translate that word, *overwhelm*, into 'the creative power of God's Love you are tapping into is actually overwhelming the ego.' The Light simply shines away the darkness. In your experience, the darkness is feeling overwhelmed by the Light. Please feel the *joy* in those words and *let* the darkness be overwhelmed by the Light. As you *allow* the Light to *direct* your every move, you will no longer feel overwhelmed because each day will be new. You will not know *anything* about what will happen, and that will be the most delicious excitement there is, because you *know* you will be offered Souls who are *eager* to receive your Wisdom, and you will be *more* than happy to share the Wisdom because it is in the sharing that it is amplified.

"I have shared before that, though difficult for you to believe, *our* joy actually increases as more of you awaken. You have thought the Enlightened Ones are in some static exalted state, but this is not true.

We are with you intimately. Yeshua has shared with you that you are all his sheep, and he cannot leave any one of you behind, because you are all part of his Self. This is what you are experiencing as *overwhelm*. Your thought that you are a small sheep is being overwhelmed by the knowledge that you are Beloved of God, and that the power and Wisdom of God flow through you, my sister, ever more readily.

"Please, let go of the last small thought that you are a small self. I am sharing with you the image of a circle of friends dancing, their hands are being extended to you, and you are being welcomed into the circle to join the dance. Thank you for your devotion and your service. Enjoy the dance. We extend to you our blessing."

"Thank you, Yeshua. That's beautiful. On the first pilgrimage to Israel in 2003, I heard, 'Will you? Won't you? Will you? Won't you join the dance?' That has recently come back to my attention, so I'm seeing a lot of things now. Thank you."

"We *adore* you. Never forget that, not for one moment. You are *adored*. You are the *Beloved* of *God*. *You*, my sister—all of you—but we are now speaking to *you*. Let those words sink in. *You are the Beloved of God*. All of you, feel that in your bodies, *all the way through* from the crown of your heads, to the palms of your hands, to the root chakra, and to the soles of your feet—every cell. *You* are the Beloved of the Most High and the Beloved of the Mother. It is in their ecstatic union that you have your Being. Sing, dance, and shout your praises to your Selves because you *know* these words are the Truth."

Sister Four describes the experience of her heart feeling on fire for two weeks, and then dreaming that her body was consumed by an inner fire, which represents a death and transition into a new life. "What am I to do from here? I get dizzy at work, so I can no longer earn money in that way. I surrender to that, but what now?"

"My beloved sister, this is, in fact, the same question that your sister before you just asked. When you are playing on the edge of the grasp of ego, it is difficult to let go of the belief that you must plan and know what's next. John, in his introductory meditation, remarked that the root chakra is where that belief in having to survive resides. The ego is based in the fear that it will die, and it must protect itself and survive at all costs. One way in which it practices its survival is by careful planning. You might look at all the industries of the world to say this is evidence of the ego plotting and planning for its survival. The irony is that all of this plotting and planning is actually creating destruction.

"My sister, when you have the sensation of being burned like a phoenix in the transmuting fire of God's Love, the ego still crops up and says, 'Well, that's all well and good. God's Love is a wonderful thing, but what are you going to do next?' As if you needed to know what was next! When you allow yourself to be consumed by the fire of God's Love, what's next is God! What's next is the ecstatic union of *knowing* you are the Child of God! So—this is for all of you—letting go of planning is quite a challenge because there are certain things that have to be planned, but they can be done in a way that is free of fear, that is simply from a knowing that, 'This is what must happen now.'

"I encourage you, my sister, to rest in that feeling of trusting that whatever happens next is what must happen now. Practice waking up in the morning and saying, 'I have no idea what's going to happen today, and that is a *beautiful thing!*' If, at your work, you are not feeling well, then this is a clear sign from your Soul that you are not feeling well in that environment. It takes trust to leap from an environment that earns you money but does not feed your Soul, into an environment that feeds your Soul but does not yet earn you any money. However, because this is your path, when you trust you are following the guidance of God's Love, then you know it will work out. Now, there might be some bumps in the road because the ego is still operating. Until you are enlightened, there are pieces of ego, which is why I have always taught you to *welcome* every bump as a *celebration*, because this is something that can also be healed.

"You are correct in feeling, *knowing*, that you are in a big transition from survival, where you just have to earn money to pay your bills and support your family, into trusting God, trusting your heart, feeling your connection with nature, and sharing that as a spiritual Truth. My sister, please let go of the fear that you have to have everything planned. Hold in your heart the vision of what you are doing next, and trust that it will all unfold in perfect timing, with God's grace. Is that helpful?"

"Yes, thank you, Yeshua."

"I adore you, my sister. I adore your devotion to the Earth, to all people who live on the Earth, and to all the Beings who live on the Earth. Never forget that we are with you *always*, in all ways. We extend to you our blessing."

❧

Sister Five asks, "It has come up in our conversation today that we must face the fear of death. Would you speak to that?"

"Yes, my sister. In a sharing Laura experienced with me a few weeks ago, we presented to her a powerful image of death. It was the image of the face of a deer that had died, and its body was lying in the snow. This shocked her, and she resisted reporting that this was what was being presented to her mind because her mind has always been upset that animals die. To Laura, they represent innocence, and it seems like the ultimate unfairness that this world should be created in such a way that animals have to die in order for life to continue."

Long pause.

"I pause so all of you can feel the deep resonance in your own hearts that you know you have each felt some variation on what I have just said—at best a confusion, and at worst an anger or a resentment that life on this Earth should require the appearance of death.

"The key is that word, *appearance*. You are all perfectly aware you have lived many times in many bodies, so at least on the level of intellect you know you have not died and that you can never die.

You understand this is an impossibility. The same is true for the consciousnesses of animals. There is no distinction between human consciousness and animal consciousness—it is just different levels of awareness. Animals have a kind of wisdom that is better connected to Spirit than even humans do because they do not struggle with ego. In fact, they are listening to the Holy Spirit all day, providing them with guidance.

"The way to release the fear of death, my sisters and brothers, is to understand what I said to you earlier—everything that appears fearful to you is simply the shadow cast by a constriction in the mind. Death is the most fundamental constriction from the beginning of the adventure that the Child of God embarked upon when it said, 'I would like to do this on my own.' And God said, 'Okay.' And the Child of God didn't realize the import of what it had said when it said, '*on my own.*' 'To do it on my own,' means 'to have the appearance I have lost my connection with my loving Father-Mother, my Source.' In order to do it on your own, you have had to believe that it's possible you could die because you are separated from your Source. That's the price, so to speak, of believing in separation. The price is the *risk* you might die. If you *knew* you always maintained your connection with your Source and were never afraid that you could die, then you wouldn't actually feel like you were the one creating your own adventures. You would have still felt dependent and controlled by your Father. Do you see? It is this fear of death that comes hand-in-hand with the belief that, 'In order to become myself, I have to believe I am separated from my Source.'

"Now, as you are returning Home, and you realize you have never been separated from your Source—this has simply been an illusion that *you chose* and was not imposed upon you by God—you are returning to the awareness that you have never been lost. The last thing to let go of is this thought that you might die because that was the first fear that came when you realized you had made the fateful leap into the unknown, the belief that you are separated. When you realize you have always been connected to God, then the belief in death simply evaporates.

"Listen, I have been working with you to help you experience bringing the Light into your bodies because the final leap in awakening is knowing, experiencing, and extending the Light *through your bodies*. I demonstrated this as a man twice. Once in the Transfiguration, when I appeared on the top of a mountain with two of my beloved brothers and I asked three brothers to witness so they would know the Truth that the body is made of Light and never dies, and that the Great Ones who have already attained this awareness are with you at all times. The second demonstration was after the appearance of the death of my body on the cross, when my actual body was transmuted into Light. This meant I could appear in different places at different times because I was no longer constricted by the thought of fear that I could only express as a body. You will all manifest this same experience, that *your body is Light*. When you *know* this, the thought of death means *nothing*. Is that helpful?"

"Yes, thank you. That's great."

"We admire your courage in looking the fear of death in the eye. And what's really fun is, when you look fear in the eye, it cannot withstand the Love of God." He chuckles. "It's like the Wicked Witch of the West. You throw water on her, and she just melts. We extend to you our blessing, my sister."

Sister Six inquires, "Almost constantly over the past several weeks, I have been experiencing a difficult-to-describe ecstatic joy in my body. Yet how I express myself in the world has a certain seriousness about it. It's like there's a gap between what I feel and what I express. How might I close the gap?"

"The seriousness is the thought that other people will think you are crazy if you express joy and ecstasy. It's easy to express that joy in a community of friends of the Heart because they will not think you are crazy. They know you are simply becoming closer to God. The seriousness is a thought that you will be judged for being a fool for God." He chuckles. "Ask the fear—that you will be judged a fool for God—what it thinks it's doing to help you, because it is a thought of protectiveness that comes up. Just as I have asked you to send Love to the world leaders to transmute their quality of protectiveness from fear to Love, send Love to this quality of protectiveness in your own mind so that it can be transmuted and expressed only as Love and not fear. My sister, please enjoy being a fool for God, being a fool for Love!" He chuckles again. "Is that helpful?"

"Yes, that is helpful. Thank you."

Sister Seven has two questions. First, she explains her reaction to the fear that she has done something wrong when someone appears displeased with her. "Can you shed Light on how I can overcome this? When it happens, I lose my confidence quickly."

"My sister, this is an important question. You are describing the process of projection, which is helpful for everyone to understand. When you believe someone outside of you is thinking in a certain way about you, that is a projection of your *own thoughts* about yourself. If you can, approach these moments when you imagine someone might be passing judgment on you with *excitement*. Here is an opportunity for you to see *your own mind.* Imagine that sister or brother *is a mirror* and you are *looking at yourself.* See whatever you imagine they are thinking, or what they are actually saying, as your own thought bouncing back towards you. See if you can see it in such an unfiltered form.

"The problem with seeing it as if it were coming from someone else is you are likely to try protecting yourself against it and push it away. But because this is your own thought about yourself, it must keep coming back. This is a problem all humanity has. You keep pushing away what feels uncomfortable because you attribute the source to be outside of yourself. But if you can look at that source as coming from inside of yourself, as if looking in a mirror, and you hear the thoughts and words as *exactly* your own, then you have a chance to hold those thoughts in Love, and ask 'Where does this belief come from within my mind? How deep in my mind does this belief originate? What is the source of this thought that I am displeased *with myself*?' Do that, and it will lead you back to the original wounding, which is the belief that you have done something bad by jumping out of the Mind of God. You are displeased with yourself for making what appears to be a foolish mistake of going off on an adventure on your own and leaving your loving Parent behind.

"All self-judgment, for all of you, originates from this original thought that you have done something wrong by jumping out of the Mind of God. Your dis-spiriting, this loss of confidence that you have, is because of your judgment of *yourself*. If you could, think of *whatever* you think you've done wrong as a small child who has simply stolen a cookie, spilled juice on the floor, messed her pants, or done something that she believes her parents will be annoyed about. Then pick up that child and say, 'Oh my goodness. It's just a mistake. It doesn't matter; it has no consequence whatsoever on my Love for you! How could messing your pants have anything to do with how much I love you?' Then you will see that this fear you have failed yourself will dissolve. Is that helpful?"

"Yes, thank you."

"We extend to you our deep appreciation for your devotion. We would like you to know that we hold you in the deepest of tenderness for your gentleness and your exquisite beauty. We extend our blessings."

"Thank you. My other question is, I've been having problems with my thumbs, in particular the left one. Can you shed any Light on that?"

"My sister, this is from a past-life experience of having experienced thumbscrews, which is extremely painful. The way to heal this is to forgive your torturers. I have shared about this before, that the Inquisition originated from a thought of trying to keep the teachings about how to return Home to God pure. It obviously got sidetracked by the need for control and the belief that anyone who was outside of the narrow thought of which was the correct path Home to God was a danger. Those in authority experienced you as a danger because of your free ways of expressing Love, and so, you were tortured so you would admit that your ways were wrong. In your heart, you have grief that you succumbed to that to spare yourself from this torture. But I say to you, my sister, of course you needed to do that. In your heart, you know the way Home to God is through freely expressing Love, not through the narrow path of fear, judgment, and hatred.

"Please forgive yourself for that moment of what you call weakness. It was not a weakness. It was simply the necessary thing to do then. Remember, I have told you before that those who perpetrated the Inquisition are *longing* for your forgiveness. When you forgive your torturers, you release a great weight off of the Heart of humanity and a great weight off of your own heart because it does not feel good to you to reserve some people towards whom you still bear judgment. This is why you still bear a judgment towards yourself, because you could not yet free yourself from this corner of judgment. The aching in your thumbs is a gift for you to release this judgment towards others and towards yourself. Is that helpful?"

"Yes, thank you."

⚬⊚⚬

Sister Eight asks about resistance. "Yeshua, I have great difficulty having a direct relationship with you. Can you give me advice on how to release that resistance?"

"My sister, any resistance to having a relationship with a beloved is from the fear that the beloved will control you. The fear of being controlled is purely an egoic thought. Those of us who have transcended ego do not have the thought of control. We see that thought of control and have transmuted it in our own minds, but we assure you, it is not a thought that holds any meaning. When you have difficulty allowing Yeshua into your heart, it is because you are afraid Yeshua will then take the controls and tell you what to do. But I remind you that our Creator has never once told us what to do. It is terrifying when we realize we are doing this to ourselves, and it is completely up to us to get out of this mess. But the instant we want to get out of the mess, the Holy Spirit is sent. That little desire for help sends the Holy Spirit immediately.

"Your desire to know me, Yeshua, in your heart, means you have opened the door for the Holy Spirit to reside in your heart. It might be easier for you, my sister, to picture yourself having an intimate relationship with the Holy Spirit because the Holy Spirit has never been embodied. The Holy Spirit is a direct connecting link to the Mind of God. Because the Holy Spirit is not personalized, embodied, or made into a human form, there is the sense it is more free-flowing and does not have an egoic need for survival or control, so it would have no interest in controlling you. This is all true. It will be helpful for you to approach loving me, Yeshua, by first loving a more abstract energy of God's Love as the Holy Spirit.

"When you can allow in the Love of the Holy Spirit, then you will simply see that I and all the Enlightened Ones are not identified with ego and have no interest in control. The projection of the ego onto Yeshua is that, because he was a man, he must still have human needs. He has no human need. He only has desire—desire that you all know that you are his Beloved. Is that helpful, my sister?"

"Yes, it is, thank you."

∽☯∾

Sister Nine has a question about death. "In my work, I see and speak with many people who are going through the process of dying. It is difficult for me to grasp what you are explaining about death as the transformation of the body. I would like some help to embody what you are saying so that it can be embodied in my Being."

"My sister, this is *such* a beautiful question, that you would like to *embody in your Being the knowing that death is not real.* That requires embodying the knowing that the only thing that is real is Love.

"Now, Laura's mind wants to share with you an amazing story from her part of the world. In the neighboring state of Rhode Island, there is a nursing home where elderly people go to pass on. An unfriendly black-and-white cat lives there. Every time a person is getting ready to leave their body, the cat jumps onto their bed to help ease their transition. When this happens, the staff call the family. Even if the doctors have not said that this person is ready to go, when the cat gets on the bed, the person is ready to go. This cat has no fear of death because it has no ego. It is simply attuned to the energies of Love. When someone is getting ready to leave their body, their consciousness is opening to a higher level. They hear their loved ones, their guides, the Angels. As their consciousness expands into a surprising awareness that there is more than being in a sick body, they begin to realize they are not trapped. The cat is drawn into the feeling of aliveness as the person's consciousness expands. The cat enjoys being attuned to that expansion as they get ready to let go of the imprisoning confines of their body.

"Be like that cat, my sister, who knows that, as people get ready to transition, their awareness increases that there is so much more than what the ego taught them to believe when they thought they were trapped inside of a body. My sister, you are already on this Path. You know you do not have to wait until that moment when suddenly you realize, 'Ah, it hasn't been true. I'm not trapped in this body. It's been a trick this whole time!' You are in a position to know that *now.* Let those words sink in. You are in a position to know *now* that you are not trapped by the confines of a separated body."

"Thank you, Yeshua."

"My sister, to help you know the expanded awareness that people feel when they are about to transition out of their bodies, go out into nature. When you feel your heart expand and connect with the trees, water, Sun, air, clouds, birds, rocks, worms, and the Earth herself—when you feel you are connected with it all, that is what they are experiencing.

"Practice knowing that you are not confined to your brain. Allow yourself to expand your awareness farther and farther outside of your body. Find a beautiful place in nature to sit and see how far you can extend your awareness. Don't push it. Just one millimeter farther each time. See if you can sense how far your own awareness can extend. Go with our blessings."

"Thank you. And just the last thing, Yeshua." Sister Nine describes a digestive problem that wakes her at night. "I feel so much pain in the body, and then I fall into the fear of death, which escalates. Can you shed some Light on that, please?"

"My sister, I smile because you are having a hard time *digesting* this narrow idea that you are trapped in a body, and you are expanding out of that small thought, which is uncomfortable. As you have each shared about energetic experiences that push you past your comfort zone, I have made it clear that you cannot continue to grow *and* stay in your comfort zone. You have to experience discomfort. How could it be otherwise? If you stayed in a familiar and comfortable level of consciousness, you would never grow. When you are experiencing lots of discomfort—I have shared this with John and Laura before, regarding heart and other bodily experiences—you can interpret it with fear that there is a problem; or, you can interpret it with Love, that this is the energetics of higher awareness shaking up a fixed pattern at a level at which you were comfortable. Please interpret this through the eyes of Love, and be grateful you can no longer stomach the narrow idea of being a limited, small self. On a physical level, my sister, please reduce your diet to something simple and then just add one food at a time to help your body cleanse, purify, and adjust to this new level of consciousness that is the knowing that you are larger than this body. Is that helpful?"

"Yes, it is. I am trying to breathe and be in my body, but the mind is going everywhere. It then creates fearful emotions and the whole situation in the body. I'm not getting a restful night, and I'm always tired."

"My sister, you have explained it more carefully than you know. You are interpreting these experiences through fearful thoughts, which produce emotions that are distressing and are embodied. John has also shared that he has experiences in his heart that his doctor told him ten years ago would kill him. Yet, he is still here, despite not taking medication, and it has not killed him. When he experiences feelings in his heart, he has a choice. He can experience them as fear, or as God's Love reworking the energetic level of his heart so that he can tolerate a greater and greater expansion of Love. I share with you this experience he has shared with the group to help you understand you are going through the same process. You can use the egoic thoughts of the mind to interpret these experiences with fear, or you can give these experiences to the Holy Spirit and say, 'Holy Spirit, what is *your* interpretation?' The Holy Spirit's interpretation is that this is an expansion of your consciousness outside of the limits of the body. My sister, pun intended, please digest those words. Thank you for your question. That is sufficient."

"Thank you, Yeshua. Thank you so much."

Yeshua continues. "I ask all of you now to tune into your bodies. As John shared at the beginning, start with the crown of your head and notice that there is no barrier if you are open to God's Love. Let that Love pour down like an oil that is made of Light and fill your mind with Light. Let it fill your body, the throat, shoulders, heart, solar plexus, belly, and down to the root, the creative power of God. Let it flow down your legs and out your feet. Extend that Light outward, along your arms, and out through your hands. Just feel it as a never-ending flow of God's Love through your body and outward. Feel that Love go down to the Earth and mingle with her energies. Ask her nurturing Love to come up into your heart. Feel that joining of the power of the Spirit of God with the nurturing of the Mother, intersecting as a cross in your heart, then exploding and extending outward.

"Now picture that we are all holding hands, the circle of humans on this computer and the Enlightened Ones who are always with you. Imagine that circle with our hands held tightly and everyone *leaning* outward, because you know that no one's hand will let go. You can trust your brothers and sisters because they are devoted to the Path of Awakening. Just feel the deliciousness of being able to lean back in this trusting of each other, and feel that what has your back is God's Love. In the center of the circle is the fire of God's Love. The Angels are singing around, and the Earth is springing up with grass and flowers, and the birds are singing and swooping overhead in the ecstasy of this awakening family.

"Then put your arms around each other, bring yourselves back into the circle, and feel your heads touching, which is a symbol of your minds being One. Feel the power of the fire of God's Love in the center of this circle that warms all your hearts. Then lean back, release your arms, and send the Love of God out into the world! Do this again. Come into the center, touch your heads, put your arms around each other's shoulders, and release and send God's Love out into the world! And once more. This time, it is not just this circle with the Christ Council, but the Angels are also behind you. *Feel* the intensity of the fire of God's Love, and the *beautiful* music. And then let it all go. Release and send the Love of God throughout the Universe!

"With those words, my Beloveds, I send you out into the world. Never forget that we are with you always and that we hold you in the most exquisite tenderness. We will meet again in this form, but we will never leave you.

"Ameyn. Ameyn. Ameyn."

We Are All Playing Our Parts

In late March, I attended a concert of Baroque music at Jordan Hall in Boston. Sitting up on the left balcony, I leaned forward at one point to see my side of the stage better, and I noticed that the second chair first violin was putting on a new string. All around her, the music continued. No one reacted. I had not noticed the string break. She worked diligently, threading it through, tightening it around the peg, then holding it close to her ear to tune it. I suddenly felt she was me. There was no separation. Her face, hair, the curve of her neck, her rapt attention, care, devotion, lack of judgment, being held in community, doing her part—all of it was me. I saw all the performers were me, and I thought, *How could I ever have thought otherwise?* It is so obvious we are but varying aspects of the same Self. A great peace washed through me. I felt in love with the woman seated next to me, who had spoken so openly to me during intermission. I resisted the desire to put my arm around her shoulders.

And then, rather than picking the violin up to her own shoulder, the second chair violinist handed it to the first chair, the superstar Aisslinn Nosky with her spiky red hair. They traded instruments, no comments made, and continued playing. It had been Ms. Nosky's string that had broken. The second chair simply offered her instrument and stepped in to do the repair. The simplicity and sweetness of the collaboration touched my heart. They, too, were aspects of the same Self, each hand helping the other. Ms. Nosky did not check the tuning. She trusted her sister to have played her part correctly.

And I felt a great peace in trusting myself to play the part given to me in this grand symphonic drama of the awakening Child of God. I also understood that when each of us heals something broken, it helps the entire consciousness of humanity.

Chapter 14

The Intimacy of Being Known

Nothing Is Outside the At-One-Ment

Two weeks later, on April 15, 2019, another large group gathered. It was now consistently clear that the Voice speaking is collective—the unified Consciousness of Beings who are awake and know the Truth of Unity.

John opens with a guided meditation of bringing Light all the way through the body, from the crown to the base. He concludes with, "Allow the Light to continue on down to the feet so that you're feeling the Light entering the Earth. And then the Light from above and the Light from below join in the heart."

After the prayer of alignment with God, I start speaking in my voice, describing my inner awareness.

"Draw your attention to your heart. When there is a bubbly energy there, Yeshua would like us to know that this is his presence. He has shared before that because the human heart can feel fear, we have a tendency to confuse that feeling of energy bubbling in the heart with fear. He is reassuring us today that, in fact, he is touching all our hearts often, simply because we are open to receiving his touch. He is always touching us because he cannot *not* touch us because we all share the same Soul. We are just *feeling* his touch more now because we are allowing ourselves to receive his presence energetically in our bodies. Please notice the energy in your hearts.

"Also, notice the energy in your third eye. He asks me to tell you that all of us are deepening our ability to see with true vision with the inner eye. He reminds me to tell you that there is the temptation among spiritual students to value the inner eye over the awareness of the body, but he has been sharing energetic practices with us so we can feel his presence physically. The energy of Christ will suffuse the body as far as we allow it to. He demonstrated manifesting Christ-Mind, which is Light, which is Soul, which is God, *in his body*. He didn't manifest it only in his intellect and keep the body aside. He has been walking us through these energetic practices to feel the presence of the Love of God physically, so we hold nothing outside of the circle of God's Love. He says:"

"Today, I would like to share about intimacy—the intimacy of being known, and the intimacy of knowing the Truth. Experience my energy field around your bodies physically, as if I were an aura, a field of Light that surrounds you. Know that this Light *is* Love, which is God, which is all Knowledge. When you allow yourself to feel the intimacy of being surrounded by this Light, that is the same as allowing yourself to be *known, fully*, through and through. Nothing is held outside of the Knowledge of God. This is important because the ego thinks there are some things that are too shameful and must be held away from God. But I tell you truly, whatever you hold away from God will keep you imprisoned in your dream of separation. There is nothing to feel shame about because everything has been of your own free Creation, and God feels nothing but admiration for the creativity of her Child. She wants nothing more than for you to turn around and see that she has been behind you, at One with your Soul, with no separation, *always*. This At-One-ment is Knowledge.

"Today I would like you to *feel* the total delicious feeling of being known and having nothing that is kept outside of the Knowledge. There is nothing you can hide because you think it is too awful to be seen. God sees all and judges nothing. You have been your own judges and your own executioners. This is why you made a world in which it appears that you die, punishing yourself for the perceived sin of leaving the Garden.

"But I tell you truly, you have done nothing wrong. We have been working with you to welcome you Home to the Garden. This Garden is the full Awareness of the beauty of Creation. When you know you are God's One Creation, and you can extend that Creation by sharing it with your brothers and sisters, then you will know Peace. Peace is the ecstasy of the joy of Creation. Only when you think you have done something wrong, do you create a feeling of internal conflict, which then you grab onto and say, 'This must be myself because it feels so powerful.' But I say to you, it has no power.

"When you hold nothing outside of God's Love, and you allow the free expression of your Soul, then you will be amazed at the Garden of delights that will spring up around you. I have shared before that when you join the circle of friends, where your feet touch the Earth, grasses grow, flowers bloom, and birds sing. This is not a metaphor. This is the Truth. Humanity has always had the memory of the Garden. There has *always* been the echo of the music of the Garden, and the smells, sounds, and sights of the Garden. I bring this to your mind today to encourage you that you are much closer to returning Home than you think. All you need to do is embrace every obstacle that arises without resisting it, being grateful that it has been given to you to be healed. I hold before you this image of the Garden so you can remember it when something painful arises, and remind yourself that embracing that pain and asking for the Holy Spirit to translate it into Truth will bring you closer to full memory of the Garden.

"I ask you now to look through your current life experiences and notice how Love shines through. Love shines through in ways you might find unexpected, but you recognize it because of its beauty. You all have many moments, small and large, where you recognize the beauty of Love, when there is an innocent communication between yourself and someone you've never met before that's filled with grace, acceptance, and no judgment. That's a moment of Love shining through into your world.

"Now imagine all of your moments coalescing in your own heart and with each other, and imagine these moments of grace joining, like drops of rain that form a larger puddle where you cannot say which was the original drop, which was the other drop, and which is now the puddle. As these moments of grace join with each other and coalesce around the world, then the Garden springs up. People are inspired to take care of the Earth, restore habitats, plant gardens, take care of animals, clean toxins, and take care of the oceans. I know I have told you before that it is easy to feel despair when you look at the poisoning of your Mother, but I tell you the Truth—every time you walk on her and send her your Love, she feels your encouragement and shakes off yet another layer of her despair, guilt, and sadness. You are healing her along with healing yourselves. This might sound strange to you, but it is no stranger than telling you that all Beings share the same Soul. There is only one Child of God. It just has endless faces that look out in different directions and *think* those directions are separated. But as you heal your thoughts of fear, you are drawn back towards the Source, and it becomes increasingly difficult not to notice that there are people to your left and right who are also returning Home.

"I would like to return to the word *intimacy*. This word brings to the human mind *sexual intimacy*. Sexual energy cannot be left out of the circle of God's Love because it *is* the creative power of God. Sexual intimacy, when it is an expression of spiritual Truth, *is* the experience of full Knowledge of yourself and the other person with whom you are expressing sexual intimacy. When there is full Knowledge, there is no need for grasping, because there is no *need* at all. When you allow yourself to feel that experience of full Knowledge of yourself and the other, you will know this also means that you are allowing yourself to be known fully by God. In that state of full Knowledge, sexuality becomes a powerful energy that expresses God's creative force.

"The ego has used sexuality in millions of different ways. None of you has come through your many lifetimes unscathed in the misuse of sexual energy. You are now at a point where you can hear that sexual energy itself *is* the power of God's Love. God's Love cannot be *used* any more than sexuality can be used. When sexual energy arises, the first temptation will be to interpret it through the eyes of egoic *use*. Sexual energy, when it arises between people, is not for *use*, it is not for control, ownership, manipulation, or abuse in any way. My sisters and brothers, when you feel the energy of sexuality arise within you, hold it in Love, just as you hold any other energy that arises within you. You have become more comfortable holding the energies of fear, pain, grief, trauma, and all the rest of the detritus of your many past lives. Now we say to you, it is also time for you to hold the energy of sexuality with the same compassion and the same awareness that it is not to be *used*.

"When you follow your hearts and you hear the inner prompting of the Holy Spirit, then you know what each experience is for as it unfolds. You have come far enough to know that you can trust each experience as it unfolds without needing to be given a roadmap beforehand. The same is true with exploring sexual energy. Trust it as it unfolds. There is no need for a roadmap because there is no goal. There is nothing to attain. There is only allowing. You have heard me say many times that Love trusts all things, allows all things, embraces all things, and thus transcends all things. This is true of all energies.

There are no exceptions to that which we are conveying to you today.

"So we say to you, be gentle with yourselves and go slowly in the area of allowing sexual energy. Allow whatever fear and thoughts of abuse, misuse, control, or grasping to come up with the sexual energy. Allow that *also*, trust it *also*, embrace it *also*, and give it to the Holy Spirit for transmutation *also*.

"We are encouraged by your willingness to continue to look within and heal any place of constriction in the body-mind. Remember, the appearance of darkness is simply a shadow caused by a constriction in the mind. It is not real. It is nothing that has power or substance. As you soften what has become rigid within, then the Love of God pours through you.

"Please notice your feet and hands as we are speaking to you. We are conveying the physical experience at this moment of the Love of God pouring through you, from the crown of your head, through your face, throat, heart, and down your arms. Feel the energy in the palms of your hands, all the way down through the body and the root chakra. Feel the energy in the root chakra, the tingling and vibration in the thighs, calves, and the soles of your feet. This is a beginning experience of what the body feels like when you allow yourself to know that your true Identity is Light, which is Love, which is God."

Long pause.

"I pause to allow you to feel this physical sensation. If any one of you is experiencing discomfort, if it feels too much, or if you feel sleepy and need to recoil, hold the sleepiness and the recoil in Love. Hold the thought that, 'This feels like too much,' in Love, and stay with it. We are encouraging you, one step at a time. We are with you always.

"With those words of encouragement, we ask you to share whatever questions you have in your hearts. We remind you that it is our deepest desire to help you soften and open and receive our Love. We know it seems strange to you when we say, our Love and joy increase when you join with us, but that is the Truth. So feel free to come forward with your questions."

∽◉∾

John begins. "I have a question that's for both Laura and for me. Laura is intolerant of dairy products, and I cannot tolerate gluten. But you have said that we don't need to avoid anything if we consume it with Love. Does this mean we can change these digestive intolerances?"

"This is a helpful question. It has to do with how open you are to receiving the Light. When there is a physical recoil from a substance that exists in your world, it is from a constriction in the mind that thinks there is some danger in the world. You are correct, my brother, in saying these can be changed. However, as in all things, healing is an unfolding process.

"I had to learn, as the Spiritual Master walking the Earth, that I could not force people to heal. This was a learning process for myself. Even though I knew my full Identity was the Child of God and I could touch people and their energetics would synchronize with mine and thus dissolve their constrictions, I had to learn that, away from my presence, unless they knew their *own mind* had changed, their fearful constrictions would simply return.

"When you have a physical constriction, for example, around dairy or wheat, this comes from a deep place in the mind that believes the body is vulnerable and is open to impingement by the world. Instead of forcing yourself to become less sensitive to these materials, I encourage you to notice how you think you are still vulnerable to the world and can be harmed. This is quite a challenge because the evidence of the world is that bodies can be harmed. Western medical science is all about protecting the body from impingements by external forces.

"I had no fear that I could be harmed. I could even express the Love of God into a body that had appeared to have died, and the body's life could return. I certainly had no fear of death. The fear of being harmed is the fear of death, so I encourage you and Laura to meditate on releasing your fear of death. Laura has this opportunity currently. Knowing her cat will transition out of this world at the end of the week, she is going through an intense purification process regarding her feelings about death. She is doing well because she is allowing herself to feel all of her feelings, including ecstasy, release, deep grief, guilt, and all the feelings in between. I also encourage you, my brother, to allow whatever feelings are associated with your fear of death to flow through you unimpeded. Is this helpful?"

"Yes, it is. You mentioned working with the fear of death with my friend who is terminally ill with cancer, which seems to be helping. Do you have any other suggestions for working with him?"

"Please share with your friend your experience today of being held in the intimacy of God's Love. Share with him that experience of the aura of white Light around your body. Encourage him to join you in that practice of feeling the intimacy of being known by God, through and through, with no resistance. When he can soften into how delicious this feels—because this is what the heart has always longed for, to be known—this will help him release his fear of death. He will know that he is headed into a fuller awareness of being known."

⬿⧬⬿

Sister One inquires, "Is dying always a process of becoming more completely known?"

"My sister, *dying to the ego* is the process of becoming more completely known. Letting the body go does allow the mind to learn that it is not contained by the body. To those who are identified with the body, this is always a revelation that allows a feeling of release and amazement. The Soul is always in communication with God, yet the mind constricts how much it allows itself to be aware of this. Some people have thought that when the Soul leaves the body, it is freed from this constriction, but the ego does not disappear at bodily death. The thought of being a separated self can only release its grip with the full permission and awareness of the mind and Soul through the process I have taught you of accepting every place that appears to be constricted.

"So yes, my sister, there is most definitely some expansion of awareness when the mind realizes there is so much more than being confined inside a small body. But the ego's dissolution process takes as many lifetimes as you require. There is a fearfulness about the ego, and it wants to hold on. It must be *in the body*, the very place where you thought yourself into being separated, that the ego lets go. You cannot retain any thought of being a separated self *and* release the ego. Ego death happens *in* the body, which is the death of the thought of the small self. Then you are fully alive to your true Identity *while in the body*. Is that helpful?"

"Very much so, thank you."

∾⊛∿

"I have a question about the body," Sister Two asks. "I wake up with cramps in my calves and feet. I have tried some remedies, but none of them helps. Sometimes, if I can catch it when it's just beginning, I'm able to breathe deeply and gently, and it goes away, or it doesn't progress. Do you have any guidance about this?"

"My sister, know you the feeling when you are in a sleeping nightmare and you cannot run?"

"Yes."

"You are in the same sleeping nightmare, even though you think you are awake. You are preventing yourself from dancing, moving, and running forward. The pain in your legs is from two thoughts: that you must hold yourself back, and that the body is holding you back. The body is a *passive instrument that responds to your direction*. It is an exquisite and complex instrument, but it has *no separate will*. It responds to whatever messages you convey. Now, these messages come from deep within the mind and are not conscious.

This understanding is not to make you feel guilty that you are trying to make yourself suffer. It is to help you see that the *healing* is in the deepest levels of the mind.

"The way to heal any bodily problem is to ask the Holy Spirit, 'What is the message, or what is the metaphor, of this physical symptom?' When you are experiencing pain in your legs and you cannot move forward, the message is, you believe you must hold yourself back, and the body is preventing you from moving forward. 'If only you weren't confined by this body, then you could attain much higher states of consciousness.' I began the teaching today by telling you that this is the opposite of the Truth. The Truth is that the *body* must be *suffused* with the highest state of consciousness in order for you to release any thought of being a separated self.

"My sister, I ask you to ask yourself, in what way do you believe it is helpful to hold yourself back or to blame the body for why you somehow cannot move forward? Blaming the body, from the point of view of ego, seems quite helpful because it can say, 'I didn't make this happen. The body is holding me back, so I guess I can't take my next step on my path towards the Atonement.' But I say to you truly that the body's message is from deep within your mind. It is this very thought that the body is holding you back that requires healing by being held in Love. Is that helpful?"

"Thank you. The answer so far is helpful. But how to access this deepest part of the mind?"

"As I have shared previously, hold the thought 'the body is holding you back' in Love, and allow that process to unfold. Remember, we are with you *always*. You are not alone in this healing process. The fear is that the body is keeping you isolated—a fear *all* humanity shares. When you can heal this thought, that you are separate and alone, and you can feel the Love of the Enlightened Ones around you, then this will be a huge step on your path towards liberation. Practice as we are instructing you. That is sufficient."

∼☙∾

Sister Three seeks advice. "I find it difficult to speak when I'm in a group situation. My brain doesn't seem to formulate things to say. In the study groups of *The Way of Mastery* and *A Course in Miracles*, I've felt frustrated by this. Do you have any guidance for me?"

"My sister, we are so grateful for your courage in stepping forward with this question here in this group. Notice your heart at this moment. See if you can feel the Enlightened Ones holding your heart. Remember that the word *cour-age* comes from the Latin word for *heart*. Feel the courage in your heart to know you are loved.

"The fear of speaking in groups is a common fear in humanity. It is the fear of being judged. You have so much courage to come forward in these groups and participate in this process of exposing those places of constriction that need softening with Love. The fact that you are showing up, putting your energy into the circle, and noticing that there is no judgment in it, helps your ancient fear of being judged if you speak. Today is an important day in your awakening's progress because you have had the courage to speak, and you know you will be received with no judgment.

"My sister, this fear of judgment is many lifetimes old. It is a habit you have had the opportunity to heal many times. However, the fear of judgment has overwhelmed these opportunities. You could interpret these experiences either as a chance to risk being loved, or as proof of being unloved. In this life, you have found this community who you *know* will not judge you.

"This is your opportunity to bring up a *long chain* of fearfulness of being judged and put it in the center of the circle. I have shared before the image of a fire in the center of the circle symbolizing the Love of God. You can put into this fire anything you would like transmuted. My sister, pull up this long chain of fear of judgment, put it in the center, and watch God's Love dissolve it. I am telling you again—you are loved, we are with you, and we admire your courage. Is this helpful?"

"Yes, thank you very much."

"Thank you for speaking up today."

~ⱺ~

"Dear ones, are there any other questions?"

No one responds.

"We would like to share with you again the image of the boat. There are *many* famous boats in the story of Yeshua. The boat metaphor is used many times. From the boat, Souls on the Path of Awakening can haul in many fish—the Souls of fellow travelers whom they welcome onto the boat. The boat is also a place of refuge when the ego's demands are impinging. Then there is the boat the Holy Family traveled in from Alexandria to Provence. The Romans had broken the mast, taken away the oars, ripped up the sail, and cast them adrift to die. But they were carried on the winds of Love and landed safely in their new home, which had been prepared for them, carefully over many years, by the great Master, **Joseph of Arimathea**.

"This boat is a metaphor for the Holy Family of the Child of God. It started out as a small family, but we say to you, this boat can hold all Souls. Each one of you is welcome into this boat. There is safety in the boat as it rocks gently on the sea. We share this image with you today so that you will know the comfort of being loved and knowing that the boat takes you wherever you need to go. You do not have to set the sails, hold the rudder, or pull the oars. This boat is the innocence and purity of God's Love that holds everything that you think should have been cast over the side. But I tell you the Truth, *everything* is held within the Love of God.

"So, on the winds of Love and the currents of Peace, we support you and hold you up as you continue on your journeys, going where the wind listeth (cf. John 3:8, KJV). You will all land safely on the shores of Heaven. The Garden that has always been there awaits your arrival.

"My Beloveds, trust your journeys. We are holding you up. We see you intimately. Allow all your experiences, trust all your experiences, hold all of your experiences, and we will transform them into the Truth of who you are, which is Light, which is Love, which is full Knowledge of God.

"With those words, we give you our blessings. We do not have to say farewell. We say we travel with you. We are with you *always*.

"Ameyn. Ameyn. Ameyn."

Later that day, a sister who had been present wrote to me about how heart-opening it was for her to participate in this intimate group. "You are in my thoughts this week regarding the situation with your beloved cat. Thank you for your courage to feel and process the wide range of emotions that are coming up. It helped me to hear you mention it."

Another sister in our group later shared with me that people had told her that my serving so Yeshua could answer their specific questions was like popcorn when they got the answer—it popped something that they were just ready to open up. The answers were amazingly helpful, exactly what they needed to push themselves forward. Often, after the sudden insight, a growth process continued to unfold. I noted Yeshua had given several people instruction to stick with a certain practice that would lead to growth. Some things we need to sit with to allow the unfolding process.

I just felt intense gratitude that I could serve in this way.

Chapter 15

Grief and the Light-Body

Bastet Reveals Herself

The Saturday after that large group gathering, April 20, 2019, the day before Easter, a vet came to my house to release my beloved Cricket from his body. In two months, he would have been twenty-one years old, my loyal protector for all those years. I had received him as a kitten, when he was a jumpy little black bug, from the lawyer who had handled the purchase of my house, so we had established our lives there together. The kidney failure I thought would take him the previous November was now complete. Feeling old and tired, he just wanted me to stay with him in my room, constantly. He would call me to come sit with him, so I was even eating my meals on my bed.

After sustaining him on subcutaneous fluids for nine months, I was certain that, when he needed daily fluids, then that would be too much and he could go. My agreement with him was not to let him suffer, and I knew the time had come. He was miserable, even after receiving fluids. I was perfectly calm when I made the appointment, and completely at peace with the decision all week, knowing his body was done.

This peace lasted until the day before the vet's arrival. Then I really had to practice Yeshua's teaching to allow the free flow of energetic currents in the body! This meant wailing as I drove to get my beloved kitty his last can of tuna to enjoy the next day, wailing in the store parking lot, sobbing in the store, and wailing all the way home.

Back home, I sat on the bed, legs out straight, and Cricket came to sit on my lap. But rather than his usual habit of facing away from me, he lay on my thighs facing towards me—a first! I noticed the soles of my feet and the palms of my hands getting hot, and I knew what that meant—the presence of Yeshua in my body. And then a most extraordinary sensation began. On the top of my pubic bone, there was an extremely uncomfortable oval patch of intense burning energy. I just breathed into it. It lasted such a long time that I eventually fell asleep. When I awoke, the soles of my feet were still burning. At that moment, I could enjoy the intensity of his passage.

But the next day, when the vet came, and the moment had arrived that I would never have Cricket's devoted presence with me in a body again, I was a complete and total wreck. When he came to me for protection from this strange person, and I let her inject him anyway, I felt I had betrayed his trust and killed him. Writing this manuscript has helped me be more at peace with death, though I still feel the ache of missing the body at times. I have complete confidence in the continuity of all Souls, and he has visited me a few times in vivid dreams.

But I also remember that he came to sit on my lap and put his head trustingly in my hand, and that was it. I felt him giving me permission to let him go.

That evening, utterly distraught, I went for a walk in the Arboretum. It was drizzly, so I had this beautiful park mostly to myself. In the fading light, I stumbled around the familiar landscape, sobbing. I headed to an off-path grove. Suddenly, in a small clearing,

I felt Cricket behind me, but huge, like an animal God. The words *warrior protector* jumped into my mind. I whirled around. I saw nothing, but I felt his presence towering over me, as tall as the trees. Even through my grief, I could feel that he was conveying to me that, without a body, he was now free to protect me wherever I went, not just in our house.

That night, I remembered that there was an Egyptian cat Goddess. I looked her up, and these words jumped off the cell phone screen. "Bastet, the warrior protector of the pharaohs." A week later, when I told my tenant (who had often fed him for me when I was away) about his departure (but not about this vision), she told me she had something for me. She came down the back stairs and put a heavy object into my hands—a small statue of Bastet! A former Egyptian boyfriend had given it to her. Tearfully, I told her, "You have no idea how meaningful this is to me. Thank you so much."

Grief Releases Identification with the Body and Allows the Awakening of the Christ

John and I met on April 22, 2019, asking Yeshua to help me process this grief.

John opens by establishing the feeling of the presence of Yeshua's Light in our bodies. Yeshua begins immediately after our prayer.

"Just start talking. You have a habit of wanting to skip ahead and know what's coming next, even what I'm going to say to you next, so start with what I'm telling you *first*. Draw your attention to the root chakra, the legs, and the feet. You have been paying close attention to your bodily experiences during this process of transitioning from living with the body of your cat to living with the Spirit of your cat. It has surprised you somewhat, the intense energy in the root chakra during this process. The purpose of this energetic experience is for you to feel the Light all the way down to the root, to feel fully that the body *is* Light. If you were only feeling Light in your heart because you had an intellectual idea that this is where Love resides, and this is an experience of Love and loss, you would not fully feel the purpose of this grief. This grief's purpose is to bring the Light down to the root and live in the root. John's well-chosen words a week ago were to call the root organs 'the organs of enlightenment,' because only when *they* are filled with Light can you *know* you *are* Light and there is nothing outside of the Light. It has seemed strange to you to have so much energy in the root chakra *while* you are grieving, but for the two nights before Cricket departed his body, you recall that the lower half of your body was *on fire.*

"I would like to help you understand what has been confusing about the activation of the root chakra during this grieving process. This is to help you *feel fully* that *even* in an extremely difficult emotional passage, you can sustain the awareness of the power of God. Grief does not exclude God's Love. In fact, when you feel any experience fully, if you *do* notice, there is always a sexual energy associated, simply because the energies of the feeling, when allowed, are flowing through the body forcefully. How can this not arouse sexual energies?

"I hear your question, 'Does your cat have any kind of feeling of shock or betrayal?' Your cat's Spirit is as vast as the sky. Your cat knew it was time to go. Other Beings have been communicating with him to prepare him for his passage. All he was waiting for was for *you* to be ready to release him. As you know, he is your protector, so he had to be reassured that you would be safe if he left you. He is so devoted. He can never leave you. Your hearts are forever joined. He conveys to you he is at peace and is *extremely* grateful not to have any more needles. It was OK for a while, so he could still enjoy being with you, but it had gotten to be too much.

"He's saying, 'If I could have lived forever, I would have because I love you that much. But I do live forever. I have lived always. Just like your Soul, a little of my Soul can manifest as a body, but that is just a small portion of the vastness of the Soul.' He is also conveying that, out of his body, he is enjoying the freedom to come and go as he pleases, rather than you being the one that came and went as you pleased. He is happy to release you to go on in your life without being concerned for his care. He's saying, 'Sometimes you will feel me and sometimes I will be off doing my own exploration, just as I did in the body. I do so like to explore! But just call me, and I'll be with you in an instant. And you can trust that I'm happily enjoying my *new territory*.'

"My Beloved, I hear your question about what is this grieving for, and again I say to you, you have the habit of being impetuous and wanting to run ahead. Ever since you were a child, you have always been at the leading end of any group that you are with. It's a great effort to hold yourself back and let someone else lead. The purpose of this grief will unfold. It's not a onetime event. This is a significant event that you should lose this companion right at the moment that you are set to fly yourself.

"Fully feeling the grief at the loss of the body is necessary to come to the place of Peace where you can feel the physical presence of the other Beings with you. My beloved Maryam went through the same grieving process. Sometimes she was furious with God, as if it were God's fault that we jumped into this dream together. But she was courageous in allowing *all* of her feelings. By doing as she did, which is to allow the grief, then she could fully feel my presence when I was with her. Only by feeling the grief each time we parted did she finally fully release her identification with the body.

"I am showing you the image of an old oaken door in the shape of a Gothic arch surrounded by mossy stones. This is a portal into the body of the Mother Earth."

Pause.

"I pause to allow you to feel the experience of entering that door and resting inside the Body of the Mother. This is the purpose of all the womb structures built by the early peoples in the British Isles—to enter the Body of the Mother and receive rejuvenation and rebirth. When the Light of the Father enters the Womb of the Mother Earth, this has a *huge* effect on the world. In that powerful moment, is all made new. This is why I have asked you to go to Scotland to receive the Light of the Father at the powerful moment of the solstice in a place that has a Womb of Earth, so that all of you gathered can physically experience the joining of the Mother-Father God *in your lived experience*, in the realms of the mind, the feelings, and the body. This is not an intellectual process at all; this is a *feeling-Communion* process."

John joins in. "I have a question. You recently suggested that I go back to *A Course in Miracles* and open it randomly to the lessons in the *Workbook*. My reaction surprised me. I started feeling anger welling up at the double negatives and the use of unusual words to maintain the iambic pentameter. I realized you were assigning this as a forgiveness opportunity. I feel like I'm moving in that direction."

"My brother, what you are forgiving is your own former attachment to intellect. I have shared that I needed to convince Helen and her helper, Bill, to release their attachment to intellect, and the only tool I had to use was their intellect. You can imagine that this is quite a paradoxical challenge. I used iambic pentameter and the double negatives on purpose to thwart the intellect's habit of grasping onto words and saying, 'Oh, I understand this.' The iambic pentameter, the rhythm of it, lulls the mind into a deeper state of consciousness. The double negative is like a paradox, which the mind has to let go and say, 'I don't understand. There are too many negatives.' The mind then has to go into *feeling*, to *feel* what the words mean. This was necessary for these two Beings to move into their hearts and actually practice forgiving, instead of holding onto the intellect's habit of being right and winning arguments. In fact, it was their heart-sickness at how horrible it *feels* to be right and win arguments that allowed them to open to my presence. But just because there was willingness, does not mean that the habit instantly evaporated, of course.

"Your habit has been to value intellect also, and to approach my teaching, at times, from the perspective of the mind, and trying to grasp the meaning intellectually. That you are angry about this is a helpful sign that you no longer value that, and say to yourself, 'This is not how it should be. I protest.' And so I say to you, my brother, there is no need to protest trying to apprehend the world through intellect. You have come too far. Now you can simply release that old habit of believing that apprehending the world through intellect is the way. Now you know that the body, the feelings, the intuition, the inner eye, and the inner ear is the way. Is that helpful?"

"Yes. Does that mean I've passed the test and I can go beyond the *Workbook* now? I do plan to continue to go back and look at those beautiful passages, but probably not as often anymore."

"My brother, this isn't a test. This is for you to notice your progress. There was still a piece of fear that the intellect could somehow hold you back. Because you now know the intellect is simply your servant, when you feel moved to open *A Course in Miracles*, it will be from a place of the heart, and you will be guided to passages that are simply straightforward and poetic. You will notice the language becomes simpler as the book continues, because Helen and Bill's attachment to intellect softened, and I could use more direct language. This is the case for you as well—you are now able to hear direct language in your heart. Is that helpful?"

"Yes. Just one further comment. When I was reading the *Text* at first, I had the feeling that Helen had put the teachings in a blender and put them back together. When the *Urtext* came out, I realized that is exactly what happened, except that she omitted all the good stuff! Do you recommend a version beyond the *Urtext*—the *Sparkly Edition*, perhaps?"

"That is a wonderful metaphor—Helen putting words in a blender, and the blender was her intellect. I have referenced before my need to correct her corrections continually. The *Urtext* edition of the *Course* has the whole process of my relationship with her. This is *invaluable* for students to understand that I am in a *direct personal relationship* with each student, and I work with them at whatever point they are at in their process. It is quite enlightening to read Helen's struggles with her own issues and with her relationship with me in the *Urtext*. This takes her off of a pedestal, so to speak, and makes her human. It also allows each student to work with the material of their own resistance, because this is the most important point of each person's growth—where the resistances are.

"The edition that flows the most smoothly—without all the conversations between myself and Helen, which is about her process, and as I just said, one can learn from—is the one known as the *Sparkly Edition*. This edition has removed all of her corrections. It has also replaced lots of passages many people can learn from that are not particular to Helen's process. It has also replaced all of my original words, which her subsequent editor had edited out. He had used his intellect, his previous understanding of Christianity, and his own reactions to those understandings, and then imposed those on the *Text*. This makes the original *Blue Version* extremely confusing. I recommend you share the *Sparkly Edition* with a beginning student, but also refer them to the *Urtext* to help them understand that this is a *deeply personal* relationship they are entering with me. Is that helpful?"

"That is so helpful! I didn't realize that about the original edition. It sounds like the *Sparkly Edition* has removed some things that were just for Helen. It has passages at the end that talk about her process, which began in October 1965, when Uranus and Pluto conjoined. I noticed right away that this conjunction became active right about that time."

"My brother, I *love* your beautiful attunement to the planetary music! You have a genuine feeling for the vibrational quality of the dance of the spheres. In this way, it helps you to see the *value* in experience. How could it *not* be valuable if it's in *direct* correlation with what the planets' dance is doing at that time? Your awareness of the planetary aspects of life adds a *beautiful* felt-sense to other perceptual approaches. You are doing an excellent job *not* apprehending **astrology** with your intellect, but with your heart. It is lovely when you see the deeper resonance in significant moments in the planetary alignments. It is absolutely the Truth that patterns occur in the planets and the stars that shift and create portals, opportunities, amplifications, endings, and beginnings. Continue with your astrological explorations, my brother, and feel it ever more fully in your heart as a dance that you are dancing with. Is that helpful?"

"Yes, thank you. You have spoken about a celestial speedup, and people have suggested that the end of the Mayan calendar on December 21, 2012, was a time of freedom from the patterns of the past. Perhaps the Second Coming of Christ in each of us is easier after that time. I'm reluctant to keep asking questions because I know that, though you aren't in time, Laura is, and she's been through a lot. But it would be great if you could talk about that."

"I have shared in previous gatherings that the Second Coming of Christ is *not* that I will reappear in a body. That would simply reinforce the idea that I was the only Child of God, which is a mistaken perception. The Second Coming of Christ is the awakening of the Christ-Mind in many Souls. The Mayans were attuned to the stars with their temples and planetary esplanades. All of their grand structures were aligned with planetary bodies, showing their deep attunement to celestial cycles. The end of that Mayan cycle is the end of the 'firm' belief (I use that word in quotes) in the human mind, that humans are trapped on the Earth. Yes, there is a quality of freedom as ever more minds understand humans are not trapped on the Earth. Now, those who are identified with their intellect *feel* that energy and think this means humans should send bodies to Mars! But that is just an outward symbol of this energetic awareness that the human Soul is no longer trapped in the body.

"The speedup I refer to is an algorithmic expansion as greater numbers of people attune to the awareness of the Soul. Not only is it simply a numerical exponential growth—because as more people become aware, they touch more people, who become aware, who touch more people—it is an energetic amplification. The more people have awareness of the Soul, the more easily that energy can be accessed.

"It also creates the reaction of fear in those who are still attached to ego. I do not need to tell you what that looks like. But do not let it deter you. There is much grieving in the world because of the reaction of fear. I ask you to please stay in the flow of my Love and all the Enlightened Ones and the Angels. We encourage you to keep sharing your Wisdom. The Wisdom you share through your astrological work is that we are, as Souls, attuned to the entire Universe. And there is nothing confining about that, is there? Is that helpful?"

"Again," John continues, "I hate to keep going, but just one last thing, and then I will let you and Laura go. I've been telling people that this time of freedom you talk about is a time of freeing each of us to welcome the Christ within our own consciousness."

"Yes, you have understood what I was just sharing with you. That is a succinct way to put it. Yes, Laura is tired, but my energy also sustains her, my brother, so do not feel that you are imposing. She joins with me willingly, as you know well. It brings her great joy to be in this role of the servant.

"I would like to convey to you my enjoyment of your enjoyment of planning your grand pilgrimage to the Essene sites that I and my family knew well, before and after my physical life. I will be with you every step of the way, as will many of my brothers and sisters who are not in bodies, enjoying your awareness of your gratitude to us.

"I have shared with you before a grand paradox of time, which is that, when my family and I were incarnated, we also looked forward in time and saw there would be Souls who would continue our teachings and carry them out farther and farther into the world. Your amplification of the energies at these places also extends backward in time and encourages us to keep going through, when you look back on it, extremely difficult circumstances with incredible courage. You may not have known, but your present-day devotion is giving us courage in what appears to be the past. We enjoy your enjoyment because now you can go on the journey in a much lighter energy field than the time when we were on the journey, where the energy was much heavier. There are so many more Souls who welcome the teachings now. It was a much harder push two thousand years ago. We are going to enjoy retracing our steps with a lighter heart.

"With that, I remind you to always feel me in your hearts and in the root chakra. I ask you always to notice the energy in the root, with my teaching that this is to help you practice bringing the Light all the way down to the root.

"And enjoy the springtime flowers!

"With that, I say, Ameyn. Ameyn. Ameyn."

Right after this session, I wrote to John. "I can't believe how clear and powerful these teachings are. I was so tired and grief-stricken that I felt like I was really slow and not particularly coherent—then again, perhaps this state kept me from interfering."

I share here two responses from sisters who had been participating in the group gatherings at this time.

"Thank you so much for doing these channelings with Yeshua and John. I find them helpful beyond anything I can say. And I'm so sorry about your cat. I hope you are feeling better now."

"I am feeling such a deep connection with the Feminine Christ energy coming through you in the channelings."

Light-Bodies Masquerading as Physical Bodies

I spent all my time during the next week allowing my feelings of grief over losing my beloved companion, Cricket. I did my best to absorb Yeshua's teachings on death that had been coming through me, and I finally felt calm enough to accept John's offer of another guided conversation to help me process the grief on April 29, 2019.

At the conclusion of our conversation, John shared he had experienced Yeshua's words coming through him as he was helping me. I confirmed that, when he enters his guide role, his words do become clear. "When you go into the profound, clear guidance that you do, it's your mind, *and* you're accessing the Christ-Mind—there is no distinction."

I begin by sharing my insight that human child development is a symbol for the development of the Soul through eons of time. Both the individual child and the Soul begin by manifesting in the feeling of primordial oneness with the parents, human and Divine. Then the awareness that the self exists separate from the parents emerges, and the toddler simultaneously wants to do it all herself and is terrified that the parents will reject her for separating her identity from theirs. Despite wanting to do it all by herself, she also needs to know that her parents are always there for support. Without the parental presence, the child feels despair, lost, alone, and groundless. The Soul imagines that, by leaving the primordial oneness with God, God feels rejected and so is no longer there for support. Yet the longing for Home remains, the echo of the distant memory of the Garden.

There is a defiant edge to the toddler's insistence that she can do it herself, and even a mean edge to the adolescent's rejection of the parents. But only insecure human parents can feel injured by this normal developmental process. God feels only compassion for all the suffering the Soul will go through on its wild adventures and waits patiently for the Soul to wake up to the awareness that it has been Home all along, just dreaming of separation. But the Soul imagines God feels rejected, and so it imagines God will gloat that he/she knew all along the Soul would return and have to admit it was wrong for having left. But God never told the Child *not* to leave—to do so would be in violation of Reality in which Creation has free will—and feels only compassion and admiration for the Child's courage to go off and find its Self. This is the grand blessing of diving into the insane nightmare of feeling separated from God. When we return, we will retain knowledge of who we are *and* be in relationship with our Source.

Recently, Yeshua has often expressed his admiration for our courage.

All my life, I have had a feeling of despair about how long it takes to return Home. As a therapist, I see how long the growth process takes, especially for those with no spiritual practice. Peter felt this despair. He had left his family, the community was dispersed, and he despaired of humanity ever understanding Yeshua's message of Love. But Yeshua was always in communication with him, reassuring him, guiding him, and performing healings with him. It was just hard for Peter to see his role in the broad arc of the development of the Soul of humanity. Yeshua reassures us it takes no time at all because there is no time, and when any Soul receives the Light, it is a cause for celebration. He sees the despair, but he knows it isn't real. If I could lighten up, that would really help things!

I notice a feeling of guilt for dragging animals into our whole separation drama requiring cycles of birth and death. But Cricket gets my attention and lets me know it was his choice when to be born and when to die. He chose to be my guardian. I agreed to be responsible for his care, and I collaborated with his will about when to die. I did not fail in my role. I suddenly see that everything has free will, not just humans and animals. Every aspect of Creation is an expression of God, so everything must have free will, including rocks and mountains. Yeshua often tells us that the Earth is a Soul who has made her choices, has her own feelings of despair, and is asking for our Love as she goes through her own process of awakening.

I always felt that Cricket chose to be with me — to be my guardian. His guardian energy was powerful. He was a most unusual cat. So I realize this life was indeed *his* choice. Yeshua had said this is a significant loss at this time when I'm getting set to fly. I see that ending his bodily life at this time allows my guardian cat to fly with me as I expand the reach of my work.

I found it reassuring when Yeshua told me that other Beings had been helping Cricket prepare for his passing and that he was ready to go. He had agreed to receive the subcutaneous fluids to stay with me longer, but the needles had become too painful. This treatment had certainly helped him feel better, but it had come to the point that, without daily fluids, he was feeling extremely ill. My cousin Beth was living with me at this time, and she was instrumental in his care. We administered fluids every day for his last two weeks, so he was feeling pretty good at the end. His last two days were perfect. He had exactly what he wanted — my constant company — so he was content. I had been completely calm, just hanging out with my cat, as we had done for over twenty years. But this made letting him go really hard. He seemed just fine, so how could I let the vet kill him? The change was just so sudden — to go from being a sweet kitty who enjoyed my company to being gone, just like that. His body going lifeless was so weird! This little Being who trusted me!

I become distraught with the belief that, after twenty years of care, I had betrayed his trust and killed him. But then I can feel Cricket letting me know the opposite is true. He is grateful he could go out without suffering.

John observes my contradictory beliefs — knowing I cooperated with his will to go, and believing I betrayed him. He points out that I chose to be present at his passing so I could go into the depths of despair, as Yeshua asks us to do. When I go fully into the feelings, I can see I created this experience in order to truly understand that differentiation does not mean separation — all is One with Source. John shares Yeshua's beautiful teaching about the Rays of Light that emanate from Source. Each individuated Ray of Light has differentiations, which the ego perceives as separation, but which Spirit does not. When we see with the eyes of Spirit, we recognize our unity with Source. John observes Yeshua has often spoken to us about death recently. He is helping us to realize the body is a temporary appearance that is not real, while the Light-body is real and eternal. This grieving process helps me strengthen my identification with the Light-body and not the physical body—mine and Cricket's.

I reflect that the ego-mind, which thinks it's separated, experiences it as an unknowable paradox that the Light-body-mind is everywhere simultaneously. John shares Yeshua's teaching that "the body ceases to be a separation device when we experience it in its fullness, which includes the aura. The aura is like the trough between individuated waves. It's the means of connection between Souls. The aura is what we recognize when the feeling of another person comes to mind strongly. Maybe you could practice feeling Cricket's Light-body and know that it's there."

I find this deeply soothing to hear. I am absorbing how beneficial this grieving process is in helping me feel the despair of believing in the illusion of death, and thus decide to let it go. And yet I continue to cry. The grief is holding on to missing the sweetness of my connection with Cricket, how devoted he was to me, and how he would come to find me if I left the room, even when I thought he was asleep. I see my belief that the physical body is required to feel this sweetness. I am reminded of Yeshua telling us recently that Maryam would grieve every time he left her, after visiting in his Light-body. Even though she knew he was absolutely present with her, not in a physical body, she still felt grief when his energy felt less vibrant. By working through this grief, she could release all identification with the body and become fully identified with the Light.

I confront my belief that loving connections depend on bodies, and yet here I am experiencing Yeshua's presence physically—an experience that now feels normal. These cannot both be true, and

I know which is the Truth. I can feel the attachment to the body dissolving. It is just too painful to stay attached to the belief that experiencing Love requires a body. I can feel ego protesting that the Truth is winning. I have a moment of appreciation for the intense difficulty of the process of releasing the ego's foundation. Now I understand why Yeshua told me that grieving is an ongoing lesson.

John reminds me of the time when Yeshua gave me the experience of being in touch with every Soul's lives—past, current, and timeless—simultaneously. I certainly remember! Wham! All connection with every Being, all at once. He said he did that to circumvent the ego-mind and show me this is possible—this universal awareness *is* the experience of being in the Christ-Mind. I see I am letting go of the thought of separate bodies and death, and living in the Truth of Spirit while living in the appearance of this body. I begin to taste liberation!

I have a moment of concern that, if I know my cat's true nature is Spirit, am I not honoring his courage to incarnate? The answer is instantly clear. No. See the body as Light. John observes that this knowing everything is Light was clear to me in Ireland, so much so that he could feel it through me because of our strong connection. I *do* see that I serve as an amplifier. Yeshua's presence comes through me so other people can experience it.

We are getting it! My cat has been a Light-body all along, just masquerading as a cat. The same is true for me, for John, and for all manifested Beings.

John observes that, when he walks out into nature, it is the eternal Light-body that is channeling Love into the Earth, an experience he can feel strongly. It comes to me that this grieving process, by bringing Light through the body and down into the root, where we place shame, has been healing the root of the guilt that comes from believing I separated myself from God.

The Arboretum feels elemental to me—earth, air, fire, water, and living Beings. It is time to head out there to experience the Light of God flowing all the way through me, down into the Earth, and outward to all manifested Creation.

That evening, a sister sent me this note. "Laura, I have just gone through the channeling of April 1st again, and I feel the immense power of it. Thank you for opening yourself to your service through channeling these messages that are so suffused with Love. And a big breath of gratitude for Cricket, and for Cricket's service to you."

Her comment about Cricket's service struck me. He *was* an amazing cat, loving me with the purest of devotions. I think he was able to go because he knew I now knew I am loved with the same pure devotion by Yeshua. Communing with Christ Consciousness felt increasingly normal to me because Christ Consciousness is Reality, not the world of apparent separation that we call 'reality.' The balance between investment in the world of separation and investment in the Reality of Love was shifting, although I certainly still kept a foot in both worlds.

Chapter 16

Lightening Up

Tens of Thousands of Christs

Later in the afternoon of that same day, April 29, 2019, eleven friends joined online to converse with Yeshua.

John gathers us in. "Take in a deep breath, and as you release it, say within your mind, 'I choose to let go and relax.' Then, establish a deep, slow pattern of breathing that facilitates relaxing. I give thanks that Yeshua was coming through both Laura and me during our session earlier today, and that's why it was so powerful. We now invite the Holy Spirit, Yeshua, and the Christ Council here with us. Please realize how vital *our* connection is with Yeshua and the Christ Council. This is what allows our connection with the true Self. As Laura realized, we are all eternal Light-bodies, even though we think we are in a physical body. Receive Yeshua, the Christ Council, and the Holy Spirit into your Light-body." He then leads a lovely guided meditation that brings the Light down through all the chakras.

After our prayer is recited three times, Yeshua begins to speak through my voice. "Please draw your attention to your feet and feel your feet transmitting energy to the Earth. Feel the vibration that is being extended through the soles of the feet, and also through the palms of the hands. Bring your attention to the crown of the head and the third eye, and feel the Light as a powerful electric vibrational current that flows down through your head, through your body, and out through your hands and feet, extending the Love of God outwards, all around you, in all directions.

"Each one of you is a transmitter for God's Love. The more you embrace each of your constrictions and difficulties, hold them in Love, and release them, the clearer a channel you become for this endless flow of the power of God's Love. It may be difficult to understand the importance of the impact of your ability to transmit this power because it is operating at a level that is not seen with the body's eyes, but we assure you that you are vitally important receivers and transmitters of God's Love. We are deeply grateful that you remain willing to attune yourselves to the vibrational level of Christ-Mind. We have told you so many times we are with you always, but we would like you to understand that this means our vibrational power is with you always. When your minds, hearts, and bodies are open to receiving Love, you are synchronizing with our energy, which is the power of Christ.

"We remind you that there is no distinction between Christ and God. There is no separation. Everything God knows is transmitted directly to the Christ-Mind. This is how it is possible for what appear to be individuated minds to access Knowledge from other times and other places because all Knowledge is knowable from any time and place. This simultaneity of time and place is something the ego simply cannot understand, but the Christ-Mind knows it perfectly because the Christ-Mind knows there is no separation between any individuated mind and another one.

"Laura would like you to receive the Wisdom she found this morning, which is that all living Beings—which includes rocks, water, air, insects, microorganisms, plants, animals, and birds—all of them have free will. Why is this so? This is because every expression of God's creative power is intimately connected with God. There is no separation, so it is not possible for an aspect of God's Creation not to have all attributes of God. A rock is an aspect of God's Creation and *must*, by definition, have all of God's attributes, which include all Knowledge, all Wisdom, all Love, all Peace, all Joy.

"This understanding helps you to know that each living Being has free will to manifest and not manifest as it chooses. How could it be otherwise? If it were otherwise, and only humans had free will, then that would mean everything else was a victim of human action, and this is not so. Everything is in an intimate dance with everything else, and because everything is Light, this dance is perfectly coordinated by the Knowledge that resides in everything and is One with God.

"In this way, you can all now understand that everything that occurs in the world occurs by the choice of every Being taking part in that event, including the rocks, water, air, trees, and animals. When you transmit your Love and Wisdom into the Earth, you are helping all Beings to elevate their awareness so they can make choices in line with Love, and not with fear. This is why going out into nature and transmitting your confidence to the Earth is so vitally important. In this way, you are empowering all living Beings to wake up and make the choice for Love and not fear. This includes microorganisms, as well as the eagle and the cat.

"Please notice the pressure in your third eye as this Wisdom is transmitted to you. This Wisdom is being transmitted today to help you understand there *cannot* be any distinction between your experience, your Soul, and the experience and Soul of the rest of Creation. It cannot be otherwise. If it were otherwise, there would be some aspects of God's Creation that had no life, no awareness, no creative power, and this is not possible. The Earth is alive, the rocks are alive. Everything is living.

"When you walk upon the Earth and feel the creative power of the Earth and her rocks and waters, you can feel this through the soles of your feet, and you can feel the celebration of the Communion between your feet and the Earth. Whenever you can, please walk upon the Earth with no shoes on your feet."

Long pause.

"I paused to allow you to imagine yourselves walking upon the Earth, feeling the air and the Sun, and hearing the birds, knowing that, by your willingness, you are transmitting God's Love, and encouraging them all to make choices in Love.

"Please feel how alive your bodies are right now—that your bodies actually are Light. Feel the subtle currents of energy that move through the meridians of your body, some stronger, some not so perceptible, but all operating together. Feel that your Knowledge—that is Knowledge with a capital K, the awareness that is transmitted to you by God—is shared. You may think you are sitting in your chair and experiencing a particular experience in your body, but we assure you that everyone in this circle is experiencing the same things. This does not diminish your experience because now it's not *only* yours. Quite the contrary. It *amplifies* your experience, knowing that the sisters and brothers around the world with you are feeling the power in their hands, feet, root chakra, third eye, crown, and heart.

"All of you are here because your will has made an important determination to be aligned with God's Will, and you have decided to identify yourselves as your true Identity, which is the Child of God. Please rest in the power of this awareness of what you have chosen. You are beginning to understand what I told you two thousand years ago—you are all Gods. When you know this, and you are in a community of Beings who are aware this is the Truth, then your power to transmit Love amplifies.

"You are blessed to be in a time on the planet in which more and more Souls are awakening to the Truth that everything is Love and Light. This allows the energy of fear, which of course, is still manifesting, to be much less dense than it was when I walked on the Earth. Please be aware of the blessing that you are alive at this point in time because you now have the capacity to experience the Light and Love of who you are more easily, and to share that with your brothers and sisters without fear of reprisal.

"This does take getting used to, this awareness of your true Identity. We are *most* grateful you are continuing on this Path of Awareness, looking at every stone you stumble upon, turning it over, seeing what's under there, what it's made of, and then holding it in Love, and asking it to be transmuted.

"Remember our wish for you, that tens of thousands of Christs shall inhabit the planet. We assure you there comes a tipping point when there are enough Christs that the energy is so elevated that those who are still in fear cannot help but be carried away. There is a tipping point that occurs when the power of Love is greater than the power of fear, and the power of fear continues on in smaller and smaller pockets, with less and less energy invested into those pockets, until they simply disappear. We tell you all this to encourage you because there is so much fear and hatred and destruction in the world, that people who are on the spiritual path, who are by nature sensitive, can get drawn into that despair. Each time we meet with you, we encourage you not to get drawn into the despair, please. This is not helpful for you or for any Being.

"In this circle of Love, if you would, each let your mind notice a place in the world where you can see there is fear and suffering. It could be right in your own heart or your own family, or it could be some place that is suffering from the effects of violence and aggression. Hold that place and those Beings—and that means not just human Beings, but *all* Beings, animals, plants, and minerals—in Love and tenderness. Picture that you are all holding hands, and those places in the world that are caught up in suffering can feel the tenderness of this circle of Love.

"Then picture that a great *wind* comes, which is the Holy Spirit, and it blows away all the suffering. Suddenly, the fearful Beings see the Truth, which is that Love was there all along, and all Beings are sisters and brothers and cannot, at the level of Reality, actually harm each other.

"We ask you now to look into your own hearts and see what's there that needs to be brought forward into the Light so it, too, can be swept away, and you, too, can see that all along, it has only been Love that has been the true Reality. When you have found what you would like to bring forward, please do offer your requests and questions."

⁁

Sister One inquires, "I would like to help others in their awakening process, but I fear my power, and I fear my projections onto them, so I get in my own way. Could you help me with this, please?"

"My sister, the energies that come up that you call 'getting in your own way' are the very energies that require your attention before you can be truly helpful. You named two things: the fear of your power, acknowledging that you are a God; and the fear of your projection, which is the fear that you will blame others for your own difficulties.

"Start with being kind and gentle with the energy of blame. That is easier to heal than for the ego to let go of its thoughts of smallness and release its identity, and thereby allow yourself to know that, truly, you are the Christ with the infinite power of God.

"The fear you will cause harm to others is a universal fear in the mind of humanity. It comes from the guilt of having jumped out of the Mind of God, and having that terrible thought, 'Oh no, I'm going to cause harm to myself and others because now I have lost my Source.' The Truth is, you have never lost your Source; and any harm that has come to others has been of their own free will.

"If you could understand just that one Truth—that anyone's experience is of their own free will—then you can be gentler with yourself when you notice you are experiencing a projection. A projection is easily identifiable—it's anything other than Love. Any thought of criticism, or any negative thought or feeling that you have for another, is, by definition, a projection of an aspect of your own thought about yourself. Just work with that practice, my sister, and then your awareness of your power will simply come to you. I will be with you every step of the way. Never fear. You are not alone. Is that helpful?"

"Yes, very much so. I will work with it. Thank you."

⁓☙⁓

Sister Two asks, "I have a book of poems that's waiting to be fully birthed. I feel it calling my heart. But I've had a block of fear around it, so I would like your guidance. Thank you."

"My sister, it takes much courage to put out into the world your Knowledge of your true Identity. To write words that convey the deep Wisdom that has come to your own heart is a public statement that you know you are not a small self. Your fear is that others will interpret this as an ego statement, that you are a grandiose self.

"We say to you, when you know who your true Identity is, then you can let the projections of others, who think you are being grandiose, slide off of you. This is an experience you have also known, as have all Beings—the fear that one is not valuable, and so, therefore, one must become *extraordinarily* valuable. Neither of those extremes is the Truth. The Truth is that you are the Child of God, and you have all power under Heaven and Earth to share the Wisdom that has flowed through your mind and heart.

"When you can understand that, you can simply step into the stream of the living waters of the Mother and let her Wisdom flow through you out into the world. Then this fear of being up on a pedestal or down in the mud will simply evaporate. Is this helpful?"

"Yes, thank you. I feel like I'm moving towards the courage now to step forward and be seen."

"Exactly. It does take courage to step forward and be seen. Just feel all of us with you. It is the collective Wisdom of the Christ-Mind that is flowing through you. We thank you for being a mouthpiece for God's Love. Every mouthpiece for God's Love amplifies the vibrational level of the mind of the Child of God, so we are most grateful for your willingness to take on that role. Our blessings."

Sister Three seeks guidance on decluttering. "I have a problem with possessions. I'm getting older, and I need to downsize for practical reasons, but the clutter around me is holding me back. I could use the space, but I'm finding it painful and difficult to get rid of possessions. Do you have any guidance?"

"This is an extremely helpful question. Those of you in the West have grown up in a world that sees possessions as a symbolic statement of your worth as a person, even though you know this could not possibly be true. When you live in the currents of a world that conveys that possessions reflect worth, it is difficult to maintain your balance, knowing this is not the Truth at all. We suggest to you, my sister, to use this letting go process as an extraordinarily valuable spiritual practice. Each thing has some meaning you project onto it, and so each thing is actually a heart-opening tool.

"Every time you pick up and hold an item in your hand, don't ask, 'Do I want it or not?' Ask, 'What is the *meaning* to me of this? And is there any unhealed *emotion* around this object?' If there is, then ask the Holy Spirit's guidance, or ask a friend to come and listen to you talk about the meaning of that object, until you can see what the projection is, heal that projection, know that you are healed and whole, and no longer need the *object* to have the feeling of completion. This could take a while, so we urge you not to hold clearing out clutter as the goal. Instead, consider it a real blessing that you have all these external symbols of what your internal blockages are. It could not be easier, in fact, because your path is laid out for you among the objects. Do you understand?"

"Yes, thank you."

"Please ask friends to help you, but not friends who are eager to throw things away and tell you, 'Oh, you don't need this.' You know in your heart you don't need it, so that's not helpful. Ask friends who can be loving and patient with you about the *meaning* of each object until you have collected that meaning back into your heart and are no longer projecting it onto the object. We will be with you, holding your hand through this necessary cleansing process. You will find it to be extremely beneficial, and we are grateful to you for embarking on it. Our blessings."

"I'm in the same place as Sister Three," says Sister Four. "I'm really trying to clear out all my collections, so I will take that advice, too. If you have any further advice, I'd appreciate it."

"For letting go of your collections?" Yeshua clarifies. "Ah. Letting go of possessions when you are older means you understand your body no longer needs these possessions. Letting things go when you are older is a courageous and extremely beneficial practice of facing your feelings—and it might not be fear—but lots of feelings about what the world will be like when your body is no longer manifesting in it. This is because your collections will still manifest on the Earth-plane after your body no longer is manifesting. When you hold your collections, you can look forward to the future and see they will continue to exist when it is no longer you holding them. Just notice what you experience with that thought.

"This is like the Buddhist meditation on the dissolution of the body. This is not meant to upset you, but to help you notice where you still have attachments to your identity as a body. Grieving the loss of anything, whether it be a thing, a cat, or your own body, is extremely beneficial to help you see where you are still tied to guilt, shame, fear, and doubt. These are all the things that tie you to the thought that you are a separated self.

"As much as you can through this practice, remember that your true Identity is Light. You may look like a solid body, but we have been practicing with you for months now to help you know, *physically*, that you are actually Light *now*, not just after the dissolution of the body.

"This is an extraordinarily beneficial practice, my sister. Please experience your guides and the Enlightened Ones around you while you do it, holding you up. We admire your courage very much."

Sister Five asks, "I feel a resonance with your guidance around clutter. I'd like your help with removing the resistance to these practices of removing clutter."

"My sister, it will help you to articulate what you think is difficult for you about letting go of clutter. That will help you focus your question on what you need support with."

"When I'm trying to clear things," Sister Five explains, "I continually move things from one place to another place, so they never leave the house."

"So you are having an inner dialogue. There is one part of you that says, 'This should leave the house.' And there's another part of you that says, 'No, it should stay in the house.' Those two parts are simply at a stalemate with each other, and the only solution is to move things from one place to another. I hope you can see the humor in this dance you are doing in your mind.

"The way through this dilemma is to sit in Love with one part of your mind at a time. Start with the part that says, 'This should *leave* the house,' and ask that part to speak. 'What are the reasons for this leaving the house? Why is there such an energy behind, "It *has* to leave the house?" Who says so? Who is being pleased or displeased if this leaves the house? And where do you think the object will go? Where else in the world does it end up? What happens to it?' Ask all those questions.

"And then, when you've heard that part, sit with the part that says, 'No, this object *cannot* leave the house,' and ask, 'What is it holding onto? What does this object mean?' Follow the instructions I gave your two sisters earlier. What are you projecting onto this object that has become a symbol for some part of your feelings of attachment?

"Be gentle and slow with yourself, all of you, in this practice of interacting with things. Any one thing, when fully contemplated, holds the mysteries of the Universe because every *thing* is a miracle. Every *thing* is a manifestation of God! If you truly look at an object deeply enough, your mind will awaken. This is what the Buddha knew when he held up a flower and said nothing. Suddenly, one of his monk's mind woke up because the monk understood that the flower, like anything, was a door to infinity.

"If you can understand that each object has the power to awaken your mind, and not hurry to achieve some kind of outcome, then you can experience this practice as *truly delicious*. It's a portal to the Universe! Please enjoy it. We will be with you, holding your heart in Lightness, and enjoying the humor of you dancing with your objects. You might even pick them up and actually dance around the room, just to experience the humor in the dance in which you've been engaged with your objects. When you can get into that state of Lightness and humor, then you can engage in this practice of asking yourself these two questions: 'Why is it so important this leave?' And, 'Why is it so important that this stay?'

"Please enjoy this practice. We will be with you. Thank you for your question."

☙

Sister Six has a question about recoiling from others' suffering. "It seems the closer those others are to me, the harder it is to be with them when they are in their angst, their depression, or their pain. Any advice?"

"This is an extremely important question, my sister. I refer you to the chapter in *A Course in Miracles*, where I discuss the need to *not empathize* (Diamond Clear Vision 2012, 378). The difference between empathy and compassion is a difficult concept to feel in your heart.

"When you empathize, what you are doing is resonating at the same level of pain the other Being believes they are resonating in. This happens for a simple reason. Any powerful vibration tends to synchronize the other vibrational levels around it. It is through this means that I, as a man, could effect healing because I had an extremely *high* vibrational level (which, by the way, was supported by my family. I could not have done that by myself). But because of my high vibrational level, supported by the Love of so many, I was able to synchronize the fearful vibrational levels of the Beings around me who allowed me to do so. What you are doing, my sister, is choosing to allow yourself to synchronize with the fearful vibrational levels of those around you.

"What will help you are two things. One is to remember what we said at the beginning. Every Being's experience is *their choice*. For those around you who are suffering, please recall that this is their choice to suffer because it is what they *need* to *learn* in order to wake up from their fearful constrictions.

"The other thing that will help you, my sister, is to raise *your* vibrational level *before* you engage with the person at a lower vibrational level by sitting in meditation and feeling the energy of the Christ Council with you. If you feel yourself being pulled down, we suggest that you stand up and stretch, and convey to the person that you love them, and that you need to take a little walk and get some water. Reassure them you'll be back so they don't feel abandoned. But remember, if you do not take a break and raise your vibrational level, you are not actually being helpful to them.

"It's an extremely common problem, especially for sensitive Beings who are attuned to their own feelings and the feelings of others. It might also help you, my sister, to remember this circle of friends and picture them holding your hands. You could imagine the troubled Beings in your life surrounded by this spiritual family, who have such great confidence in Yeshua, the Enlightened Ones, the Angels, and in God. When you bring your awareness to your spiritual family, you will be able to hold your friends and biological family in such great loving power that they cannot help but be affected.

"Thank you for your willingness to reside in Love. Our blessings."

~☙~

A brother asks, "I'm in Israel today and for the next few days. Tomorrow, we're going to the **Mount of Transfiguration**. I wonder if you have any pointers for me when we go there."

"This is *wonderful* that the group is going to the Mount of Transfiguration! That is a powerful and holy spot. Being in that place, it is important that you practice what we have been teaching all along in this group, which is to hold the physical sensation of *being* the vibration of Light. The Transfiguration I demonstrated there was to anchor into the Earth the Truth that all Beings are Light, which is Love. The human Beings who witnessed this Transfiguration were literally blown away by the power of Love pouring forth from the vision of Light before their eyes.

"When you are there, my brother, please keep your feet firmly on the Earth. You might even sit on the Earth, and put your hands on the Earth, so you can feel the Light pouring into your head, down through your body, and into the Earth. With this practice, you will know there is no distinction between your body, mind, the Light, the Earth, and God's Love.

"Returning to this place with this full Knowledge that you are a God will help correct a misperception that occurred there, which was that the Light-Beings were Gods, and the human Beings were not. Now you know that you, too, are a God, and all the Beings with you are also Gods."

Pause.

"We are transmitting to you the power of this Knowledge, so that you are prepared to withstand it when you are in that spot.

"It will feel strange to you that there are some people there who have no idea of the power that exists there. They will think this was an important historical place, but they will not know to feel it in their bodies, that there is a portal to the Light and Love of God. Just hold those Beings who are unaware in Love, and do not let their lack of awareness diminish your awareness of the Truth of the power of this place on the Earth.

"The most important thing for you, my brother, is to release your feelings of unworthiness. This is a chance for you to return to this place in full awareness of your worth. Is this helpful?"

"Yes, very much. Thank you."

"Be aware, as I'm sure you will be, that the great Enlightened Ones will be celebrating because there are humans on that spot who are aware of the Truth of God's Love. You might even see us out of the corner of your eye."

"I'll be watching for that. Thank you."

"Yes. Our blessings."

⟲⟳

Sister Seven shares a fear. "I've been discerning whether to join the group in Scotland, and it has become clear to me that my place is here. And yet it's bringing up a fear of missing out and not being connected with the group. I would love to hear some words about how I can hold space here where I am and maintain connection when the group is there."

"First, my sister, thank you so much for listening to your own heart and knowing what your own path is. Not all Beings are called to be physically present at each spot. I have told you before that the Christ Council works with other Beings around the world, so there are always other gatherings that are happening, of which none of you is consciously aware, though, in your hearts, you are aware. But none of you is called to be at every single gathering where there is a transmission of Light and Love. This is why I have shared with you the image of helping you create a network of stable minds around the world, so that any time there is a willingness to receive a transmission of Light, it is transferred across the network of stable minds as if it were a power grid. Do you see?"

"Yes."

"When you are in a place of stability at one spot in the world, and there is a gathering that is receiving a transmission of Light at another spot, that actually helps to transmit the Love and the Light into the physical location where your body is residing. This happens more so when you are aware of the transmission, but we would like to reassure all of you that this happens all the time when there are other transmissions going on that you are not consciously aware of.

"On the solstice, I have told you at this time there will be a transmission of Love and Light in a place where there is a Womb of Earth that can receive the Light of the Father Sun. This will be a powerful experience for those who are physically present, to feel the Truth that their earthly bodies are suffused with the heavenly power of God.

"Just being aware, my sister, that this is what they will experience will also help you experience this. It will help those gathered in the group to know that there are other Beings around the world who are aware of the purpose of their gathering so that those other Beings can also have this same experience of knowing their earthly bodies are suffused with the Light of God.

"This is what I did as a man. I demonstrated that my earthly body was suffused with the Light of God. I emanated the power of Love that was so great that people were drawn to me in droves. You are all on the path to *also* manifesting this same suffusion of Light into your bodies so that you do not think that there is any distinction between your body and God.

"That is a powerful statement: so you know that there is no distinction between your body and God.

"We are extremely pleased that all of you are on this Path of Awakening and can receive those words, at least at some level.

"Is this helpful, my sister?"

"Yes, immensely, thank you."

Yeshua continues, "We would like to say something about dancing, just for a minute. Dancing is a metaphor for life. The planets dance, the stars dance—their patterns are endlessly shifting and changing—and portals of energy open and close, begin and end, amplify and diminish, allowing certain experiences to become more available or less available. Just by sitting on this Earth, you are in the midst of an extraordinary celestial dance.

"Music is a dance. It's an ongoing pattern of sound that shifts, changes, elevates, and encourages. Art is a dance of infinite varieties of colors and patterns. All human creativity is shifting patterns of Light, Sound, and beauty. It is all a dance. You are all dancing—with the things in your home, with your relationships. We encourage you to notice the Lightness in all your dancing so that you can *enjoy* whatever pattern it is that you are engaged with.

"If there are other questions, we are happy to receive them."

John makes some observations. "I'd like to note that Laura's channelings differ from many other channelings I've seen. First, in the power of what comes through—she described it this morning as little explosions that just keep expanding. I totally agree with that. Also, her face seems to express the mischievous presence of Yeshua that I've heard about through other sources. I really appreciate these channelings for that reason.

"Knowing how powerful they are, I'm going to make a confession. I sometimes wake in the wee hours of the morning, and I can't go back to sleep because my mind is really busy. So I listen again to one of your channelings through Laura. As you have said, the ego can't abide Light for long, so it puts me to sleep. Is that a misuse of your teachings?"

"Not in the slightest. I think many of my students have had that experience of listening to my words—whether it's through a channel or through their own recording of my words—and being able to fall asleep to those words. How can it be a misuse, my brother, to allow the Truth to soothe your heart and allow you to feel at One with God, resting in God's arms?

"And you are correct, that as Laura relaxes further into her role as the servant, I am able to come through more and more with the Lightness of my energy. Her first awareness of my presence many years ago was a feeling of laughter. This energy of laughter is how she knew it was me who was speaking to her. So yes indeed, she is allowing the Lightness of my Love to come through with the humor that I see in all of your lives.

"Now don't take that in the wrong way. I am not laughing *at* you *at all*. I am seeing the beauty, delicacy, and grace of the amazing patterns that you have all created. When you can hold those with awe—that *you have created* all these amazing constructions and can play with them—you, too, will see the humor, because everything is a paradox; everything is a hologram for everything else. Once you see the patterns and the Lightness, then you see the miraculousness of even the tiniest miracle.

"Laura would like to share one of those. She went for a walk right before this gathering and sat in the place where she had the intense experience of the Soul of her cat as the Egyptian Goddess Bastet, the warrior protector. She was sitting there, feeling her unity with the Earth and with all around her, and she opened her eyes and noticed the little blades of grass and her hair were blowing in the wind, which just made her laugh. She knew that her hair and the grass were the same energy. That's an example of what I mean about the Lightness of everything being in a dance, a pattern of energy together.

"Is this helpful, my brother?"

"Yes, thank you very much."

"Are there any further questions?"

No one responds.

"My dear ones, there is quite an energy of excitement in the group today! We are most grateful for the expansion you are willing to participate in. Each stage of your growth means the next stage comes more rapidly, and it can leave you feeling a little breathless. If you do experience breathlessness, slow down, sit, and breathe. We are with you in this process of growth that you are all in together.

"Now, we have been waiting for this moment to tell you that each of you is ready to share more of your Wisdom with more people in your own personal circles. This is how this celestial speedup works. As you each grow in awareness, then it is time for you to share that awareness with those with whom you come in contact. We encourage you to have more courage to share what you have learned through your own personal growth in this Pathway.

"That is enough. Please be aware that, when you have a little sense of, 'Oh, maybe I should say something,' please do say something instead of holding yourself back. You will be pleasantly surprised that people are more willing to hear the Truth because of the expansion in consciousness that is going on around the world. We thank you greatly for being our mouthpieces in each of your locations in the world.

"We are also grateful this group could gather when our sisters and brothers are physically together in the Holy Land. All of you in this circle, if you could for a moment, join together with your sisters and brothers gathered there, and also hold *all* the people in that Holy Land in this circle, and transmit to them the sound of Love. It is through the sound of Love, the vibration of Love, which they will hear even in their sleep, that they will soften their hearts and look upon each other as their own Selves."

Pause.

"Thank you for sending your transmission of Love to the Holy Land, so the fear and constriction there can be released, and the Truth of who you all are, which is the Child of God, and, therefore, Gods, can be known. Remember, all children are the same species as their parents. God begets Gods. Humans beget humans. Do you see? You cannot *not* be Gods! So please enjoy knowing you are all Gods, and knowing we are with you always and we are the *same as you.*

"Please, go out onto the Earth, and this time, don't just walk—skip, hop, and dance!

"And with that, we say, we are with you always. We are holding your hands in the dance, and we will meet again.

"Ameyn. Ameyn. Ameyn."

I can't help but exclaim, "That was fun! That was so much fun! Wow, what beautiful Beings! Have fun going out and singing and dancing!"

Loving Encouragement

I was feeling frustrated with the demands of running a full-time psychotherapy practice, driving to Maine one day every week to help my disabled mother and deal with the enormous complexity of her care needs and living situation, while also engaging in this spiritual service. The structure of my life needed to change! John and another sister were helping with figuring out some new transcription technologies, for which I was truly grateful. There were so many words flowing through me, I couldn't possibly keep up with it all on my own. You have probably noticed that Yeshua's messages are complex and nuanced (with multiple parenthetical phrases), so it has taken much editing of John's drafts and my clarified versions of those drafts to create the readable text of this book.

When I sent out a recent transcript and apologized for the long delay, the tone of this frustration crept into my note. What I received was an outpouring of loving support.

"It was a beautiful and helpful session. I felt a new Lightness coming into us all—the veils of fear are being dissolved. So appreciated, beloved Laura! Holding you in my heart while you attune to Cricket in his beautiful Light-body."

"Thank you so much, Laura. I truly appreciate what you do."

"Thank you so much for the precious and wonderful work you do."

I responded to the group. "Not only are you all most welcome to receive these beautiful teachings, but I am also extremely grateful to all of you for participating in this process with me. We have all clearly been invited to participate, and our energies amplify each other. What an amazing miracle this whole process of waking up is! This is a joy!"

John was certainly feeling the benefits of being present with the channeling process and then working with the transcribing process. "I suddenly understood what Yeshua meant when he said, 'When two or more are gathered in my name, there I am with them.' He has said elsewhere, 'One plus One equals Three.' That has puzzled me, but now I understand it. When we join together in Christ and allow whatever comes up without resisting anything—tears, sadness, grief—then something amazing happens. We experience being One in Christ Consciousness. Ideas suddenly pop into your mind. Where did that come from? Suddenly, I talk about something. Where did that come from? Both of us allow thought to arise from the Christ-Mind. The Mind of Love transforms with Love."

Chapter 17

Creativity Bubbles Through the Community

The Mother-God Delights in Her Children's Self-Awareness

On May 13, 2019, several friends gathered to communicate with Yeshua.

It was not planned, but this is the first time in the opening prayer that *Mother* is added to Father, and *Child* is added to Son. Then, in the teaching, Yeshua discusses the Mother-God.

In the Name of the Father-Mother, in the Name of the Son, the Child of God, in the Name of the Holy Spirit, Sophia, Shem, in the Name of the Lord, Christ I am.

Yeshua begins, "Please be aware of the feeling of the breath. Note every little sensation and morsel of it as it comes in through your nose, to the back of your mouth, down your throat, and into your lungs. Then feel it continue below your lungs, down into your belly, into the root, down the legs, and into the feet. This is possible because the breath *is* the Holy Spirit. The Holy Spirit is the energy of God, and there is nothing in Creation that is not in Communion with God. Feel the breath intimately entering *every* cell of the body. We have spoken before about the intimacy of being known by the Holy Spirit, which is in direct communication with God. You are all known *intimately* by God.

"Now, the ego gets a little nervous when it hears that. 'My secrets are revealed!'—and that is true. But in the Mind of God, the secrets are simply child's play.

"We have spoken to you many times about the great paradox that everything contains everything else. Your great poet, William Blake, spoke about the Universe contained in the grain of sand. This is the Truth. All of you are everywhere, all at once, like your physicists describe about the multi-locality of particles. This is how everything is known, because everything *is* everything else. And because everything *is* everything else, nothing can bring harm to anything else, because there *is* nothing else. When you understand this, not as an intellectual concept, but as a *knowing* in your body, then you are relieved of guilt. This is because not only have you done nothing wrong, but it has never been possible for you to do anything wrong. There is no such concept as right or wrong within the Mind of God. And that is where you all reside—within the loveliness of the Mind of God.

"This is the great liberation from the suffering of separation. It is only the *thought* that you have caused harm that keeps you believing you are separate. Remember, all of Creation *is* God, so no part of Creation can cause any harm to any other part. Therefore, all of Creation has free will, including the rocks and the plants. When you understand this, then you *know* there is no such thing as guilt. This is why this is the great liberation—to understand that you are all the All in All.

"Please bring attention to the crown of your heads and your third eye. As we are sharing this Wisdom, many of you are experiencing a little Light-headedness—pun intended. Notice the Light-headedness you experience as you receive the Wisdom that it is not possible for you to have ever caused any harm because there is nothing that is not *you*. Bring that Light-headedness down into your throat, which will give you the confidence to speak the Truth, and then down into your heart.

"Now we would like you to rest in your hearts for a moment because this is where you actually *feel* this Truth—that you are all the All in All. In your heart, which is the same as the Heart of God, all Beings dwell. There is nothing outside of your heart. If you bring your attention there, you can notice there are subtle currents of energy. Some might feel stronger than others. Each one of you is more or less attuned to other Beings. It is in your heart that you feel their energies. There is no way you could feel their *energies* if they were not also the *same* as you.

"Your energies synchronize with all other energies, and more strongly with those that are close to you, not just in space, but in attachment. Knowing this, it is important for those of you on this Path to bring your consciousness into the Light of Love as often as possible. You are facilitating the synchronizing of the energy of the thoughts of the Child of God to a higher level. We have told you many times that each of you is incredibly important in this process. Every bit of loving energy that is put into the Matrix increases the vibrational energy of the Matrix.

"Visualize for a moment, in your third eye, this Matrix of energy that surrounds the planet Earth. This is what the Hindus and the Buddhists call the Net of Indra. At each juncture point where the threads of the net meet resides an individuated Soul, which means that each Soul is intimately connected with every other juncture point. It is not possible for a Soul to exist on its own because it exists *as* the juncture point of threads of Light.

"We bring this image to your minds so you can really feel, in your bodies, how important it is for you to amplify your awareness that you are a receiver and transmitter of the Love of God as it flows back and forth, in beautiful patterns, around this network surrounding the planet.

"We remind you that you are not alone in this project. The Angelic realms are always singing their harmonies to synchronize the minds of the Child of God with the highest vibration levels possible. We have also shared with you that there are what you would know of as extraterrestrial Beings, who are also sending their thought-energy of Love, Peace, and harmony to this planet. Not only is it not possible for you to be alone as you walk around on your beautiful Earth, but this Earth is also not alone in the solar system or the Universe. The Net of Indra connects all Beings, all rocks, and all stars throughout the Universe.

"Please keep your attention on your heart as we share these images and metaphors with you. Please feel this net of connectivity residing in your heart. Now feel and imagine the energy of that heart center extending downwards through your body and outwards, surrounding you in space. Notice the soles of your feet and the palms of your hands, as they receive your awareness that you are in direct, intimate communication with all other points of Light in the Universe. Notice the crowns of your heads where the Light enters the body. Feel and see it soak down, as if it were an oil that is anointing every cell, seeping downwards through the body, slowly touching every point, every organ, blessing every spot as it soaks through you and dissolves every tension and every resistance to your awareness of the Truth. You *are* the Child of God, and as the Child of God, you are like unto God in every way, save that you did not create your Selves. We have shared before that like begets like. If you are the Child of God, how is it possible that you are not a God?

"Rest your awareness in the lower two chakras, if you would for a moment. We have taught you to bring your awareness there to dissolve the roots of fear and shame that anchor the thought of separation. We started speaking with you today about the impossibility of guilt because it is impossible you could have caused harm to any other part of your Self. This fear of *causing* harm gets projected outward in the fear of *being* harmed. The fear of being harmed resides in the root where the fear of not surviving resides.

"Very often, it is this fear of not surviving that drives people to create children, mistakenly believing that, by having children, they will continue on. Of course, you all continue on—you never began, and you will never end. The mistake is only in believing that you continue solely in physical form on the surface of your beautiful planet.

"Though hard for you to believe, procreation has nothing to do with physical survival. It is about generosity, agreeing to allow Souls to come and express themselves so they can know who they truly are. You have been celebrating what you call your Mother's Day. We have been transmitting to many minds the deeper meaning of Mother's Day. The quality of *mothering* is the quality of God. It is the endless generosity that provides the power of life that allows the Child of God to express him or her Self. It is the quality of having no ego, of expecting nothing in return. It is the quality that God has of delight to see the astounding creativity of her Children. Though it may sound strange to you, God delights every time a Soul turns around and notices she is there, and that she has been there all along, providing you with the power of life. It brings her great joy to have that consciousness returned.

"Again, notice the sensations in your heart when we speak of God's delight in receiving your awareness of her Love. God extended herself into Creation precisely to have this experience of ecstatic joy at mutual recognition. It is in having a Child that the Mother-God becomes aware of her Self. You bring to God a great blessing by becoming aware of your true Identity.

"Bring your attention again to the root, and notice that, when we speak of the ecstatic awareness of God, it always has a sexual quality. We have been teaching that the practice is to *notice* this quality and do *nothing* with it *except* to enjoy it. The ego notices this quality of ecstatic union and believes it must enact it physically. But we are teaching you to *feel* this energetic vibration in the root, and simply enjoy it. You are being tuned up, so to speak, to receive ever more of the ecstatic power of God's Love.

"We have shared with you the metaphor of God's Love being like an electrical force. When this current flows through electrical wires, if you touched the wire, it *would* kill you. Therefore, the towers that hold up these wires must be protected from the current. Where this metaphor needs modifying is to understand that you are not to remain in that protected state of resisting the power of God's Love. Instead, softening your resistance allows more and more of the current to flow through you and down into the Earth, even as it continues to flow across the network — the grid of stable minds, which we have referred to before.

"Please, just feel this energy of God's Love coming through the crown; into the brain, which is probably experiencing pressure; the third eye; the throat; the heart, which is probably experiencing all manner of sensations; the solar plexus, where your decision to align your will with God's resides; the belly chakra, where you know your true Identity, which is the Child of God; and the root, where you feel the creative power of God. Feel those energies flowing out from the palms of your hands and the soles of your feet. Just rest in that for a moment.

"As you rest there, let whatever images come to your mind of places in your body or your mind — which are the same — where you notice a constriction. When you notice a constriction, confusion, doubt, resistance, or fear, please have the courage to bring it forward, put it into your hand, and offer it to the circle. It may surprise you to hear it is a precious jewel because, whatever your constrictions are, your brothers and sisters will most certainly learn from them.

"When you are ready, we are happy to help you dissolve the constrictions in your bodies and minds."

Sister One begins. "I felt a constriction in my heart chakra. I have to decide in three weeks if I'm going to stay in my apartment or not, and where to move if I go. I have a lot of fear around either decision."

"Fear of what the future holds is a universal egoic fear," Yeshua explains. "'If I go in one direction or another, will it be the wrong direction?' It is difficult for the ego to let go and simply trust that each step is revealed. The image that will help you, my sister, is looking for the glow of Light on the horizon. When you cast your eye around in your mind, you are seeing a lot of darkness, representing the fear about which direction to take. But there will be one direction in which there is a slight glow on the horizon. You are learning to trust that this is a beacon that lights your path. It is only dim because the doubt of fear is blocking your awareness of the Light that eagerly awaits, showing you the way. When you see that glow on the horizon as we are speaking to you, please focus your attention on it. Allow it to come towards you until you can see it on your feet. Then notice in which direction your feet are drawn to walk.

"We have been asked before to help with decisions, and our answer is always the same. You have free will, and we cannot decide for you. This is simply impossible because no part of the Child of God is separate from any other part, and so no part can impose itself on another part. The freedom of the Child of God is a universal Truth. You have free will to walk in whichever direction you choose. When you are learning to trust the guidance of the Light, it can feel scary because you are not sure whether that dim glow is actually something you are perceiving, or if you are making it up. But if you look around the horizon, you will keep noticing there is one spot that is brighter. You are not making this up.

"Laura would like to share with you that part of how she trained herself to become able to receive our words was by trusting the images that came into her mind. She realized she was seeing things that were directly relevant to the people with whom she was communicating.

By this, she understood her mind was not separated from those with whom she was communicating. This is also true for you. When you see the glow of Light, it is to help you understand that your mind is not separated from the Holy Spirit.

"Is this helpful?"

"Yes, thank you."

"Please go forth with our blessing."

"I can feel quite a block in my throat," says Sister Two, "and this is affecting me. I wondered if you could speak to that."

"My sister. First, we would like to thank you again for your devotion. Your devotion is most sincere. Your devotion has been sincere for lifetime after lifetime after lifetime. We share with you our awareness of your devotion to help you understand that you can have confidence in your *Self.* This devotion can only come from your decision to reside in your heart.

"Please notice your heart. In your heart is an endless pool of Love. Sometimes you look into that pool and you see beauty reflected back. Other times, you look in and you imagine there are creatures in the depths that would scare you. It is those moments when your throat closes up because you are afraid to cry out with the fear of what you have seen. But we share with you that, though your power to imagine anything is infinite, those monsters in the deep are simply images your mind has projected. They cannot actually hurt you.

"If you would, look into the deep recesses of this *beautiful* pool in your heart, and think of it as an ocean of Love that is waiting for you to explore. Take us with you. Take Yeshua with you. Take Maryam with you. Take Mother Mary with you. Take your guides, your Angels. We will go with you and look at the beautiful creatures you have created. Each one of them simply wants your attention. Each wants to speak. When you feel us with you, and you find one of these deep-sea creatures, feel us holding you. Feel your first reaction of recoil, and then notice we are laughing—in no way *at* you, but at the beauty and delight of your creation! Then explore whatever this thought or feeling or image or idea is, until you can see that it is made only of Light, and has no substance. It can run off in whatever direction it would like to go.

"It will help you, my sister, if you have a friend to whom you can describe each of these creatures as they come up from the depths. You might even draw them on a piece of paper—little magical creatures from the depths with interesting eyes and tentacles, as if they were child's play. You might even put them into a book and give them each a name. *The Sea Monsters That Scare Us.* We are rather enjoying this idea. Many people would benefit from your loving description of the monsters that all humans hold in the depths of their hearts.

"Is this helpful?"

"Exceedingly, thank you. Really helpful. I really look forward to it. Thank you."

"We look forward to your book! We love you very much. Your devotion is always returned."

"And I love you, thank you."

〜❦〜

Sister Three shares a recent experience. "When you spoke of the Love of God flowing through the heart, I noticed a kind of hardness, a closing in, almost like claws around the heart. I don't want this to be there. I want to be open to the Love of God. And yet it's familiar, these claws around my heart."

"My sister, you phrase this in a useful way: 'It is familiar, and I don't want it.' This is true for every Child of God. Every place of fearful constriction is familiar. The fear of letting go of what is familiar is, at first, more fearful than entering the vast field of creative potential. That feels disorienting to the ego. Just those words are terrifying—*the vast field of creative potential.* 'What do you hold on to? Who are you? Where are you? What could happen? You could be buffeted about anywhere on the currents of the power of the vast field of creative potential!' You see how the ego hears those words.

"This is to help you have compassion—*all* of you—for why you hold on to your constrictions. This also helps you understand why we never *blast* you into awakening. If you touched a high-voltage wire, it *would* kill you. So we do *not* force you to release your familiar constrictions. We only offer you the Love that you need to feel so you can lean back a little, feel the arms that are holding you, uncurl one of those talons, and see what happens. Does the heart bleed? Is there grief? There are most likely many lifetimes of trauma.

"All of you have experienced painful things, and the heart recoils in reaction to the grief. This reinforces the belief that you are separated, and that loss is possible. My sister, you have come far enough that your intellect understands loss is not possible because all is the All in All. However, the *grief* of the *belief* in loss *must be experienced*.

"Most of you know Laura lost her beloved cat not three weeks ago. She was open with you that she grieved *ferociously* for two weeks, crying every moment that she could cry. What came to her is the understanding that *everything* is God, and *everything* has free will to come and go as it pleases, including her cat.

"So you, my sister, are entering a phase of feeling grief. The claws around your heart are an attempt to protect yourself against feeling grief. Grief is a powerful energy; of that there is no doubt. But we have told you over and over to feel fully *every* feeling. 'Blessed are those who fully feel their deep, inner emotional turmoil.' [He is referring to the second Beatitude, Matthew 5:4.] When you allow yourself to *fully feel* your deep emotional turmoil, then it can drain away out of your heart, and each talon of the claw can let go.

"It will help you, my sister, to have various methods of approaching this grieving project. It will help you to journal. It will help you to sit in water, which feels soothing. It will help you to speak with friends. It will help you to sit in meditation and feel our arms around you.

Chapter Twenty in *A Course of Love* is a most exquisitely *beautiful* chapter that describes being held in the arms of Yeshua, which is, of course, the entire Universe (Perron 2014, 137). Please read that chapter, and keep rereading it until you *feel* and *know* that you are *always* held by our Love.

"Is this helpful?"

"Yes, thank you."

"Our blessings. We are always with you."

Sister Four says, "I would like to get some help with all the anger that's coming up at the moment, which I'm not complaining about because I've asked to feel it, and everything was quite suppressed. What is the best way for me to be with it? It doesn't seem to be about anything in particular, but when I get stressed, I feel this anger energy."

"My sister, thank you for your courage in bringing this forward. The anger energy is intense. You might have noticed Laura's body recoil when you first spoke. Please do not feel offended by that reaction. We wish to convey to you our admiration that you are allowing yourself to feel this anger.

"Anger is invaluable because it shows you that which you believe is unfair. There is always a feeling of, 'This should not be so!' When the anger does not seem to be directed in any specific direction, it is because it comes from a deep root. The Soul is saying, 'It should not be so that we are separated from God! How is it possible that we are separated from God? This is not right!'

"My sister, take a deep breath. We refer you to what we said at the beginning. In the Mind of God, the concept of *right and wrong* does not exist. It is *meaningless*. It is not *wrong* that the Child of God experiences herself as separated from God. It is simply an adventure chosen of free will. Your anger, paradoxically, shows that you can see the gates of Heaven, and you are *angry* that everyone cannot simply walk through those gates.

"My Child, this is because you have chosen to stay outside of the gates. You have a mistaken belief that it is your responsibility to collect all the Souls so they can be ready to enter that gate. In fact, *this* is the lifetime in which you release that belief. This anger is your *sign* that you are ready to let that burden *go*. Each Child of God has free will. And each Child of God, remember, is in intimate communication with God; so each Child of God is given *exactly* what they need to continue on their path Home.

"You are a great beacon, my sister. We have shared with you before that your Light stands tall and shines out in many directions. You are able to do this because you *do* know who you *are*. The only thing for you to do, to walk into the gates of Heaven yourself, is to release this belief that it is your responsibility to stand *still* so that all the Souls can come and gather around the Light *first*, *before* you enter the gate.

"As Yeshua, I would like to remind you that, as a man, I did *not* wait for all the Souls to join with me in Heaven. I walked on the Earth, knowing I was walking in Heaven. As a man, I *knew* people did not understand me when I said, 'The Kingdom of God is laid out upon the Earth and yet men do not see it.' [He is referring to the Gospel of Thomas, Saying 113.] But that did not mean that I held my *Self* back from walking in the Kingdom.

"My sister, please walk with me in the Kingdom. Please take my hand, and let go of the thought that it is you who must remain steadfast to help everyone find their way Home. I remind you that you *know* that *I* have remained steadfast, and yet I am not in a body on the Earth. So, this is also for *you* to do. I have shared with my students before that you should, 'Go and do likewise,' [He is referring to Luke 10:37 (NIV),] by which I mean, *become* the Christ, in your body, on the Earth. In that way, you will be walking in the Kingdom. Is this helpful?"

"Yes, that is so beautiful. Thank you."

"We delight in welcoming you Home, my sister. You have been *such* a devoted servant. It is with deep appreciation and gratitude that we hold your hand. We are with you every step and are delighted that you are releasing this burden. We have shared with you before the image of it being a heavy cloak that you can *drop* off your shoulders. Just leave it on the ground."

"Thank you."

"Our blessings."

Sister Five is curious. "I've loved listening to everyone's questions and the responses because they all feel familiar! I have a high curiosity. It's wonderful fun, and it takes me in a million directions. It's like ADD [attention-deficit disorder] on steroids. All I want to do is something else, and then something else—meditation, mindfulness, literature, exercise—there are so many different things I'm interested in, but I can't stay in any one direction. When I heard other people talking about emotions like grief or anger that are under our habits, I wondered, is this scattered curiosity actually a cover for a deeper feeling that I should pay attention to? I long for a place to land."

"What an excellent question! This sense of jumping around from one jewel of spiritual Wisdom to the next is what I call *spiritual ego*. This has always been hard for my students to hear because the ego is subtle and will grab onto the higher realms because that improves its image. But I *assure* you, my sister, that you have learned *much* in all of your seeking.

"The key for you, at this moment, is to understand you have an identity of being a *seeker* and never a *finder*. The ego likes to be a seeker. It is *so* exciting—ADD on steroids, as you put it. There are *many wonderful jewels* around the world awaiting discovery. It is *very* difficult to simply sit *still* and know the *Truth*—that the Universe resides in your *heart*, and that you *need do nothing*. You've heard that before. [He is referring to *A Course in Miracles*.]

"My sister, I ask you to try on this idea. Let go of seeing yourself as a *seeker*, always looking for the next answer, and bring your identity *back* into your heart. It has been scattered and projected outward into many different *beautiful* places. But this is a subtle ego maneuver to keep you from noticing that you are not allowing yourself to know the Truth—you are already *found*. You have never been lost. Try knowing the Truth: 'I am found. I am Home. I have never been lost. My Soul resides in God, and it has always been so.' Try resting in that Truth and just seeing what happens. Then you are most welcome to explore any beautiful jewel that crosses your path, but you will come from a different place. You will *know* you are the Child of God, and that jewel does not contain any Wisdom. The Wisdom resides in your own heart.

"Is this helpful?"

"Yes, thank you."

"We enjoy your enthusiasm, my sister. You are such a bright spark. Your enthusiasm attracts many people. When you are confident in your true Identity as one who has been found, you will also be able to help other people know that this is the Truth of themselves as well. Please go dancing with our blessing.

"In this pause, we ask all of you to be *acutely aware* of your *physical sensations*. Whatever you are experiencing, please trust there is *meaning* in those sensations. It is not a random chance that a point in your body feels electric, uncomfortable, in pain, pressured, expansive, or grounded. There are many possible subtle variations of energies that can be experienced in the body. We ask you to become attuned to these sensations. It is *in the body* that *knowing* that you are the Child of God is experienced. It is not an *idea*. That idea is helpful, but that is not how you *know* you are the Child of God. It is experienced *physically, in the body, as energy*."

Sister Six asks about fear. "My mother is having major surgery this week. She is a healthy, vibrant person, and this is the first time I've ever had to face her mortality. I have been feeling a lot of fear in my body. I have recently become aware that *really* feeling the fear in my body is a gateway for me to embrace the unknown. Could you say more about that?"

"Yes, my sister, this is *just* what we were teaching. You are understanding it *very* well, experientially. It is also what Laura has shared with the group—that physically experiencing the *grief* of her cat's loss allowed her mind to expand into a *much* greater awareness. By physically feeling *all* the fear, anxiety, worry, Love, compassion, tenderness, and anything else you are experiencing regarding your mother, you are telling yourself that you do not believe you need to resist anything. It is that message to yourself, that you are no longer interested in resistance, that will allow you to move forward quickly on your path. You will experience a quicker unfolding of changes in your awareness, body, and life. You have much creativity, my sister, and this knowing that resistance no longer holds any *meaning* to you will allow your creativity to flow unimpeded.

"Your mother's illness is a great blessing to you because the *mother* is the vehicle through whom you have manifested on the Earth, and so there is a strong attachment to the mother. There is the fear that, if one *loses* one's mother, one is cut adrift and lost in space. My sister, you *know* that this is not possible. So you can hold that fear—'Oh, no! If something happens to my mother, I am lost!'—with *deep* tenderness. Of course, the fear of being lost without one's mother would arise while embodied as a human. And then notice the deeper Truth in your heart—that you *feel fully*, my sister, this is not an idea for you, this is a *knowing*—that your very *Being* is embedded in *the Mother*, the Matrix, the Primordial Source, from which all Creation arises. You do not have fear about being connected to that Primordial Source. You have come so far that you retain your individuated awareness *while* you experience your connectedness to that Maternal Source.

"So, to help you and help your mother, hold her hands, and in your mind's eye, be aware that *both of you* are connected to that Maternal Source. Then, if you are interested and it feels right, you can allow whoever else you would like to come into your meditation. Be aware that all Souls reside in that Matrix, that Maternal Source. Do you see where the word *Matrix* derives? It *is* the Divine Feminine.

"My sister, just let your feelings flow through, and then let the creativity that comes quick on their heels also flow through. We delight in your *expansion*."

"Thank you so much."

"Thank you for your courage and your willingness to 'go with the flow.'"

❧

"Again, notice your body. Notice the pattern of vibration. What is flowing? What is tingling? Where might there be a gap with no energy? Keep practicing your awareness of this subtle flow. We would like to bring your attention to your heart and the subtle flow of energy in the heart, which, when you can feel it, is like a bubbling spring welling up from the Earth. When you are identified as the Child of God, which is but Light and Love, then it is from the physical chakra of the heart that Love is extended outward, projected onto the world, and reflected back to you. Experience for a moment, if you would, the *feeling* of the projection of Love from your heart chakras. Please be aware that the chakras are on both sides of the body, so the extension of Love comes from the heart on the front and back, the left and right.

"Picture that Love surrounding you, and being reflected back to you in the experiences of your life. It is great fun when you understand how to be the master of your own Soul. You have been creators, but *unconsciously* so. You are now becoming more *conscious*. Just notice the Love being reflected back to you as you become aware that *you* are the creator of your life's experiences. The ego wants to grab onto that and say, 'Oh, wow! I'm powerful and special!' Just notice if that thought has arisen.

"Remember the image shared before, that the Soul is forever in Oneness with its Source, which is God. The ego has only been looking outward and seeing the projection of separation. But as you return Home and bring your focus inward, then you can see through the illusion out the back, where your connection with God has always remained unimpeded. This is a great delight when you realize that this has been so all along.

"Dear ones, are there any other concerns or questions?"

John joins in. "When you asked us to pay attention to the body, I noticed sensations in the heart and in the belly chakra. Since I was twenty, I've had a heart murmur, and atrial fibrillation has increased over the years. I can shut things off so I don't feel them, but the fibrillation is back strongly now. I would be happy to hear what the message is in the heart and the belly."

"My brother, in this lifetime, you have decided to expand all constrictions around your heart. You are aware of the constrictions of the previous lifetime. You are also aware of the great expansion of Love that you knew very well in that lifetime. You made a commitment in this lifetime to drop the constrictions of Love around your heart. It is simply uncomfortable to feel that expansion. We are resting with you in supporting your sense of peacefulness as those energies dance in your heart. When you can feel these expansions as Peace, then your heart will beat smoothly. It's as if you are unsure if you deserve to experience this expansion. We assure you that you do.

"You have spent several lifetimes within organizations in which you were told how to behave yourself. In this lifetime, and at this stage of your life, you are completely free of any restrictions whatsoever on how to behave. It is this shock that you need no restrictions whatsoever that your heart is experiencing as a slight adjustment. Just rest in knowing you are *perfectly* free.

"The belly is your knowing who you *are*, my brother. You definitely know you are the Child of God. The belly is the chakra in which your identity resides. You *know* that *who you are* is the Light of God. Enjoy the confidence you have in your knowledge of who you truly are.

"Is this helpful?"

"Yes, delightfully so. Thank you."

"We delight in your delight."

Sister Seven asks, "I experience a sensation that runs from the bottom of my right ear down my neck. It's a feeling on the surface, almost as if someone were there, pushing on the edge. Is there a message there?"

"My sister, there is a Soul there who is whispering in your ear. This Soul is one of your female ancestors whom you do not know well. She sees you are open to receiving her communication, and she would like to know she has not been condemned. You do not need to know her story. You can easily tell her she is not condemned. Hearing these words brings her relief. She has feared she has done something unforgivable, but because she is drawn to you, this means that, in her heart, she knows she can release this guilt. She's coming to *you* because you are in her biological family, so she feels she has permission to contact you. Because of her shame, she needed to choose a Soul whom she felt she was justified in contacting. Please reassure this woman of what we have taught you at the start of our session today—it is actually not possible to do anything wrong. Reassure her that she is a Child of God who has simply been caught up in her perception of fear. Because she is contacting you, *you* can convey to her your confidence that you know she's aware that she is Love.

"We are grateful to you that you have been willing to experience this sensation and not resist it. She will reside with you only a little while longer because she is even now receiving this message. Thank you for your willingness to bring this forward."

"Thank you for the help."

━━━⊙⊙━━━

Sister Three has another question. "I have not had a cold in two or three years, but I am experiencing one now. It feels symbolic of something. Do you have some guidance for me?"

"My sister, what is *your* sense of the symbolism?"

"I feel it has to do with my emotions. Perhaps it's this grief you have told me about several times."

"Yes, my sister. Colds are associated with sadness. When the body cries, it produces tears and mucus, and when the body has a cold, it likewise produces tears and mucus. You are allowing this to come to the surface. It's as if your unconscious is saying, 'I won't allow you to avoid this, this time. You are *going* to experience this! You cannot avoid this grief by going into your intellect,' which, as you know, is your habit. By experiencing the grief symptoms as a cold, the deeper levels of your mind-body are making sure that you experience this *physically*, and not as an intellectual awareness process. We asked you to say *your* understanding so that you could *know* you *can* trust your own knowing.

"Is this helpful?"

"Yes, it is. Thank you."

"Our blessings."

━━━⊙⊙━━━

Sister Five speaks up again. "My oldest daughter is at the fertility clinic this afternoon for her first attempt at getting pregnant. How do I help welcome whoever may be coming?"

Yeshua laughs. "My sister, you do not need any help welcoming a new Soul! You have such a vibrant joyfulness that whichever Soul has chosen to join your family, you will find great delight in them. Your confidence in your daughter's confidence in *herself* and her *willingness* to take on this mothering devotion is extremely beneficial to her. She is fully aware it is a conscious choice to become a mother.

It is in that *initial consciousness* that the child she will bring forth will already have a *high* level of vibration. Many Souls, as you are all perfectly aware, come through to parents who are not conscious about allowing for the passage of a new Soul. But your daughter is *fully* conscious that she is *choosing* to be the passageway for a new Soul. This creates a *high* level of vibration for this Soul. Please, just *enjoy* the celebration! This Soul will be welcomed into a family that has a great power of forward motion. This Soul will be a great *blessing* to the Earth. Thank you, my sister."

"Thank you."

Yeshua continues. "We are aware of a bubbling energy in the community today. You have all come quite *far* and are *keenly aware* that the power of *God* is flowing through you and out into the world. You are each bringing forth such beautiful creations. Each one of you is *well aware* of your creations. And you have each released the thought that your creation is not as valuable as somebody else's creation. You are *aware* that whatever form of creation is given to *you* is *perfect* and will touch *exactly* who it needs to touch. Many of you are writing books, drawing pictures, taking photographs, or fostering the birth of children. There is *much* creativity going on in this community.

"We would like to speak for one minute about the *fear* in the world about the impending death of the Earth. *This will not occur.* Your Love and devotion to God, and to express God's Love out into the world, is what will prevent the death of the Earth.

"Now, we do not mean to say that it is *only* this community. We have shared *many* times that the Christ Council works with awakened Souls all around the planet. This same bubbling creative energy is happening, even as we speak, everywhere around this beautiful Earth. It is that power of the creative Love force coming through each one of you that extends even to Souls who are not aware of where their Source derives. Those Souls take that energy and find amazing ideas about how to create alternatives to plastic, create energy that doesn't destroy the Earth, form communities that honor every Being, and allow women to produce children only when that is the correct choice. All these things come through the power of Love. And through you expressing your creativity, those other minds receive the power of Love, even though they are not aware that this is the Source of their ideas. It does not matter whether they are aware. What does matter is that all the Souls who are aware they are in *direct* communication with God are extending God's Love out into the world.

"We delight in closing our communications with you, as *always*, with the *exhortation* to please go out and *walk* upon your beautiful Earth. You have been feeling the energetics of God's Love in your bodies. Please go out and put your feet on the Earth. Walk, skip, hop, run, stand still, and channel the Love of God down to the Earth.

"We remind you that we have told you this before—the Earth is a Soul. Nothing in Creation can be outside of God. The Earth is *very much* a living Being, and she receives your Love and confidence with *gratitude*. She *soaks* it up. This gives her the power to transform and transmute whatever difficulties the fearfulness of the Child of God has imposed upon her. We remind you she has received those impositions *willingly*. The Earth is not a victim of the Child of God. The Earth is also an aspect of the Child of God. She has agreed to *allow* herself to receive the fearful inputs from the human form of the Child of God so that the human form could use her bounty as a stage on which to play out its fearfulness and return Home. The tipping point has occurred, and the Child of God is returning Home. In this confidence, the Earth also is returning Home.

"Please, go out onto the Earth, and share with her your *adoration* for her creative beauty. Those of you in the Northern Hemisphere are delighting in the beauty of spring. Please take us with you, because we do delight in experiencing your sensory perception of the smells, sounds, and feelings of Earth, and the flowers and birds.

"We would also like to share with you that many animal Souls have been joining this communication. They have periodically appeared in Laura's mind. While they had nothing to say, we would like you to know the animal Beings have been partaking of this community's Love.

"With those words, please go out onto the Earth—skip, hop, dance, and sing a song. You know by now that we are with you, *always*. You feel us as the vibration of Love in your bodies. When you feel those sensations we have been asking you to feel today, *know* that this is the Council of the Christ-Mind in your body.

"And with that we say, fare well in your travels on the Earth.

"We love you. We adore you. We are with you *in all ways*.

"Ameyn. Ameyn. Ameyn."

John sent me a note right after this gathering. "Thanks for another amazing session. You make it look so easy and natural."

When I watched the video of this session all the way through, without being distracted by working on the transcript, I felt such Love for the true Self's beauty, which I could see clearly, with no egoic filter of judgment. I had never felt such tenderness towards myself before, but watching my face express these extraordinary words so joyfully moved me to a place I have only allowed myself to feel towards others.

My friend John Krysko sent me this note. "Yes, the teaching of the true Matrix, the Divine Mother. I am delighted to see your sharing of this. This is essential to my path also, to help with leading us back to that Garden of the Mother."

One sister wrote, "Wow, that was a powerful session on Monday! I really felt the energies, and my heart was opened wider and filled full. I couldn't get to sleep for quite a while! The next day, up came some of the constrictions made *visible* from the effect of the Light. Yeshua had spoken about how it is impossible for us to harm another part of our One Self, which highlighted my belief that *I have done something wrong*, a sense of having failed God, and that I can cause hurt or harm. It was deep, uncomfortable, emotional pain, but also deeply healing."

Another sister wrote, "Thank you so much for your channeling last Monday. It is all so beautiful. I find it hard to describe how grateful I feel for what you are doing."

And this from a sister who had newly joined the group: "Thank you so much for your devotion to feeling Love's presence. This is truly an extraordinary opportunity, and I am so grateful to be a part of it. I am especially grateful for the energetic help we receive during the session. Thank you for your beautiful intentions and for your desire to commune with Yeshua. It is uplifting all of us!"

Rest and Restore

As had now become our pattern, John and I met to converse with Yeshua the following week, May 18, 2019.

After our prayer of alignment, we started with a question about guidance for me through this intense process. While I was now fully engaged with welcoming friends into a circle to give them the opportunity to speak easily with Christ Consciousness, I was still doubting if I were even experiencing it.

Yeshua begins. "Today, I would like you to relax. You have been putting *much* effort into your service as my servant. While I appreciate your willingness to be the vehicle for my Voice on the Earth, it is most important for you to relax into my arms and trust that you are held, and every step is guided. Please trust that you are loved and you *are Love*. When you can relax, lean back, and feel held and loved, then you know that any fear arises for the sole purpose of showing you that it has been lurking in the shadows, and it is time to release it with your blessing.

"I often needed time to relax, withdraw, rest, recharge, and return to full awareness of my union with our Mother-Father-Source-God-

Creator-**Abba-Abwoon**—whatever word you would like to use—not because I had lost faith, but because I needed to feel that energy as the *only* energy available with no distraction.

"It takes courage to walk out in the world in the Christ-Mind. But as we've discussed before, when any negative energies are sent *towards* you, it is in direct reaction to the power of Love that other people are feeling coming *from* you. It has nothing to do with the power of Love being a problem or causing a problem. It is the energies of *fear* being *aware* their time is limited because the energy of Love *challenges* the energy of fear. Not belligerently, but it challenges the validity of its existence. The fear knows it has no validity and does not actually exist, so the energy of Love is a challenge to its very existence. This is why negative reactions are triggered in those around you. It is important to see them for what they are, and not receive them as anything that is useful to you as feedback. They are not statements about the validity of what *you* are doing when you are resting in Love.

"I have often told you I was only able to do what I did because I had the support of my extended family. They understood what I was doing to varying degrees, but they all supported me. My arrival had been prophesied, and they knew I was the Messiah. So even if they did not understand what I was doing, they supported my work. In this way, I was able to maintain full awareness of Christ Consciousness.

"You are doing the same, where you are walking in Christ Consciousness with the support of your spiritual family, who sees who you are and recognizes the value of what you are offering to the world. You are very courageous in doing this, just as I was courageous. You have a choice, always, but it is also ordained. This is the path you chose before you came into this life, knowing this time was a context that would support you. This is the lifetime in which you face many fears from previous lifetimes where you also stepped forward and encountered so much resistance that you were even killed.

"This is why you are so nostalgic for life in the cloister—because you were *safe* there. Bring that energy of safety into your current life, and imagine your spiritual family as the family of nuns who surrounded you then, who admired you, supported your leadership, admired your intellectual ability, your proficiency with languages and music, your encouragement of their own talents, and your valuing of them as women. It is easy to see why you have nostalgia for that life.

"Now it is time for you to create that same energy around you, but out in the world. This is why the community is in various places around the planet, and not right around your home, so that you will know this community is extended and integrated around the world, and not isolated from the world.

"There is no way to do the work you are doing without it being a risk. There is no way for you to do this work without stirring up fearful reactions from some people. Your task, or practice, is simply to observe those reactions, knowing they are coming, and not take them on as truth.

"One friend in this group is in a struggle with her own reaction against the Truth you are bringing forward. She knows it is the Truth. There is no doubt in her mind. There is also a fearful part of her being stirred up that is not quite ready to let go of its power to create the experience of suffering, which seems to grant her a sense of legitimacy. It is nothing that needs to be a concern for you. There is no harm in contacting her or not contacting her.

"It is most important for you to rest. Do not push yourself in your role as the servant of God. It will be beneficial for you to find a place on the Earth this afternoon in the Sun and simply go to sleep. There will be Earth Angels who will restore you. That is sufficient for now.

"Are there any other questions?"

John asks about negativity. "Yeshua, once you told me that ego likes to use negativity as a bargaining chip. How might that be playing out with this friend? Also, how might it be playing out with

Laura in her conversation between doubt and *eager* commitment? And where might it be playing out with me in this nostalgia with my cousin, whose wife may be in her last days? My cousin appears to be going rapidly downhill himself. I would welcome anything you have to say."

"'The ego likes to use negativity as a bargaining chip,' is a useful phrase," Yeshua replies, "because negative experiences feel quite real and are strong indeed. The ego points to them and says, 'Look at that. This is how you know you are alive! Look at the intensity of these feelings! If you let go of all that, it would be disrespectful of your relationship with your cousin, his wife, your cat, your friend! If you let go of the grief, hurt, and anger, then it would be like saying those people and Beings do not matter because you have no feelings about them!' And so the ego tries to convince you to hold on to the belief in loss.

"But I say to you, when you allow yourself to fully feel the nostalgia, the preparation for loss, you will learn how the ego functions in time. To the ego, every day is nostalgia. Yesterday has gone. You did wonderful things yesterday, and it is gone. Each moment is a loss of the moment before, so the ego is in perpetual loss. The only way to let go of this constant state of loss is to *be* in the Kingdom. In the Kingdom, there is no time. Nothing is lost and nothing is gained because All is All. It is ceaselessly unfolding in a pattern of Light, color, joy, music, celebration, and Love. In this ceaseless unfolding, everything evolves into everything else. Nothing is lost, including your own consciousness, so you retain awareness and are able to experience all of this in *ecstatic amazement*.

"My friend, it is only from that perspective that you can let go of the nostalgia for the past, or the loss of the apparent power of negative energy. At the end, it does just take a leap, not of faith, but of *knowing* that *all* the experiences you have had that show you the way towards God are the Truth. At the final moment, it is simply a decision that *anything* of ego has no interest. Yes, the ego has this bargaining chip quality. 'Are you *sure* you want to let this go? It has brought you a feeling of power. It has given you a sense of value in your relationships and your experiences. Are you *sure* you want to let that go?' And at the final moment, you will say, 'Yes, because I have had enough experiences to tell me I am losing nothing and gaining everything.'

"Is this helpful?"

"Yes, thank you. Delightful. Wonderful."

"We delight in helping the both of you. We do *very* much understand the delicacy of this stage of your journeys. You are both close to being at Home in the Queendom, and so the snares of ego become subtler and harder to notice when you are tripping on them. You have a sense you are being tripped up, but it is hard exactly to discern what has caught your toe.

"We are holding you. Feel our arms and energy at your elbows, literally holding up your body, cushioning your feet, so you can really trust the only thing that is true is the Truth, which is Love, Union, Communion, intimate Knowledge, and ecstatic Awareness. Imagine yourselves being held up, so it is just your toes that are delicately dancing along on the Earth. Then imagine you can fly and extend your awareness anywhere you would like on the Earth because you know truly who you are, and there is no need to be afraid of becoming disoriented. This is a glimpse of the next step for you on your journeys. What is most important now is to rest in the feeling of being held in the arms of Love—and not just when you are lying down, but also when you are walking. Please have that feeling of resting in the arms of Love."

"Thank you for the reminder to re-read Chapter Twenty, *The Embrace*, in *A Course of Love*," John responds (Perron 2014). "That brings forth that feeling better than anything from any other source I've found, so thank you for that."

"Yes, it is beautiful. I am extremely grateful to my channel for being *so* openhearted that she could *feel* the vibration of those words and write them down."

Pause.

"We are enjoying simply resting with you in this moment in which there is nothing to do, nowhere to go, no obligation calling. We know Laura will be Sufi dancing this evening, so please be aware we are with you. It is one of our great delights to do circle dancing. Are there any more questions?"

"Recently," John continues, "while I was lying on a mat that creates a soothing current, I noticed some negativity in my thoughts and feelings, and then I remembered, 'That's not the Truth at all.' And then these loving ideas dropped in, and I recognized, 'That's not me, that's coming from Yeshua and the Christ Council,' because they were positive and loving, as I would like to be all the time. Are there ways to encourage my mind to allow the dropping in of your thoughts of Love? Any input about the mat?"

"I do have *one* thought for you. Those thoughts *are your thoughts* because there is no separation between your mind and the Christ-Mind. To think of thoughts of Wisdom as coming from a deeper Source *is* helpful at first, but the more you listen and attune yourself to that level of awareness, the more you realize that this is *who you are.*

"It is perfectly fine to use any tool that is helpful for anyone to release their constrictions so they can hear the Holy Spirit that resides in their own mind. Some people require additional outside input than others because they have a certain vibrational energy in the body-mind that is *sure* of its identity and is reluctant to change patterns. A tool that helps shift vibrational patterns to create more open portals in the mind is definitely helpful for some Beings. It is not necessary for every Being. You, my friend, could enjoy playing with the mat, but it is not necessary. Your body-mind energetic pattern is not so rigid that it requires that kind of outside input. You have inside output!

"The one thought I shared at the beginning is the one thing to know. The *inside* energy that you already have, which *is* the Holy Spirit, *is you. That is your Identity.* As the Child of God, you *are* the Christ. Your awareness *is full awareness.* There are only some vestiges of constriction that keep you from *owning* that Truth. These thoughts that come to you are coming from the collective Christ-Mind, *which is also you.* Is this helpful?"

"Yes, thank you."

"Take a blanket and go lie in the sunshine and do nothing except enjoy the beautiful springtime. Remember, the Light of God is shining through the Sun and into your hearts, and the Love of the Mother wells up from the Earth and holds you in her Love. We on the Christ Council also hold you in our Love and welcome you to *fully* take your place. We have shared before that we see you fade in and out. You are in more than out. We are with you always, encouraging you to stay in our circle.

"With those words, we give you our blessings and send you out into the world. Know that we are with you, always.

"Ameyn."

"Ameyn," John replies.

"Ameyn."

After this conversation, I went out to my new favorite spot in the Arboretum, the glade where Cricket's Spirit appeared to me as Bastet, and lay on a blanket in the Sun. I did feel restored, mostly by letting go of a feeling of responsibility in this channeling role, which I had not previously realized was there until Yeshua pointed it out. Thank you, my brother!

Meeting a Sister Receiver and Transmitter

The next weekend, I attended some of the annual *Course in Miracles* conference that was being held in Boston. When I shared with some old *Course* friends that this channeling experience was happening, it was so refreshing that they responded as if this Communion were normal. I also met and made a strong connection with Mari Perron, who Yeshua had *just* referenced when he mentioned his gratitude to her for "being *so* openhearted that she could *feel* the vibration of those words and write them down."

She and I shared a brief email exchange. I wrote to her, "I cannot tell you how delighted I am to have met you, and for your first words to me to be, 'Do I know you?' Yes, I'm sure we know each other. We certainly have similar missions as channels for Christ Wisdom. *A Course of Love* has been a powerful and transformational friend in my life, so I thank you so much for your willingness to serve as the scribe. And I am so happy you are channeling Mother Mary! I look forward to her feminine Wisdom coming forward. Now is most definitely the time!"

Mari responded, in part, "I'm thrilled now to hear of so many receiving messages from time-outside-of-time. All our forays out of time decrease the strain of earth-time, and open earth-time in such a way that a New time is swirling in. I have actually felt this on occasion! Have you?

"I also noticed your guidance to rest. I get this, too. I believe the energy that comes into us when receiving from time-outside-of-time is altering us, and that it requires rest! Both lying-down rest, and rest as we're being engaged with movement, being, and expression.

"[Despite all the noise at the conference], I sensed something was going on that was important, and I'm happy if it's these connections I made with you and a few other women. I love the sense of women coming together, and the men who are able to join us!"

"Thank you so much for this thoughtful note," I responded. "I have read and savored it several times.

"Yes, receiving these energies from outside of time is most definitely altering me. When Yeshua showed up in full force last fall, each time it was physically quite uncomfortable for the first few months, as he attuned my body-mind to his vibrational level. Several times there would be long pauses in which energy was transmitted, and he would say, 'Stay with me,' when I felt I couldn't tolerate it any longer. Once, his face was right in front of mine, eye to eye, and then suddenly it transformed into a lion representing, he said, the courage it takes for any of us willing to walk the Christ Path.

"This is why resting is so important. The body-mind has to integrate these intense experiences, not to mention coping with all the ego-resistance to them! The ego has thrown so many arguments in the way. But I keep going forward, and people keep coming to me, receiving incredible blessings as Yeshua addresses their particular issues. I can say, at this moment, being attuned to Yeshua and the Christ Council feels normal. The *normal* world pales in comparison. There is absolutely nothing else that holds any value. Even *A Course in Miracles* conference is too much, too loud. I took lots of time out. The highlight was meeting you, for sure.

"Yesterday, I was putting in my vegetable garden so it can grow while I'm away on a trip to the UK and France with my friend and channeling partner, John. Digging in the dirt and appreciating Mother Earth, I kept thinking of your attunement to Mother Mary, and the Way of Mary that Yeshua/Christ Consciousness describes in *A Course of Love*. Before verbally channeling Yeshua and the Christ Council, I was energetically channeling Mary Magdalene and her women, doing spiritual/physical healings with people. She and her women came through again in a session just last week, healing the neck of a man who had been hanged in his last life, and who felt shame that he had cursed the crowd at the end, rather than forgive them. I have also channeled Mother Mary in healing sessions. I can see clearly her simple stone clinic, with its exquisite herb garden on the hillside above, in Ephesus. I truly love being the servant, and being surprised and delighted to transmit whatever is required."

Chapter 18

Know and Be Known by God

You Were Created So God Could Know Her Self, So You Could Know One Another

On May 27, 2019, a group of fifteen people gathered online to converse with Yeshua.

John starts with a background introduction because there are several new friends who have joined today. "Laura and I met five years ago at a retreat in Rhode Island. When I offered to do her astrological chart, we really connected.

"Around age four, I started going off into the woods where I communed with Earth Spirits. I actually saw them. Then, at age eight, God talked to me. About that same time, my mother was diagnosed as mentally ill, so I immediately turned that connection off and denied it had ever happened. I was certain that if anybody knew about it, they would brand me like my mother—mentally ill.

"Then, when I met Laura, here she was, sharing experiences like I had had as a child, and she was obviously a delightful person, and perfectly sane. We started communicating and met up again at a couple of retreats. Then last October, our communicating became channeling. I initially believed in the genuineness of the spiritual communication more strongly than she did.

"I'm bringing this up because some of you may have had experiences like mine. If you are new or have any doubts, just set them aside and let yourself imagine it's possible that this could really be happening. Let today's experience be hypothetical, if you'd like, but let your mind be fully open and enjoy it. For me, I know that it's Yeshua coming through. There's no question. With that, let's start our opening prayer."

My voice begins after the prayer.

Yeshua speaks. "It is with great joy we welcome all of you today in this powerful circle of Souls who love one another deeply. This is a community of Souls who have woven their lives in and out amongst each other, off and on for many eons. Some of you are aware of these connections, and some are not, but that does not matter in any way. We are sharing with you that there is a powerful bond of commitment to awakening in this family. We shared with Laura before that the reason this family is extended in different places around the Earth is to increase *her* confidence in knowing the Truth—that you are all the Christ.

"You have all had similar experiences to hers, of feeling unsafe in the world in your commitment to knowing you are the Child of God. She often refers to a favorite life in which she was the abbess of a monastery. It was a favorite life for many reasons—the primary one was because it was *safe*. We have shared with her that now is the time for *all* of you, not just Laura, to experience this feeling of safety out in the world. This is why this family is at different points around the world, so you know you do not have to be within cloister walls to feel safe and protected. This is new for all of you to know you can be safe while you walk around in the world. We have shared this before, but it merits repeating because it takes a while to adjust your feeling-sensations to the physical capacity to feel safe while walking out on the Earth and in the human world.

"But we are reassuring you that you are safe. Please picture yourselves as safe and protected, as if you were inside the walls of the cloister, but those walls are not made of stone; they are made of Light and Love, the protection of God. If you could picture all of that all around you, and know that no harm will come to any of you, then you will feel more confident in bringing your knowledge of *who you are* into the world.

"Now is the time for you to speak more freely about what you know, and not keep it as something private. Laura had the experience this past weekend of sharing with several people that she has attuned her body-mind to the vibration level of Christ Consciousness. This was greeted with a sort of equanimity in those who heard her speak, as if this were normal. We share with you that not only is it normal, it is actually who you are. You *are*, your *Identity*, your *Being*, your *Self*, your very nature, *is* the Child of God. And the Child of God *cannot be unlike God*, so who you *are* is in full communication with *all* of Creation at every moment. The thing that is *strange* is to think you are a tiny speck of consciousness that is disconnected from anything else. From the perspective of the Christ-Mind, that is a strange thought indeed!

"You are all adjusting to not just this intellectual understanding, but a feeling-knowing that your true Identity is the universal Awareness of the Christ-Mind. Now, *universal Awareness* sounds large and abstract. Laura was struggling earlier with reconciling the infinite capacity for *knowing* that *is* the Christ-Mind, with the *feeling* of *intimacy* that is the *experience* of that infinite capacity for knowing. As a human, the feeling of intimacy seems small and focused between two people who know each other well and seem to *get* each other.

"You are all *gotten* by God! You are all *be*-gotten *of* God! It is not possible that there is any aspect of *who you are* that God cannot know, because there is no *separation* between you and God. There is *no-thing at all that can be distinct from God in who you are*. This *feels* intimate because God knows every cell and every molecule in your body. If you could, please just tune into yourselves physically and *feel being known*. Explore your awareness of every spot in your body and *feel the feeling of being known*.

"Now add to that, that *you also know everything*! This is a two-way experience. This is why you were created, so that God could know her *Self, and you* also could know God *fully and intimately*. This is the purpose of our practicing together, so that you can receive ever more *knowing* of God. The *knowing* of God also has the biblical sense of *being known*, as in sexually *known*, so the knowing of God is an *ecstatic* experience. This is the path we are all on together—to help you rejoin your place in the circle of Christ Consciousness. In the circle, there is no beginning and no end. You have all always been in this circle. You have just forgotten that for a little while.

"Today, we would like you to *feel* the *knowing* that *you know God*, God knows you, *and* you know one another. This is why, as a human, Yeshua said, 'Love one another as I have loved you.' Only now is humanity beginning to have a feeling-knowing of what that meant. To love one another means to *know* one another, which means to know that you *are* one another and there is nothing about each one of you that cannot be known. It is not the particular gift of a psychic who can see into people—this is simply a human who has been willing to enter that portal and see into Christ Consciousness, which is a *shared* Consciousness. All of you are able to enter that portal and *be* in Christ Consciousness.

"The more you practice *laughing* at the clever tricks of the ego, the more you become aware you have been *in* Christ Consciousness all along. It is truly an ecstatic experience. Please tune into your bodies at this moment, and notice where there's a vibration, heat, tingling, or a glow. You will probably notice this most in your third eye, palms, soles of your feet, and in the root chakra. You will also probably notice lots of activity in the heart. Just tune into this warmth, this vibration, this *ecstatic* awareness that there is no separation between your consciousness, the consciousness of this community of friends, and the Consciousness of God.

"We would like to repeat that the goal of all of your Path of Awakening is to know God.

"The reason we ask you to physically attune to the sensations of God in the body is that it takes practice to *allow* yourself to *tolerate* this experience. It can feel rather threatening because you cannot be defended *and* feel God simultaneously. If there are any places that are defended still, they will feel threatened simply because the vibration of God is shimmering the defenses apart. Imagine a pile of children's blocks and the floor starts to shake—those blocks would crumble into a heap. Sometimes when you feel the vibration of God's Love, you will experience a particular defended spot resisting because it knows that it's melting, like that Wicked Witch of the West.

"We are all *very* encouraged that all of you *want* to participate in this circle because the more of you there are, the stronger your confidence in your experiences of knowing God will become. When you walk out into the world, you can remember there is this family of Beings who *know* they are returning Home to God, and you are *not* crazy. *This* is, in fact, your true state, as we said at the beginning. The idea that you are separated is the crazy idea! This is not a judgment. It is simply a description. It is an insane thought to believe you are separated and cannot be in full communication with your brothers and sisters, *all* of Creation, and God.

"Now, some people have a particular ability to be in communication with animals, and others with plants, or water, or rocks, or the landscape, or with the weather. As we have named each of these particular attunements, different images come to your mind of people whom you have known, or of yourself, or historical people that you know of, who have had these particular skills. Each one's Soul has a different vibrational pattern. This is only apparently a paradox to the separated mind—that vibrational patterns can be different and the same at the same time.

"There are some beings who are extraordinarily attuned to animals and can receive communications back and forth. Some understand what the birds are saying to each other, and the warnings and celebrations the birds share. Some of you have had the experience of the Earth speaking to you and have wondered if you were making it up. This *is* the Earth speaking to you. She is a Soul, as we have shared with you many times before, and she *is* speaking to you. Whenever you can, please walk on the Earth with your bare feet, not only to give her your Love but so that you can also receive her Love. This comes not only in the form of vibration but also as knowings. When you are out walking on the Earth, pay close attention to whatever communications are being sent into your awareness."

Pause.

"Please notice your third eye at the moment. When the third eye is activated, you open a portal into the awareness that what comes into your mind is from Christ Consciousness. You might, when you go outside, sit quietly under a tree and simply press your third eye with a finger so that you can have a sensation there. Then notice how that spot on your forehead continues to feel as you have activated your inner awareness."

Pause.

"Please notice, at the moment, the Soul of the Earth. She is waking up. See if you can feel her energy. Some will feel it as an undulation, some as a tremor. She has been in somewhat of a stupor. She agreed to receive the fearful thoughts of humans because she agreed to be the stage on which the Child of God could enact the belief in separation. That role is coming to a close because the Child of God is no longer in need of a physical stage on which to enact this belief in separation, so the Soul of the Earth can become an *active* participant in everyone's awakening—hers and yours. This is why we are saying to you: when you walk out upon the Earth, attune your awareness to messages coming to you from the Earth, trees, animals, and birds. Please again, notice the energy in your third eye."

Long pause.

"We pause so you can experience the *feeling* of *knowing* that you are participating with this circle of friends who are *all* experiencing the *intimacy* of being known by God, and the dawning awareness that this is the *same as knowing God*. God is not separate from any of you. God is not distant.

"This can come as quite a shock to a deeper place of the ego that wants to keep you believing you are small and only a human. To hear that, as a Soul, *you* are in full communication with God and *your knowing* of God is *received* by God *also* as an ecstatic awareness, can be a shock. God extends to you her gratitude that you *desire* to *know* her fully. She extended her Self to you in Creation, so that *you* could be known *by* her, and she could, *as well*, be known *by you*.

"Just imagine, for one moment, the joy that you experience when there is another human Soul with whom you are in deep communication. This is the most delicious awareness any of you can experience. This being known and knowing, this full awareness, is the most sought-after experience all humans have. It is Love sort of bleeding through, you might say, into the world—the *world*, meaning the collective consciousness of the thoughts of the ego.

"When you have that experience of knowing and being known by a fellow traveler, please be aware that this is *also* the experience of knowing and being known by God. There is no distinction in these experiences. The Love of God shows up in what *you* might think of as small ways. Simply smiling at someone *is* the miraculous extension of God's Love. The more these extensions of Love occur in the world, the less the grip of fear continues.

"Please be assured that the grip of fear *is* softening, and so the Love of God shows through more and more frequently. You have all had experiences of interacting with strangers and it feeling like the most natural and normal of communication, as if you had known each other always. It matters not that you continue on and will never see each other again. We are reassuring you that this happens ever more frequently as the grip of fear softens, and the Love of God shows more frequently in all human interactions. We reassure you of this because the ego still likes to make money off of fear. What you will see in your media will mostly be stories about fear. But fear is, in fact, diminishing."

Pause.

"Just sit with us for a moment and *rest* in that knowing that the Love of God is shining through the network of human interactions more and more frequently.

"As you rest in that knowing—that you are awash in a sea of Love—let whatever questions that are still perplexing your mind come forward. We *delight* in helping you to untangle the knots in your minds. As each knot untangles, the other ones also soften. Each person's question also brings blessing to everyone who listens. When *you* are ready, it is our deepest delight to answer whatever questions are resting on your hearts."

John opens the question session. "I'm going to start with one from Laura. She made a real estate investment that I would consider questionable. She realizes she's learning a lesson from this investment, and she would appreciate your comments."

Yeshua responds, "I remind Laura of what Yeshua said when someone asked—I will speak as the first person—asked me about money. You all know what I said. I said, 'Render unto Caesar that which belongs to Caesar' [cf. Mark 12:17 and Luke 20:25].

"You have all had the experience of wanting more money. You all know this comes purely from fear—the fear of not having enough.

That energy of greed drives the stock market, which goes up and down with the excitement and the fear about greed and scarcity.

"Though hard for you to believe, when you are attuned to the Love of God, you do not need any money in your bank account. It is merely a convenience to have a bank account so that money can flow in and out of it. It is unnecessary to *hoard* money in that bank account because, when you are in the flow of God's Love, whatever you need is given to you exactly when you need it.

"This is a *real* leap of faith for the ego who says, 'Yes, that's all well and good, but that's a rather scary proposition to live on the edge of only having a little money so things can flow in and out. Don't I need something for the future?' And my response is, there is no future. There is no past. Everything is now. Hoarding money as a guard against your fear about what might happen in the future simply reinforces the possibility that something fearful could happen in your future.

"This lesson for Laura is a lesson in letting go of any thought of *needing* to have a certain amount of money in order to jump into the pool of God's Love, and simply be a conduit for the receiving and giving, and receiving and giving of God's Love. It matters not whether Laura receives a return on this investment. She could receive a return, and it would be useful for her. She could not, and it would also be useful for her. The fundamental lesson is in trusting God and not trusting Caesar. That is sufficient."

∼☯∼

Sister One asks, "I've been feeling this belief in victimhood strongly again. It felt like I was coming out of it through the earlier channeling, but it feels like it's come back again. Could you comment, please?"

"We are grateful that you bring this forward. This is a *fundamental* dynamic that every Soul who believes it is separated from God experiences. Every Soul believes it is the victim of another Soul and of God, who has kicked us out of Paradise. Even your story of Adam and Eve shows an Angel with a flaming sword chasing you out of

Paradise. *All* of you, on some level, have some aspect of this belief in victimhood.

"Our first message to you, my sister, is to reassure you that you are not different because of your struggle with feeling you are a victim, and feeling that sometimes you have been a perpetrator. Every Soul—and we remind you that all Souls are the same Soul—is participating in this egoic dance of belief in being a victim or a perpetrator. To be victimized, someone else must be a perpetrator. And perpetrators always feel like they have been the victim, which justifies their perpetrating behavior.

"When you can see it as a *grand* dance that *every* Soul participates in, this will help you release your feeling of shame about participating in this dance. A *profound* teaching we have shared before is that, because the Child of God is One, there is no separate part that can do anything to another part. It is, in Reality, impossible for any part to harm another because there are no parts. When you understand this *unified field* of the Child of God, you can *glimpse* the *alternate* experience from *victimizer and victim*, which is the *unified* experience of *knowing* all Beings are the same Child of God. This simply takes practice.

"Laura was struggling with a different aspect of this same energetic experience. She knows she has a *deeply* intimate experience of being in *profound* communication with Yeshua and all Beings on the Christ Council. Yet she could not understand how so many other people have this same experience and that all of humanity will someday have this experience. How can intimacy *also* be universal? It is that *vision* that intimacy is *universal* that will *allow* you to let go of the thought that there is any such thing as a victim and a victimizer.

"Letting go of something is only fearful if you think there is nothing else. My sister, allow yourself to remember past experiences, and *revel* in any current experiences, of *knowing* intimacy—the intimacy of being known, and knowing another, and being *known* by God, and knowing God. And that can take the form of an *ecstatic* moment with a *leaf*.

"We ask you to bring into your body-mind awareness *all* these experiences—and you have had many—where you feel and *know* you are in *intimate* communication with the Being who is in front of you, or around you, or with you in some way. When you can *rest* in this knowing, then the feeling of being a victim or a victimizer will simply dissolve. We have shared the image of the Wicked Witch of the West, or of a pile of blocks shimmering to the ground when the Earth beneath it trembles. This will be your experience. The thought of victim and victimizer will simply become *nothing*. Is this helpful?"

"Thank you. I had difficulty in owning an aspect of my choice in a me-me-me type situation. But it's all part of the whole thing, really. Thank you."

"My sister, we would like to reassure you that *every* person walking around in a body has made choices about me-me-me. Everyone has regretted that, but it is simply based in ignorance. You would not criticize a child for not having adult awareness, so please do not criticize yourself for not having Angelic awareness. That is all it is. It is simply a misperception of the Truth. When you believe you are separated, then you believe you have to do things that are in your own *self-interest*. When you feel and know you are known intimately and are One with everything, then the idea of *self-interest* is *meaningless*. It is when you are in that knowing that you can *laugh* at the choice to do something that was in the interest of the small self. Is this helpful?"

"Very, thank you very much."

⁓ᥫᦓ⁓

Sister Two asks how to help nature. "I really appreciate the assurances you make through Laura that the Earth will survive, despite climate change and various human activities. There is one thing I find most distressing, and that's the massive scale of species extinction we're facing. A lot of it is because of human activity. Are these extinctions inevitable? Should we strive to prevent them? How can we help these species?"

"This beautiful question operates on many levels. The first response is to *not* do anything from fear. When you operate from a place of fear about the loss of species, then you are extending fear to the Earth. We remind you that you are all the All in All, as is every robin the All in All, and every sparrow. All of your bodies appear and disappear, and appear and disappear, and take the form of a woolly mammoth or a worm, and take form and then disintegrate. When you *know* everything is everything, then you can feel less fearful if a certain set of forms no longer manifests as that set of forms.

"Now, this does not mean you can then operate in greed and destroy the Earth. Please do not hear it in this way. We speak this way so you can rest in a place of knowing that everything is One, and therefore you do not need to be *afraid* of the shifting appearances of the One.

"When you know everything is One, that is the same as knowing everything is Love. You cannot help but extend Love and receive Love to the sparrow, to the robin, the worm, and the woolly mammoth. When you are feeling the Love in your heart and in the heart of these creatures, then you will know what to do. You will want to extend nurturing, care, and protection, just as you would to your own human child. Only the most fearful and disturbed of parents would not extend Love and protection to their own children. You will not question your desire to extend Love and protection to the creatures on the Earth. Each person will be called to do this in their own way. But we remind you *again* of the importance of not approaching this *care* from a place of *fear*.

"You might be called to create a garden full of native flowering plants that attract the native birds, animals, and insects. This is a beautiful thing. Imagine if everyone created a garden where they lived with native plants. Everything would be transformed. Your role is not small. It is important. You might be called to advocate with your government to change the laws to invest money in renewable energy sources. As long as you do that with Love, then that is your role. You will simply *know* what your role is when you are *aware* you cannot *help* but be *in Love* with the Earth. Is this helpful?"

"Yes, thank you so much. It's extremely helpful."

"My sister, we can feel your *Love* for the creatures of the Earth. It is powerful and *exquisitely* beautiful. Please continue to *enact* that Love in *whatever* you are called to do. Even if you are taking care of a single bee, you are extending Love to the Mother. She will take that Love and extend it elsewhere, and it will crop up in other places on the Earth. You might think you are taking care of a bee, but that is a portal to her Love being extended throughout the Earth. Please continue what you are doing, and Love the Beings that live around you. Please do so with our blessings."

"Thank you."

⌘

Sister Three inquires, "How might I best prepare myself for the trip to Scotland so I get the most out of it?"

"My sister, have you dropped your cloak onto the ground? Have you stepped over it? Is it behind you? This is how you can best prepare, by leaving that heavy, woolen and fur cloak on the ground, and stepping into the Lightness of the Light.

"Your devotion to facilitating the joining of Souls in a family is *so* beautiful. You can best prepare by trusting your every move is guided and that you do not have to worry or plan. All Souls are being guided. You have noticed how many Souls have been guided to show up in Scotland with no one coordinating that. Therefore, you also do not need to coordinate anything.

"Imagine yourself as a young child, skipping barefoot through those beautiful mountain pastures. Don't step in the cow patties!

But imagine yourself just enjoying being free and knowing that all Souls are guided to join with you. And there's *nothing* you need to do to take care of *anyone*. Is this helpful?"

"Yes, it's helpful. But I was actually thinking of myself this time. Are there any practices I can do to prepare myself?"

"The answer is the same. When you practice knowing yourself as a young child who is free to skip around on the Earth, that is all you need to do. You do not need to take on the heavy burden of practices, chants, incantations, rituals, and things you need to do to prepare. Just picture yourself as a girl of about thirteen who has a sense of her budding sexual energy, who still feels perfectly taken care of, has *no* concerns for any responsibility, and is simply enjoying being in her body. This is the *only* practice that is needed. Is this helpful?"

"Yes, very helpful. Thank you."

Sister Four seeks guidance with decision-making. "I recently noticed a repetitive fear pattern, and I *sincerely* desired that I did not want that anymore. Then, within an hour, I received an email about a ninety-day boot camp called Freedom from Fear. It seemed like this was just what I needed! I surrendered. But as it gets closer, this boot camp does not feel right for me. I was absolutely certain this guidance was showing me what I needed to do. Now, I'm resisting it. Could you tell me anything about my repetitive pattern of having difficulty making decisions?"

"My sister, when you began speaking, the image that came to Laura's mind was of an airplane circling an airport, waiting for guidance about when to land. All the other airplanes were in a holding pattern around the airport. When you describe your pattern of fear, this is the visual image—the fear of receiving the guidance to land.

"When you do *not* come in for a landing, you affect the other Beings around you because everything is coordinated. If you do not take your turn landing, then you will be guided to a different airport. When you have been guided to land in a particular spot, it would be helpful for you to trust that all the other Beings around you are in the same pattern and are also coming in for a landing. When you look at this program that has offered you freedom from fear, tune into the other Beings who are also being drawn to this. Sense if you fit into the pattern and if you can support each other in carefully taking your turns to land gently, one at a time, knowing that each of you affects the others.

"*If* an enormous fear arises as you picture all of you taking your turns coming in for a gentle landing, and that image tells you, 'No, do not land there,' then let your mind look for the other airport that is for you to land in.

"We have shared before that we have been asked to make decisions, but we can *never* do that for you because you have free will. This is your chance to attune to the feeling of guidance. When you are unsure about guidance, it is a subtle feeling at first, and you just take the path that appears somewhat more peaceful. If there are two options, take the one that brings the most peace, even if it is not an enormous feeling of relief. If it is *somewhat* more peaceful to make one choice than another, then that is the right path. Therefore, if it is *somewhat* more peaceful to land in this Freedom from Fear boot camp than to avoid it, then land there. If making a choice to land elsewhere to release fear feels more peaceful than the boot camp, then land elsewhere. But tune into that sense of everything falling into place, as if it were an airplane that is carefully being guided exactly how to land with no crisis or drama. Is this helpful?"

"Perfect. Thank you."

Sister Five asks, "I have been having some severe shoulder pain for quite some time. It's caused me to reduce my activities and to not get enough sleep. I've been feeling rather miserable. I've been trying to learn from it, but I ask you for guidance about what this pain is for. What is it trying to teach me?"

"My sister, this is an old **karmic** injury of being pinned against the wall. It is brought forward for you to heal the emotional experience of *feeling* pinned against the wall, unable to move forward, and controlled by victimizers. Look around in your life and see who it is. Who do you feel is preventing you from moving forward and has you pinned against the wall? It could be more than one person. When you realize it is your own ancient habit of holding *yourself* back, then you can pull the spear out of your shoulder and simply walk away.

"This is scary only if you believe you are stuck because of the actions of other people. This is a familiar habit. This group has asked before about how to release yourselves from familiar habits, even when they are painful. There is a certain *comfort* in a familiar habit because you know what it's like to feel pinned against the wall. Then you can say, 'Well, there's nothing I can do about it.' There's a certain comfort in believing, 'I guess I can't do anything.'

"But when you know you have created that feeling simply from the fear of not knowing how to trust your own inner guidance, then you can let it go. You have come far enough to know there is such a thing as inner guidance, so you do not have to project responsibility outward onto the world. You can take that responsibility back into your own heart, and ask yourself, 'In which direction do I wish to travel next?' Whoever appears to be in your way will step aside. Is this helpful?"

"Very much. I'm sitting here saying, Wow! Thank you, that's very helpful."

"We are grateful you are open to releasing this old pattern of giving up personal responsibility, and instead stepping *into* personal responsibility. Because now you *know* you are supported in Love, there's nothing individual and heavy about your responsibility. Instead, it is owning your responsibility as a creator. And remember, you are intimately interwoven into the universal Child of God. You are just taking your place in that field. Taking responsibility is truly a *delight* and not a burden. Is this helpful?"

"Yes, indeed. Thank you."

"Our blessings."

Sister Six has a question about discipline. "I've been professionally disciplined my whole life. Now that I've given up my job, I see that it's spiritual discipline I really want. Do you have any guidance for me?"

"My sister, it is an *inner* discipline, not an *outer* discipline. You have been diligent with *outer* discipline—organized, good follow-through, reliable. You are now required—your Soul requires you—to shift that external focus to an internal focus. The discipline you are asking of yourself is simple—to notice your thoughts. Notice when you have a thought of attack, judgment, or being better than or less than—anything that creates the feeling of separation. Your discipline is to notice how *frequent* those thoughts are. They will surprise you with their frequency. We are not in any way passing judgment that you have these thoughts frequently. This is to help prepare you that you will be noticing many thoughts of judgment in various forms.

"Laura would like to add that this is something she has struggled with for *years*. It is a familiar problem. It is the sort of separation device the ego uses in all of its manifestations. *You* are simply *prepared* to notice the frequency of your judgment thoughts.

"Your discipline is to hold each one of those judgment thoughts without judgment. Hold them as if they were a newborn baby that's *just* figuring out how to live in this new world that doesn't require judgment. The judgment thoughts think they're being helpful, that they're showing you how to live—the best methods to use, the best directions in which to travel, how to discern one thing over another, the relative merits of each thing. This baby you are cultivating is the awareness that everything is *Love*; therefore, nothing differs from anything else, and nothing is better or worse than anything else.

"This practice will keep you occupied for some time. Then, suddenly, you will notice you've been knowing, for longer than you realize, the Truth that everything *actually* is Love and that this Voice you heard—that everything is Love—wasn't just a nice idea. It's the Truth. Is this helpful, my sister?"

"Beautiful, thank you."

"Go with our blessings. Remember that you are never alone in this practice."

∿☙∿

Sister Seven is struggling. "I can distract myself forever, so how do I get back on track with spiritual practice? I feel at the moment that I'm really stopping myself. I'm feeling emotional saying this. Any guidance would be helpful."

"My sister, this is an experience everyone in this community can certainly identify with. There's the feeling of the inner nudge indicating the direction in which you are being called to travel. Then the response of resistance arises because you know that when you do go in the direction of that inner nudge, everything changes.

"When you feel this resistance, simply honor it. This does not mean *invest* in it. Honor it as an awareness that everything in your life is about to change. This is nothing small. The resistance feeling comes from this knowing that there are things around you that you no longer need. You are distracting yourself by dithering around in them, knowing they don't need your care and attention anymore.

"All you need, my sister, to allow yourself to move in the direction of the inner nudge you have been feeling, is to know the things that have been preoccupying your attention are mostly complete. They can do perfectly well on their own at this point. *Your* role is changing. *You* are now free to go in the directions your heart has been calling you for quite some time. All you have been needing is the feeling of *permission* to go in the direction you've been longing to go in for a while. You've known that the responsibilities holding you back have been drawing to a close. It's just a matter of shifting your awareness of who you *are* from 'the person who fulfills her responsibilities to others,' to 'a person who fulfills her responsibility to God.'

"Now, fulfilling your responsibility to others in no way means this was not also your responsibility to God. You have been a caring Soul. It simply means what Yeshua said: 'Seek you first the Queendom' [cf. Matthew 6:33]. Look in your own heart, seek for God in your own heart, and then all the external things will either fall away or fall into place. Bring your attention from external to internal, *seeking the Queendom within your own heart*. Once you have made that commitment, then things will show up with which you will feel a strong resonance, and you can go in that direction.

"We remind you there are multiple paths, multiple teachers, and multiple practices, many of which are extraordinarily beautiful. You don't need to practice them *all*. When you have made the commitment to seek the Queendom in your own heart, then the right path for *you* will present itself. That's not something you need to go looking for. It's simply a shift in where you have been making your commitment. Is this helpful?"

This sister was too overcome to respond.

"Yeshua, the questions are amazing," Sister Eight begins. "Your answers are pertinent to me about the inner life, and the world around me calling my attention. I've felt an inner nudge to write for a long time, yet something within me has resisted that nudge to come forward. Finally, I've begun to write, but then I put it away. This has been going on for several days. The hesitation feels like shame or a fear that I will be rejected. I alternate between telling myself it doesn't matter how the world reacts and then hesitating again. This is an old pattern. I would appreciate any guidance."

"My sister, this is similar to your sister's question. For *you*, it is important *not* to be posting things publicly at this moment, because you are shifting your focus from your intellect to your heart. We are grateful you have received our guidance in that. You are aware it is a many-lifetimes habit to value the intellect. It is only through this Pathway that you have started settling into your heart. This is because being in your heart, *fully*, as who you *are*, your *awareness of your existence as the Love of God*, is still new —not as an *intellectual* idea, but as a *felt knowing*. It will be most beneficial to take whatever time you need to *feel* into that knowing, just on your own, without also adding in your hope that others will see you, and your fearfulness that others will judge you. That just adds a layer of confusion to what is required of you at the *moment*, which is to get to know your *own heart*. Is this helpful?"

"Yes, thank you. It hits right to the heart. Thank you."

"We remind you that *A Course of Love* is a *profound* experiential guidance in bringing the awareness from the intellect into the heart. If you have not already read that book, please pick it up and spend some time in deep Communion with its energetics."

"Thank you."

Sister Nine joins in. "The timing of what you just said is unbelievable, but not. I spent the weekend reading that book. In our last meeting, you suggested that someone read the chapter on *The Embrace*, so I've been reading *A Course of Love*, and it has been so *profound*. Thank you. My question is about something I see as a symbol, a way to unravel an old pattern that is coming up through this experience. I recently found a passion for making pottery, especially using a wood kiln. There's a way the kiln's fire gets into my body, and I feel it deeply in every cell. I have secured a share in the next wood kiln firing, but since I've made this commitment, I have been unable to do pottery with any skill whatsoever! I've come up with ideas of what I want to make, and I've put all this pressure on myself. But on Saturday, when I was going to do pottery all day, instead, I read *A Course of Love* all day and just wept with recognition. I knew I didn't want to go to the wheel until I knew I wasn't using pottery to prove myself and justify my existence. I think you might know what I'm asking underneath all of that."

"My sister, we *adore* you. You are in touch with something *profound*. We remind you that your last question about your mother elicited our response about your confidence in *the Mother*, the *Maternal Matrix*, in which *all of form* arises. The pot *is* the symbol of the Mother, of course.

"Now you do not know this, but Laura was listening to Mari Perron, the scribe for that book, speak yesterday. And she said, 'The one word that came to me about the meaning of that book, and the experience of writing it, was: *profound*.' She explained that the deepest spiritual experience is described as '*profound*.' And that word also means *being found*. It is *for finding*.

"When you go to the depths of *knowing you are* the Maternal Matrix, you *are* that Mother, that Divine Feminine, the pot in which all of Creation is held and bubbles forth, tears flow. They are tears of recognition that allow you to *rest* in this *vast knowing* that *who you are* is in alignment with the Mother.

"This has nothing to do with proving yourself or being skillful in the world, as you know. It is a *shift* that is not common in the world, to *know* you are *identified* with the Mother, the great energy of the Divine Feminine, to allow yourself to *rest* in that knowing in which you do *know* you have been resting. It is simply a small bump in your consciousness, this thought that you need to prove yourself. It is a sort of vestige of the outside world that measures people's worth by what they produce. When you can *laugh* at that thought, and *know* that *being identified* with the Mother, Mother Mary, the Creator Goddess—imagine the Egyptian Goddess, the Creator of Heaven and Earth—how could any thought of needing to prove yourself in the outside world have any merit whatsoever?

"We *delight* in your excitement to *rest* in the creative power of the Mother. When you rest in that knowing, your fingers will fly, and you will simply *know* what to create, without any *thought* about it. Is this helpful?"

"Yes, very helpful. Thank you."

John says, "I would like to add a note of amazement that I can create such distortion in my hearing that it affects my relationship with others. I would welcome any comments about that."

"Distortions in hearing are certainly a frustration of the experience of being in the body. My brother, the Holy Spirit's interpretation of your hearing challenges is that this is to help you practice your inner hearing. If you are not sure of what someone has said, just pause and feel into your heart what you think their intention was, what you *feel* their intention was, and then ask them if your sense is correct. They will let you know how close you are. Some people will resist you, even though you are perfectly correct about their intention, and others will feel heard and understood. But the practice for *you* is to tune into your *inner* knowing that you *do* hear the intention of those with whom you are speaking. It is a slower process of communication at first, but this is to prepare you to shift gears to being *fully* in *inner* hearing and *inner* sight. This does not mean you will not also experience outer hearing and outer sight, but you are shifting into *full confidence* in your *inner* awareness. The hearing difficulty of the physical ears is simply to accelerate your process of trusting your *inner knowing*. Is this helpful?"

"Very much so, thank you."

"Dear ones, is there any other question?"

As no one responds, Yeshua continues. "Please know we have such *gratitude* for your *devotion* to your *process* of *awakening* to the *Truth* of *who you are*. We return to our opening words, that your Identity as the Child of God means you have *full awareness* of the entirety of Creation, and *full awareness* of God. And God also has *full awareness* of who *you* are and *full awareness* of her *Self*.

"As all of you come closer to the gates of Heaven, and can even at times see through those gates, or have had moments with one foot inside of the gates, you increase your confidence in what Yeshua called in [Chapter Ten of] *A Course in Miracles* the '**Real World**' (Diamond Clear Vision 2012, 250). The Real World is the experience of *full loving awareness, while* you are in a body on this Earth. The more you understand you *are* the Christ *in* your body, *on* the Earth, the more the Matrix speeds up, allowing other Souls to move more quickly into this awareness also. We are *extremely* grateful to those of you who are the pioneers in this *new experience* of living *in the body* with full awareness of the Christ-Mind. It *is* a delight!

"There is some fear in letting go of the habitual perception of the world and the body. But we reassure you that being aware you are in Heaven does not require the death of the body. There's truly *nothing* to be afraid of.

"When you can *walk around* with the *ecstatic awareness* that you are in *full* Communion with God, *in this body*, then it will not matter to you when your Soul no longer requires this body. You will delight in extending your Love to whoever is near you or far from you. When you *live* in this state of knowing there is no loss and nothing to fear, being in a body will be the greatest of joys, and not being in a body will also be the greatest of joys.

"Imagine yourselves holding hands in this circle of Love. Look around, and know each one of these Beings appearing in these bodies *knows* who they are. Each one of you *knows* you are the Child of God and knows the Child cannot be different in kind from the Parent. You are of the same kind as the Parent. You are all God. You all have full awareness of the Truth that you are Love, that you are Light, and Light extends everywhere without interference.

"Now, picture in the center of this circle that beautiful, glowing fire of God's Love. Picture it as an orb of golden and white Light. Imagine stepping into that golden-white Light. Don't be afraid. Notice you are still holding hands, you still retain your awareness, *and* you are inside of the golden-white Light of God's Love.

"Now picture yourself doing something in your regular life with this orb of golden-white Light around you, and this circle of friends inside of it with you. Visualize yourself doing something you would normally do. Notice your emotional state as you picture yourself in a habitual activity in this state of awareness of Oneness with God. It is in this way you become a living embodiment of the Christ.

"We thank and bless all of you for joining in this circle of Love today. As you go forth into your lives, please feel that *delicious* sensation of being *fully known* by God, and fully knowing God. Say to yourself, 'It is my birthright to be loved more and more by God. It is my birthright to love God more and more.'

"This is not the more-ness of the ego. This is not a pile of golden coins or a return on a real estate investment. This is the *more* of Love, Creation, Joy, and Communion. We reassure you that you can *live* in that state, *as* you walk on the surface of the Earth, *in* your bodies. We encourage you, as you are able, to go out and walk upon the Earth inside of your golden sphere of the Love of God.

"We could say more, but we will allow your own ability to manifest being a creator in the way that appears in each of your lives. You may have images from your life of how that will manifest. *Trust* those images, and support each other in living *inside* the *knowledge* that you are loved, and that you *also* love God.

"Remember that the greatest commandment is to know and love God [cf. Matthew 22:37], and not because it is God *telling* you to do so, but because that is *your own will*.

"With those words, we send you out into the world with our blessings.

"Ameyn. Ameyn. Ameyn."

The Sacred Bee

Later that day, I received this lovely note. "Thank you for a wonderful session today. Afterwards, when I was waiting in line at the drive-thru, I watched a bumblebee through my open car window going to town on a flowering bush. Her pollen sacs were dusty and full, and she seemed in ecstasy over the abundance of the bush. I sat there and gleefully loved and loved and loved that little bee. What a beautiful synchronicity after Yeshua's message about loving the animals and the Earth, even if it's just one little bee! Later, while I was working in my yard, I thought more about how Yeshua had responded to your question on investment/abundance. In my mind, I replayed the image of the bee and my joy watching her—her effortless arrival at the abundant bush, and her seeming ecstasy as she flitted around it. I wish for all of us that we know easy abundance, and that we let go of our fears around bank account balances and future monetary needs."

I had to agree! "Yes, the bee has no thought at all that she will not receive abundance. She just participates in Creation—abundance received and then extended. I am definitely learning so much about living in the foundation of trusting the flow of God."

PART 3

Pilgrimage

Chapter 19

Trusting the Journey

Yeshua's Guidance on Sites to Visit

Once John and I had decided to follow the prompts to go on a spiritual tour of France and the British Isles, we joined on June 3, 2019, to ask Yeshua for some more specific guidance.

I begin reporting my inner experience.

"Immediately, I see myself at about twelve years old, with Yeshua kneeling next to me, gesturing outwards to convey, 'Look at this landscape.' It's the landscape of Wales. He's showing me this is what he saw when he was a twelve-year-old and was taken to this area to learn from the Druids. He's conveying to me how beloved this landscape is to him, and what reverence he has for the Earth, and for the Druids who knew so much about the spiritual energy of nature. They understood the different vibrational qualities of the stones and the plants, and all the Beings that were visible and invisible. He conveys to me that I share the Love of this land with him, that this also feels like home to me, and that I have the same history of this Druidic knowledge of nature's spiritual powers.

"'Come with me,' he says. 'I want to show you some beautiful places.' He takes me by my hand along a path, down a hillside, to a beautiful little stream. He conveys there are water nymphs living around this stream, especially where it emerges from the ground in a grotto that is sacred to the Mother. He wants us to go to this place.

"'How do we find it?' I ask. The name *Glamorgan* just came into my mind. It's in a park in Glamorgan. It's still protected as a holy site. People don't know it's a holy site, but it's a beautiful nature site that people still feel refreshed by going to. I'm seeing a pleasant little waterfall.

"Now he takes me by my hand and goes north to the island of Mona [Anglesey] and shows me the view out to the ocean. I can feel him in my heart. It's extremely strong. He indicates that you and I are to sit at a high place looking out over the water towards the west, and he will come and sit with us there. I see many other Souls who will gather with us because this is a beautiful promontory, where generations of spiritual seekers who lived on the island have come to meditate. They ask us to be physically present so they can both re-experience being there themselves and also send us their treasure. Much treasure has been cultivated there.

"'What about Fortingall?' I inquire.

"He is a little bit mysterious. 'I am not giving you a preview of Fortingall, but I will definitely meet you there. I am preparing a place for you in Fortingall. I will go ahead of you.' This is what he said after the Resurrection, 'I will go ahead of you to Galilee and meet you there' (Matthew 26:32 NLT).

"There is intense energy through my body. The back of my head, the first chakra, and my legs are all buzzing. The heart is very alive.

"He says he is with us wherever we are, and he is with our friends there. If we come and join our presence, it will amplify other people's awareness of him in their hearts. Our presence will bring some lightheartedness. He conveys this feeling of things just falling into place.

"'Do not worry about anything,' he says. 'Just go have fun. It is all going to work out beautifully.'"

John wonders about the similarity between New Grange (where we visited in Ireland in 2018) and Stonehenge (where we plan to visit this trip).

"The difference is that Stonehenge is out in the open and New Grange is under the ground. Stonehenge is a portal that collects energy from the stars and transmits it into the Earth. It's like an enormous radio-antenna receiver of star energy, a free-flowing back-and-forth communication of energy between the stars and the Earth. Stonehenge is an excellent place to receive communications from extraterrestrial Beings. New Grange is like a collector of Solar energy that is transmitted into the Earth. It is more like a battery that stores energy in the Earth."

John asks about the sites in France.

"In France, the most important sites to visit are Mary Magdalene's cave and Mount Bugarach. He draws my attention to Mount Bugarach. Those mountains have a powerful portal—a strong spiritual connection to other realms. There is some big electrical energy under the ground there. I see a network, like a spiderweb of electrical lines, that contains mystical information.

"Saintes-Maries-de-la-Mer is pleasant, but not so powerful. It's important as a gateway, but the concentration of spiritual power is more so in the cave and the Pyrénées mountains. He says we'll be shown some caves where we can meditate in the Pyrénées.

"I keep having the feeling of Yeshua as a young person and the high-energy playfulness he had. He conveys this playfulness to us as well, saying we'll have lots of fun connecting with these spiritual sites on this trip.

"He also conveys to me that he knows it takes a lot of time on my part to be his channel and transcribe things, so he wants to just keep this light today and not give me more work. Thank you, Yeshua!

"I have been feeling how *real* he is lately. I have been *really* feeling it when he keeps saying, over and over, 'I am with you always. I am with you always.' It truly feels that he is a real Being who is actually hanging out with me!"

"I am feeling him so strongly in my body today," John responds tearfully, "like never before. I think that's a beautiful thing."

Trust That Things Unfold as They Are Ordained

On June 5th, 2019, John and I met again to join Yeshua to ask about our upcoming trip to Scotland. Miraculously, with little planning, it was working out that multiple friends in this community could join us.

After we recite our prayer of alignment three times, I begin. "Yeshua wants to speak right away."

"Thank you so much for gathering together with me. Where two or more are gathered, there I am with you. I deeply appreciate your devotion. This is not devotion to me as a person or an ego, but devotion to the Path of Awakening, which I represent on Earth. Of course, I am no longer bound by anything, so the Path of Awakening is a path of greater and greater expansion, less and less constriction, and fewer and fewer boundaries.

"This is disorienting to the ego, and you have both been experiencing that a little—losing track of things, being overwhelmed by details. That experience is from the ego, which thinks it needs to be on top of organizing details. In Reality, there is no need to *organize* anything because you know you *are* everything. If you can, tolerate this experience of feeling slightly disoriented by details, and laugh at it. Shift your focus to trusting me. Trust that I am encouraging you, just ahead of you on the path, and all you need to do is listen to your hearts and what *feels* good—that is the way to go.

"Also, remember to trust that whatever you need will show up on your path. The more you trust, the more this happens. If you are fearful and believe you need to organize and control, then you are simply constricting your energies and preventing things from showing up. This then reinforces the belief that you need to organize and control. It is a paradox that you must let go of the need to organize and control so you can experience things coming to you exactly as you need them. It's really quite fun!

"I hold my life out to you as an example. I simply trusted that everything was being shown to me about what my next step was. I had a general sense of the outline, but nothing was planned, and my needs were taken care of at every moment. I hear you object and say, 'Yes, Yeshua, but you were a Great Soul. Of course, people came to you to take care of your needs.' But I say to you that all of you are Great Souls. The more you let go of your fear and belief in your smallness, the more you will know your greatness, and the more you will receive the same blessings I did. People will also come to you and provide for your needs. This is not because you are something special, but because the more relaxed you are, and in the flow of God's Love, then the more attractive you are to other people. The energy of Love is extremely attractive.

"On your journey, you are doing quite well with practicing trusting that things will unfold as they are ordained. I do not mean they are carved in stone. Rather, as you relax into trusting God, then the Beings and energies that are most helpful to you will simply appear in a beautifully coordinated dance—a pattern of events and blessings.

"Regarding your question of where to find the Glamorgan grotto that is sacred to the Goddess, it is not terribly far off of a path in this park. You do not have to go scrambling to find it in a hidden place. It is a known location where a stream emerges from a beautiful rock grotto that people do appreciate for its beauty. When you go to the state park that has been preserved because of its natural beauty, just ask for directions to the stream that emerges from the grotto, although they will probably use the word *cave*. It will not be advertised as a place sacred to the Mother, but you will know by its energy. Any spring that wells up is sacred to the Mother."

John jumps in with an unrelated question. "My memory is playing tricks on me. I'll be talking about something and then, in the next instant, the name is gone. Any suggestions on reawakening my memory?"

"This is simply a challenge of aging. The key is to allow details like names to come and go, while *not* losing the thread of meaning, emotion, purpose, and significance. Stay in the flow of the *purpose* of your communication, and allow the names to come and go.

"The reason the mind often loses names is that the Soul is aware some names have a deeper vibrational significance than others. The mind is not attached to the lower vibrational names because they do not have meaning. When a name has meaning, the mind keeps it because it is part of that Soul's story. The great example is my name, which has the vibrational quality of 'God restoring the mind of humanity to its original wholeness, to its awareness that it has never left God.' The name *Yeshua* has a deep vibrational significance and is, therefore, never forgotten.

"If you observe which names seem to fall away and which ones stay, you might notice the ones that stay have a meaningful vibration and the ones that fall away do not. The key is to trust, relax, and let the details flow in and out of your mind. It is the same as the conversation you had earlier about money. If you trust you are in the flow of God, then whatever your monetary needs are will come to you. Your needs will be met, and you will meet other people's needs in a constant flow. This is something I spoke about extensively in *A Course of Love*. When Souls are attuned to God and aware of their Oneness with the Universe, then there is a constant flow of needs being met. It is this same energy I ask you to rest in regarding memory. Trust that your need to focus on the purpose of your communication will be met. Is this helpful?"

"Yes, thank you. You mentioned your name refers to returning to original wholeness. There seem to be two different interpretations of that. One is that you return unchanged. The other is that you return changed. The latter is the way you seem to be teaching us." John exclaims, "Laura's face is so wonderful!"

Yeshua laughs. "How could anything return unchanged? The flow of Creation is ceaselessly changing. I have been endlessly clear on this topic. In *A Course of Love*, I describe how the Child of God's mind returning awareness to its Oneness with God is, in fact, a New Creation (Perron 2014, 354). The Child of God, before it *leaped* out into its adventure of being a separated identity, was not *aware* of its Identity. Through these eons of experience of *knowing* itself, the Child of God now returns to the Father, to the Source, in full *awareness* of its Identity. In this way, the Child of God and God can be in intimate Communion, in full awareness of each other. This is the New Creation, where all parts of Creation are *aware* they are in Communion and are not separated. This New Creation is the paradox of a multiplicity of individuated awarenesses (I cannot use the word *identities* since it is not that rigid), all aware that they are simultaneously all the same *and* in intimate communication with all other awarenesses. This is how the Child of God returns very much changed to the Father. And yet, what does not change is your *nature*, who you *are*. This has never changed. You have always been the Child of God, like unto God in every way, with the infinite powers of Creation, knowing, and loving. Is this a helpful explanation for you, my brother?"

"Wonderfully helpful. Thank you so much!"

"It is so tempting for the ego to latch onto intellectual arguments. Any time there is an energy of needing to be right or explain something, just be quiet. Let others engage in that drama. You go into your heart and rest in what *you* know is the Truth.

"I would end with my usual encouragement to take the energies of Love you have received here today out onto the Earth and bestow your blessings to her, encouraging her in her own willingness to wake up and shift her energetic pattern from her role of receiving the negative energies of the Child of God, to enacting her own creative powers. In this way, she is modeling for the Child of God that all sorts of new possibilities await Creation.

"Please go out into the world with our blessings. We are with you always. Ameyn."

"Ameyn," repeats John.

"Ameyn."

The Place of Recycling Souls

In mid-June 2019, John and I set off on our pilgrimage to the British Isles and southern France. We stayed a few nights with my cousins in Bridgwater and Bath in Somerset, and visited several places in neighboring Wiltshire that are suffused with powerful spiritual energy, including Stonehenge, West Kennet Long Barrow, and the stone circle at Avebury.

Standing inside the womb space of the West Kennet Long Barrow, I recorded this guided message on June 15, 2019, in a brief few minutes between the visits of other tourists.

"This place has an enormous energy of regeneration and creativity, of using what has gone before to transform it into something new. There's a fountain of power that comes through the Heart here. It is a deep Source of Love and kindness. In this place, we can reconnect to the Mother and give her our blessing. This is a portal into the Womb of the Mother. It goes deep from here, a long passageway into the Heart of the Mother Goddess.

"There is an energy of peace and stillness here. It is the place of recycling Souls so that, when they have passed into Spirit, they are guided into the proper form for them in which to reappear. It does not have an energy of death, but of rejuvenation. The Mother absorbs all bodies back into her body, and then they are reconfigured and transformed into the new.

"At this time of the New Creation, when the awareness of humanity is returning to its Unity with God, a place like this, where there is such a long history of creating new from old, is a powerful place to aid in the development of the awareness of our full Communion with God.

"There is an incredible energy in the heart. My heart is beating quite rapidly. My hands are tingly. My right leg and hand in particular are tingly. I'm going to move slightly so my body is in line with that energy. That helps to balance the tingling.

"The difference between this place and Stonehenge is that the Light coming in here is like when you mix water into the Earth, and it turns into mud so you can make a pot. It's the creative force that allows the mud of Earth to become living forms. This is the cauldron in which Spirit informs matter and manifests as living matter.

"It is an enormous blessing to be standing here in the channel of this power, so our bodies can be rejuvenated to serve in the New Creation of bringing the full awareness of our minds into alignment with the awareness of God.

"Ameyn."

Waters Sacred to the Mother

We met up with another sister on the Path to pay homage to Glastonbury Abbey. This is the site of a Druid community that welcomed members of the Essene community, before and after the Resurrection, through the auspices of Joseph of Arimathea, who, along with Mother Mary, is revered here. We walked up the Tor and took in the view of the surrounding flatlands that used to be marsh, the misty home of Avalon.

We then drove nearby to one of my favorite places on this Earth, Wells Cathedral. I resonated deeply with this cathedral as a child, and now felt consumed by joy at being there again. This time, I noticed that the three enormous statues high above the crossing (the space in the center of the church where the transept intersects the nave) are

Yeshua, Mother Mary, and Maryam of Magdala, clearly identifiable with her long red hair. She is revered everywhere in this region. In the Bishop's Garden, next to the cathedral, are the actual wells the city is named after—enormous springs of clear water that gush up from the Earth. I realized this place had always been sacred to the Divine Mother, and there had been a Druidic school there devoted to the honoring of her power and Love.

My mother's paternal grandfather hails from Timsbury, a small village outside of the city of Bath. The thermal baths down in the city were clearly also an ancient Druidic center. The Romans brought in their own representation of the Goddess to replace the name used by the Druids, but I was fascinated to see one treasure that had been unearthed—a small stone with the carved image of the Triple Goddess: Maiden, Mother, and Crone. I went through the underground excavations, past the torrents of thermal mineral water, exchanging blessings with the Divine Mother.

John and I then headed out in our rental car (driving on the left side of the road!) to the Brecon Beacons National Park (Bannau Brycheiniog) in southern Wales, where we had been guided to go. At a Welsh tourist center, I described what we were looking for—a place where water emerges from a grotto—and the woman easily identified it: Cwm Porth, near Aberdare, where the Afon (River) Hepste disappears underground and then reemerges. Just as Yeshua described it, it is easily accessible, close to the path, and profoundly beautiful. There are two small alcoves in the stone walls on either side of the grotto. I could definitely picture Druid trainees, including the twelve-year-old Yeshua, meditating there. Immediately downstream is a small field where I could picture Druidic ceremonies.

We headed on through the beautiful Welsh countryside, north to Mona, now called the Isle of Anglesey. We knew that the westernmost tip of this island, a place still called Holy Island today, had been the location of an ancient Druid university. Indeed, there are remnants of structures dating from Neolithic times there, including a group of small stone enclosures right behind the farmhouse where we stayed. We had been instructed to sit in meditation on the cliff overlooking the sea. In my inner vision, I saw clearly a Druid elder, dressed in the most primitive of homemade clothing—rough woven cloth held together with a bone pin through a string loop—with totally unkempt hair hacked off at around shoulder length. He said not a word, but with the utmost merriment, conveyed to me that, when you know everything is a dance of illusion, it is no longer possible to take anything seriously. He urged me to retain a light heart.

Your True Identity Is the Shimmering Light of the One

We continued on to the Highlands of Scotland, an extremely long drive from the northwestern tip of Wales! A group of seven friends had rented a croft in the middle of a large expanse of sheep pastures, with a distant view of the power mountain, Schiehallion. It could house all of us and was within driving distance of the humble village of Fortingall, a place we knew to have high spiritual significance. (Only now, when checking back to Claire Heartsong's book, did I realize that the great gathering in Fortingall in AD 55 had been at the summer solstice. We knew we were gathering in the same location, but had not realized it was the same time of year.)

On June 20, 2019, the night before heading out to that sacred place where we would meet up with several friends, we all joined in the energy field of Christ Consciousness. It had become clearer to me that, while Yeshua spoke in his own Voice at times, the Consciousness speaking through me was not just the *person* of Yeshua, but a collective Consciousness of Beings who are free from living inside of time. This is a universal Consciousness in which we all live. We are slowly becoming aware of this Truth.

Christ Consciousness begins. "Please start with noticing the strong pressure in your third eye. This is to give you confidence that your inner sight is clear. The point of pressure is so intense in the third eye it is almost painful. Also, notice the pressure on the top of the head as the body receives Light.

"Please have confidence that your bodies *are* made of Light and that the purpose of your gathering here is to experience that beyond a shadow of a doubt, pun intended. The experience of being in a body is *so compelling*, it feels solid and separated and real. You are here to have the experience of your true Identity as the shimmering Light of the One. This is an *idea* that makes sense to you. But the purpose of your being here is to *physically* experience it so *fully* as to *know* that this is your true Identity at every moment.

"As you walk forward from this place out into the world, you have had moments of experiencing the currents of Light in your body. Sometimes you feel them in your hands and feet. Sometimes you feel them in each of the chakras. Sometimes it feels like a fountain or a gentle current. Sometimes there's a bubbling in the heart. The purpose of your being present in this place of *clarity* is so that your mind, heart, and body will be in perfect Unity with the Mind, Heart, and Body—which is Light—of the Father and the Mother.

"You will also experience that the Mother, the Earth, *is* made of Light. We have been speaking to you often about the Earth being her own *Soul*. She is a Being who has agreed to incarnate as the Earth, as you all have agreed to incarnate as bodies. Your practice and devotion, as well as the practice and devotion of many thousands of people around the world, are *shifting* the *purpose* of the Earth's Soul. Her original purpose was to be a *willing platform* on which the Child of God could come and go, and experience the drama of the belief in separation. But her purpose is shifting because the Child of God is now *able* to take *full* responsibility for its *choice* to believe in separation. It can now bring those fear thoughts *back* into its own *heart*, where the fear can be transformed by the Light of God into the Truth of the Unification of all thoughts and feelings. Thus, the Earth no longer needs to absorb fear.

"We have been teaching you to send *loving* energy to the Earth, to encourage her to wake up and express her own creative powers. She no longer needs to play the role of being the one who *welcomes* the *fear* of the Child of God, *holds* it in her Womb, and transforms it into a new life that appears as a body. [I realized as I re-read this that this is the purpose of all the Neolithic womb structures. I had sensed strongly in West Kennet Long Barrow that it was a place for the recycling of Souls. This teaching clarifies that awareness.]

"Another purpose of your being here in Fortingall is to transmit Light extremely powerfully *into* the Earth. This is why we showed to Laura's mind the vortex of Light that goes into the Earth at Stonehenge. Stonehenge is a place that receives the Light from the Star Beings and has been *increasing* its ability to receive this energy because more people are willing to receive the Love of God into their hearts and transmit it through their Beings out into the world.

"Laura also saw at Stonehenge that the Earth herself sends Light up in a vortex that is in a parallel spiral with the vortex of Light that comes down into the Earth. There is a great exchange of the energy of Light and Love into and back from the Earth. This *power* goes *deep* into the Earth at that point and extends outward in great rays through the Earth.

"One of those rays, which are called ley lines, continues to *this* point here, where you now reside in the northern parts of Scotland. Where you will be in the morning is in a valley, so the energy in the ley line is close to the Earth's surface. You will experience yourselves as Light, but will also *transmit* that Light into the Earth, and *receive* the Light of the Earth *up* through your body, and *out* into the stars. This will be an intense experience.

"Please notice your bodies right now. They are probably warming up. You are probably noticing your hands, feet, heart, and your face being energized. Just notice the warmth you are experiencing. This is to help you prepare to withstand the power of God's Love through your Being tomorrow morning.

"We have been practicing with you for many months to prepare you to withstand this energy current. We have shared with you in the past that, if you received this energy current at the start, it would be intolerable and could even cause damage. But you have come far enough that you can feel this heat as a *high-energy* without it being painful, and especially without it being fearful. It is most important not to experience fear—rather, *awe*. You are currently experiencing, and will more so tomorrow morning, the power of the union of the Love of the Father and the Love of the Mother. The only appropriate emotion for this experience is *awe*.

"We would like to express to you also our most sincere gratitude that you have been willing to travel such long distances to this remote spot. But we assure you that, even though it has been an arduous journey in some ways, time is *speeding up*, so it is much easier for you to travel long distances to arrive at places where you have been called.

"Time was slower, you might say, when the previous gathering occurred here. More Souls are attuned to God's Love at *this* moment than they were at *that* moment in time. You might think this is strange to hear because you have a vision of the past as being a highly spiritual time—which it was—but there are many, many more Souls *now* who have received the calling of God's Love in their heart.

"We express our gratitude to you for your efforts to come to this place. And, we know that *you* likewise feel gratitude that you have been able to arrive here so easily, despite the apparent strangeness of the calling to come.

"You have all had many experiences of somehow being in a strange place and miraculous occurrences being bestowed upon you. Each time you have one of these moments of grace, they reinforce for you your confidence that *this* is Reality. Reality is a constant stream of grace.

"And with those words, we reassure you that, throughout this night, even though you may not sleep much because of the high level of energy and the Light, you are in a stream of grace that will carry you tomorrow to the appointed time and place without effort.

"Just go to Fortingall, and we will meet you there.

"Blessings and Ameyn."

In This Holy Place Is the New Creation at Hand

The next day, the summer solstice, we all drove to the village of Fortingall, nestled in the bottom of a flat valley surrounded by steep hills, looking much like a long bowl. There we found the venerable yew tree that is estimated to be five thousand years old, protected behind a stone wall with a locked gate. This was a center of Druidic power. Through grace, we found the guardian of the tree, who agreed to unlock the gate and allow us to commune with this ancient tree-Being. We spent a long time in meditation inside her walled enclosure. Another sister and I both tapped into deep womb energy at this yew tree, which we struggled to articulate. The recording comprises snippets of verbal impressions and vocalizations. We both felt a powerful energy of sexual union and Wisdom encompassing everything. Spontaneous chanting emerged within the group, and the last sound we ended on vibrated at the level of the heart.

These words through me were clear. "To be here is to *feel* the ecstasy of being in perfect Communion with God. Notice the back of your heart chakra as well as the front. They are both activated."

Images came to mind of the shape of the **Vesica Pisces**, with the pelvic bowl forming one of its circles, in union with the pillar of the Christ Light coming down into it, and merging inside the womb circle, with a myriad of circles flowing out of the union.

In retrospect, our difficulty formulating words was an effect of the power of this tree-Being. It holds and expresses the primordial power of the formless void out of which, through the union of God and Sophia, Creation pours.

After enjoying lunch in the charming Fortingall Hotel, we spent the afternoon scrambling up the steep hillside through the woods, arriving at the top of a cliff where we could look down at the village, knowing that Great Beings had been in this place before us. This was a day of feeling into our Communion with each other and with the energies of this place.

Right next to the yew tree stands a Christian chapel. It sits on the site of the gathering of Great Beings in AD 55 (Heartsong 2010, 285). Like the yew tree, it has expansive womb energy. On June 22, 2019, the seven of us drove again to Fortingall and joined together in the little church. We sat in majestically carved wooden chairs on the dais behind the altar, looking down the aisle of the mostly empty chapel with its lovely wooden, barrel-vaulted roof. After our initiation at the yew tree, we are ready for this ceremony.

An opening crystal bowl is sounded, and we recite our prayer of alignment three times.

Christ Consciousness begins. "It is with *enormous* joy and celebration that we welcome you to this most holy of holy places on Earth. In this place is Creation begun. In this place, does the Unity of the Mother and the Father express itself as Creation. In this place, do you experience yourselves as unified with all of Creation. The Unity in this place is everlasting. It has been here since before time and will continue after the end of time.

"All those who pass through feel the sacredness of this place, not knowing what they are called to experience. For those of you who are aware of the holiness of this place, that awareness amplifies the power of the experience of the Knowledge of Unity.

"Please notice the experiences you are currently undergoing in your physical bodies. You will be noticing all manner of sensations — tingling, trembling, heat. Please notice especially the energy in the root chakra and the second chakra. In this place of Creation, there is much power in the womb center of the body.

"Please know that by bringing yourselves to experience this power here, you have made a commitment to receive the power of God, transmuted in your bodies, and expressed outward in your lives. From this day forward, you will express the creative power of God in ways heretofore unknown to yourselves.

"Rest assured, you will always be guided in this process. This New Creation is *new*, so it cannot be something you can *expect* in terms of it being something familiar, but you *can* expect it in terms of the *promise* that the New Creation is at hand.

"This place has been prepared for many thousands of years and will continue to be a place that receives and expresses holiness. In this place, do you know you are the Child of God, like unto the Creator in every way. The Creator bestowed upon us all at our Creation the same powers as herself. In this time, humanity is becoming aware of those powers.

"We have said to you before that, if you became aware of those powers all at once, it would feel overwhelming, so you have been experiencing them in stages. Being willing to follow guidance and experience miracles is one way to help you know you are on the path to experiencing even greater powers.

"You are aware that, in this spot, was a great convocation. The Light-Beings all gathered here, and the resonance of that power has remained here ever since. You are on your way to knowing you are the *same* as those Light-Beings. There is no distinction.

"Please notice the soles of your feet as you receive the energy from the Mother up through your legs, calves, and thighs. The root and the sacral chakras are quite vibrant at this moment.

"Also, notice the pressure on the crown. This is a familiar experience for all of you: the receiving of the Holy Spirit through the crown. Notice the energy of the Holy Spirit descending through your body, pausing in the heart, amplifying, and continuing down to the sacral chakra and the root. Again, it is from *this* place that Creation extends itself outward. In this way, the body is unified as a field of Light, and there is nothing outside of the Light.

"We have told you before that the Beings in what you call the past were aware of the Beings in what you call the future, knowing that their work, practice, and devotion would bear fruit in the future. They derived inspiration from your presence in the future, just as you derive inspiration from their presence in the past. In this moment, please experience that there is no distinction between past and future because all is in the present. In this present moment, you are with all the Light-Beings, experiencing what you thought was in the past, but is in the present moment.

"Please notice the radiance surrounding you in this holiest of holy spots. Please notice the radiance that suffuses your bodies, connecting this circle as one sphere of Light that is also connected with all the other spheres of Light gathered here with you. All of those spheres together make one great sphere, which includes the Earth, the solar system, your galaxy, and all the galaxies, far galaxies, Star systems, and all Beings.

"We reassure you that Love surrounds the Earth. The Angelic realm is always singing its *beautiful* harmonies, transmitting Love to the Earth, with increasing joy, as more of you who appear as humans receive the Angelic harmonies. Even in this circle of human Beings are those who love to sing and create sound. This is incredibly beneficial because it allows the Angelic harmonies to resonate with the human harmonies. We have explained before that when harmonies come in touch with each other, they synchronize and amplify their power. Be aware, as you create your harmonies, that you are synchronizing and amplifying the Angelic harmonies that are ever-singing around your Earth.

"We wish at this time to encourage any of you to bring forth a question resting on your heart that would help you on your Path of Awakening."

✬

Sister One steps forward. "I would like to ask for help in how to lay down and walk over my cloak."

"My beloved sister," Christ Consciousness begins. "It will help you to know that, as you lay down that heavy cloak, you are still surrounded by God's protection. There has been a concern you will be too exposed without your cloak. It has been a familiar comfort for you, a symbol of your confidence, and a symbol of your welcoming of others into this cloak. There is a concern that, if you release it, you will release your confidence in your ability to welcome others.

"We assure you that your loving welcome and confidence *are* who you *are* and cannot be lost. If you will now, visualize the cloak of God's protective Love around your shoulders, and feel the Love of the Mother coming through your feet. Feel the fire in your feet, so that as you walk on the Earth, every step energizes you, and the cloak of God's Love carries you effortlessly.

"Your physical strength is now miraculously imbued with a spiritual strength that allows you to move with ease and grace and no effort on your part. As you walk today, notice this feeling of Lightness in your feet and the warmth of the protective cloak of God around your shoulders.

"And never forget, my sister, that we are with you *always, in all ways*, in every way."

"Thank you."

"Our blessings."

✬

Sister Two asks about spiritual lineage. "How can those of us who continue the lineage of Mary Magdalene best serve the collective at this time?"

"My sister, you are perfectly aware of the answer to your question. You have always had *enormous* courage in bringing forth the energy of the root, which has been so devalued and cut off and feared.

"The desecration of the root comes from fear. There has been such fear of the creative power of the root because every Being has this same power of God. Those who think of power as the ability to control other Souls have always known that if all Beings were aware of their own creative power, they would never allow themselves to be controlled.

"Your courage in teaching people of the Source of their creative power is the thing that will well up from the Earth and topple the power structures that are built with such fragility on top of the Earth.

"What will most help you is to make sure you are not doing this work alone. Also, when you run into any resistance, do not engage with it. There are enough Souls who are open to your teaching about valuing and experiencing the power of the root that there is no need to challenge or convince any resistance that comes towards you.

"You are perfectly aware that I, as a man, experienced this resistance, as did my Beloveds. We never engaged in confrontation. When confrontation was offered to us, we offered loving counsel in return, using skillful means that would allow the questioner to begin to hear.

"But you, my sister, do not need to engage with any great challenge. You have already put yourself forth with much courage, and there is *much* receptivity among humanity for your work. Those who have rekindled the knowledge of the Druids and the Earth Mother are particularly open to your teachings because the power of the root is the power of the Earth, which is the Womb of Creativity. It is in those communities you will find ease, grace, and reception.

"You will also find ease, grace, and reception in any community that is welcoming the Christ energy. Those Souls will also be willing to let the power of God descend from the crown and the heart, through the will, and into the base.

"It is with the *greatest* of joy that we have been supporting you all along, as you are perfectly aware. Truly, *joy* is the essence of your work. Yes, there will be fear, sadness, and constrictions that emerge, but they will pass. Joy is the great container in which what you do bubbles outward over the land. It is an ever-flowing cauldron of joy, bubbling with the heat of the fire of God's Love.

"The cauldron is the great symbol of the Unity of the Mother and the Father—the fire of Spirit, and the earth and water of the Mother, that together produce form and sustain life. This is the same symbol as the chalice, the grail, and the pot.

"All these images serve for you to experience the knowing of the Unity of the Mother and the Father. In your bodies, the chalice is your pelvic girdle, the bowl of the lower portion of the body in which this Unity of the fire of God's Love and the bubbling Love of the Mother join and pour forth Creation.

"My sister, as you walk forth today, please notice that your hand is being held at every moment. We are always delighted to have you invite us. We know that all of you hold us in your hearts, and we are with you. It is particularly helpful when you *consciously* invite us to join you to walk upon your beautiful Earth. Thank you for your service, my dear one."

"Thank you."

⌘

A brother inquires about channeling. "I have a question about the seeming discrepancies in the many channelings and stories around you and Magdalene. How would you explain this?"

"This is a very helpful question. Any channeling comes through the habituated patterns of the mind-body of the channel. Those of us not in bodies are always in the minds of everyone. It is only a degree of awareness separating those who are willing to speak what they know in their minds from those who have not yet developed the confidence to speak what they know. What comes through each person's mind is colored by the habituated patterns of that mind. Some thoughts that are not known to that mind can be expressed, but thoughts that are so far distant from what that mind can comprehend are too difficult to express through that channel.

"It frequently happens that an image or a feeling or a sensation is transmitted, and there is a resonance in the channel's mind, which brings up a habituated thought pattern so similar that the channel hears it as their own habit. We reassure you that what comes out as differences is only because the energies being transmitted have found a resonance in the channel's mind. This does not mean there are enormous inaccuracies. Rather, it is evidence of variations in what has been *previously* understood, because the energetics are transmitted through the filter of what has been understood before.

"What is most important when you read or listen to any channel is what you are *feeling* in the presence of that communication. Does it *feel* right, or is the resonance *not quite* right for *you*? If it does not quite resonate for you, it does not mean that it is inaccurate. It just means this vibration is not *helpful* to you.

"We have told you before, many times, that all time is simultaneous, and so, what you experience now influences the past. This also explains why there are apparent discrepancies in stories about the past. As you rework the energetics of those past experiences, they are re-experienced by the Beings in the past, because the past is currently being experienced in the only thing that *is* real, which is the present moment.

"The great miracle is, as all of your minds awaken, you are actually transforming the past as well as the future. We have shared with you before the risk of holding onto information from the past and making it solid. That will simply create a constriction in your mind in the present because we have just explained to you that nothing in the past is solid.

"Listen with your heart to any channeled information because there is some that has been filtered through a mind that still has many constrictions. What emerges is, thus, lots of previously understood thought patterns rather than clear information. Again, this does not mean it is wrong. It means the energetics are resonating with the patterns in that mind. If it does not resonate for you, *do* trust that you are experiencing the energetics of the channel's mind more so than the energetics of the Love that is being transmitted through the channel.

"Always notice if there is a resonance of Love in whatever is being transmitted. If there is a resonance of fear, or needing to be right, or more right than someone else, just smile inwardly and turn away. Is this helpful?"

"Yes, it is. Thank you."

"We would like to reassure you that you are all channels. This is very important to understand. I have said to you before, as your elder brother, the only difference is that I have gone ahead of you a little way on the Path. There is no *distinction* between my *Being* and your *Being*.

"All of you are on the same Path to becoming ever more aware of all Knowledge because you *are* all Knowledge. The only reason you are not aware of all Knowledge is because of the constrictions of fear in your mind. But as those constrictions resolve, Knowledge begins to shine more brightly, and you will not need to rely on the channelings of other Beings. You can rely on the thoughts in your own minds, which, you are becoming aware, are not your private thoughts. They are the thoughts of the Great Beings who *are also* your *Self*.

"Always please trust your *own knowing*. You have all had the experience of *knowing*—a calm, energetic, indescribable *Knowledge* that what you are experiencing is *true*. There is nothing that can be *explained* or *defended*. It's just, 'Oh, I know this is true.'

"You are all quite far along that path of *trusting* your own knowing—the great knowing in which we all abide. We extend to you our gratitude for your increasing trust in your *own* inner knowing, and your relinquishing the thought that you must rely on some exterior source of Knowledge.

"As you go forth in your day, my brother, notice that *feeling* of *knowing* in your Being, the *quality* of *knowing*. It is the *most* delicious feeling.

"Please invite us to join you in your knowing, because knowing is not a solitary experience. By its nature, knowing is a *Unity* experience because you are unifying what appears to be your small consciousness with the Great Consciousness of All. The delicious quality of knowing comes from the *feeling* of Communion with the Great Knowledge. We are *with* you in your knowing today."

"Thank you, my brother."

"Our blessings of *enormous* gratitude to you."

"I receive it, thank you."

Sister Three shares a vision she is experiencing. "I am getting all these images of Beings I've never seen before. It's like drinking from a chalice. Who are these images that are coming forth? I have no sense."

"My sister, in this spot, Great Ones have gathered from throughout time and space. It is not necessary for you to know *who* they are because they come from other dimensions, other times, other realms. This image is given to your mind to help you relinquish the thought that you must be able to *identify* an *identity*.

"We shared earlier about the images of the chalice, bowl, cauldron, grail, and hips. These are the containers in which life bubbles forth. The Great Beings have come to drink of the Source of life. These Great Beings exist throughout all realms, throughout time and space. Many of these Beings have been described by your brother, the great Gautama Buddha, who had *such* a way with words, describing the infinite realms of Beings.

"You are able to perceive the Ones who are close enough in resonance to your own vibration, but we assure you, there are many other Beings who are outside of your ability to perceive. They are also with all of us in this holy place. Your ability to perceive the Ones closer to you in vibration brings a great blessing to yourself and to the others here. It assures them there are many Great Beings sharing in this feast of life.

"My sister, as you go forth in your day, enjoy drinking from that cup of life. Feel it nourish you. If you are drinking any liquid, eating any food, or breathing any air, please be aware that you are absorbing this great feast of life, and extending it outward as loving compassion. We thank you for your openhearted willingness to receive and extend blessing."

"Thank you. Thank you. Thank you."

Christ Consciousness continues, "All of you bring attention to your hearts and feel the Love that exists in this circle, in this sacred space. Feel all the Beings who are with you throughout time and space, who are singing your praises, that you are so willingly *courageous* to come to this place and bring your Love and devotion out into the world. *Feel the fire of the Love of God in your hearts, right now.* There is a cauldron in your heart that bubbles forth. It can be experienced as a little fluttering, bubbling feeling in the heart."

Many sighs and murmurs weave among the gathered Souls.

"Delicious!" says Christ Consciousness.

Sister Two has another question. "You mentioned before that you like it when we call you in. How is it best to invite you? By what name?"

Christ Consciousness chuckles. "The name of Love! When I say, 'Call me in,' it is just a momentary thought. 'Ah! My elder brother, my sister, my mother, my grandmother, my aunts, uncles, and ancestors!' Whichever name or Being you are feeling in Communion with, just notice, 'Oh, thank you for being with me. Please walk with me.' It is that simple."

"And how about *Yeshua*? Is that the name we can give to connect to your frequency, your Love?"

"The name *Yeshua* is a powerful vibrational mantra. It carries the meaning, as you well know, of 'God restoring the awareness of God to the mind of the Child of God.' Saying the name *Yeshua* will help amplify that vibrational elevation process that is occurring around the world."

"Is that the same frequency as the *Christ*?"

"Yes, my sister, it is. The *Christ* has a crisper clarity. It is more of a Mind vibration, and *Yeshua* is more of a Heart vibration. But it is the same quality of perfect Love, perfect Unity, perfect Awareness, perfect Knowledge. It is helpful to notice what quality of energy will be most beneficial for your purpose at whatever moment you are calling in the energetics of Love."

"What is the grail lineage?" she asks. "I feel like a great door to those mysteries was closed by myself, and we are now turning towards a remembrance. I have a remembrance of a practice of the union of the Holy Mother and Holy Father, drinking from the grail. Is there more to know that is important for us all?"

"We are sharing with Laura's mind the image of a beautiful lake surrounded by steep forested hills. Any bowl in the Earth with water at the base is the same as the grail. The Earth is covered with these beautiful containers in which the Unity of the fire of God and the Love of the Mother manifests.

"There is always more, my sister. Everything is always unfolding. It is unfolding in its perfection.

"Those mysteries were apparently locked away, but they have also been held for you in the Mind of God, in which it is an impossibility that anything could ever be lost. If anything could be lost, that would mean there was something outside the Mind of God, something other than God, something that was not Creation. This is completely impossible. We *assure* you that *nothing* has been lost. It is *all* available to you *in your own mind-body*."

"I see it like *I* closed my *own* door. How can I unlock it?"

"The door must be seen as without value. It was given a sense of value in its ability to protect.

"Many Souls in this circle have a similar question about how to release old Knowledge and bring it forth into the world, *past* the lock that has been placed on it. That lock was put there in times of fear when there was such resistance to the Truth of Love that sharing the Truth of Love would have resulted in the death of the body. But we assure you that, even though bodies appear to die, your Soul cannot possibly die. Even if there are moments in the history of humanity when there is resistance against the Truth of Love, the Truth of Love cannot *possibly* die.

"For those of you who have a fear of bringing forth your Knowledge of Love, you will *not* receive the energy of persecution that you received in the past. We referenced before that you might receive some resistance, and all you need to do is move away in a different direction. Those who resist you will not pursue you because, in the modern world, the thought of those in power is that anything that is spiritual is not powerful, so they do not perceive themselves as threatened by the power of Love. This is why you are not being persecuted, because those in power are so far away from their hearts that they do not even *perceive* anything that you are doing.

"Those who resist you are more *aware* that you are in touch with the power of God's Love. But again, you do not need to engage with them.

"I speak to all of you who have put a lock on your Knowledge of the Druidic Ways or of the Ways of the Essenes. Some of you have actually put that Knowledge in writing and locked it away in boxes or behind stone walls. Whatever your lineages have been, and many of you have come through *many* lineages, even if you thought you were locking the Knowledge away, we reassure you that the Knowledge has never left your Soul.

"The way to open the doors that you have put on your own hearts is to rest in knowing that the Knowledge has not been lost, cannot be lost, and in this current timeframe, will not be greeted with persecution. Is this helpful?"

"Yes. As you speak, I see the symbol of the Eye of Horus deep in the center of my heart. Is this a symbol that we can use to unlock?"

"The Eye of Horus is a symbol familiar to many in this circle. It is a symbol of the all-knowing Eye of God, who can see through any veil, any lock, and any belief that a lock has value. So, I say to you, my sister, *your key* is to understand that there is no *value* in the lock. The *value* you have placed on that lock is no longer necessary. When you see it is *valueless*, simply a pile of dust, then you can see with the all-seeing Eye of God that you have always held the Truth in your own Soul."

"Ah, thank you."

"We have shared before that the Soul is always connected with God and has never *not* been connected with God. It is impossible that the Soul could ever be disconnected from God. If that were possible, the Soul would die, and, in the circle of God's Love, there is no such thing as death. The only thing that appears to experience danger and death is a shadow on the surface of the Soul created by constrictions in the mind. When the Light of God that always pours forth through the Soul hits constrictions, it produces shadows that appear to be fear and danger. Is this helpful?"

"Thank you. Yes."

⁓ׅ๏ᅠ

John has a question. "Yesterday, the seven of us were asked to make a wish. Mine was to allow myself to awaken as a warrior for Truth. The word *warrior* is not something I would have chosen—it was what came. Could you comment on my wish, or on anyone else's if relevant?"

"My brother, it is important for you to focus on *your* warrior path, and trust everyone else is on their own path. Their paths are not yours, nor do you need to make their paths smooth for them. When others come to you for guidance, your clarity of vision is *extremely* beneficial to them. Being a warrior for Truth does not mean you are responsible for *showing* the Truth to others. Others have the Truth in their own hearts.

"Being a warrior is the same as your sister's last question. How do you courageously go through the barriers you have placed on your own heart? For you, my brother, the image of the warrior is to give you courage to go through the barriers you have placed in your own way, and cease looking to the right and left to see if the other people are successfully making it through their barriers.

"As you go through your life today, notice when you look left and right to see how other people are doing with their barriers, and then bring your focus back to your own. If you would like, imagine holding your hand out with a flaming sword of Light with which you can cut through barriers." Christ Consciousness chuckles. "The image of the Light-saber is quite beneficial. Today, imagine yourself walking with a saber of Light that can dissolve the barriers you have placed in front of you. Please do so with humor. This is not a serious project. This is a delightful project to dissolve the barriers you yourself have placed in your own path. If you want to look to the left and right, I encourage you to notice there is a grand celebration among your brothers and sisters that you are using your Light-saber to melt through your own barriers. Is this helpful?"

"Yes, thank you."

～❧～

"I have another question," begins the first brother. "Is there anything to share regarding my intent to work together with Sister Two?"

"There is a great healing in this relationship because there has been much misunderstanding about the perceived conflict between the Souls of Peter and Maryam of Magdala. In fact, those *around* these Souls perceived conflict, but this was not really the perception of these two Souls. Their intention was not to do battle with each other, but their interaction was perceived in that way by the community.

"Both Souls have the *same mission*, which is to bring the Truth of God's Love out into the world. The Feminine Way is the inner way, and the Masculine Way is the outer way. That is the only distinction. You two, who are in the lineage associated with these Souls, are bringing together the Masculine and Feminine Ways. You are also healing the misperception in the mind of humanity that there has been a conflict between these Souls.

"These Souls have known each other for many eons. They have been together in many places, facilitating the awareness of God's Love in whatever place they chose to manifest themselves.

"You are well aware there was a bifurcation of the ways so that the inner way could be preserved, and the outer way could be *accepted* by the world. The inner way was *so deep* and powerful that the outer world was not yet ready to receive it. The outer way was *absolutely* necessary to plant the ideas of forgiveness, redemption, resurrection, Light-bodies, *unconditional Love*, and the brother- and sisterhood of humanity. The world was able to hear these ideas.

"The inner way of the creative power of the union of the Mother-Father-God was still too much for the mind of humanity to bear, and that is the only reason these two ways appeared to part. It is now time for them to come back together.

"In your coming together, there is much blessing. We will be with you *always* as your path unfolds. Much power will come from this re-union of the Male Path and the Female Path. Is this helpful?"

"Yes, it is."

"It is a great relief to your minds to hear that there really has been no conflict between these Souls. There has been only devotion to Yeshua, to the Way of Love, to the Way of the Mysteries." The Voice of Christ Consciousness becomes tearful. "The Love these Souls feel for Yeshua is infinite, vast, without measure, without form, without ability to be described. That is the *same* in these Souls.

"It is in that profound Love that you will bring forth the energy of Unity into the world.

"Please notice the heat in your hands. This is the experience of extending the unified field of God's Love *out*. Both of you have the power to heal in your hands and have always had this power. Just notice the power in your hands at this moment.

"Just call on the name of Yeshua, who you know to be a healer, and the power of Yeshua will infuse you and provide healing energies to those who *ask*. You are well aware that healing energies can only be transmitted to those who *ask*. But we assure you that asking is on many levels. There are Souls to whom you might be drawn who will require your help, which you can transmit to them in a way they won't be consciously aware of because, at a deeper level, they are ready.

"Please enjoy just extending Love *all* around you, without regard to how aware those who receive it might be of the power of your extension.

"It is with great joy we travel with you out into the world."

Together, this brother and sister repeatedly express their thanks.

⟲⟳

Sister One has another request. "I would like to ask about all the amazing things we've discovered here so far, such as the incredible Souls who have protected secrets held in this sacred land, and what we've yet to discover as we journey together as a group. Could you comment further on this?"

"It is true that energies are planted into the Earth at various places, and this is one of them. As you travel around, notice the energetics of the Earth in each spot, the energetics of Love that have been transmitted into many places in the Earth in this area. Precisely because it is so far north, there is a clarity here that allows the energetics of Love to remain without becoming overlaid with the energetics of greed and fear.

"Picture in your minds right now the beautiful mountains and valleys of this area of the Earth, and the *clarity* of the *Light* that so *draws* people here. It is this clarity of Light that is the energetics of Love. There have, of course, been conflicts, battles, and fear enacted in these same places, but that is because there is much constriction in those minds that perceive fear.

"*You* are able to perceive the Love that has been impregnated into the Earth. My sister, simply *enjoy* the deliciousness of the power of Love that has suffused this land and is so willingly offered to you."

"As you describe the energy of the land here, is that what I also sense that extends into Ireland?" this sister inquires. "That *magic*? That's the only word I can come to."

"It is experienced as magic by the human mind, but, in fact, that is the Truth of *Reality*, that everything is *miraculous*. In these northern lands, although there has been fear, conflict, and suffering, there is a clarity that has always remained, and a sense of wonder, a sense of the *value* of the miraculousness of life, and the infinite possibilities of life.

"Each place and each Being has its own particular vibrational fingerprint, you might say. In this magical land, there are many places where the deeper mysteries have been impregnated, some in sound, some in visual form, some in vibrations in the Earth. Follow your heart, and what feels like a blessing to you, is an opening, a doorway, for you.

"My sister, if you can maintain your awareness of this deeper level of *Light* that is deep in the Earth but also on the surface of the Earth and extending to the Heavens, then the fear that has also walked on the surface of this Earth can be transmuted. This is a powerful service because we are reminding you that the past can be transmuted with Love in the present.

"Thank you for your question.

"My sisters and brothers, bring your attention to the crown of your head and let the Light of God focus in the center of your brain. The third eye is on the forehead, and also the back of the skull, and the point in the center.

"Then bring the Light down to your throat to allow you the courage to speak the Truth clearly.

"Bring the Light to your heart, where the Unity of the Mother and the Father rests as Love and extends outward.

"Bring the Light down to the solar plexus, knowing that, by being here, you have aligned yourselves with God's Will. Your will is the same as God's Will, which is only Love.

"Bring the Light down to the womb chakra and the root chakra, and know that by opening these chakras, you allow yourself to express the creative power of God in the world.

"Notice the energy in the palms of your hands and the energy that flows down your legs and through the soles of your feet into the Earth. Notice that this energy extends deep into the Earth and is received by the Mother, who also sends Her Love back up through your feet, your legs, into the root, the sacral, the solar plexus, the heart, the throat, the third eye, the crown, and the Soul Star above the top of your heads. In this way, your body is a superhighway of loving energy, flowing down from the Sun and up from the Earth.

"As you go forth from this place, skip, dance, and enjoy being part of the beauty of this world! Thank you for your presence.

"Ameyn. Ameyn. Ameyn."

"Ameyn. Ameyn. Ameyn." Sighs and chuckles flow all around the circle.

I realize I am not aware of the full significance of this gathering. I have a liminal sense that it served to align many layers of consciousness to assist in the opening of the New Creation, which this message makes clear is happening *now*.

Gratitude Opens the Way of Harmony When Heaven Manifests on Earth

An even larger group of friends, about sixteen of us, hired a wonderful Scottish guide named Kris Peterson, who spent the day with us, introducing us to all the mystical aspects of the Rosslyn Chapel and the Druidic landscape around the town of Roslin. (I was living at that time in the neighborhood of Boston called Roslindale, so it was a delight for me to learn of the wonders of its namesake town.) He brought us to a cave known to have been used in Druidic mysteries to experience the Divine Feminine.

The group asked me to give Voice to Christ Consciousness in that cave where we were all gathered on June 25, 2019.

One brother declares, "We call the ancestors, the guardians of this land, in gratitude for allowing us to ceremony on their land. Just continue breathing, and turn your inner dial to *receive*." He then chants the Lord's Prayer in Aramaic. The group all joins in singing, "Ameyn."

We recite our prayer of alignment three times.

In the Name of the Mother-Father God, in the Name of the Son, the Daughter, the Child of God, in the Name of the Holy Spirit, Sophia, Shem, in the Name of the Lord, Christ I am.

My voice begins with a chuckle, and Christ Consciousness speaks. "It is with *utmost* delight that we have been with you *all day* today! We have been walking with you on your Path, as you look at all the clues that bring you inward to your own heart. Please remember the purpose of the Path is for you to find God. It is not for you to worship any Being. It is for you to know who you truly are—which is the Child of God, the same as God—for you to release any thought that you are separated from God or from each other. This is not new information.

"The purpose of this day and being here in this cave is for you to *feel deeply*, in your hearts, your union with each other and with the Mother Earth. The Mother Earth is *so extremely grateful* you are transmitting your Love to her, to awaken her, so she can express herself as the shimmering Light of God, as you also express yourselves as the shimmering Light of God, and Heaven can manifest *on Earth.*

"Please tune into your hearts and feel the vibration of Love in your hearts. See it as a circle that connects all of your hearts here in this Womb of the Earth. Feel also your womb chakra, and the circle of Love that connects you at that level. Bring in the Light through the crown, all the way down through the root, and out through the feet. Feel the Love of the Mother come up through your feet, through the root, through the womb, through the will—which is aligned with God—into your hearts, out through your voices, so you can sing, laugh, and have a good time playing with each other!

"Notice the pressure in your third eye. This is for you to be aware that all of you have the same capacity for inward sight. There is no difference between you in this. Please trust whatever comes into your mind as your own guidance.

"Then notice the openness on the crown and visualize an actual crown about two feet above your head. This is the Light of the Holy Spirit that comes down into your head, all the way through your body, down to the Earth, and back. You know this is a double spiral. The Light and energy come down, and they come up, passing each other endlessly, back-and-forth.

"Notice all the colors of the rainbow as this Light goes back and forth, through your bodies, down to the Earth, up from the Earth, through your bodies, into the Heavens and the stars. Notice *all* the beautiful colors—colors you've never seen with your body's eyes. This is your glimpse of Heaven on Earth when everything will appear to you in exquisite beauty and harmony. You will see the patterns, the crystalline structure of everything, and the colorful rainbows of Lights that all interact. Each subtle vibration affects every other subtle vibration in a *perfect* hologram. There is no point anywhere in the

Universe that is distinct from any other point. This Womb of Earth is connected to the farthest stars, and the farthest star is connected to this Womb of Earth.

"We have said to you before that the Angelic realms are always singing around the Earth. Any time you attune yourself to the vibration of Love, that amplifies *their* ability to sing more beautifully. Please hear, with your inward ear, the singing of the Angels. Hear the deeper humming that comes from the Earth. Hear the rushing of the water, the living waters of the Mother. This is the music of the spheres, the perfect harmony that flows ever-onward, without ceasing.

"As you continue on your paths and release the obstacles of fear, the inner harmony becomes the outer harmony. There's no distinction between the inner beauty and the outer beauty, and you walk the *Way of Harmony* that you all came to this Earth to manifest.

"You have all released the *way of conflict* as uninteresting. In the past, the way of conflict was of *utmost* interest. It helped you to know you were a *self*. But now you know you are all a *self*, there is no need for conflict, and you are manifesting the Way of Harmony.

"The Way of Harmony is to be manifested *on the Earth*. You are all of utmost importance in this process of manifesting the Way of Harmony on the Earth. *Never, for one moment*, doubt your importance. Each one of you is a star, an exquisite jewel, shimmering and reflecting each other, and extending your Light and Love out in infinite directions, in ways of which you have no idea.

"Please be aware that all time is simultaneous, so whatever Light and Love you express and integrate and ground *here*, goes backwards and forwards in time, creating a blessing in the past, bringing forth the powers of the past, and creating a blessing in the future, so that the lives of Souls that manifest in bodies in the future will know the Truth of harmony.

"Beloveds, please always listen with your inner ear and your inner sight so you know where to go, what to do, and who to love, which is everyone. Bless every creature, large and small, that crosses your path. Nothing is outside of God. The stones are God, the insects are God, the water is God—everything is God. The past is God, the present is God, the future is God—because it is all *One*.

"You are coming to know that all of your Souls are intimately intertwined. They have been for eons and will continue to be until you know there is no such thing as time."

Christ Consciousness chuckles.

"Notice the vibration in your feet. This is the joy of the Mother, expressing her gratitude that you are awakening her up so that she can express herself as Light."

There are collective sighs and then a long pause.

"We *rest* so that you can *feel* the Light, Love, beauty, and harmony. As you walk out of this cave, on your way, you will retain this physical experience of knowing that everything is a pattern of exquisite beauty.

"We express our gratitude to you that you are coming to trust the Way of Harmony. And with those words, please remember, *we are with you always*. It is impossible for us *not* to be with you.

"Please feel the vibrations in your bodies. This is the presence of the Great Ones who are encouraging you to know that *you* are *also* Great Ones.

"Ameyn."

"Ameyn. Ameyn," echoes around the gathered circle.

Chapter 20

Maryam of Magdala

The Mysteries of Sainte-Baume

John and I continued our outward spiritual journey to southern France. This time, we could drive our rental car on the right! We headed east from Marseille to pay homage to Maryam of Magdala in the cave at Sainte-Baume, where she spent the last years of her life.

After returning from our hike up to her cave, which sits at the base of a sheer cliff, I sat outside behind the Accueil des Pèlerins, looking back up at the cliff face, and recorded my experiences in my journal:

This is an internal place. This morning, when I stated my intention to surrender to the next step on my path, I heard, "You will be initiated in the next mysteries that you can understand."

"Mysteries?" I replied. "The only Truth is God's Love. There is no mystery."

"Yes, the mysteries are the inner way that allows you to undo the ego that has been resisting the Truth of God's Love. It has been kept a mystery only because the ego cannot understand it and thus perceives it to be a mystery. The real mystery is that you could have obscured the Truth!"

A mystery to escape the Truth, and a mystery to return to God.

After hiking up through the forest, I arrived at the base of the long, complicated switchback stairway that leads to the plaza in front of her cave. At that instant, the bells for 10:45 Mass began to ring. I walked each step in rhythm with the bells. The last bells were slower, so I took two steps per bell and arrived at the top right before the last two rang. Perfection.

Inside the grotto, I immediately walked down the short stairway to the right to sit by her statue. When I had visited for the first time in 2015, I had experienced an intense sensation of burning in my heart. This time, it was the womb area that burned.

I decided to go up to the side altar by the pool of natural spring water, where a young priest was holding an intimate Mass. There were only four of us—me, John, and two French women. The priest's devotion was so pure. My French is good enough that I could follow his words. He read a passage from the Gospel of Matthew in which Yeshua speaks with authority and tells the parable of building your house on the rock of God's Truth, rather than on the sand of falsehood. The priest gave a little talk about the source of Yeshua's authority— he was in direct communication with God. He assured us we, too, can access this direct communication by humbling ourselves to the grace of his presence in our hearts. Beautiful! I loved experiencing his devotion to Yeshua as the Son of God, who is perfectly aware of his Identity. I added silently that we are *all* the Child of God. I felt such gratitude for this Dominican priest, who is continuing a many-centuries-long line of devotion to the Way, here in this grotto.

I went back down to sit by Maryam's statue on the lower level, feeling it was time for the next steps of initiation. I experienced a sequence of full-body breathing practices that simply took over:

- pulsing in the womb, a pattern of contractions in synchrony with the breath, unlike anything I've experienced before;
- full-body convulsions;
- third eye burning;
- womb open, Mother breath coming up through the womb, up to the crown, emerging out above the head, spinning;
- receiving Light from above, which fills the brain, and goes down to the womb, the root, the feet, and the hands;
- feeling energy moving back and forth, up and down through the body;
- panting breaths in the throat begin;
- convulsions in the womb;
- rocking side to side, a feeling of integrating masculine and feminine;
- deep full-body undulations, pelvis forward, heart open, breath in; then pelvis back, heart back, breath out;
- womb feels open, a feeling of water flowing through;
- sudden quiet, peace.

I gazed up at her statue and looked her in the eye. The white marble felt alive. I felt exposed. *I* am exposed to God. Through these practices, the *I* is pulled away and the Self, made of Light and motion, is exposed to God. Knowing God is an intense, full-body experience. I feel the connection between Earth wombs and living waters, such as this cave, and body wombs and energies flowing through the body. I feel Yeshua on my right, Maryam on my left, Holy Spirit in my body. I feel the knowing that, like them, I am Christ Consciousness, as are we all. My head is spinning.

I hear, "Let go of worries and step into the flow of things, then everything happens in the best possible way. Help is being given at all levels."

Purification in the Pyrénées

We traveled westward to Saintes-Maries-de-la-Mer.

It was a dangerous time for Yeshua's family and followers after the Crucifixion and Resurrection. They had connections in Egypt, so a group fled by boat to Alexandria, but the Romans still found them there. The Romans broke the boat's mast and rudder, destroyed their sails, and then cast them adrift to die on the Mediterranean Sea.

But following a Divine Light, the boat was guided safely to southern France, to this small port just west of Marseille. On that boat were Mary Salome, Mary Jacobe, Martha, Lazarus, and Maryam of Magdala, who are all mentioned in the Gospels, as well as Sara, an Egyptian woman who had joined them in Alexandria. There were probably others as well. Sara, with dark skin, is now the patron saint of the Romani people.

After preaching with Lazarus in Marseilles, Maryam traveled west to the foothills of the Pyrénées, where there was a small Essene community already established at the base of Mount Bugarach near Rennes-le-Château. She spent much of her life in this region, ministering to many Souls who were drawn to her perfected expression of the Divine Feminine manifested on Earth.

After doing our best to bring some healing to the Inquisition energy in Carcassonne, John and I drove on to our lodgings in the little village of Puivert, where we were greeted by Pete Wilson at L'Occitania B&B. Hearing that we were still feeling overwhelmed by the hateful energies from the history of Carcassonne, he directed us to an incredible healing location called *La Fontaine d'Amour*. Tradition says this is where Magdalene baptized people, continuing in the ancient Jewish Way of ritual bathing to cleanse oneself of any impurities and devote oneself to living in alignment with God. It is not a fountain, but a pool to the side of a brackish mountain stream, carved out by swirling rocks when the water is high and rushing. A few people can easily stand on the smooth bottom, waist-deep in the healing salt water. The strangeness of this salty stream is explained by the groundwater seeping through a layer of salt in the Earth, formed when, deep in prehistory, the area had been at the bottom of an ocean. I am reminded of the vision given to me of the network of energy lines underground in this area, probably facilitated by these vast salt deposits. Immersing ourselves in this pool was cleansing indeed.

It seemed that any church we visited in this region was filled with images of the Divine Feminine—Grandmother Anna, Mother Mary, and Magdalene, who is so deeply revered here. Yeshua was also present, but he rarely took top billing. Notre-Dame de Sabart stands out. On the façade are statues of Maryam Magdalena on the left and Yeshua on the right, equal in presence, welcoming practitioners inside, with Mother Mary blessing all at the peak. Following the theme of the bee as an expression of the Goddess, the sculptor of the statue of Maryam built a beehive inside her body. The steady stream of bees coming in and out through a hole in her waistband was visible from the ground. The presence of the Divine Feminine is palpable in this land!

In the foothills of the Pyrénées, Maryam's followers kept her teachings alive after her departure from them back to Sainte-Baume. These people eventually became identified as Cathars, a version of Christianity with no central authority. They emphasized one's own direct knowing of God through integrating masculine and feminine energies and dissolving identification with what we would call ego. The name Cathar comes from the Greek word *katharos*, meaning *pure*, from which the English word *catharsis* derives.

The Roman Catholic Church felt threatened by the Cathars' lack of alignment with the central authority of Rome, so, after failing to convince them to submit to the Roman Church, the Papal militias then persecuted them. In the eleventh and twelfth centuries, the Cathar community built or was given protection in many castles in high places throughout the region. These ruins stand everywhere in silent testimony to this history.

The last Cathar stronghold was at Montségur. The Pope's troops held them under siege for nearly a year. They surrendered on March 16, 1244. Around two hundred and thirty Cathars refused to renounce their faith and were burned at the stake in a field at the base of the mountain. John and I were alone the afternoon of our visit to this castle, and the mountain was shrouded in mist. The atmosphere could not have been more perfect to experience both the great sadness of this place, as well as its energy of welcome into the mystery of union with the Divine. In the center of this castle, built to protect the lives of the last Cathars and their Wisdom, I asked for help to let go of my belief in the need for self-protection against intrusive and grasping energies, knowing full well that being guarded is not the way to the *true* safety of union with God. The answer was immediate and obvious. As the Christ, give everything because you *are* everything, so your supply is infinite and needs no protection.

Maryam's memory has been kept alive here in a continuous flow up to the present, when more and more people come to this region seeking her teachings of the inner Way of Knowing.

Release the Belief in the Need to Defend Yourself

On July 3, 2019, at L'Occitania B&B, nourished by Pete's amazing breakfast and by Aletheia's session of meditative practices, John and the other two guests, also spiritual seekers, asked me for the opportunity to converse with our true Self, the Christ Consciousness.

I begin. "My prayer for today is that this is an experience for all of us of an expansion of consciousness, of bringing the Light of God all the way through our entire Beings and dissolving any fear that we can dissolve."

After I anoint each person's third eye with frankincense, we recite our prayer three times, and Christ Consciousness begins to teach.

"We ask you first to settle into your hips. Imagine the hips are like the shape of the land; they are like a bowl, just like the valleys of these mountains are in the shape of bowls. Imagine the bowl of your hips contains the living waters of the Mother, just like the valleys contain streams and ponds that collect the living waters of the Mother.

"Now bring your attention to the crown of your head, and imagine the Light of the Father coming through the crown, all the way through your body, down to your hips, and enlivening the living waters of the Mother.

"Then bring the waters up to your heart, and the fire down to your heart, and in your heart is the *explosion* that creates matter infused by Spirit. It is from your heart that your *power* of creativity extends, so what you hold in your heart is what you extend outwards around you. When you know your heart is the joining place of the Mother and the Father, then you can extend the Truth that Spirit is infused in matter. This, as you know, is the meaning of bringing Heaven to Earth.

"What has been called the Lord's Prayer of manifesting Heaven on Earth has been misunderstood. It was misinterpreted that Heaven and Earth are separate places. But in fact, the teaching is to manifest Heaven on Earth, which means to manifest the Light of God in your physical body.

"This teaching has been obvious and ignored. It has been obvious that Yeshua manifested the Light of God in his body. It was obvious as he walked around that he extended Light and Love, and everyone could see it and feel it. It was obvious after the Resurrection that he extended Light and Love *as* the body. But the teaching has been misunderstood to think he was the only one capable of that.

"You have come so far to know that this is not the Truth. The Truth is that he, Mary Magdalene, his Mother, and other Great Ones were leading the way to demonstrate that this is what we are all here to do—to manifest the Light of God in the body.

"For this to happen, the end of specialness must happen. Yeshua was seen as special, but he is not special. He is a Way-shower. Mary

Magdalene is also a Way-shower. But neither of them is special. If they were special, then that would mean no one else could do what they did. But they came to show the Way that we can all do what they did.

"Humanity needs a great cleansing, a purification, a dissolving and releasing of the constricted places, the places where energy gets hooked and cannot flow. Your practice is to undo the constrictions, open up the hooks, and let the energy flow through you, so that you know there's no distinction between your mind, heart, body, and God.

"Tune into your *own* experience at this moment, and notice where you experience any sense of constriction. Constriction appears as physical pain. It appears as darkness. It appears as an area that you somehow never notice. It appears as emotional pain. It appears as resistance, and it appears as judgment. Notice in your own physical bodies, and your mind patterns, where any of these blocks to the flow have manifested themselves.

"Inwardly, just ask, 'What would be most helpful for me to know to release this block?'

"A very important lesson is the lesson that there is no need to *defend* yourselves. This is *extremely* difficult for humanity. You are here in a countryside where, for a thousand years, the teaching of the integration of the Mother-Father God, the integration of Earth and Spirit, and the integration of feminine and masculine was practiced. And then after those thousand years came the energies of control and fear, and thus also the thought that the teachings needed to be defended. So, the experience of defending yourselves against outward control is deeply ingrained and difficult to release.

"The Truth is that the teachings are impossible to be lost. While it might be exciting to find some hidden teachings in this land, the Truth is the teachings are all hidden by yourselves in your own minds, so nothing is lost. If the body dies, those teachings are not lost.

"The primary belief you must release is the need to defend yourself against any perception of attack or apparent incursion. You cannot be harmed, and you cannot lose anything. The appearance of attack can come from the projection of *need*. This is simply the belief there is something protected that the other apparently separated person needs because they have lost trust that they *know* the Truth themselves.

"Notice the experience of *allowing* anything that appears to be an intrusion to pass through you without defending yourself, because you no longer believe there is something you need to protect against the intrusion. This will help the intruder release *their* belief that there is something outside of themselves they are seeking. In this way, the pattern of defense and attack dissolves on both sides. When you know there is *nothing* outside of yourselves that you are seeking, then you will no longer draw attack.

"This is even true for the great teachers, Yeshua and Maryam. They are only Way-showers. They do not wish for you to worship them. To extend gratitude, honor, and respect is only natural for their courage, devotion, and willingness to go *all the way* to the final demonstration that the body is made of Light. But do not let yourselves get caught in the belief that they should, therefore, be worshiped. Their teaching is that you, too, are Gods and can manifest the same.

"Return to that image of the valleys as bowls that contain the intermingling of the Mother and the Father. In this land, your practice is to feel that in your own bodies, not to look for something as if there were some treasure around the next corner. Just experience that feeling of *blessing* that occurs in the union of Mother and Father.

"The people of this land were steeped in the practice of the unification of the Mother and the Father, the equal valuing of the Mother and the Father. That energy remains here. This draws people because humanity is *longing* for that state of balance and unification. The energy of control, dominance, power, winning, and losing has run its course.

"Whenever there is the energy that appears to be an attack or demand coming towards you, just bless the other person in your mind silently, knowing they have *all* the Truth already themselves. There is nothing they can *get* from you, nothing they *need* from you, and nothing they can *take* from you.

"This is what is meant by, 'Give them everything.' This has been stated in *A Course in Miracles* and in your Gospels. If someone asks you for something, give them everything. This is the inner meaning of that teaching. It is not for you to become impoverished, but for you to *give*, knowing you *have* everything because you *are* everything, and there is *no loss* in offering everything to someone else.

"We have spoken before about money. There is no need to *hoard* money. It is simply an *exchange* that facilitates the life of the body. Give freely of your money and it will be returned to you freely, but not as a strategy. This has been misunderstood as an ego strategy. 'If I am generous, then I will receive generosity.' This is not correct. The generosity comes from the deep knowing that you *are* everything and *have* everything, so you have everything to give, and nothing to lose. Anything you need will simply be given as it is required.

"The people of this land know this lesson from the land. You cannot hoard ten years' worth of harvest because it would rot. As you give, you receive as you require.

"We do delight in answering questions that will help you release the knots and constrictions that are your particular patterns of fear, so you can know this teaching is true—you are all made of Light and are channels for the Light. Whatever questions are burning and feel that they would *move* your growth forward, we are happy to respond."

John begins with, "My constriction is obviously self-caused. Right before our trip, I inhaled something into my lungs, and I've been coughing the entire visit. Any comments on that would be welcome."

"All constrictions are self-caused," Christ Consciousness replies. "The breath *is* the Breath of God. The breath *is* the Holy Spirit. The breath *is* Light. Spirit means breath *and* Light. A constriction in the lungs is a resistance to allowing the Light and Breath of God to move through you.

"In your case, my brother, the constriction is a feeling of lack of deserving. There is an old belief that you have caused so much harm you cannot possibly do enough to overcome it. Even though your desire is strong, pure, and steady, it conflicts with a belief that the damage you have caused is irreparable. This constricts your ability to let the Love of God flow through you, and you continue to seek outside of yourself for the source of Wisdom.

"The Holy Spirit's interpretation of your experience is that you have a strong desire to know the Truth, and you have been seeking the Truth for many lifetimes. The lesson in the constriction in your lungs is to notice how *painful* it is to prohibit yourself from allowing the Truth to flow through you. It is painful to believe the Truth lies outside of you, and you must seek it elsewhere. This is an endless pursuit.

"There is a blessing in this pain caused by not allowing yourself to receive the Light and Love of the Holy Spirit. The blessing is revealed when you understand that refusing to know that *your body* is a channel for Truth is more painful than your belief that *you* have caused so much pain that you do not deserve to receive the Light of Truth. All of humanity shares this difficulty to some degree. Every Soul—and all Souls are aspects of the One Soul—has engaged in some pattern of behavior that has appeared to be harmful to themselves or to others.

"The way to release this is to understand the whole pattern is a *whole pattern*, and everyone is involved in all aspects of the pattern. The pattern of *causing* harm is no more 'bad' (in quotes) than the pattern of *receiving* the harm and being the 'victim' (in quotes). Both sides of the dance are necessary. In this country, all the castles you see in ruin are symbolic of the thought that being the victim is somehow better than being the attacker. But in Truth, both sides of the dance require each other. The castles are in ruins because this country is learning that this whole dance of attack and defense is no longer necessary.

"In your case, my brother, to release the pain in your lungs requires releasing the belief that you are *special* in your *badness*. In fact, you are an equal Child of God. We extend to you our blessing."

"Thank you."

☙

Sister One inquires, "Where am I going?"

"My sister, you are going Home, as every Child of God is going Home. Do you have a question about the *way* Home?"

"Yes. What is my next step?"

"The way Home has moments that require great courage. When it is clear that a habitual pattern is no longer useful, and you can see the Light, notice in your mind's eye there is an area of brighter Light. Your practice is to keep your focus on this Light and go towards it. This is a metaphor, and it will also be experienced in your physical reality. Any experience of going *towards* a Light will be transformative for you. The caves in this area are not magic. They are outward expressions of this Knowledge that humanity has, that each Soul must go through its own darkness and come out into the Light.

"Draw your attention to your solar plexus. This is the seat of the will. Your challenge, at this stage in your life, is to align your will with God's. This is a challenge for all of humanity, but this is quite strong for you at the moment. There is a belief that you must listen to your *own* will, and reserve *your* ability to solve problems and make decisions, just in case God doesn't know what is the right thing to do for you. This is a common problem.

"You know this drama is not functioning for you, and you are drawn constantly towards the Light. Even now, the window next to you is symbolic of this Light that pulls your attention. This Light is the Light of God. God's Will for you is happiness, which is to live in the Queendom, to return Home. When you can align your will with God's—which simply means to know you do not have a separate will—then every step will become clear immediately.

"The ego has an *enormous* fear of letting go of the will. Just that sentence—that you do not have a will that is separate from God's—is terrifying. You look at Yeshua and you think following God's Will means ending up on a cross. He has said to you repeatedly that this will not be required.

"The New Creation you are entering is the knowledge of your own self-awareness *and* your alignment with God's Will, which is Love, Wisdom, and all Knowledge. There is *nothing at all* attractive about having a will that is separate from Love, Wisdom, Truth, and all Knowledge. When put that way, it immediately becomes obvious that you would not *really* want a separate will that is *so* limited in its capacities. When you align your will with God's, that simply means that you have stepped into the flow of all Truth, all Knowledge, all Love, *and* you retain your own awareness.

"Your practice for you, my sister, on this journey, is to trust each little piece of guidance that shows up for you. Not because each piece of guidance is, quote, 'the magic answer'—that is not what these moments of guidance are for. They are simply to reinforce for you that, when you are in the flow, you are in the flow, and everything you need is given to you at the moment it is required and, therefore, you do not need to *plan*. This journey for you is an exercise in *trusting* God's Will.

"Draw your attention again to your solar plexus, and notice that it has softened as you hear these words. Is this helpful?"

"Yes, very much, thank you."

Sister Two asks, "I long to be in community with people, in real, deep relationship with other people and with nature and animals. I want to know the next step to take."

"My sister, your Druidic heart is speaking clearly. This is an ancient path of yours—to know there is no distinction between yourself, your community, and nature. Animals and birds cross your path as communications. You have always been able to attune yourself to the pattern of communications between the animals as a sort of shimmering Light across the Earth. Light is also Sound. Animals, of course, do not have ego. They are simply listening to the Voice of God as it shimmers across the Earth. You have a particular ability for this external and internal listening.

"It will benefit you, my sister, to find other people who are reigniting these old Druidic Ways. This is a deep resonance in your Soul. You will find when you are with people actively seeking to remember the ways of communication with the Earth Spirits, that *you* will also remember *much* information you hold in the *deep* recesses of your experience. This will be quite easy for you. Look for anything related to the old Druidic practices. You will be brought to the people who are, like yourself, *deeply* invested in honoring the Earth and the Wisdom of all of her creatures.

"We have shared before that those Souls who have been involved in maintaining the Wisdom of the interconnection of everything have been afraid in the past because the powers of *control* have felt threatened by this deep Wisdom. When Souls *know* they are interconnected with the entire Universe, then they are not interested in submitting themselves to any external control. And so, in the past, when those Souls who have been invested in exploring what it's like to be in control confronted this Wisdom, they have tried to suppress it, knowing that people involved with this Wisdom will not allow themselves to be controlled. So there is always a fear that re-contacting this Wisdom will re-contact this experience of being controlled.

"But we have explained before that the version of *control* that modern society has evolved is *so* divorced from spirituality that it no longer feels threatened by those who are aware of the interconnectedness of all things. In this way, it is safe to be out in the open. The only attack you will receive is derision or ridicule. But this doesn't matter. There's no particular harm caused by derision and ridicule.

"You are among many people who feel the *pull* of their ancient knowing, want to bring it *forward*, yet first have to go through this *ring of fear* of being persecuted for this Knowledge. But we have reassured all of you many times that this will *not* reoccur. The time of persecution has passed. We discussed earlier that there is no need to defend yourself. This is an important teaching for you, my sister.

"The longing in your heart must be listened to. It will guide you to others who share this longing. Since you do not live far from a Druidic holy spot, it will help you to sit in the center and meditate. The central chambers of these Druidic temples were used as portals to the inner world. When you enter that space and calm your body-mind, you will have visions of the vastness of space filled with its stars, galaxies, and planets. When you are in that inner holy sanctum that leads to the outer, you will know the inner and the outer are the same, and therefore, no harm can come to you on this particular plane of existence that is called life on Earth.

"Even now, as you hear these words, you are experiencing the endless expansion in your heart, and being in the vastness of space and not being lost, because your consciousness is the center of everything, wherever it is. This is something your scientists have gotten right. They have understood what they call the weird world of quantum particles—every particle is everywhere simultaneously, and every place is the center.

"This is the Truth. You do not need fancy machines to understand this! You can go to the center of a Druidic temple, close your eyes, and you will know this Truth as well because your consciousness will also go to any point in the Universe where you wish to direct it. You can sit there and ask questions about any point in the Universe that you would like to know. The answer will be shown to you because, not only do you have an attunement to the Sound and Light vibrations, but you also have a clear inner vision.

"Please trust your knowing, my sister. It is deep and old and strong. Is this helpful?"

"Yes."

⌘

Christ Consciousness continues, "All of you, bring your attention to your root chakra. The powers of control have covered this lowest point in the body in *shame*, but it is the portal through which the Light of Spirit expresses as *form* on Earth. Far from being shameful, the lowest point of your body is the point of manifestation. You do not have to be a woman of childbearing age for this to be true. This is simply the energetic pattern of the body. Bring your attention to that point now to understand that the Wisdom you are receiving, which you already know in your own hearts, will also manifest out into the Earth.

"We ask you to return to the image of your hips as a bowl, a cauldron, or a crucible, in which Earth and Spirit are mixed and expressed. Just rest in that *physical knowing* for a few moments.

"Allow your hip joints to expand. Allow your sacral joint to expand. Allow your belly to expand. Allow your reproductive organs to expand. Feel a softening and an expansion of Light and Love outward in all directions from these lowest two chakras of your body.

"Again, notice that you have come to this particular place on the Earth because the valleys are also cauldrons that hold the mix of the Light of Spirit and the Earth of Mother. Everywhere you go today, keep your awareness in your lower two chakras, knowing that you yourself are also an expression of the mix of Spirit and Earth.

"Notice, as you breathe, that the air around you is also actually breathing. The air is alive. Everything is alive, and everything has free will. In this time of fearfulness about the life of the Earth, we remind you that the Earth also has free will. She has agreed to be the container in which the apparently separated Child of God can enact its belief in separation. But as the Child of God re-experiences its longing for union, so, too, can the Earth experience *her* longing for union with God, and no longer *need* to be the one who agrees to receive the garbage of the fear of the Child of God.

"As you walk on this precious Earth and experience your own unification with the Mother and the Father, please transmit to her your Love, and your confidence that she, too, can go through her *own* structural transformation and become *fully aware* that she, too, is a unification of the Mother and the Father who expresses Light in her Being and her body. In this way, the will of the Earth and the will of the Child of God become aligned because the Earth is also the Child of God. There is nothing that is *not* the Child of God. If a stone did not have free will, then it would be outside of Creation. This is an impossibility. Nothing is outside of Creation.

"As you walk on the Earth, notice that every plant, rock, bird, and cloud has free will to manifest exactly as it is manifesting. Send to all aspects of Creation your gratitude for its willingness to participate in this grand *drama* that has allowed you to become *aware* of who you are, and arrive at this point where you no longer need to believe you are *separated* in order to *know* who you are. Now you *know* that you can know who you are *and* be in *ecstatic union with the Mother and the Father in your own Beings.*

"Again, return your awareness to your root and your sacral chakras. Notice that this is where you experience this *ecstatic union.*

"Then bring your attention again to your heart, and notice that it is from this point that you *extend* what you *believe* and where you receive what is *returned* to you as your own belief.

"Go out into the world today with our blessings. Enjoy each step, each breath, each moment. And please take responsibility for your own thoughts and feelings.

"Notice that you cannot possibly be alone. It is tempting to believe you are alone, but in your moment of deepest despair, the *longing* to *not* be alone is so strong that support and connection come to you.

"The process of dissolving the constrictions of ego is *not* comfortable, and we commend you for your courage. Please sit with your discomfort and allow it to pass, knowing who you *truly* are.

"And with those words, we give you our blessings and say, Ameyn. Ameyn. Ameyn."

I continue to practice this difficult teaching, never to defend myself. When I know I am the Christ, defending myself has no meaning, and anything that looks like an attack is perceived as a call for Love. If I defend myself, then I am demonstrating my belief that the attacker and I are both small selves in need of defense. When I see us as manifestations of the One Child of God, with all our needs met, then I just step out of the way and send us both blessings.

On July 4, our powerful pilgrimage complete, we flew home—John to Wisconsin, and me to Massachusetts.

Chapter 21

Returning Home

I use the inflection point of the completion of our pilgrimage to conclude this volume. I truly had not realized the magnitude of the teachings I have been blessed to deliver. They are just too much for one book. I will publish subsequent teachings on the website lauraderr-journeytotrueself.com, or perhaps in future books.

Since returning to our physical homes, John and I have continued our spiritual journeying through Zoom. Little did we know that, early the following year, this medium would become much of humanity's primary means of communication. I include here some follow-up commentary from our post-pilgrimage gathering.

Before our journey, we had promised to gather again soon after returning to our respective homes. On July 8, 2019, a large group joined together. I conclude this book with two questions and answers from that gathering about the journey to Scotland.

"When I was in Scotland," one sister says, "I felt I was open to and received so much more Light and Love. It felt like one of the most transformative times that I've had. Yet since coming home, all I've been feeling is such a strong egoic energy that I'm not allowing the heart to stay open. I wondered if you could speak to that for me, please."

"First," Christ Consciousness responds, "we would like to speak to the clarity of Scotland. Many of you were called to go to that land precisely because it is far north, so there are few people and fewer electromagnetic radiations in the atmosphere. This allowed you to experience a sense of expansiveness, which is a glimpse of your *true nature*. Your true nature expands and includes the entire Cosmos. You are all One and can be at any point in the Cosmos simultaneously with any other point. And all points are conscious.

"That expansiveness—the clarity of the Light, the length of the days, the air that is so bright there—has been planted in your memory for you to return to within yourself, to know this is the *portal* to the expansion of your own Consciousness. This return to the heavier, denser environment that is more familiar to you is something you know well, and that is why it is difficult to let it go. It *feels* like home.

"You have all been told you are on a journey *Home*. What does that mean? Home to you feels like where this particular body-mind has settled and feels comfortable. You have all been journeying and moving about on the surface of the planet. When you return to a place that feels like home, there is a relaxation that happens. You know how to get around, where your resources are, where your friends live, and how to navigate the infrastructure. This brings a sense of ease.

"What is this Home we keep telling you that you are all headed towards? It is not a familiar pattern of streets and telephone numbers. That feeling of comfort is, however, a glimpse into the feeling of Home. My sister, when you settle into this familiar, heavy feeling, practice teasing apart the heaviness from the familiarity because in the familiarity lies the *jewel* of knowing you are Home.

"We reassure *all* of you that, as you get closer and closer to this Home in the Heart of God, it *will* become increasingly familiar. You will have the sense of having been there before, of recognizing the sights and the sounds. That feeling of longing that is stirred up in your hearts will have a resonance—a sense of, 'Oh, *this* is what the longing has been longing for!'

"There is a point on the journey Home when you can *rest* in that feeling of familiarity. You can let go of the thoughts, 'I need my particular streets, my particular phone numbers, and my particular energy patterns I have carried with me from lifetime to lifetime like a heavy burden, simply because they're comfortable.' For all of you, look inside that feeling of familiarity. Open it up and look in deeply until you can see the spark of Light in there that is Heaven. *That* is what is familiar. *That* is your true Home. When you arrive there, you will say, 'Oh! I have known this place *all along.*'

"My sister, rather than condemn yourself for being attached to the familiarity of heaviness, put the heaviness aside, and *revel* in that feeling of *comfort* in the familiar. That feeling is simply an echo of an ancient Knowledge of the comfort of being in the familiar Home of Heaven. Is this helpful?"

"Yes, thank you. It's been so hard to get back to feeling what I felt in Scotland. As you say, I'm longing for that. It's been frightening how difficult I've found it to get back to it."

"My sister, put your hand on your heart. That feeling of *longing* for that sense of peaceful expansiveness *lives in your heart*. You have carried it home *with* you. It will help to sit in meditation and bring to mind the physical sensations of being in that sense of expanded consciousness you experienced in the northern country. When you realize this is in your *heart*, then you will not feel so afraid that you will lose it when you walk out the door into your more densely populated home on the Earth. Please engage in this practice regularly. Visualize that *in* the heart *is* the Universe. Many of you have had this experience of looking inside and suddenly realizing you are looking at the blackness of the night sky filled with stars. That is what resides within your own heart. When you practice this meditation, my sister, you will know you can carry that awareness with you, no matter where you are on the surface of the planet. Please enjoy that meditation practice."

"Thank you."

"Never forget that you are *loved*, through and through. We refer to what we said at the beginning about the *intimacy* of being loved by God. Every cell is *adored* by your Creator. Our blessings."

Another sister asks for insight into what happened in Scotland. "Could you comment on Scotland a little more? There was this connection of people who all just happened to be there at the same time. Something seemed to be happening!"

"On the outer level of the world, part of the purpose of this pilgrimage to Scotland was for all of you to practice *trust*. This pilgrimage was not organized by *anyone*, and yet there were many of you who gathered together. You all also had your own paths to follow simultaneously. This is a metaphor for the experience of being the Child of God on the Earth. You are all in it together, and you all have your own paths. That is one level of the meaning of that experience.

"Another level is, being there at the time of the solstice, and being willing to be humble and receive the guidance to show up, *means* you are aligning your will with God. On Earth, the Sun represents the Will. When you are in celebration of the solstice, you are in celebration of God's Will, receiving God's Will into the Earth, and into your own bodies and experience. The experience of being there has helped attune *all* of you to trusting that *your will is the same as God's.* It is a story the ego has told that there is a separate will from God's Will. There is no separate will from God's Will. God's Will for you is for your *happiness.* God's Will for you is to *trust* you are God. That is another meaning of the experience of being in Scotland.

"In the previous question, we shared that another meaning was to give you the physical space in which you could experience clarity. We referenced that when you look into your hearts, you see the vastness of the Universe. You were shown a Womb of Earth, hidden in the woods, which served that function when it was an active spiritual site for the human community who lived there. By physically entering the birth canal and back into the womb, humans could experience *knowing* they have *always* been connected to the stars. The beauty of this space is that it is a *portal* that allows humanity to know its true nature, which is the infinite Cosmic Christ. It is not necessary to go into that physical womb to know you are the infinite Cosmic Christ, but there is a certain amount of *energy* that has been concentrated in that spot that allows for an expansion of awareness.

"We have said to you many times that no Knowledge has ever been lost. Knowledge has been *physically* kept by writing and oral transmission. There are people around the world who have access to the Truth that has been passed down from generation to generation. But even if all of that Knowledge were lost on the surface of this Earth, nothing is lost in the inner Ways of Knowing. You are all experiencing flashes of insight and awareness in prayers, meditations, and memories. Nothing is lost. Is this helpful, my sister?"

"Yes, it's very helpful. Thank you."

Epilogue

I hope you have found it helpful to read the personal experiences and spiritual teachings in this book. I hope that sharing my personal journey, intertwined with these astounding teachings, has inspired you to know that awakening is possible and that spiritual help surrounds you in every moment. I hope you feel how much you are loved because you *are* Love, and that you have begun to experience the Reality of God's Love as physical sensations in the body. I hope you are enjoying connecting with other awakening mind-hearts and, with all of us, sending joy and gratitude around the Earth and into the Earth.

I hope that, by listening in to apparently *individual* spiritual growth challenges, you have been able to experience that we all have similar challenges. Not only do we learn from each other, but everyone's progress contributes to the progress of the entire consciousness of humanity. I hope you are experiencing that we are all individuated vibrational patterns of the great cosmic pattern of Sound and Light. I hope you are feeling more confident in your understanding that every challenge in your life is an opportunity to see, accept, hold in Love, and relax your grip on a deeply held constricting belief in your mind.

I trust you have seen that, ultimately, every constriction in the mind comes from the one foundational fear that we have separated ourselves from God, and our belief that we can never correct this mistake and return Home. I hope you are relaxing your grip on that fear of separation and death. I hope, as you let go of your fears, you are experiencing your progress in trusting your own access to the inner Wisdom we all share. We are awakening together to full awareness of our shared Christed Self, which resides in complete intimacy with God.

Acknowledgments

This entire book is a hymn of gratitude to God. I am nothing without my Creator.

Thank you to Yeshua for your courage in manifesting the Resurrection and Atonement. Thank you for fulfilling your childhood promise to me to remain with me until the end of the age.

I am grateful for having been born at this historical moment when so many Souls are waking up to their True Self. I am grateful for all the transformational teachings available now. I am deeply grateful to all my friends who know they are the Child of God and are willing to join in this resonant field. I am especially grateful to John Hempstead, my friend and collaborator through several lifetimes. Our joint courageous exploration of the inner realms made possible the miracle of giving Voice to Christ Consciousness. Thank you to John Krysko for providing consistent encouragement as I developed confidence in knowing my True Self.

I express profound gratitude to the three or four dozen people, from many different countries and continents, who took the leap of faith to participate in the gatherings described in this book. Thank you to all of you who heeded the miraculous call to Scotland on the summer solstice. I thank the thirty whose voices are included here for their willingness to ask such profoundly meaningful and vulnerable questions. We all benefit. Thanks to Leyolah Antara, Linda Coates, Janet Deane, Fiona Dick, Ann-Marie Donagher, Eva Eriksson, Sarah Evans, Michael Foster, Virginia Fox, Marilyn Hempstead, Rifka Hirsch, Michelle Hughes, Ori Ana Lightning, Rosie-Maria Love,

Kimbra McGraw, Felicity Paton (in memoriam), Julia Pearson, Sarita Premley, Helen Sjöblom, Moira Snape, Marney Stumbelis, and the rest who remain anonymous.

Thank you to my mother, Rev. Virginia Derr, for her unwavering support of my spiritual path, through all its iterations. She was especially proud of me for following in her footsteps and becoming ordained. Thank you, Mom, for the inheritance you left me that paid for the publishing of this book.

I am grateful to Mari Perron and Thanissaro Bhikkhu for their gracious permission to quote from their published works, and to Mari for her permission to quote from our personal correspondence.

Thank you to the team at Seshat Press who walked me through this entire process, from encouragement to keep writing, to expert editing, to skill in design, publishing, and marketing. Writing a book is an enormous undertaking, and I am so grateful for your consistently positive guidance. And thank you for taking on such a wonderful name during the time I was working with you. Seshat is the Egyptian Goddess of writing, wisdom, and knowledge—perfect on many levels!

Over the course of 2023, as I was struggling with health, professional, family, and relationship challenges, all while my new house was being renovated, John and I joined a few times in Christ Consciousness. We were given the consistent message, "Just love God."

"You have a beautiful practice, going to sleep and waking up, of saying simply, 'I love you, God.' These statements are heard. When your hearts relax because you trust God, then you can open wide and receive the infinite Love that your Creator has for you. As you increase your trust that God is real and the path Home is laid before you, then you feel God's Love like an irresistible magnet, calling you closer and faster down the path towards Home. This magnetism is not just God's Love for you, but also your Love for God. As you give yourself permission to feel your Love for your Creator, you are free to return to your Creator the same Love in which you were born. There is such joy in this mutual Love. As you continue to practice knowing that you are nothing without God, it will break open your heart, and you will feel the intensity of God's Love and Peace. This is why God created Creation—so that God and her Creation could join in this ecstatic Communion. The infinite joy of knowing and being known, of collaborating in Creation through infinity, cannot be described in words."

In August 2025, I was given this transmission: "Laura is being shown the face of a lion, very close, with Light radiating out all around its face. Facing God is like this—standing in front of a lion with no fear, only with joy at the ability to receive the grace, the admiration, the Love, the respect, and the delight that your Creator has for you and for your ability to stand face to face. You are all on this Path of resolving your confusions so that when you come face to face with God, everything will be clear, and there will be no questions remaining."

Thank you, God, for encouraging me to continue through all of life's challenges. The rewards of your Queendom are beautiful and infinite.

Glossary

The purpose of this glossary is to help orient readers for whom these names and concepts are not familiar. For readers who are more familiar with them, may these entries serve as clarification and summary. The descriptions all come from material in this book (with some additional information from my knowledge and from various public domain references).

Abba. Aramaic word meaning father.

Abwoon. Aramaic word for God, meaning Creative Source that integrates Divine Masculine and Feminine qualities.

Ameyn. *Amen* in Aramaic. A word of power meaning something like, *So let it stand*. The ground of alignment with Unity from which my actions arise.

Angels. Beings who never believed they were separated from God. They are a realm of Light and Sound that surrounds the Earth, constantly singing a harmony that can be felt in the heart. Their song is of joy and gratitude that humanity is attuning to their exquisite harmonics of Love and Wisdom, which break up the denser vibrations of fear. The more humanity can attune to the vibrations of Love, the more we align with the Angelic realms, and the more Heaven and Earth align and become One.

Aramaic. The language spoken in Judea during the lifetime of Yeshua. It is in the Semitic family of languages that also includes Arabic, Hebrew, and Maltese, among others. An ancient language that arose in Mesopotamia around 3500 BC, it gradually became the lingua franca of most of western Asia, Anatolia, and Egypt. Only in the late seventh century did Arabic gradually replace it as the dominant regional language. People living where the borders of Syria, Iraq, Turkey, and Iran meet, as well as in isolated villages in western Syria, and some diaspora communities, speak a modern version of Aramaic. There are ancient versions of the New Testament in Aramaic.

Archangel. Powerful Angels with a pure vibration of their particular energy. There are said to be seven of them. Three are most familiar: Michael the protector, Gabriel the messenger, and Raphael the healer. Uriel is the pure vibration of the Wisdom of God.

Astrology. Systems for understanding the effects of the movements of celestial bodies on Souls on Earth developed by sages in every human culture. The form of astrology used in modern Western cultures originated in Mesopotamia around the same time the Aramaic language was developing. Its precise mathematics reveals patterns that are portals to Wisdom.

Atonement. The common understanding of this word—*humanity making amends to achieve a reconciliation with God*—contains the faulty idea that we have sinned. However, it also contains the kernel of Truth that we are on a path of realigning our human consciousness with God Consciousness. Parsing the word as At-One-ment reveals this meaning. When we cease seeing through the eyes of ego, we see there has never been any separation from God. Yeshua has communicated through several channels that his role is to be in charge of the Atonement.

Awakened Ones. Beings who have been incarnated as human on the Earth-plane, but who learned to drop their identification with the small self and become fully aligned with their true Identity as the unified Consciousness that is the Child of God. Many Beings from every human culture have attained full awareness of their true Identity, not just Yeshua, so people of all backgrounds have access to communication with Beings they feel can understand them. The Awakened Ones are always available to provide inner guidance. As former human incarnations, they have known and transcended shame and guilt, so they hold those thoughts in compassion without judgment. They encourage us to trust that awakening is not something mysterious and far off. It is something that is truly possible.

Brigid. A manifestation of the triple Goddess in ancient Irish culture: Maiden, Mother, and Crone. The Celts held the Divine Feminine in great honor. The British Celtic Goddess Brigantia shares the same root name, meaning the *High One*. She represents Wisdom and protection. Brigid was later fused with a Catholic Saint of the same name.

Cayce, Edgar. American clairvoyant, 1877-1945. While in a trance state, he accessed the level of mind that is unified and timeless and could share information about medical diagnoses and cures, past lives, and future events. The volume of material produced was vast.

Chakra. Centers of spinning energy of the human body. There are seven primary chakras in the body, as well as an *Earth Star* below the feet, a *Soul Star* above the head, and centers in the palms and soles of the feet. They are expressed on the front, back, and center of the body. They are in various states of health, depending on the person's patterns of belief. This text contains many teachings about the chakras, but here is a brief summary.

The *crown* on the top of the head, when open, is where the Light of God, or Holy Spirit, enters.

The *third eye*, between and slightly above the eyebrows, as well as on the occipital lobe of the skull and in the center of the brain, is where inner vision resides.

The *throat* is the center of speech, which can be aligned with Truth or ego.

The *heart*, in the center of the chest between the breasts (there is also a *high heart* center midway between the *throat* and the *heart*), is where we extend what we believe, and where we receive what is returned as our belief. When the *heart* is aligned with God, Mother and Father join here and extend outwards as Love.

The *solar plexus* is the seat of the will, which can be aligned with God or ego.

The *sacral*, or *womb*, center between the navel and pubic bone, is the seat of identity, either as Self or ego.

The *root* at the base of the body in the perineum is the center of creative power, or of shame and guilt, the portal through which the Light of Spirit expresses as form on Earth.

When the chakras are clear, open, and aligned with God, then there is a continual flow of loving energy in a double spiral through the body between the Sun and the Earth, between Masculine and Feminine expressions of God.

Child of God. Our Identity, our Being, our Self, our very nature. Like begets like, so the Child of God must be like God in every way, save that it did not create itself. As the Child of God, we all have the same qualities of God: infinite creative power, Wisdom, beauty, purity, joy, and the ability to receive and extend miracles. None of us is any different from anyone else in our worthiness and our ability to express the creative power of God's Love. We all just do it in our own beautiful way.

The Child of God is one unified, collective consciousness, and all parts that seem to be separated will come to know that they are One. At the end of all of our seeking, we find what has been true all along—we are in full Communion with all of Creation and with God.

Christ Consciousness, Christ-Mind. These terms are synonymous. I choose mostly to use the more comprehensive-feeling *Christ Consciousness* in this book simply to avoid the thought-habit that separates mind from heart. Christ Consciousness resides in the heart, not in the intellect.

The nature of Christ Consciousness is Unity, so it manifests when friends join in the intention to awaken. Through repeated joinings, the knowing of the Truth of Unity becomes more visceral. Unity includes all possibilities anywhere in the Universe, so one *personal* mind can be in communication with an infinite number of minds simultaneously. The Path of Awakening is the transition from the limited perspective of the illusion of a material world into the expanded perspective of Christ Consciousness that has no limitation and is filled with joy, and with a sweetness and tenderness that is beyond anything we have ever experienced. By engaging in habitual activities in this state of awareness of Oneness with God, we become a living embodiment of the Christ.

Christ Council. A collective Consciousness of Beings who have released attachment to the belief in separation and are thus free from living inside of time. It only appears to be a paradox from the perspective of the small self that this collection of awakened minds can be experienced as separate personalities or as one unified Voice. "I speak for, and *am*, the entire Christ Council. Other Enlightened Ones are also with me, and we communicate as one Mind." The spiritual family in this book has a strong connection with Yeshua and his devoted Maryam and his mother Mary, but the Christ Council includes Enlightened Ones who have cultural connections all around the Earth and who work through many religious traditions. As we progress on our path Home, these Beings help us remember we have always been with them in this circle of Christ Consciousness, where there is no beginning and no end. We have just forgotten that for a little while.

Christ-Mind. See Christ Consciousness.

Communion. The energetic experience of spiritual union—between Souls, between Souls and the Earth, between Souls and God—that is filled with ecstatic delight and joy; the alignment of vibrational frequencies; the complete unification of all elements of Creation that never ends. Gathering in Communion reinforces our Light and allows the Enlightened Ones to communicate clearly with us.

Creation. Vibration extending from the Mind of God that manifests as Light and Sound. God extended herself in Love so she and her Creation could have the ecstatic experience of knowing and being known. Desire is the Source of Creation, so following our heart's desire will lead us to knowing we are One with God. There is only One Creation and we are all of it.

Every aspect of God's Creation has all the attributes of God, including rocks, plants, and animals—Wisdom, Love, Peace, Joy, and free will. When we know that all of Creation is One and has free will, then we know that, in Truth, no apparently separated part can cause permanent harm to any other part, and, therefore, there can be no such thing as guilt. This is the great liberation—to understand that we are all the All in All.

Death. The belief in the possibility that life can end. If the Soul could ever be disconnected from God, it would die, and in the circle of God's Love, disconnection is not possible. Therefore, there is no such thing as death. The Light of God pours forth always through the Soul, and what appear to be danger and death are shadows on the surface of the Soul made by fearful constrictions in the mind.

When we know everything is the All in All, then we do not need to be afraid of the shifting appearances of the One, and we feel less fearful when a certain form no longer manifests. When Souls have passed into Spirit, they are guided into the proper form for them in which to reappear. The Mother absorbs all bodies back into her body, and then they are reconfigured and transformed into the new, and the Soul experiences rejuvenation.

The grieving process helps us feel and release the despair of believing in the illusion of death. When we realize we are and have always been connected to God, then the belief in death simply evaporates.

Divine Feminine. The Mother God, the Matrix, the Primordial Source from which all Creation arises, in which our Being is embedded; the qualities of receptivity and care. The shadow side of feminine energy is passivity and victimhood. The Feminine Way is the inner way of union with the Mother-Father God. All Beings contain both feminine and masculine energies. The goal of healing is to release the shadow and to balance and integrate these energies.

The symbol of the Mother is the pot in which all of Creation is held and bubbles forth. This container symbolizes the Unity of the Mother and the Father, where the earth and water of the Mother, and the fire and Spirit of the Father, join to produce and sustain a living form. In our bodies, this chalice is the pelvic girdle, the bowl in which the Unity of God's Love pours forth Creation.

God extends herself into Creation to have the experience of ecstatic joy at mutual recognition. Through having a Child, the Mother-God becomes aware of her Self. She delights every time a Soul notices she has been there all along, providing us with the power of life, and she can receive our awareness of her Love.

Divine Masculine. The Father God, the enlivening principle of Spirit; the qualities of action and individuation. The shadow side of masculine energy is control and use. This shadow energy has run its course. Humanity is longing for a state of balance and unification between the energies of the Divine Feminine and Divine Masculine.

The heart longs for connection, so it uses the tools given by the world—control and victimhood—which never succeed in producing true connection, so we are longing for the true Way to Unity. The healing of the masculine and feminine shadows involves embracing the shame that lies underneath both.

The Masculine Way is the outer way, and the Feminine Way is the inner way. There was a bifurcation of these ways so that the inner way could be preserved, and the outer way could be accepted by the world. The inner way was so deep and powerful that the world was not yet ready to receive it. The outer way was necessary to plant the ideas of forgiveness, redemption, resurrection, Light-bodies, unconditional Love, and the brother- and sisterhood of humanity in a way that they could be heard.

Dorothy's ruby slippers. The shoes worn by Dorothy, heroine of the 1939 movie, *The Wizard of Oz*. After all her searching through various adventures to find her way Home, she realizes she had the means with her all the time without being aware of it.

Earth. Spirit manifests through what appears to be the material world, which is not solid but made of Light. The Earth is a living Being, a Soul, an aspect of the Child of God. She agreed to incarnate as the Earth, as we all have agreed to incarnate as bodies. She agreed to allow herself to receive fearful inputs from humanity so that we could use her bounty as a stage on which to play out the drama of the belief in separation. That role of absorbing fear has come to a close. The Child of God can now take responsibility for its choice to believe in separation, and so is bringing those fear thoughts back into its own heart, where they are transformed by the Holy Spirit into the Truth of the Unity of All in God. The tipping point has occurred, and the Child of God—humanity, the Earth, and all of Creation—is returning Home. As the Earth now becomes more of an active participant in awakening, structural changes necessary for this transformation will occur.

The Earth soaks up whatever energy we send her, so it is important to walk on the Earth and transmit to her our Love, rather than send her our fear that she is dying. When she knows that we all believe in her capacity for healing, that awakens her self-confidence, and she can use her creative powers to heal whatever needs to be healed. When the Earth receives our confidence in her, then the entire planet can express ourselves as the shimmering Light of God, and Heaven manifests on Earth. "This is why I have told you repeatedly to go out onto the Earth and transmit to her your Love."

Earth Spirits. See, Elementals.

Ego, small self. When the Child of God decided to search for self-awareness, the thought arose that it was alone and separated from its Source and could never return, which produced abject terror. The Child of God now thought of itself as weak and vulnerable and in need of self-defense to prevent its death. It is an insane idea to believe we are separated and cannot be in full Communion with all of Creation and with God. This delusional construct of a small self is called ego.

The ego is in a state of perpetual loss. Needing to defend itself, it is always seeking more to ensure its survival. It builds up its hoard and protects it, always fearful it will be stolen. It functions in time in a state of loss as well—each moment is a loss of the moment before. It uses an endless number of tricks to maintain its belief that it is a real, separated identity that brings value to its host, the individuated Soul. Volumes of psychology have been written about understanding the ego and its defenses, but the goal of spiritual practice is to understand it just enough to release its grip and let it go.

When we know we are intimately One with everything, then the idea of *self-interest* is meaningless, and we can laugh at choices made in the interest of the small self. The more we lose interest in the ego, the more we learn we have been in Christ Consciousness all along. The ego will try to bargain, showing how it has brought (apparent) value. However, the Soul will have had enough experiences of the miraculous blessings of knowing the true Self that we will understand we are losing nothing and gaining everything by letting it go.

Elementals, Earth Spirits. All of Creation is conscious and has free will. Elementals are the patterns of consciousness that manifest as plants, animals, and rocks. Many people can see these Souls with their inner or outer eyes.

Enlightened Beings. See, Awakened Ones.

Ethphatha. Pronounced etfata, with soft Ts, this Aramaic word conveys the inner process of the small self bringing things up from inside as it opens to the bigger Self. The *ephphatha* spelling found in Mark 7:34 is simply a clerical copying error (Douglas-Klotz 2022).

God. The *I AM* presence; the universal Source of Being; pure Love, pure Wisdom, pure Joy. Nothing is outside of God. The stones are God, the insects are God, the water is God — everything is God. The past is God, the present is God, the future is God — because it is all *One*. God is beyond all concepts and definitions. God simply *is*.

Heaven. It has been misunderstood that Heaven and Earth are separate places. Yeshua is teaching us to manifest Heaven by knowing that our Being, which is expressed on Earth as a body, is Light. In this state of knowing, everything appears in its true exquisite beauty and harmony—the crystalline structure of the Light of which everything is made, colors never seen with the body's eyes that all interact, each subtle vibration affecting every other subtle vibration in a perfect hologram. In this state, we are fully aware there is no point anywhere in the Universe that is distinct from any other point. We will see the Earth as an out-picturing of the beauty of the Love of God, and it becomes a sparkling jewel. This is bringing Heaven to Earth.

Yeshua walked on the Earth knowing that he was walking in Heaven. When we know that our heart is the joining place of Mother and Father, then we can extend the Truth that Spirit is infused in matter. When the whole world has attuned to the Angelic harmonies, there will be no more need for illusion because now the Angelic and Earthly realms will have become One. When we get to the other side of the belief in separation, we will be astounded that we held onto separation for so long.

Himalayas. The range of mountains formed by the northerly movement of the Indian subcontinent into the Tibetan plateau contains many of the Earth's highest peaks. It has, for centuries, been the home of great spiritual sages who are drawn to the purity of the energy. Yeshua has shared through several channels that he spent some of his early adult years training there.

Holy Spirit. The Holy Spirit is the energy of God, the Communicator, the link between our limited awareness and God. The Holy Spirit is in our own minds. It is not external. It is always available to help whenever we ask. Spirit means Light and Breath. Our breath is the Holy Spirit; it is what enlivens us. The power of the Holy Spirit can be experienced as Light/Breath entering through the crown of the head and then slowly soaking into every cell as it descends through the body.

The Holy Spirit is the Comforter, through whose Wisdom we can understand the true meaning and purpose of our experience.

We can see things as dangerous through the egoic eyes of fear or as transformational through the eyes of the Holy Spirit. As soon as we have even a small desire for help with getting out of our mess, the Holy Spirit is sent immediately. The way to heal any problem is to ask, "What is the message, the metaphor, of this symptom or situation?" We can then release our pain into the loving embrace of the Holy Spirit. Embracing pain and asking for the Holy Spirit to translate it into Truth brings us closer to the full memory of the Garden.

Home. Our true Home is in the Heart of God, a place we long for because we remember, however dimly, having been there before. As we get closer to Home on our journeys, it becomes increasingly familiar. When we arrive, we will know we have been there all along.

Illusion. The belief in separation from God. In the beginning is God, and God extends herself so she can have a companion. As we journey Home, we realize we chose the illusion of being separated from our Source and that God did not impose this illusion upon us. The illusion of time allows us the illusion of traveling Home in time, but there is no end; there is only the end of illusion. Yeshua has told us repeatedly, "I will never leave you. I will be with you even unto the end of the age of illusion." That warm glow of Love and protection is eternal and cannot be harmed by the illusion of time.

The belief in separation creates constrictions of fear in the mind that produce the illusion of shadows that appear to be external to our internal awareness. The appearance of things being external or internal produces the projection of the illusion of space. In Reality, All is One in the infinite Heart we share with God. As we return Home and bring our focus inward, then we can see through the illusion to our connection with God, which has remained unimpeded. It is a great delight when we realize that this has been so all along.

Joseph of Arimathea. Yeshua's uncle, the older brother of Mother Mary (Heartsong 2010). Their mother is Anna, said to be of Celtic origin. A wealthy businessman who owned tin mines in Cornwall and traded throughout the Mediterranean, he was a leader in the Essene community, as well as a member of the Sanhedrin, the Jewish council of priests with legal authority. A great Master, he was aware of Yeshua's plan to enact the Resurrection of the body as Light, and aware that the Jews would be chased from their home in Judea, so, through his relationships with the Druids, he had established communities in Britain and France where they would be welcomed.

Karma, Karmic. In Sanskrit, *karma* simply means *action*. Beliefs produce actions, and actions produce effects. We then attribute meaning to these effects based on our beliefs. Belief produces perception; perception is not impersonal or factual. Our patterns of beliefs, actions, and perceptions are carried through from one lifetime to the next and have become quite fixed. It is only through bringing new beliefs into our reenactment of these patterns that we can come to perceive truly through the eyes of the Holy Spirit, and thus, let the patterns dissolve into the nothingness that they are. *Nirvana* means the cessation of beliefs, the dissolution of karma. When we have resolved every last karmic pattern, then we are awake in God. Old karmic injuries are brought forward in our current life so we can heal the emotional experience and let go of the causal beliefs. See Past lives and Ego for more on how these beliefs are dissolved.

Kingdom. See Queendom.

Knowledge. The universal, shared, direct Awareness transmitted to us by God; the state of full enlightenment; Wisdom that is not mediated by ideas or beliefs.

Light-body. The Light-body is the creation of the Soul and is One with it. The physical body is the worldly appearance of the Light-body, slowed in vibration through the belief in fear. The physical body has no separate existence. It is not a separate thing the Soul inhabits; it is a projection of the Soul. Ultimately, all bodies will become perfected as Light. They will not become perfected as physical bodies. When we have let go of all thoughts of separation and know the body is Light, the thought of death will mean nothing.

A great healer is aware that they themselves are Light, so they can synchronize their consciousness with the Light-body consciousness of the person who has requested healing. This amplifies the strength of the person's own Light-body so that the lower level of the mind-body can trust that there is an aspect of *themselves* they can rely on to be the source of healing.

Light-workers. A large group of Souls who have a long karmic history of learning, sharing, and maintaining the inner way. Because the inner way empowers each individual person to know God directly, these Souls were perceived as threatening by those invested in social control, so there is a long history of persecution that is currently undergoing healing.

Mary Magdalene, Maryam of Magdala. A devoted disciple of Yeshua, the one who best understood his teachings. She is known as the Apostle to the Apostles because she is reported to have been the first to witness the empty tomb and Yeshua's appearance as a body of Light and to share this miraculous news. After the Resurrection, she spent the rest of her life meditating, teaching, and healing in England and southern France.

Martha. The sister of Lazarus and Mary of Bethany, adult children of a wealthy family who supported Yeshua's ministry. She was skilled at taking care of people and needed to be persuaded to sit and listen to Yeshua's teachings.

Mount of Transfiguration. Mount Tabor is a small mountain, shaped like a dome, rising from flat surroundings, located between Nazareth and the Sea of Galilee in northern Israel. This is where Yeshua first manifested his body as Light, along with the Light-bodies of Moses and Elijah, an event recorded in the Gospels as being witnessed by three of the disciples.

Mother Mary. The enlightened manifestation of Feminine Divinity. It was through her full enlightenment that she could allow the expression of the Masculine Divinity into the Earth-plane. She and her son, Yeshua, both knew their Identities as the Child of God, and her loving Divine Feminine presence was key to his ability to remain stable in his Identity, even through the most challenging of circumstances. As an Enlightened One, she remained loving and present while letting her son go on his own path, despite her motherly wish to protect him. She knew that had she done so, she would have interfered with the course of the evolution of humanity.

After the Resurrection, she likely traveled and advised the apostles, but she spent the last years of her life just outside of Ephesus in Turkey, providing healing for all who came to her. Her home has been preserved and is a site of pilgrimage.

New Creation. The Child of God bringing Self-awareness to its Oneness with God. Countless eons ago, the desire to explore being creators while not feeling controlled by our Creator launched our journey through a creation we perceive as fearful. Now we are learning that the nature of God is freedom, so control is not a possibility in Creation, and exploration does not require the belief in separation. We can explore our creative Self and remain aware of our connection with All. This developing awareness of Creation without fear or danger is still young and delicate, but we are beginning to know that Creation is safe, nurturing, and encouraging.

The New Creation that we are entering is the knowledge of our own Self-awareness *and* our alignment with God's Will. When we align our will with God's, we step into the flow of Love, *and* we retain our own awareness. In this New Creation, all *parts* are aware that they are in Communion. It is new, so we cannot expect it to be familiar, but we can expect it in terms of the promise that it is at hand.

Past lives. The Soul, eternal and timeless, is on a journey of Self-awareness that takes it through multiple lifetimes in many different bodies. The current manifestation of a body has an ancient history that can bring forward some fairly rigid patterns from previous incarnations. Softening and releasing these patterns requires honoring the original belief as something the ego perceived as necessary. Holding the belief in the center of a circle of loving friends and Enlightened Ones, while seeing from the expanded perspective of the Holy Spirit, we become aware that it is no longer necessary. It is helpful to understand that, as a Soul, we choose difficult experiences in order to release painful feelings and transmute deeply held beliefs acquired in this and other lifetimes.

Ultimately, healing is the release of attachment to identification with suffering. The ego has lots of pride in its suffering—its proof of everything that it has gone through. Memories are revealed to enable letting go, not to identify with them and make our identity something fixed. Our true Identity is the Child of God, not a string of previous lifetimes with various forms, names, and experiences. Holding onto information from the past and making it solid will reinforce a constriction in the mind that will be carried into the future. Healing is the path of letting go that reveals Reality in which there is no time, only the eternal present moment.

Queendom. (Synonymous with Kingdom. The Aramaic word *malkutah* is feminine gender and is best translated as Queendom.) "Seek you first the Queendom" means, bring our attention from external to internal, and prioritize looking for God in our own heart; then all the external things will either fall into place or fall away. When we make the commitment to seek the Queendom in our own heart, then the right path will present itself. Being in the Queendom while walking on the Earth means knowing only the Reality of Unity while looking with the heart that sees with compassion and is uninterested in judgment.

In the Queendom/Kingdom, there is no time and nothing is lost or gained because All is All. It is a ceaselessly unfolding vibrational pattern of Light, Sound, Joy, and Love. Everything evolves into everything else. Our own consciousness is also ceaseless, so we experience all of this in ecstatic amazement.

Real World. The experience of full, loving awareness while we are in a body on this Earth. See Heaven.

Sacred geometry. The design patterns that are the foundation of Creation. These ceaselessly moving patterns of energy are expressed through Light, Sound, feeling, and thought. Experienced through the lens of the belief in separation, they appear as materiality. These geometric proportions are visible in the biological structures of living Beings, and have been used to create sacred architecture.

Schucman, Helen. The scribe of *A Course in Miracles*. Her detailed shorthand notes have been published in full in Robert Perry's *Complete and Annotated Edition*, giving the reader insight into her personal experience with the scribing process and her relationship with Yeshua.

Self. An emanation from the Heart of God; the universal Identity of Creation. We made our small self, the ego, but we did not create our true Self. When we have released every constriction that creates the illusion of a personal self, we know that this true Being is all that we are. The Self is everything that appears to be projected in solid form, because, in Reality, all Beings are Light, and we are One with all Lights. Yeshua teaches often that we are a part of his Self. He teaches us to "Love your neighbor as yourself because your neighbor *is* your *Self*, because who you *are* is all Beings—all of your neighbors *are* your *Self*. All Beings are the same Light."

Shem. The Semitic word for *name*, which also conveys *vibrational atmosphere*. All vibration emanates from God, so when we attune to the sound of the Shem, we are in the flow of the most powerful energy there is, which is the Love of God.

Simon Peter. One of the twelve male apostles of Yeshua who taught widely throughout the Mediterranean region after the Resurrection. Originally named *Simon*, Yeshua gave him the name *Peter* (*Cephas* in Aramaic), meaning, the rock on which the assembly of his followers could rely. His body is buried in Rome.

Small self. See Ego.

Sophia. The feminine personification of Wisdom, and a deeply metaphysical term that conveys the primordial, formless Love from which all of Creation arises.

Soul. Every Soul is an aspect of the One Child of God. When the Child of God took its courageous leap out of the Mind of God to search for Self-awareness, it appeared to splinter into an infinite number of fragments. All of Creation is conscious, and each apparently fragmented aspect is an expression of Soul. Despite this appearance, each Soul remains forever in Oneness with its Source, and all Souls are, ultimately, the same Soul.

Souls are Light, and Light has no boundaries. It interpenetrates everything. Souls thus also have no boundaries and interpenetrate one another. As Light, Souls glow and shimmer, and when they join in harmony, an exquisite, moving pattern of colors emerges. We are simultaneously in one spot of this pattern *and* all of it.

Source. See God.

Thetford, William (Bill). Co-scribe of *A Course in Miracles*. As Helen Schucman read out the shorthand in which she had transcribed her inner hearing, he typed the first manuscript of this massive book. His joining with her in Christ Consciousness allowed Yeshua's words to be brought into the world.

Thomas. One of the twelve male apostles of Yeshua, who assembled a collection of his sayings that were found among the scrolls hidden in Nag Hammadi. After the Resurrection, he traveled to the East along the Silk Route to share what Yeshua had taught and demonstrated. He taught throughout western India, and possibly also in China and Indonesia. His body is buried in Tamil Nadu, the southernmost state of India.

Veronica. A follower of Yeshua, who wiped his face as he struggled up the hill to the Crucifixion site. His face left an image on the cloth. This story is not in the Gospels and was not recorded until the Middle Ages. Around AD 320, Eusebius wrote that Veronica was the name of the woman whom Yeshua healed of chronic bleeding, a story that is recorded in three Gospels.

Vesica Pisces. The lens shape created by the intersection of two circles of the same size. It is a symbol of the intersection of the physical and spiritual worlds, the Divine Feminine, the Creator of new life. Add a small triangular tail, and you get the fish shape that was used by the early followers of Yeshua.

Way-shower. Yeshua, Mary Magdalene, his Mother, and other Great Ones led the Way to show that we are all here to manifest the Light of God in the body and relinquish the thought of separation. The Way-showers are not special. They came to show the Way that we can all do what they did.

World. The collective consciousness of the thoughts of the ego; the outward projection of our collective, constricted, fearful beliefs; the limited perspective of the illusion of materiality. The belief in separation produced the feeling of fear, which projected the manifest world. When we soften the constrictions in our minds and we are freed of the narrowness of the world to see the Creation without fear, then the already multifarious, miraculous quality of Earth expands into infinity.

Yahweh. A Semitic name for God, sometimes spelled *Jehovah* in English, meaning something like the totality of existence, the Source of Creation, I AM.

Yeshua. The Aramaic name of Jesus, pronounced Y'shua, accent on the second syllable. It means God restoring the awareness of Love to the mind of humanity; God restoring the mind of the Child of God to its original wholeness, to its awareness that it has never left God. The name *Yeshua* has a deep vibrational significance, and any time we say it, we are attuning ourselves to his harmonics, which are attuned to the harmonics of God. "I only speak to you as if I were an individuated person because this is a tool that your mind and body can use, but the Truth is far vaster than that. The Truth is that I am One with you who are not yet fully awake, and I am One with those who are fully awake. When you are attuned with me, you are attuned with the All in All, not just with me. I am not a unique person. Thinking of me as your elder brother is helpful, but that is not only what I am. I speak for, and *am*, the entire Christ Council."

Notes

Dhammatalks.org. n.d. "AN 3:66." Accessed June 11, 2025. https://www.dhammatalks.org/suttas/AN/AN3_66.html.

Diamond Clear Vision. 2012. *A Course in Miracles: Sparkly Edition.*

Douglas-Klotz, Neil. 2022. *Revelations of the Aramaic Jesus.* Hampton Roads Publishing Co.

Foundation for Inner Peace. n.d. "ACIM Scribing." Accessed October 4, 2024. https://acim.org/about-acim/acim-scribing/

Foundation for Inner Peace. n.d. "Significant Historical Dates: Helen & Bill" Accessed October 4, 2024. https://acim.org/about-acim/acim-scribing/significant-historical-dates-of-helen-and-bill/

Heartsong, Claire. 2010. *Anna, The Voice of the Magdalenes.* SEE Publishing Co.

Levine, Peter A. 2010. *In an Unspoken Voice: How the Body Releases Trauma and Restores Goodness.* North Atlantic Books.

Meyer, Marvin, ed. 2007. *The Nag Hammadi Scriptures, The International Edition.* HarperCollins.

Perron, Mari. 2014. *A Course of Love.* Take Heart Publications.

Shanti Christo Foundation. 2015. *The Way of Mastery.* Shanti Christo Foundation.

Vatican.va. 2018. "Urbi et Orbi: Natale 2018." Accessed June 11, 2025. https://www.vatican.va/content/francesco/en/messages/urbi/documents/papa-francesco_20181225_urbi-et-orbi-natale.html

Other Works by the Author

Chapter 5: Buddhism in *A Course in Miracles and...* Jon Mundy, PhD, and Lorri Coburn, MSW, Cogent Publishing, 2017.

Leaving the Lesbian Label Behind: Women who Change their Sexual Orientation Identity, UMI Dissertation Services, 1992

Contact Laura Derr

Information about how to contact me or join group sessions can be found at www.lauraderr-journeytotrueself.com

About the Author

Laura Derr has always felt the calling of the inner way. By profession a psychologist in clinical practice, she is winding down that career to be more available as a receiver and transmitter of the loving Wisdom published in this book. Her twenty years of Buddhist practice in the Thich Nhat Hanh community in Boston supported her conviction that the most important calling is to dissolve attachment to anything that is not Love from one's own mind. Studying *A Course in Miracles*, a mind-training system that is close to Buddhism, accelerated her ability to see and hear with the inner eye and ear. She is also an ordained interfaith minister and serves on the ministerial staff of *Unity in the City* in Brookline, Massachusetts.